The 30-Day Diabetes Cure

Dr. Stefan Ripich, ND, CNP, and Jim Healthy

Bottom Line Books

www.BottomLineSecrets.com

Bottom Line Books® Edition 2011
Published by arrangement with Brainstorms, Inc.
ISBN 0-88723-637-5

10 9 8 7 6 5 4 3 2

This book is based on the research and observations of the author. The information contained in this book should by no means be considered a substitute for the advice of the reader's personal physician or other medical professional, who should always be consulted before beginning any health program.

The information in this book has been carefully researched, and all efforts have been made to ensure accuracy as of the date published. Readers, particularly those with existing health problems and those who take prescription medications, are cautioned to consult with a health professional about specific recommendations for supplements and the appropriate dosages. The author and the publisher expressly disclaim responsibility for any adverse effects arising from the use or application of the information contained in this book.

Bottom Line Books® is a registered trademark of Boardroom® Inc.
281 Tresser Blvd., Stamford, CT 06901
www.BottomLineSecrets.com

Bottom Line Books® publishes the opinions of expert authorities in many fields. The use of this book is not a substitute for health or other professional services. Please consult a competent professional for answers to your specific questions.

Offers, prices, addresses, telephone numbers and Web sites listed in this book are accurate at the time of publication, but they are subject to frequent change.

Bottom Line Books® is an imprint of Boardroom® Inc., publisher of print periodicals, e-letters and books. We are dedicated to bringing you the best information from the most knowledgeable sources in the world. Our goal is to help you gain greater wealth, better health, more wisdom, extra time and increased happiness.

Printed in the United States of America

To my patients, who taught
me the art of being a good doctor,
and my father, who taught me the
art of being a good man

ACKNOWLEDGMENTS

Many people made this book and *The 30-Day Diabetes Cure* daily plan possible, and it is with deep gratitude that I acknowledge and thank them…

- My coauthor Jim Healthy, who helped me in innumerable ways to research, write and formulate these chapters—and to publish this book.

- His wonderfully spirited and passionately dedicated staff at Jim Healthy Publications, who believe, as I do, that this sane, sensible approach to the world's most serious health threat will relieve incalculable suffering and save many precious human lives.

- Candelora Versace, whose tireless research and countless late nights gave birth to this book.

- Heidi Hough and Cinny Green for their masterful editing.

- Ryan Greendyk for his precise proofreading; Miguel Yi for layout and design; Justin Handley for his ingenious marketing and Web site construction; Rosemarie Ademulegun for her fierce positivity and the TLC she showers on our book buyers; Caitlin Martines for taking care of all the details; and Jennifer Carr for her wise business guidance.

- Special thanks to Frank Cody and Terry Rich for their superb video, editing and production talents; Pat Corpora for believing in this project and helping to bring it to fruition; and Martina Punkre for her boundless love, brilliant insights, incomprehensible patience and nonstop support.

- My many patients who believed in me…believed in The 30-Day Diabetes Cure…and believed in the unfathomable healing power within themselves.

- Finally, Terry Warrington for being the spiritual glue that held us all together during this challenging creative process. She was (and is) the wind in our sails. This book would never have happened without her.

CONTENTS

FOREWORD

A hero is no braver than an ordinary man,
but he is braver five minutes longer.

RALPH WALDO EMERSON

A FEW YEARS AGO, I sat with an elderly friend of mine named Sally who was dying from lung cancer. She'd been a lifelong smoker and now the tumors in her lungs were draining away the little life that remained in her. We both knew her time was very near.

"You know," she said in a faint, raspy voice, "I always meant to quit…but I always thought I had more time."

I recognized a tragic truth in these words—and also how emblematic it is of our human condition. Many, if not most, of us live in a similar state of denial. We're forever promising ourselves that "someday" we'll change a bad habit, lose weight, start exercising, return to school, or in some other way change the predictable course in which our lives seem headed.

Sadly, most of us run out of time before "someday" can arrive. So strong is our denial and the force of our habits that we're willing to unconsciously trade our health, future happiness, and an extra 10 or 20 years of life—which, once on our deathbeds, we desperately plead and bargain for—in exchange for the "mañana mentality" that is so pervasive in our culture today. A mentality that keeps us from making important interventions in our own lives right now.

Of course, not everyone succumbs to this. We all know people who finally said, "Enough." People who made a real commitment to change their lives in order to accomplish something amazing. And who somehow managed to stick with it when the going got tough (as it always does) and eventually make it to the other side. Somehow they found a way to get in touch with their "warrior spirit," to dig deep and activate the willpower to fight the good fight and emerge victorious.

Many of Dr. Ripich's diabetes and prediabetes patients have done precisely this, and it's what we both hope this book will help *you* achieve. I'm not naïve enough to believe this book will save the world—though that's both my wish and objective. Lots of people have good intentions at the start of a journey, but only a certain number have the grit and determination to reach their destination. We want *you* to be one of the victorious ones.

Uncontrolled diabetes is a terrible disease that causes people to literally waste away, losing important parts of themselves along the way: their mobility, eyesight, and independence. Their ability to feel anything but pain. Perhaps the greatest loss is the state of comfort most of us take for granted. In his or her final years, a diabetic's life is marked with relentless misery, sorrow, regret, depression, near-constant physical pain, and utter dependence on others for the most basic of human functions.

Now—*right now*—is the time many people yearn for when they learn it's "too late" to do anything about their diabetes except live on drugs and watch helplessly as their condition (and body) degenerates. I want you to realize how incredibly precious this present moment is so you can seize this opportunity.

Our hope is that after reading a little more of this book, you'll be inspired to take control of your health and turn your condition around with conviction and daily commitment.

Don't be like Sally and put it off until later. You may *never* have a better opportunity to sidestep a diagnosis of diabetes—or feel your diabetes if you've already been diagnosed. In both cases, you'll prevent the terrible complications of this dreadful disease.

Awaken your warrior spirit *now*—and fight like hell for your health, your future, and your life. Dr. Ripich and I will be by your side every step of the way, urging you on.

Jim Healthy
April 15, 2010

SECTION ONE

WHAT YOU MUST KNOW ABOUT DIABETES AND TODAY'S TREATMENTS

If someone is going down the wrong road,
he doesn't need motivation to speed him up.
What he needs is education to turn him around.

JIM ROHN

WILL DIABETES DESTROY MODERN CIVILIZATION?

Listen, are you breathing just a little and calling it a life?

MARY OLIVER

DIABETES IS NOW the fastest-spreading disease in human history. Its incidence around the world has doubled in the past two decades, prompting the World Health Organization to declare it a global pandemic. Diabetes and the condition that leads to it, insulin resistance (also called prediabetes), currently affect close to 20% of the world's adult population. Those numbers were expected to double again in just 16 years, but newer studies show it will happen even faster.

In the US alone, diabetes affects an estimated 30 million adults and teens, with an additional 57 million walking around with prediabetes, many of them unknowingly. Because, as it develops, diabetes is largely a disease without symptoms, most of these people won't get a diagnosis until it's too late for a full recovery.

Few people outside the medical community recognize just how dangerous a threat diabetes is to global health and economic stability. Most people view it as another unfortunate, yet normal condition of growing old, like cancer or heart disease. Many even believe having diabetes is "no big deal" because it has become such a common affliction and because so many people who have it seem to be living normal lives thanks to new drugs, glucose monitors, and injectable insulin.

NOTHING COULD BE FURTHER FROM THE TRUTH

Diabetes is raging out of control. Every 10 seconds someone is diagnosed, with official estimates pegged at seven million new cases per year.

Not only is diabetes destroying our health, it's decimating the world economy at an alarmingly fast rate. Last year, the US spent $174 billion on diabetes treatments, while another $58 billion vanished from our economy from lost productivity and sick leave. And even though the world health community spent more than $400 billion last year fighting the disease, it's hopelessly losing the battle.

Consider this: 30% of all children born after 2002 are destined to develop type 2 diabetes and will die 20 years *prematurely* because of it. Theirs will be the first generation in history to have a shorter life span than their parents. Prospects are even more tragic for African-Americans,

Hispanic/Latino Americans, Native Americans, and Asians, whose rates of diabetes are 200% to 400% *higher* than those in the general population.

THERE IS NOTHING "NORMAL" ABOUT DIABETES

And there's no such thing as a normal life for people who have it…

- Diabetics constantly worry about what they eat and how it will affect their disease. Many frequently prick their fingers to monitor blood sugar levels. Those with type 1 must inject themselves with insulin several times daily in order to stay alive—and go to bed each night fearing their blood sugar might drop so low during sleep that they won't awaken.

- Having diabetes accelerates the aging process, causing premature wrinkling of the skin and wearing out organs at a hastened pace. People with diabetes often look and actually are 15 to 20 years older biologically than their chronological age.

- Diabetics suffer more depression…have higher rates of Alzheimer's…endure more heart disease and strokes…are usually vulnerable to kidney disease…and live under the constant threat of heart attack, which is the cause of death for this disease 75% of the time.

- Add to this the horrible complications that eventually appear: Loss of vision and ultimately blindness. Insufferable nerve pain known as neuropathy. Dangerously elevated blood pressure, which often leads to heart failure. And poor circulation resulting in gangrene in the extremities, requiring limb amputations for many patients.

Tragically, during the years considered "prime" for most adults their age, diabetics will watch helplessly as their bodies and minds waste way, losing their comfort, mobility, mental clarity, independence, and body parts one by one.

THIS ISN'T THE DESCRIPTION MODERN MEDICINE WANTS YOU TO HEAR

I realize this is a grim picture unlike the one you see in those upbeat TV commercials hawking diabetes supplies—or on the glossy covers of diabetes magazines featuring lavish desserts and sweets.

But this *is* the reality and fate for the average person with diabetes. And nothing in your doctor's little black bag or the drug researcher's lab is able to change this all-too-typical outcome.

BUT IT DOESN'T HAVE TO BE THIS WAY

Type 2 diabetes, representing 95% of all cases, is the most easily prevented and reversed medical condition on today's Top 10 Killers list, often without any drugs, finger pricking, or glucose monitoring.

This is proven by numerous scientific studies and by clinicians like me who have gotten patients entirely off their diabetes-related medications...have normalized their blood sugar naturally...repaired much of the damage that diabetes had done to their tissues and organs... and virtually erased their risk of heart attack, blindness, kidney failure, limb amputation, stroke, Alzheimer's, and other serious complications.

The very same approach I use has also freed type 1 diabetics from the prospect of these terrible complications, while dramatically reducing their injected insulin by as much as 80% to 90%. This book will show you exactly how to achieve these remarkable results for yourself.

SO WHY IS DIABETES RAGING OUT OF CONTROL?

Despite numerous research studies and patient case histories proving that diabetes is easily controlled and reversed without drugs, the general public and diabetes patients aren't getting the message. Both types of diabetes continue to grow at alarming rates and this alone confirms that current medical treatments are failing miserably. So why do doctors continue to prescribe them to their patients?

The shameful reason diabetes is going unchecked and mistreated involves a reprehensible web of greed, corruption, chicanery, egotism, collusion, and incorrigible medical politics throughout the entire "Diabetes Industry."

Diabetes isn't an infectious disease like malaria that millions of people are "catching." In 95% of all cases, it's a self-created lifestyle condition that's easily defeated once patients are properly educated on how to stop doing the things that cause and worsen it—and start adopting the practices that are proven to reverse it. Irrefutable scientific evidence shows that my simple, inexpensive nondrug approach is more than *200% more effective* than current drug treatments.

The solution is just that easy, but the medical community is neither supporting nor publicizing it. Instead, it's being obscured by relentless medical hoopla about new drugs, promising new cures, high-tech monitoring equipment, and ubiquitous propaganda that puts a smiley face on living with a horribly destructive disease. A disease that, in reality, will have a nightmarish outcome for most patients, even when they follow their doctor's orders to the letter.

THE CONSPIRACY TO KEEP YOU OBLIVIOUS

I'll be blunt: You're being lied to about diabetes for reasons that will become clear as you read the numerous Special Reports you received when you purchased this book.

Powerful forces are at work to keep the public in the dark about just how easily diabetes can be conquered. It is scandalous that this utterly conquerable condition has been "medicalized" by those who are profiting handsomely from the billions spent on treatments every year—and the trillions more that will be expended over the next decade.

The explanation for this is simple, albeit shocking: There's more money to be made from *treating* diabetes than from curing it. If you find this assertion hard to accept, you haven't been reading the recent accounts of how hundreds of billions of dollars were stolen in broad daylight by the banking and mortgage industries (also once considered reputable and trustworthy) and the heartbreaking consequences of these scandalous actions that have left millions of Americans homeless, bankrupt, unemployed, without health insurance, and saddled with enormous debt and ever-increasing taxes to pay for publicly-funded bailouts of these industries.

Today's diabetes dilemma has become an enormous cash cow that special interests will continue to milk for their own personal gain, regardless of the misery and deaths those profits will create. We can't allow this to happen.

Words can't express how outraged this makes me feel. To fight back, I wrote this book to help every person who wants to escape this deadly trap while they're still able.

YOU CAN'T AFFORD DIABETES IN THIS (OR ANY) ECONOMY

Even if *you* don't have diabetes or have a low likelihood of developing it, chances are that someone very close to you does or will. Perhaps one or both of your parents. Maybe one of your children or grandchildren. Surely someone in your extended family or circle of friends. The odds are great, so this message is for *you* too because…

Today it costs $150,000 a year to care for a chronically ill parent in-home, whether yours or theirs. Because today's medical treatments are able to prolong the deterioration of diabetic patients, their slow process of wasting away can occur over 10 or more years. That's $1.5 million I'm betting you haven't stashed away for this purpose.

Diabetes-related drugs alone cost $400 or more a month. Statistics show the average diabetic requires at least $40,000 to $80,000 in additional medical care compared with nondiabetics (and I'm quoting you a conservatively low figure). Add to this the intensive physical care a diabetic parent or child requires, not to mention the overwhelming emotional and psychological stress placed on caregivers. Few people today can afford this—especially in these crisis-riddled times.

The 30-Day Diabetes Cure offers you a proven, effective, and inexpensive alternative to costly diabetes drugs and medical treatments so you won't be forced to surrender your life savings to doctors, hospitals, and drug companies. This proven nondrug approach can dramatically improve the quality of life—and the ultimate outcome—for the average diabetic, whether type 1 or type 2.

HAVING DIABETES IS LIKE FALLING OUT OF AN AIRPLANE

That's how helpless and out-of-control a person with diabetes feels. It's as though you're plummeting to earth in slow motion, paralyzed by a deer-in-the-headlights fear deep in your gut. No matter how you try to distract yourself or deny it, some part of you is always aware that you're falling faster and closer to the ground below with every tick of the clock.

The great tragedy is that 99.9% of the four million people who will die from diabetes every year never realize they're wearing a *parachute*—and if they simply pull the ring, they'd float gently down, landing unharmed (and even delighted by the descent!).

You and everyone you know who has diabetes are wearing just such a parachute right now. *The 30-Day Diabetes Cure* is a virtual instruction manual that shows you how to locate and pull the ring to save your life. Doing so will open your mind (and your chute) so you can save yourself and your loved ones from this self-inflicted plague.

What is this wondrous parachute? Foremost, it is none other than the incomparable ability of the human body to repair and regenerate itself—a truly awesome capacity that modern medicine inexplicably ignores and constantly seeks to circumvent.

The 30-Day Diabetes Cure shows you how—step-by-step and day-by-day—to awaken and strengthen your body's own marvelous self-healing power so you can wrench your destiny from the greedy clutches of the Diabetes Industry and bring it back home where it rightly belongs.

ARE YOU READY TO OPEN YOUR PARACHUTE NOW?

Please have no illusions. You'll need more than wishful intentions to succeed on *The 30-Day Diabetes Cure.* During your journey you'll encounter many of the temptations and seductions that got you sick in the first place. This is no magic bullet. It will take commitment, determination, and persistence to turn this serious condition around. But there can be no mistake: This is the best and only viable alternative you have to surrendering your life to diabetes.

And you can do it. Every single one of my patients who has followed *The 30-Day Diabetes Cure* has succeeded. It has never failed.

Modern life appeals to the "leisure streak" in all of us. Never before in history has immediate gratification been so possible to achieve at every turn. Living in these times is like being a kid in a candy store who continually stuffs himself and gets sick until he finally learns his lesson.

If you've truly had enough and are ready to reclaim your life and health, you've come to the right place. If you're wise enough to understand that the "easy way" almost always turns out to be the most difficult and painful in the long run, then *The 30-Day Diabetes Cure* is "just what the doctor ordered."

I urge you to carefully read the following chapters of Section One and all of the Special Reports you received with this book before you begin the actual 30-day plan. The scientific studies presented in them will convince you of the effectiveness of my approach—as well as the futility of following current conventional medical treatments. This intellectual knowledge will help firm up your resolve to defeat this utterly beatable condition once and for all.

More than anything, I hope these words and the real-life case histories of my patients who have succeeded with *The 30-Day Diabetes Cure* will inspire you to trust the miraculous healing power of your own body and mind. Give it a chance. It will never let you down. And if you need any extra help or inspiration, visit our free Web site, *www.myhealingkitchen.com.*

CHAPTER ONE

WHAT IS DIABETES, ANYWAY?

Perhaps everything terrible is in its deepest being
something helpless that wants help from us.

RAINER MARIA RILKE

THERE'S A LOT OF CONFUSION TODAY—even among doctors—about what diabetes actually is, and about the ideal way to treat it. What we know for certain is that diabetes is a worldwide epidemic that's growing by leaps and bounds.

The World Health Organization estimates that 370 million people worldwide today suffer from some form of diabetes, and its incidence has doubled over the last 30 years. Nations from small to large are being overwhelmed with cases. In Romania, the diabetes epidemic rages—with one in two people categorized as obese. In China, nearly 100 million people now have diabetes, and researchers estimate that an additional 148.2 million Chinese are in a prediabetic state.

The financial cost of diabetes is pummeling the global economy. In the US alone, the cost of treating this condition will rise from $174 billion today to nearly $400 billion by 2034.

What *is* this disease that now surpasses HIV AIDS in the number of people who die from its complications every year (now totaling nearly four million)? With the increase in the incidence of diabetes seen in virtually every country on the planet, this death toll could easily *double* before the next decade unless we find a way to contain and reverse this worldwide epidemic.

UNDERSTANDING DIABETES IS ESSENTIAL TO CURING IT

Exactly what is diabetes? Is it a state of high blood sugar? Is it a damaging condition of chronically high insulin levels? Is it the destruction of insulin-producing beta cells in the pancreas? Or is it the serious harm done to tissues and organs from being exposed to excessive levels of glucose and insulin over a long period of time?

There's equally as much confusion over the *causes* of diabetes. Is it caused by genetics or diet or combination of both? Is excess weight the culprit or is some fundamental hormonal imbalance responsible for the weight gain? And what's the connection to cardiovascular disease and heart attack, the most frequent cause of death in people with diabetes?

Let's start by separating fact from fiction: Diabetes is not a single disease and it doesn't have a singular cause. It is an understandable configuration of interconnected metabolic problems that will come up over and over in our discussion of the stages and types of diabetes. But let's start at the beginning…

HOW YOUR BODY MAKES ENERGY

All living things need energy to survive. For humans, our primary fuel is glucose (blood sugar), which is essential at the individual cell level where glucose is transformed into *adenosine-5'-triphosphate* (ATP), the energy that animates us—our very life force. Glucose that's not used immediately is converted into fats called *triglycerides* and stored in fat cells for use later. Remember this fact for later: *Excess glucose is converted into fat.*

Long hours of physical and mental activity, especially if they're stressful, require extra energy beyond what's needed for normal functioning. This is why your cells make sure there's always some extra fuel stored away: So you have it when you need it. In fact, your body is especially adept at hoarding fuel for the lean times—a survival function that evolved over thousands of years—because food wasn't always as plentiful as it is today.

Your body has good reason for doing this. Without enough glucose to keep you going, your cells, especially brain cells, would shut down. That's what happens when you get low blood sugar (*hypoglycemia*). Deprived of fuel, you feel dizzy, irritable, and faint; when cells don't get enough glucose, you eventually slip into a coma. Ultimately, without sufficient glucose, life is not sustainable and you die.

What your body *doesn't* have an elegant solution for, unfortunately, is *too much* fuel. Storing extra fuel for times of lack was an essential evolutionary development, honed over eons of deprivation and insufficient calories. This continued well into civilized times. The concept of the body having to cope with too many calories and excessive levels of glucose was an anomaly in human life until the last hundred years or so (with the exception of royalty, who've always had more than enough to eat).

WHAT'S INSULIN'S ROLE IN ALL THIS?

Insulin is a hormone produced in your pancreas. Its main job is to convert these extra glucose calories into fat (called *triglycerides*) and usher them into your body's fat cells and liver for storage. A by-product of this process results in lowered blood sugar.

Another one of insulin's functions is to help glucose into your fuel-burning cells so ATP can be created. In this role, it acts as a kind of gatekeeper that rings the doorbell to open the doors (called *insulin receptors*) on your cells so glucose can enter. This is how your brain, muscles, and other organs receive the energy they need.

Rising levels of blood sugar signal your pancreas to create and release insulin into the bloodstream to unlock these receptors. So when you consume foods that readily break down into glucose—most often sugary products and refined carbohydrates—the levels of blood sugar and insulin rise quickly.

The more carbohydrates you eat, the higher your blood sugar rises, which in turn triggers more insulin output from your pancreas and therefore more stored body fat. When your body doesn't have enough time (or physical activity) to burn off the calories you're consuming—or the fat it has stored—an unhealthy situation begins to develop.

INSULIN RESISTANCE (PREDIABETES)

In this case, too much of a good thing is *bad*. Your body is well equipped to deal with an intermittent but steady flow of glucose. It knows how to manage a supply that arrives in intervals, with sufficient time in between to convert the sugar to ATP energy. But your metabolism is ill-equipped to deal with a constant supply—an oversupply—of glucose.

Because your cells are unable to immediately process all this glucose, a backlog is created, sort of like a long line of coal trucks backed up at the receiving gate of a power plant (in this case, the insulin receptors on your cells). But instead of waiting in line to dump their loads, the truckers grow impatient and dump everything at the gate.

In your body, this massive dumping creates high levels of glucose in the blood. And because sugar is extremely inflammatory, it damages the tissues and organs with which it comes in contact. Imagine how much harm thousands of dusty, coal-laden, diesel-belching 18-wheelers would do to a small town's streets and air. This damage is even worse in your bloodstream. (I'll explain why a little later.)

The second health problem created by all this extra glucose occurs in the pancreas as it struggles to crank out extra insulin to clear the bloodstream. It's as if the gatekeeper (insulin) was constantly ringing the doorbell at the receiving gate of the power plant (your cells). But the supervisor inside, knowing the plant's capacity is full, ignores the ringing. This state is called *insulin resistance* (or prediabetes) and is the early stage of type 2.

The situation gets a lot worse if not corrected at this point. All that extra glucose in the bloodstream signals the pancreas to produce even more insulin. Now your bloodstream is flooded with glucose *and* insulin, a doubly inflammatory combination. Together, they literally "burn" tissues and organs (a process called *glycation*), crusting them with a layer of oxidized sugar called *advanced glycation end products* (AGEs). Elevated levels of AGEs accelerate the aging process, which is why people with diabetes have prematurely wrinkled skin and organs that are 15 to 20 years older *biologically* than their chronological age. This explains why people with diabetes tend to have a shorter life span by as much as two decades.

In addition, this extra insulin frantically creates more triglycerides to be stored as fat. This is how weight problems and obesity occur. And the larger your fat cells get, the more insulin resistant they become. A vicious cycle is developing and must be attended to properly.

Approximately 60 million Americans (that's 20% of the US population!) are walking around with prediabetes right now—and most don't realize they're in any danger. The damage that's being done to their arteries and organs from glycation and AGEs is silently taking a serious toll. See if any of the following early symptoms fit you...

THE TOP 10 SIGNS OF INSULIN RESISTANCE

Insulin resistance creeps up on you sneakily and does serious damage to your pancreas, blood vessels, kidneys, and heart long before you even suspect trouble is brewing. It is often called prediabetes because it leads directly to full-blown diabetes, in which the insulin-producing beta cells in your pancreas die from exhaustion. This is type 1 diabetes, requiring regular insulin injections for life.

Not getting your blood sugar under control at this early stage virtually ensures you will become a type 2 diabetic before long. If you have any of the symptoms below, see a doctor pronto to get the tests I recommend later in this chapter. If a diagnosis of insulin resistance is confirmed, your doctor may want to start you on medications immediately. This is usually *not* necessary however; any official treatment protocol is to put the patient on diet and lifestyle modifications first. Unfortunately, many doctors don't do this because they are unfamiliar with what really works—and they have almost no time at all to supervise and motivate your compliance.

Rest assured that prediabetes can usually be reversed with the simple, inexpensive, and highly effective step-by-step lifestyle modifications you'll read about in *The 30-Day Diabetes Cure*. Here are the telltale signs...

1. **Belly fat.** A large abdomen is an early sign of insulin resistance in men. In females, it appears as belly fat combined with prominent buttocks. It is such an accurate indicator of the improper metabolism of sugars and fats that it has its own name: *Diabesity*.

2. **Depression.** Depressed individuals are often insulin resistant because the stress associated with depression actually causes the liver to flood the body with high levels of *cortisol* (the so-called "worry hormone"), which elevates blood sugar. When depression or stress is chronic, the extra insulin produced by the pancreas can damage arteries, cells and the kidneys. If you tend to feel depressed, sad, or "blue," be sure to see your doctor and request the tests listed below instead of just taking antidepressants.

3. **Low blood sugar.** If you feel agitated, jittery and moody, and experience an almost immediate relief once food is eaten, you might be hypoglycemic (a state of low blood sugar). If this

is accompanied by any of the other symptoms listed here, especially physical and mental fatigue, you might be experiencing insulin resistance.

4. **Fatigue.** Insulin resistance wears people out. If you feel tired without a reason such as exertion or lack of sleep, it might indicate how hard you body is working to metabolize excess sugars.

5. **Brain fogginess.** The fatigue caused by insulin resistance often expresses itself as a mental tiredness. Inability to focus, poor memory, loss of creativity, and poor grades in school often accompany insulin resistance, as do various forms of "learning disabilities."

6. **Intestinal bloating.** People who eat sugary and refined carbohydrates suffer from lots of gas. This may be a tipoff that your metabolism isn't functioning properly because of insulin resistance.

7. **Too much or too little sleep.** Many people with insulin resistance get sleepy immediately after eating a carbohydrate-rich plate such as pasta or a meal with potatoes, bread, and a sweet dessert. Research published in the *Archives of Internal Medicine* found that people who sleep less than five hours each night are 250% more likely to develop insulin resistance or impaired glucose tolerance. Reason? Being sleep-deprived is stressful and triggers cortisol and carbohydrate cravings to placate it.

8. **Dental problems.** When you're prediabetic, elevated blood sugar encourages bacteria that cause periodontal disease (gum infections), which in turn increases your risk for heart problems.

9. **Frequent colds and infections.** Also slow-healing wounds. A bloodstream overrun by sugar blocks the action of cells that fight infection, causing vaginal and bladder infections and making skin sores slow to heal. Also, people with prediabetes often have reduced circulation, leaving tissues starved for the oxygen-rich blood that promotes healing.

10. **Sexual problems.** Between 35% and 50% of men with prediabetes or type 2 experience erectile dysfunction and sexual problems. Excess insulin in the bloodstream created by insulin resistance damages the endothelium, the layer on the inside of blood vessels that instructs the vessel to contract or relax. Making matters worse, the anger and frustration this usually causes is stressful, thus triggering cortisol. Some women with blood sugar problems can experience inflammation of the vagina or cystitis (bladder infection).

STANDARD PREDIABETES SCREENING

If you're experiencing one or more of the above symptoms, I encourage you to investigate the possibility of insulin resistance by requesting the diagnostic tests below from your physician...

1. **Hemoglobin A1C.** This is a standard screening test for prediabetes. It measures how much glucose has attached to the hemoglobin in your blood. If you've got a lot, you are at risk for

diabetes and heart problems. (For a more in-depth explanation of this test, please read the Special Report *Dodging Diabetes Complications*.)

2. **Triglycerides.** High triglycerides in the blood are often found in overweight persons and those on the brink of diabetes. But even those who are not overweight may have stores of fat in their arteries as a result of insulin resistance. These triglycerides are the direct result of excessive consumption of sugary foods and beverages, plus refined carbohydrate food products. These create a glucose overload, which results in extra insulin being required to convert it into body fat.

3. **Hypertension.** Insulin resistance causes arteries to become clogged with accumulated fat and other substances, which forces the heart to work harder and elevates blood pressure. Having too much insulin in the bloodstream is also linked to high blood pressure, which is why it's a telltale sign of insulin resistance. There is a direct relationship between the level of insulin and blood pressure: As insulin levels elevate, so does blood pressure. Elevated cortisol also raises blood pressure.

4. **LDL cholesterol.** Insulin resistance lowers good cholesterol (HDL) and raises bad cholesterol (LDL) levels. Healthy levels are total cholesterol below 200 milligrams per deciliter (mg/dL), HDL cholesterol above 45 mg/dL, and LDL cholesterol below 130 mg/dL.

MODIFICATION BEFORE MEDICATION

If you are diagnosed with insulin resistance or prediabetes, your doctor might want to put you on blood sugar–lowering medication such as Glucophage (*metformin*) as the first line of "defense" against developing type 2. I urge you *not* to go down this slippery slope right away. The official medical protocol calls for physicians to try diet and lifestyle modification before drugs (except in emergency situations).

Merely lowering blood sugar by forcing the pancreas to churn out more insulin (as these drugs do) isn't the solution. Your cells don't need more insulin; they need to become more *insulin sensitive*, which means they need to be better trained to use the insulin already being produced. Drugs can't accomplish this. Only a combination of reducing your consumption of "fast carb" foods (those which convert quickly into glucose) and increasing your physical activity (which lowers the amount of insulin your body requires) can achieve this. That's exactly what *The 30-Day Diabetes Cure* helps you achieve.

Numerous studies confirm that diet and lifestyle modification, such as those you'll learn on *The 30-Day Diabetes Cure*, are twice as effective as Glucophage in lowering blood sugar. More important, only diet and physical activity can reverse insulin resistance and type 2, while protecting you from the onset of diabetes' deadly complications.

THE LEPTIN CONNECTION

There's another hormone at work that triggers insulin resistance that you rarely hear about. Called *leptin*, its job is to send the "I'm full" signal (called *satiety*) to your brain after you've consumed enough calories for basic nourishment. Under normal circumstances, leptin also triggers the release of your body's stored fat so it can be burned for energy.

Unfortunately, the leptin signal gets shut down by overeating, eating rapidly, and by high-fructose corn syrup (HFCS)—a nasty sweetener widely used in sodas, fruit drinks, baked goods, and most commercial food products. In these instances, *leptin resistance* can develop and your brain never hears the "Enough, already!" signal.

- A recent study confirms that eating/drinking large amounts of fructose-containing food products causes leptin resistance and elevated triglycerides in laboratory animals. Those fed a high-fructose diet ate more and gained more weight than animals fed a high-fat, high-calorie diet.

- Research done in early 2010 at Princeton University showed rats who ate high-fructose corn syrup gained a lot more weight—and an extra helping of belly fat—than rats who ate table sugar, despite taking in an equal number of calories.[1] The reason for this disparity is that consuming HFCS blocks the leptin signal and therefore leads to overeating.

Leptin resistance also seems to be the underlying reason many dieters can't lose weight even when they follow a severely calorie-restricted regimen. Those extra pounds don't budge because the brain never gets leptin's message to burn up stored fat instead of wanting to eat again.

Worse, when the brain doesn't hear leptin's message, the pancreas keeps producing insulin to deal with all the extra glucose that's produced. The result is excess insulin in your bloodstream. If you're not prediabetic yet, you could actually become hypoglycemic (low blood sugar) from all that insulin. In reality, leptin resistance is a step toward insulin resistance and diabetes, although most doctors are completely unaware of the connection.

CENTRAL OBESITY = BELLY FAT

Whether you call it a beer gut or a potbelly, having a large waist circumference seems to be quite common among Americans in midlife (and even early ages). Despite all those ads for six-pack abs, no amount of exercise can turn this type of belly into a flat, ripped midsection if you have a damaged metabolism. This belly fat is more formally called *central obesity*.

Belly fat is excess weight around the waist, usually on people with normal-sized arms and legs. It's often called "apple-shaped obesity." This distinguishes it from "pear-shaped," where the extra weight is carried in the hips, buttocks, thighs, and legs.

---

[1] http://www.princeton.edu/main/news/archive/S26/91/22K07/

A well-informed doctor knows that when a patient's waist-to-hip ratio is high—that is, if your waist is larger than your hips—it's a dead giveaway of cardiovascular and blood sugar problems. (You may now be more informed than most doctors, though, so keep this in mind as you assess your own symptoms.)

The solution to central obesity is fairly simple: By replacing your consumption of fast-carb food products with fiber-rich "slow carbs" (explained and described in *The 30-Day Diabetes Cure*), you'll be targeting this belly fat without countless reps of sit-ups and crunches. Slow carbs are true "flat belly foods." I promise you'll come to love your tape measure, because your shrinking waistline will be the most visible evidence of your progress on my plan. The inches you lose will correspond directly to your body's reversing insulin resistance.

Remember, *The 30-Day Diabetes Cure* isn't a vanity diet; this is about your health. Your belly is a barometer of your body's resistance to insulin. Don't fall into the trap set by numerous experts who claim that losing weight will reverse prediabetes and type 2. This is a counterproductive strategy because it takes your focus off the real goal. Weight-loss diets are tough to stick with and are self-defeating. In fact, studies show that they fail 95% of the time over the long haul. And those who are lucky enough to succeed at losing weight eventually gain it all back—and then some—within three years or less.

You want to get your belly under control because it's a symptom of *prediabetes* and quite possibly *metabolic syndrome* (also known as Syndrome X, described on the facing page). Healing your metabolism through *The 30-Day Diabetes Cure* will naturally result in weight loss without even trying to lose an ounce. This is a lifestyle overhaul that you can stick with for life.

POLYCYSTIC OVARY SYNDROME (PCOS)

PCOS is a hormonal imbalance that causes weight gain, irregular periods, ovaries with multiple cysts, infertility, fatigue, acne, and excess facial or body hair. Many women who have PCOS are overweight or obese, have type 2 diabetes, and/or are insulin resistant. Scientists have uncovered an undeniable link between insulin resistance and PCOS, offering women with this array of symptoms a real chance to turn it around. If you have PCOS symptoms, see your doctor first. Then start my 30-day plan.

METABOLIC SYNDROME

The next stage in the development of full-blown diabetes is metabolic syndrome (MetS), and it's estimated that one-quarter of all Americans, or 68 million, are unknowingly walking around with it. It is a more aggravated stage of insulin resistance directly related to central obesity, which we've learned is caused by an inability to metabolize the insulin and glucose that flood your bloodstream with triglycerides.[2] But MetS includes a combination of other complications—including hypertension, elevated triglycerides, belly fat, and low HDL cholesterol—which make it extremely dangerous.

According to the American Heart Association and the National Heart, Lung, and Blood Institute, metabolic syndrome is present if you have three or more of the symptoms below. Also, if you meet three of these five risk factors for MetS, you are at serious risk for developing cardiovascular disease and type 2 diabetes—in addition to having a sudden heart attack or stroke.

SYMPTOMS OF METABOLIC SYNDROME

1. **Large waist circumference** (measured as length around the waist): Men with waists that measure 40 inches or more and women whose are 35 inches or more could have MetS.

2. **Triglycerides**. High triglycerides in the blood are often present in overweight individuals. But even those who are not overweight may have stores of fat in their arteries as a result of insulin resistance. These triglycerides are the direct result of too many sugary unrefined carbohydrates in the diet being converted to body fat by insulin. Triglycerides equal to or higher than 150 mg/dL suggest MetS.

3. **Hypertension.** It's been shown that most people with increased blood pressure also tend to be insulin resistant. It is often possible to show a direct relationship between the level of insulin and blood pressure; as insulin levels elevate, so does blood pressure. Blood pressure equal to or higher than 130/85 millimeters of mercury (mmHg) in the presence of these other symptoms indicates MetS.

4. **Cholesterol.** Insulin resistance lowers protective HDL cholesterol and raises "bad" LDL levels. Low HDL cholesterol (men under 40 mg/dL and women under 50 mg/dL) in conjunction with other symptoms suggests the presence of MetS.

5. **Hemoglobin A1C.** This is a standard screening test for prediabetes. It measures how much glucose has attached to the hemoglobin in your blood. If you've got a lot, you're at risk of diabetes and heart problems.

6. **Fasting blood sugar (FBS)** measures blood glucose after you have not eaten for at least eight hours. Levels equal to or higher than 100 mg/dL suggest MetS.

---

[2] http://www.news-medical.net/news/2007/12/18/33652.aspx

LIFESTYLE MODIFICATIONS CAN TURN THIS AROUND

Amazingly, even if your tests show that you have these risk factors, you can reverse MetS by two simple changes. First, a multiyear study at Duke Medical Center called STRRIDE (Studies of a Targeted Risk Reduction Intervention through Defined Exercise) examined the effects of increased physical activity on middle-aged, overweight men and women. The results showed that a person can lower risk of MetS by 50% merely by walking 30 minutes a day, six days per week—even if you don't make any dietary changes. Duke cardiologist William Kraus said, "Some exercise is better than none; more exercise is generally better than less, and no exercise can be disastrous."

Second, poor diet plays a major role in MetS.[3] The Dietary Intake and the Development of the Metabolic Syndrome study compared the risk of MetS between the "typical Western diet" consisting of refined grains, processed meats, fried foods, poor-quality red meat, and soda, and the "prudent diet" heavy on cruciferous vegetables such as broccoli and cabbage, carotenoid vegetables (carrots, pumpkins), fruit, fish and seafood, poultry, whole grains, and low-fat dairy (otherwise known as the Mediterranean diet).

The results were impressive. Individuals with the highest scores in the "typical Western diet" had an 18% higher risk of developing MetS compared with those on the Mediterranean diet. Individuals with the highest consumption of fatty red meat (hamburgers, hot dogs, and processed meats) had a 26% greater risk compared with those who ate the least. On the other hand, consuming dairy products seems to be protective, producing a 13% lower risk of developing metabolic syndrome. (Don't miss the fascinating discussion on healthy saturated fats on Days 9 and 11 of *The 30-Day Diabetes Cure*.) Consumption of fried foods, fast foods, and diet soda were also associated with metabolic syndrome, while coffee and nuts were not.

Several other studies[4] confirm these findings. So by following *The 30-Day Diabetes Cure*, you'll be making the lifestyle modifications that have been shown by rigorous scientific research to protect you against MetS and diabetes.

TYPE 2 DIABETES

When insulin resistance and MetS are not checked through diet and lifestyle modifications, your condition can quickly evolve into type 2, the most prevalent form of the disease, encompassing 95% of all diabetes. In type 2, the pancreas continues to produce insulin (too much, in fact), but it's no longer effective in ushering glucose into cells. This leaves large amounts of sugar circulating in your bloodstream, along with loads of ineffective insulin. Together, they're a recipe for obesity and cardiovascular damage.

---

[3] http://circ.ahajournals.org/cgi/content/abstract/117/6/754

[4] http://www.level1diet.com/reverse-diabetes.html

When insulin is rebuffed by fuel-burning cells, it converts glucose into fatty triglycerides and stores the end product as body fat. This doesn't occur immediately, though, so in addition to a bloodstream flush with glucose and insulin, it also becomes loaded with fat, which clogs it up and gets deposited as plaque on artery walls. Cardiologists love to blame cholesterol for heart disease, but too many triglycerides—triggered by excess insulin—are a far more dangerous risk factor for heart attack (the cause of death in 75% of all diabetic fatalities).

The prime areas for this fat storage are around your waist, bottom, and thighs (otherwise known as central obesity.) Under normal circumstances, the leptin response will command the body to use this stored energy for fuel. But overeating and being overweight interrupt the normal functioning of leptin, so its signal never reaches the brain, which leads to the further accumulation of body fat. That's the real reason diabetes and obesity are so intimately linked. You can clearly see that being overweight doesn't cause diabetes—*it happens the other way around.* (You can also see why sugar and refined carbs are the real cause of heart disease, not meat, saturated fat, and cholesterol as current medical thinking suggests.)

FIVE DANGEROUS SITUATIONS ARE NOW OCCURRING IN THE BODY

First, high levels of both glucose and insulin are now circulating through the bloodstream. Together, they are highly inflammatory, as if billions of tiny shards of glass were coursing through your arteries under pressure, scratching and scraping the tissue they come in contact with. This damages the delicate lining of artery walls in the same way as if you rubbed your cheeks with sandpaper until they bled. What happens next is very much like the scabbing process that would occur on your face.

In an attempt to repair the microscopic scratches and scrapes in your arteries, your body uses fats and cholesterol to seal and heal them. Layer upon layer of these fats (called plaque) accumulate and can block arteries—or can trigger a blood clot, which results in a heart attack or stroke. This is the primary reason 75% of all diabetic fatalities are caused by cardiac arrest, making it the most deadly of all complications.

Second, massive amounts of free radical molecules are generated by all this inflammation, which destroy healthy tissue—including beta cells in the pancreas. When free radical populations reach a critical mass, they overwhelm the antioxidant defense system that protects the body's DNA. Once the body's genetic blueprint is breached and damaged, cancer begins to develop. (It's especially important to note here that glucose is cancer's preferred fuel, feeding tumors just like fertilizer feeds a plant's growth.) Continuing to consume sugary carbs when you have diabetes or insulin resistance is like asking for a diagnosis of cancer.

Third, glucose molecules displace oxygen's usual (and essential) presence within red blood cells, in effect hijacking them. The result is that vital organs—among them the brain, heart, eyes, arms, and legs—suffer poor circulation. This is the fundamental cause of serious diabetic complications including blindness, gangrene, and limb amputation.

Fourth, without sufficient oxygen and with high levels of glucose, the blood becomes thick and slow-moving. In response, the brain sends out a "thirst signal" in an attempt to dilute the bloodstream. Gulping extra fluids (and, tragically, most diabetics reach for sugary sodas, making matters worse) causes excessive urination, and in the process, the body can become dehydrated. Frequent urination also flushes out precious nutrients already in short supply, further depriving vital organs of adequate nutrition. Ultimately, the body eats its own muscle in an attempt to gain vital nutrients. This is why diabetes is called a "wasting disease."

Finally, the pancreas becomes exhausted by its overproduction of insulin, and the few remaining beta cells that produce this important hormone eventually die. When the body can no longer produce its own insulin, a synthetic version of the hormone must be injected regularly or the patient will die. This is type 1 diabetes (which I'll discuss in detail in a moment).

WHY DRUGS AREN'T THE SOLUTION

Drugs have the ability to lower your blood sugar count, which will make your doctor very happy. But your pancreas won't be as pleased. It will continue to wear itself out until every one of its insulin-producing beta cells is destroyed unless you improve your eating and lifestyle patterns and heal the damage that inflammation has already caused. This is what *The 30-Day Diabetes Cure* will help you achieve.

It's important to note that everyone loses beta cells as a natural part of the aging process, but for most people this loss isn't critical. However, it's a different story for a person with type 2 or insulin resistance. Scientists now know that insulin resistance is the primary killer of insulin-producing beta cells, and thus speeds the development of diabetes and worsens its consequences. (Read more about protecting yourself from these deadly complications in the Special Report that accompanied your purchase of this book, entitled *Dodging Diabetes Complications.)*

THE GLOBAL EPIDEMIC OF TYPE 2

We know type 2 is spreading as quickly as our waistlines. And it's happening all over the world. What's causing this disaster? Study after study shows that it's a combination of our sedentary lifestyle, overconsumption of sugar and refined carbohydrates, coupled with chronic stress. Tragically, most people with type 2 take pills and finally insulin to stave off the symptoms, but this does nothing to cure the underlying condition.

To complicate matters, type 2 diabetes is beginning to show up in younger individuals—even children. Once this was a condition that developed in people over 60 (which is why it was called *adult-onset diabetes*), but no more. So many young people are being diagnosed with it that the name was changed to "type 2."

WHY SUCH A FLOOD OF SUGARS IN THE FIRST PLACE?

When scientists want to give lab animals type 2 diabetes in order to perform medical research, they usually feed them the basic components of the typical Western diet: sugar and refined carbohydrates. It doesn't take very long for the disease to develop. That's because these so-called "foods" lack their natural fiber, which has been destroyed by the refining process. This increases their shelf life considerably, because there's nothing left "alive" that can cause the product to spoil. Unfortunately, these lifeless foods cannot sustain health or life.

One of the most important components of food in its natural state is its fiber. This is their "roughage" content, which slows the breakdown of complex carbohydrates into glucose during digestion (which is why they're sometimes referred to as "slow carbs"). With the fiber mechanically processed *out* of these foods, our digestive systems have nothing left to do. Processed "fast carbs" move quickly from stomach to bloodstream, instead of spending several hours slowly being digested and releasing their sugars over time. Add a flood of sweetened beverages—which zoom into the bloodstream even faster—and you're shifting the insulin-producing beta cells in your pancreas into overdrive. And, over time, all that insulin makes your cells resistant to it.

As research has shown repeatedly, you can reverse your cells' resistance to insulin by minimizing foods that create this rush of blood sugar. Quitting fast carbs such as sweetened drinks, breakfast cereals, and white-flour products and replacing them with whole foods that still have their natural fiber intact causes energy to be released slowly, over time, and taken up perfectly by your body for fuel.

Decreasing your intake of fast carbs results in better insulin activity—and insulin resistance clears up all by itself, without the need for drugs. Add a little extra physical activity and your cells become more sensitive to insulin, so your body needs less of it. A lovely by-product of this is weight loss.

This improvement kicks in as soon as you begin *The 30-Day Diabetes Cure*. In a matter of a few days, you'll notice your strong desire for fast carbs, sweets, and processed foods will decline dramatically—because you'll be breaking the vicious cycle of "carbohydrate craving." Your blood chemistry will begin to balance itself naturally and you'll reduce overall cholesterol and triglycerides. This is the perfect recipe for reversing diabetes *and* improving your overall health.[5]

---

[5] Ibid.

THE TOP 18 SIGNS OF TYPE 2

The risk factors for type 2 build upon the ones that cause the prediabetic conditions of insulin resistance and MetS (see pages 12–14, 16). Having one or more of these factors places you at greater risk for developing diabetes:

1. Belly fat

2. Depression

3. Low blood sugar

4. Fatigue

5. Brain fogginess

6. Intestinal bloating

7. Sleep habits: too much or too little

8. Dental problems

9. Infections

10. Sexual problems

And to these 10 signs of insulin resistance let's add:

11. **Diagnosed insulin resistance**

12. **Diagnosed metabolic syndrome**

13. **Frequent urination plus increased thirst.** These effects are caused by your astonishingly smart kidneys trying to rid your body of all the extra sugar in your bloodstream via urine. And as you urinate more, the thirst center in your brain's hypothalamus sends out a "drink more" message.

14. **Dizziness plus sweating.** As your kidneys try to flush glucose from your system, the loss of fluids can prompt a drop in blood pressure, triggering dizziness and a sweaty feeling. As your sugar levels increase, so too does the thickness of your blood. And the thicker it gets, the more difficulty it has flowing through the tiniest capillaries. This can make you sweat.

15. **Numbness plus tingling in feet or hands.** High levels of glucose in the blood damage the tiny nerve endings that spider out into your legs, feet, and hands. Neuropathy is the medical term for nerve damage, which triggers these sensations.

16. **Age.** Those 45 and older are at greater risk. Over time your body—and especially your pancreas—accumulates damage from environmental toxins, nutrient-poor foods, and a lack of antioxidants in your diet.

17. **Low or inactive thyroid.** When your thyroid is underperforming, you feel sluggish and don't have the energy for basic tasks. Your metabolism slows and your insulin rises. Chronic

stress and poor nutrition can also burn out your thyroid, causing inflammation, weight gain, high insulin, and high blood sugar. (See the Thyroid-Diabetes Connection on page 24.)

18. **Polycystic ovary syndrome.** A women's hormonal imbalance (explained on page 16).

If you are displaying any of these symptoms or risk factors, I strongly suggest you make an appointment with your doctor and request the tests for insulin resistance and MetS, which I previously described. Add the following tests to determine if you have type 2…

Glucose tolerance test. An oral glucose tolerance test is one that can be performed in a doctor's office or a lab. The person being tested starts the test in a fasting state (having no food or drink except water for at least 10 hours but not greater than 16 hours). Test results between 140 and 199 mg/dL indicate prediabetes or worse.

High-sensitivity C-reactive protein (hsCRP). This test determines whether you have the systemic inflammation associated with all chronic diseases. Average risk is 1.0 to 3.0 mg/L; high risk is above 3.0 mg/L.

THE CARDIOVASCULAR CONNECTION

Here's a frightening statistic: 75% of all diabetes-related deaths are due to heart attack or some form of cardiovascular disease.[6] All that glucose, insulin, and fat circulating in your bloodstream can eventually destroy your eyesight, nerves, kidneys, and other organs, but diabetes takes a special toll on the heart. Half of all heart attack victims are found to be insulin resistant, meaning they're already in a prediabetes state and on track to develop full-blown diabetes, usually without their knowledge. Also the percentage of cardiovascular patients who have insulin resistance or MetS may be as high as 50%.

SHOULD DIABETICS TAKE DRUGS TO CONTROL HEART PROBLEMS?

According to recent research, the answer seems to be a resounding "no." In the March 2010 issue of the *New England Journal of Medicine* (*NEJM*), research called the ACCORD study (Action to Control Cardiovascular Risk in Diabetes)[7] theorized that lowering the high blood pressure of people with diabetes would reduce the risk of cardiovascular disease.

Half of the 4,773 diabetes patients in the study took drugs to lower their systolic pressure (the top number) down to 120, which is considered normal. The other half had a more modest goal of 140, which is higher than normal. Shockingly (at least to the doctors who assumed it would), the lower blood pressure numbers *failed* to prevent heart attacks and cardiovascular

---

[6] http://www.americanheart.org/presenter.jhtml?identifier=4726

[7] http://www.nhlbi.nih.gov/health/prof/heart/other/accord/

deaths. And dangerous side effects from the drugs were plentiful, including the toxic load from taking up to three drugs just to lower blood pressure.

The same issue of *NEJM* reported on yet another failed study to lower blood pressure, this one involving 6,400 type 2 patients trying to reduce their systolic blood pressure to 130. The result was a 50% *increase* in the risk of strokes, heart attacks, and death.

Another aspect of the ACCORD study confirms that the current medical obsession with drugs and numbers does nothing to save diabetics from heart attacks. Lowering cholesterol is a common tactic cardiologists have tried—and it fails. Prescribing cholesterol-lowering drugs called *statins* is the preferred conventional treatment, although these drugs have numerous adverse side effects and little to no evidence proving their ability to prevent heart attack or heart disease.

In this most recent study, doctors wanted to add a triglyceride-cholesterol drug called a *fibrate* to their patients' cocktail of pharmaceuticals, in concert with a statin drug. The results showed that combining the fibrate and a statin drug for diabetic patients did *not* produce any lower risk of cardiovascular disease or death as opposed to those taking only one or the other.

Having healthy cholesterol levels and low blood pressure are certainly good for the health of your heart, but tinkering with blood pressure and cholesterol in a patient who already has dysfunctional blood sugar metabolism is not, in my view, the way to treat either the cardiovascular risks of diabetes or diabetes itself. Rather, I've found that reversing the underlying insulin resistance with proper diet and lifestyle modifications reduces all cardiovascular risks, including high blood pressure and high triglycerides. In most cases, drugs are unnecessary and counterproductive.

THE THYROID-DIABETES CONNECTION

Having an underactive thyroid can contribute to diabetes, but it's a risk factor that's often overlooked. I'd consider it a disservice to my patients to assume anyone's diabetes was caused exclusively by poor food choices. To ensure there isn't an underlying thyroid problem that needs to be corrected as we work on my 30-day plan, I have my patients take a complete Thyroid Hormone Panel. Not surprisingly, some of them have indeed had low thyroid function (hypothyroidism). This means that the thyroid gland isn't producing enough hormone to keep the metabolism revving optimally, resulting in exhaustion, weight gain, brain fog, and vulnerability to viruses and frequent colds. Low thyroid also affects insulin's ability to effectively move blood sugar into cells, where it's needed for cellular energy.

In some people, the immune system attacks the thyroid gland mistakenly, interfering with thyroid hormone production and producing weight gain, inflammation, and elevated insulin. If thyroid dysfunction is at the root of your blood sugar problems (and statistics do show a direct correlation between high blood sugar and low thyroid function), it can easily be treated with supplements, nutritious foods and, if necessary, medication. When your thyroid starts functioning normally again, blood sugar abnormalities usually improve or disappear.

GESTATIONAL DIABETES

There's a form of type 2 diabetes, usually temporary, that occurs in about 5% of pregnant women in their third trimester. It's called *gestational diabetes* and it requires more prenatal attention than normal pregnancy. The symptoms are the same as those for prediabetes and type 2. The causes are:

- A family history of gestational diabetes (i.e., your mother, grandmother, or sister had it)

- You have previously given birth to a large baby, weighing over 4.5 kg (9 lb)

- You are overweight or obese

- You have polycystic ovary syndrome (PCOS)

Diet and exercise are the standard treatments for gestational diabetes, but about 1 in 10 women won't be able to lower their blood sugar this way. These women may need oral insulin.

After delivery, blood sugar (glucose) levels generally return to normal. Doctors recommend that mothers breastfeed the newborn within 30 minutes of delivery to keep his/her blood sugar at a safe level and then every two to three hours after. This form of type 2 diabetes is not to be taken lightly. A woman with gestational diabetes is more likely to need a caesarean delivery, and 25% of women develop type 2 diabetes within 15 years. (This may be related to poor diet and exercise, which caused the temporary diabetes to begin with.)

TYPE 1

Type 1 represents 5% to 10% of all diabetes cases. It occurs when the immune system attacks and destroys the insulin-producing beta cells in the pancreas, rendering it incapable of producing the hormone. Type 1 diabetics must inject supplemental insulin, though by following *The 30-Day Diabetes Cure,* my type 1 patients have been able to cut their dose considerably.

Doctors have long believed type 1 is caused by a malfunctioning immune system and is genetically based, but new theories call this into question. One thing is certain: The incidence of type 1 is rapidly increasing. Here are some speculations as to why…

A family history. Anyone with a parent or sibling with type 1 diabetes has an increased risk of developing the condition.

Genetics. The presence of certain genes indicates an increased risk of developing type 1.

Geography. The incidence of type 1 diabetes increases as you travel away from the equator, suggesting that a deficiency of vitamin D ("the sunshine vitamin") encourages the disease. For example, people living in Finland have the highest incidence of type 1—about two to three times higher than rates in the US and 400 times that of people living in Venezuela. Other research shows that vitamin D is indeed protective against type 1.

Antibodies. These are white blood cells that target the body's own cells, believing them to be foreign invaders. Their excessive presence can predict with relative accuracy whether a healthy child will develop type 1 in the future.

Viral exposure. Exposure to Epstein-Barr virus, Coxsackie virus, mumps virus, or cytomegalovirus may trigger the autoimmune destruction of the islet cells—or the virus may directly infect the islet cells.

Environmental toxins. Strong research suggests that numerous toxic chemicals present in today's environment do damage beta cells, perhaps signaling their destruction by the immune system because they need to be "cleaned up."

Other dietary factors. Omega-3 fatty acids may offer some protection against type 1 diabetes. Drinking water that contains nitrates may increase the risk. Additionally, the timing of the introduction of cereal grains into a baby's diet may affect his or her risk of type 1 diabetes. One clinical trial found that between ages 3 and 7 months appears to be the optimal time for introducing cereal.

TYPE 1 ON THE RISE

Provocative clues abound that suggest that type 1 is not exclusively a genetic disorder. Evidence shows that the incidence of type 1 was relatively low and unchanging until the second half of the 20th century, when there was a statistical increase followed by a dramatic leap in the mid-1980s. It's currently estimated that the incidence of type 1 has doubled in children since the 1980s and is now 10 to 20 times more common than it was 100 years ago.

What could be causing this increase? Researchers theorize it might be reduced exposure to sun, which drives down levels of vitamin D, increasing pollution, and the increased weight and body fat of children as a possible accelerator of type 1 due to the stress it places on the pancreas's insulin-producing cells. Some researchers think a lack of exposure to pathogens that were formerly prevalent—meaning we're just too clean—may be causing hypersensitivity of the immune system, resulting in the body's own white blood cells destroying insulin-producing beta cells in the pancreas.[8]

---

[8] http://www.eurekalert.org/pub_releases/2010-01/kp-iot010410.php

COMPLICATIONS OF TYPE 1

The complications of type 1 diabetes develop gradually, and the earlier you develop diabetes, the higher the risk of complications. Unfortunately, these complications eventually become disabling or even life-threatening. Here are some common complications that must be monitored closely and guarded against:[9]

Heart and blood vessel disease. Diabetes dramatically increases your risk of various cardiovascular problems, including heart attack, coronary artery disease with chest pain (angina), narrowing of the arteries (atherosclerosis), heart failure, stroke, and high blood pressure. As mentioned before, 75% of people who have diabetes die of some type of heart or blood vessel disease, according to the American Heart Association.

Nerve damage (neuropathy). Excess blood sugar injures the walls of capillaries that nourish your nerves, especially in the legs. This can cause tingling, numbness, burning, or pain that begins at the tips of the toes or fingers and gradually spreads upward. A type 1 diabetic can eventually lose all sense of feeling in the affected limbs. Damage to the nerves that control digestion can cause problems with nausea, vomiting, diarrhea, or constipation. For men, erectile dysfunction may be an issue.

Kidney damage (nephropathy). The kidneys contain millions of tiny blood vessels that filter waste from your blood. Diabetes can damage this delicate filtering system. Sometimes this can lead to kidney failure or irreversible end-stage kidney disease, requiring dialysis or a kidney transplant.

Eye damage. Diabetes can damage the blood vessels of the retina (diabetic retinopathy), potentially leading to blindness. Diabetes also increases the risk of other serious vision conditions, such as cataracts and glaucoma.

Foot damage. Nerve damage in the feet or poor blood flow to the feet increases the risk of various foot complications. Left untreated, cuts and blisters can become serious infections. Severe damage might require toe, foot, or even leg amputation.

Skin and mouth conditions. Diabetes may leave you more susceptible to skin problems, including bacterial and fungal infections. Gum infections also may be a concern, especially if you have a history of poor dental hygiene.

Osteoporosis. Diabetes may lead to lower than normal bone mineral density, increasing your risk of osteoporosis.

---

[9] http://www.mayoclinic.com/health/type-1-diabetes/DS00329/DSECTION=complications

Impaired wound healing. Because diabetes compromises blood circulation, the supply of oxygen and vital nutrients is severely reduced. The result is that wounds heal very slowly—and sometimes not at all.

Pregnancy complications. The risk of miscarriage, stillbirth, and birth defects are increased when diabetes isn't well controlled. For the mother, diabetes increases the risk of diabetic *ketoacidosis*, diabetic eye problems (retinopathy), pregnancy-induced high blood pressure, and preeclampsia.

Hearing problems. Hearing impairments occur more often in people with diabetes.

WHAT CAN YOU DO IF YOU HAVE TYPE 1?

A person with type 1 diabetes must monitor blood sugar and take insulin to stay alive. But there's much more you can—and must—do. Every step in *The 30-Day Diabetes Cure* works together to heal the damage done by diabetes and to prevent complications from developing.

Most doctors believe it's not possible to repair a damaged pancreas, but I'm not so sure they're right. They said that about brain cells and heart cells, only to have those beliefs overturned by recent discoveries. Never underestimate the human body's remarkable ability to heal itself. Besides, there's been some promising new research indicating that the pancreas may in fact be able to be repaired, thus reversing diabetes naturally…

- Beta cells were able to be regenerated in laboratory animals, according to research published in 2004 in the journal *Nature* involving Harvard scientists who clearly demonstrated it could be achieved successfully. Although similar studies have yet to be performed on humans, this is an exciting development.

- Several human studies already have shown that both weight loss and exercise can reduce insulin resistance by increasing cell sensitivity to insulin. This means that less natural insulin is required for glucose management, thereby de-stressing your beta cells and boosting their potential productivity and longevity.

- In 2008, the journal *Obesity* published a study examining the effect of exercise and weight loss on a group of obese, elderly adults. After just six months, their insulin sensitivity doubled. Losing weight and being active not only significantly lowered their odds of developing type 2 diabetes but also increased the participants' insulin sensitivity and improved beta cell function.

In *The 30-Day Diabetes Cure*, you'll also discover supplements that have been shown in preliminary research to enhance the function of your remaining beta cells—and perhaps even regenerate new ones. To learn more, be sure to read the Special Report that accompanied your purchase of this book, entitled *How to Heal Your Pancreas*.

NEW FORMS OF DIABETES

Although the following types of diabetes don't have universal definitions and treatments, it is fascinating to note that this disease keeps evolving in different patterns and influencing different parts of the body.

Type 1.5 diabetes. Relatively new, this condition is diagnosed in adults who do not immediately require insulin for treatment and have little or no resistance to insulin. When special lab tests are done, patients are found to have antibodies that attack their beta cells. It is sometimes called Slow Onset type 1 or Latent Autoimmune Diabetes in Adults (LADA).

About 15% to 20% of people diagnosed as type 2 seem to have type 1.5 as well. They are often diagnosed as type 2 because they initially respond to diabetes medications and have adequate insulin production. The first line of treatment is diet and exercise. If that is ineffective, standard type 2 medications are given and many type 1.5 patients usually end up on insulin injections. Curiously, many individuals who have type 1.5 are often slender and physically fit and do not exhibit typical signs of type 2 diabetes, such as the MetS cluster of high triglycerides, low HDL, or high blood pressure. In addition, their insulin sensitivity is normal. Luckily, when their blood sugars are controlled, people with type 1.5 have less risk for heart problems found in type 2 diabetics with high cholesterol and blood pressure.

Type 3 diabetes. This is a newly identified category of diabetes that is "brain-specific." A study from Northwestern University found a link between insulin problems, type 2, and Alzheimer's disease, with excess blood sugar being the cause. In fact, some researchers refer to Alzheimer's disease as "diabetes of the brain." They believe elevated blood glucose levels create tangles in the brain matter called plaques, which block neurotransmitters from communicating with each other, thus causing memory loss and other cognitive dysfunction. Type 3 is associated with other forms of diabetes. Researchers discovered that an earlier onset of type 2 diabetes—usually before age 65—is a risk factor for dementia and Alzheimer's.

All stages and types of diabetes are very serious, requiring your immediate and continuing care. Numerous studies show that diet and lifestyle modification is the most effective way to halt and reverse all diabetes-related health problems (with the exception of type 1, although here too they are very helpful). *The 30-Day Diabetes Cure* makes it easy for you to adopt a diabetes healing lifestyle on a step-by-step, day-by-day basis.

CHAPTER TWO

THE MEDICALIZATION OF THE DIABETES "EPIDEMIC"

The doctor of the future will give no medicine,
but will interest his patients in the care of the human frame,
in diet, and in the cause and prevention of disease.

THOMAS ALVA EDISON

DESPITE OVERWHELMING EVIDENCE, the medical industry—including the American Medical Association (AMA) and American Diabetes Association (ADA)—remains "unconvinced" that diet and exercise can reverse both prediabetes and type 2 diabetes. Of those doctors who do recognize the power of diet and other lifestyle changes, most believe the modifications involved are too strict for the average patient to follow long enough to make a difference.

This certainly hasn't been my experience. I've never met a patient who didn't want to get better without drugs. Nor have I ever had a patient with prediabetes or type 2 who hasn't been able to withdraw all glucose-lowering medications, in addition to a host of other diabetes-related drugs, including those for high blood pressure, high cholesterol, depression, and kidney protection (to name just a few). And this has been a relatively easy matter for the vast majority of them.

So what's really stopping doctors and medical associations from going all out to promote this easy, inexpensive, and effective (as proven by numerous scientific studies) approach? I believe the underlying motivations behind the medical community's resistance to a nondrug diabetes protocol have more to do with politics and economics than with science-based results.

Our US health-care system focuses on acute care—emergencies requiring immediate and often dramatic attention. Western-style doctors excel at these heroic surgeries and interventions. From removing a ready-to-burst appendix to unimaginably intricate brain surgery, we get top-notch care in this arena from modern physicians.

But most doctors are far less effective in the face of chronic medical conditions. And they fail miserably at preventing them. This is tragic in several ways, but perhaps most of all because multiple studies show that up to 90% of all chronic medical conditions could be prevented or alleviated with proper patient *education*.

DON'T BLAME YOUR DOCTOR

The truth is, doctors don't get paid for educating their patients. In our profit-based health-care system, insurance companies won't reimburse them for it, so there's little incentive for doctors to teach their patients how to manage and heal their conditions without drugs. That's just one of the ways our health-care system works against you in your attempt to heal yourself of diabetes naturally. Here are some others…

Few physicians specialize in diabetes treatment. Since reimbursement for assessing, educating, and treating diabetes patients isn't very profitable, there's minimal appeal for young doctors to specialize in diabetes. In fact, 85% of diabetes patients are treated by general practitioners who have little training in proper diabetes management.

Most doctors don't know much about nutrition. MDs get about four hours *total* (!) of nutrition education in medical school—and zero hours on herbal remedies, supplements, and alternative medicine. But they *do* know about prescription drugs, and that information comes not only from drug reps and salespeople who wine and dine physicians into prescribing their products, but also from the very medical schools at which our future doctors are trained. A study published in the prestigious *Journal of the American Medical Association* reported that almost two-thirds of academic department heads surveyed at US teaching hospitals and medical schools have financial ties to the drug industry. Drug companies "are involved in every aspect of medical care," according to the lead author. [10]

Today's physician is time-crunched. Doctors spend an average of 8 to 12 minutes with each of their patients—barely sufficient for diagnosing the underlying cause of the problem, let alone mention providing adequate health education for eliminating it. Even if your doctor were aware of the nutrition and lifestyle changes that could reverse your diabetes, there's simply not enough time to educate you and keep you motivated. Physicians don't even have the time to listen to patients. A recent study found that a doctor interrupts his or her patient a mere 23 seconds after the start of their conversation. Check your watch at your next office visit.

To be fair, this isn't your doctor's fault either. Doctors simply don't believe you'll follow through. It's common knowledge that most people have a hard time committing to changing their diet to reverse or successfully manage a disease. Likewise, after an initial burst of good intentions, gym memberships often go unused. Because of this, many (if not most) doctors simply don't believe patients like you will stick with a diet or exercise program, even though it could save you thousands of dollars a year—and even save your life.

But the real reason many patients don't stick with a diet and exercise plan is because their doctors don't provide enough specific information in the first place or any ongoing support so patients are inspired to continue. It's not the doc's fault, really. The real blame lies with our profit-driven

---

[10] http://www.msnbc.msn.com/id/21333262/print/1/displaymode/1098/

health-care system. Most doctors are bright, caring, idealistic people who enter the profession with the idea that they'll be helping others. But the practice of medicine has morphed into the *business* of medicine. The pressure on doctors to use drugs as their primary treatment is overwhelming.

Your doctor could lose his or her license. Doctors are scrutinized very closely by licensing boards. By recommending an "unofficial" treatment, physicians run the risk of lawsuits and losing their medical licenses if a patient complains. It's much safer to "go by the book" and follow the Standard of Treatment protocols, which almost always involve prescribing drugs. The patient may not get any better, but at least the doctor won't wind up in court.

Investors—and doctors—stand to make a bundle. Health industry "insiders" are counting on the diabetes "boom" to generate loads of new revenue and profits. The US already spends $174 billion every year on diabetes care alone, and that number will multiply as diabetes continues to spread like wildfire. Doctors have kids in college and mortgages to pay, too.

Big Pharma exerts a powerful influence over doctors. Billions of dollars are raked in every year from diabetes drugs alone. And that means the pharmaceutical industry has plenty of money to spend on encouraging physicians to prescribe their products. Market analysts are forecasting that the market for diabetes drugs, devices, and monitoring systems will grow at double-digit rates, reaching a value of more than $55 billion by 2016. The market for insulin will grow more than 18% next year alone. Anything that might reduce these sales (such as widespread adoption of lifestyle modifications) is a threat to Big Pharma's bottom line and will be discouraged and discredited whenever possible.

THE NEW SURGICAL "CURE"

But it isn't only drugs, drugs, and more drugs. Surgeons want a piece of the diabetes pie, too. Medical experts are now recommending bariatric (gastric/stomach bypass) surgery as a treatment option for patients with type 2 diabetes, *even if they are not obese*. The financial enticement is powerful: Gastric bypass costs $35,000 and a slightly less invasive procedure known as gastric banding (called Lap-Band) can run as high as $30,000. And Medicare will pay for both procedures when they are deemed "medically necessary."

Does the surgery reverse diabetes? It seems to. Research published in the *American Journal of Medicine* analyzed 600+ studies involving more than 135,000 patients. Results? Seventy-eight percent of diabetic patients who underwent gastric bypass surgery required no diabetes medication. And 86.6% experienced improvements in their diabetic symptoms.

In fact, bariatric surgery is the only "cure" the medical community will endorse. And it's undoubtedly more effective than pharmaceutical treatment, which offers multiple drugs that merely slow down the fast pace of deterioration while doing nothing to reduce a patient's risk of developing serious complications. But is it as safe, inexpensive, and effective as simple diet and lifestyle modifications? Not by a long shot.

HOW IT WORKS

Gastric bypass surgically reduces the size of the stomach, making it impossible (in theory, anyway) to overeat. Once the stomach has been modified with staples, bands, or partial removal, it can hold only a small amount of food, producing impressive weight loss due to mandatory calorie restriction.

Doctors are claiming this to be a promising development, and more type 2 diabetes patients—even those who aren't overweight—seem to be taking the bait. There were 220,000 bariatric surgeries performed in 2008. Analysts forecast that number will continue to rise this year, despite the economic downturn.

But like all surgeries, there are risks of complications, infections, and deaths on the operating table or afterward. And the results aren't as "guaranteed" as advertised. I have a 38-year-old patient named Spence who had the surgery, lost weight, and then ballooned back up to 320 pounds by stuffing his new smaller stomach with food until it expanded to its former size. His A1C (blood sugar) level skyrocketed and his diabetes returned.

What surgeons *don't* tell you about bariatric surgery is that you have to follow a sensible diet and exercise program after the surgery. In fact, you have to be even more careful about what you eat because your stomach size has been reduced so much that you have less room for nutrient-rich foods. Bariatric surgery or not, in the aftermath, you must still eat foods that will help repair the damage done by all the diabetes-induced inflammation. Plus, you also have to take steps against heart disease. In short, you have to eat a diet similar to my meal plan in *The 30-Day Diabetes Cure* and increase your physical activity level anyway. So why not give that a try before going under the surgeon's knife?

With gastric bypass surgery, you'll also face the problem of what to do with all that loose-hanging skin after you've lost 100 pounds or more (something that doesn't happen when you lose weight with proper nutrition and physical activity). This extra skin often requires yet another type of plastic surgery called *corset trunkplasty,* which re-creates an hourglass figure in formerly obese women and gets rid of love handles in men who have rapidly lost massive amounts of weight.

THE LATEST MEDICAL TRICK

Coming soon is a new nonsurgical bariatric procedure known as the *endoluminal sleeve.* Surgeons basically slide a tube down your throat until it reaches the small intestine, where it blocks the absorption of carbohydrate-converted glucose into the bloodstream. Since most refined carbs are broken down into glucose in the small intestine, this effectively blocks their release and conversion into body fat.

It's a slick idea, but you can accomplish the same goal by simply avoiding refined carbs and by eating more "resistant starch" foods, so-named because they resist digestion in the small intestine and are metabolized instead in the large intestine. Result? No glucose surge.

If you'd rather not willingly climb up onto a table to have a tube thrust down your throat and into your gut, you can learn all about glucose-resistant foods on Day 14 of *The 30-Day Diabetes Cure*.

DOES THIS SEEM RIDICULOUS—OR IS IT JUST ME?

Let's step back a moment from the relentless beat of the diabetes-surgery drum and look at where we are. Re-engineering the small intestine is a Frankenstein-like experiment. Medical science has no experience with the effects of shunting so many sugars away from the small intestine and into the large intestine. To bypass the complex workings of an endocrine system that functions beautifully when provided with the proper fuel—essentially using a scalpel to try to remove diabetes as if it were a tumor—seems to me a bizarre and extreme approach. Especially when the problem is so easily repaired with a few simple lifestyle changes.

Bariatric surgery may be a necessary, life-saving option for a person who is morbidly obese, but to recommend it for people of normal weight reveals just how broken, perverse, and distorted the current medical trend for treating diabetes.

CAN YOU AFFORD TO HAVE DIABETES IN THIS ECONOMY?

Medicalizing diabetes is an expensive strategy that our economy simply can't afford. The US health-care system is already overloaded with medical problems that could easily be prevented and reversed with commonsense lifestyle modification.

Nearly 47 million Americans don't have health insurance. Medicare is nearly broke. Insurance premiums are skyrocketing along with deductibles. Medical resources are stretched to the breaking point and will undoubtedly soon be rationed because there simply aren't enough to go around. At this very moment, we have the power to eradicate diabetes in a single generation with aggressive public awareness programs and patient education.

In fact, it's just a matter of time before economic restrictions force many of us to resort to a simple, safe, and inexpensive diabetes cure. Why wait when you can save yourself the unnecessary expense, suffering, and disappointment right now?

CHAPTER THREE

CAN DIABETES BE REVERSED?

Your mind is like a parachute;
it only works when it's open.

ANTHONY J. D'ANGELO

WHICH OF THE FOLLOWING statements about diabetes do you believe is correct?

- Prediabetes, or insulin resistance, is a common blood sugar abnormality you can live with "normally" as long as you monitor your glucose levels and keep them controlled with medications.

- Type 2 diabetes is incurable and irreversible (unless you have bariatric weight-loss surgery), but researchers are closing in on a cure.

- Type 1 diabetes is a purely genetic misfortune. There's nothing you can do about it except take your insulin injections and hope for a pancreas transplant—or a new research breakthrough.

- Diabetes is no big deal these days. By closely monitoring your blood sugar and following your doctor's orders, you can enjoy a normal life and escape the horrific complications of diabetes, including nerve damage, going blind, and losing limbs through amputation, not to mention heart attack, stroke and Alzheimer's disease.

SURPRISE: THEY'RE ALL FALSE!

Not only are all of these statements false, they're extremely *dangerous* if you have diabetes or are on your way to developing it. I realize you've probably heard each of these pronouncements from numerous respected sources: your doctor…the American Diabetes Association (ADA)…the pharmaceutical industry…and the mainstream media.

But every one of these popular beliefs about diabetes is dead wrong, and in a moment I'll show you clinical research that disputes each of them. Furthermore, *The 30-Day Diabetes Cure* will introduce you to actual patients of mine who are living proof that modern medicine's beliefs about diabetes and its treatment are unnecessarily complicated, expensive, risky, and doomed to fail.

Here's the critical fact: The medical establishment has failed to contain the current diabetes epidemic. In *The 30-Day Diabetes Cure,* I will give you a positive, renewed sense of hope for your condition and your future health.

TYPE 2 AND PREDIABETES *CAN* BE REVERSED

While you aren't hearing this from The System, plenty of scientific research proves that both prediabetes and type 2 can be reversed with a few simple diet and lifestyle modifications, just like those presented in *The 30-Day Diabetes Cure*. For example: In 1982, nutritional researcher Kerin O'Dea restored a group of severely diabetic Australian aboriginal men to good health simply by getting them off the typical Western diet of refined carbohydrates and its accompanying sedentary lifestyle (the two major causes of type 2). Not a drop of medication or insulin was required.

The men were badly overweight and insulin-resistant, with seriously elevated cholesterol, triglycerides, and high blood pressure (all major risk factors for heart attack and stroke). They were headed for a shortened life span with miserable complications, including gangrene, blindness, heart failure, various cancers, and amputations of digits and limbs caused by nerve damage. After just seven weeks on her plan, O'Dea drew blood samples and discovered these dramatic changes…

- Blood triglycerides, glucose, and cholesterol levels had plummeted into the healthy range.

- Blood pressure had dropped significantly and normalized.

- The men had lost an average of nearly 20 pounds each.

In O'Dea's own words, "All of the metabolic abnormalities of type 2 diabetes were either greatly improved or completely normalized." The markers for diabetes and heart disease were completely gone!

This discovery, in my view, was as significant as some of the most famous in medical history, ranking right up there with Lister (sterilization), Pasteur (germ theory), Fleming (antibiotics), and other medical superheroes. Like the work of these brilliant earlier medical pioneers, O'Dea's discovery could have prevented unnecessary suffering and saved millions of lives had it been heeded and adopted in mainstream practice. Instead, her research was buried because of medical politics and food industry pressure.

OTHER OPTIMISTIC RESEARCH STUDIES

Other research has confirmed O'Dea's finding regarding the prevention and reversal of type 2 and prediabetes, notably...

- In 1984, the journal *Diabetes* reported on a clinical study done at the University of Vermont College of Medicine proving that increased physical activity boosts cell sensitivity to insulin, thus reversing the insulin resistance that is the precursor to (and underlying cause of) type 2 diabetes. These findings were confirmed by a 2003 study published in *Diabetes Care* demonstrating that sedentary adults who simply added walking to their daily routine cut their risk of developing insulin resistance (prediabetes), even if they didn't lose any weight.[11]

- Researchers at the UCLA School of Medicine found that 50% of type 2 patients were able to reverse their diabetes in just three weeks by making small changes in their diet and adding moderate exercise. "The study shows, contrary to common belief, that type 2 diabetes and metabolic syndrome can be reversed solely through lifestyle changes," according to lead researcher Dr. Christian K. Roberts.[12]

- In 2001, the *New England Journal of Medicine* published research showing that even the simplest dietary changes can reduce the risk of developing type 2 diabetes by nearly 60%. Subsequent studies (which included switching to the delicious, healthful foods you'll discover in *The 30-Day Diabetes Cure*) improved this reduction in diabetes to greater than 95%.[13]

- In 2001, the largest study ever conducted to test the ability of diet and exercise to prevent prediabetes from turning into full-blown type 2 proved to be a smashing success. Doctors at 27 medical centers around the country enrolled 3,234 people and assigned them to receive the drug *metformin* (Glucophage), a placebo, or a lifestyle program involving classes and coaches who kept track of their progress. After three years, the lifestyle program cut the participants' risk of developing diabetes by more than 50%—a much better result than metformin provided. "I don't see this as out of reach for the 10 million people who are at high risk for diabetes," said Dr. David Nathan of Massachusetts General Hospital. (That figure has grown to 60 million Americans alone.)[14]

---

[11] Lindström, Jaana, et al. (2003). The Finnish diabetes prevention study (DPS): lifestyle intervention and 3-year results on diet and physical activity. *Diabetes Care,* 26(12).

[12] Roberts, Christian, MD, et al. (2005). Effect of a diet and exercise intervention on oxidative stress, inflammation, mmp-9, and monocyte chemotactic activity in men with metabolic syndrome factors. *Journal of Applied Physiology.* http://jap.physiology.org/cgi/content/full/100/5/1657

[13] Hu, Frank B., MD, et al. (2001). Diet, lifestyle, and the risk of Type 2 diabetes mellitus in women. *New England Journal of Medicine,* Volume 345:790-797, No. 11. http://content.nejm.org/cgi/content/short/345/11/790

[14] Chang, Kenneth. Diet and exercise are found to cut diabetes by over half. *New York Times,* August 9, 2001. http://www.nytimes.com/2001/08/09/us/diet-and-exercise-are-found-to-cut-diabetes-by-over-half.html

- A 2007 Duke University Medical School study found that type 2 diabetics who reduced their consumption of carbohydrates achieved better blood sugar control and more effective weight loss than those who went on a typical calorie-restricted diet. After just six months, the low-carb group had lower hemoglobin A1C results and lost more weight, with 95% being able to reduce or even completely eliminate their diabetes medications. Plus, as little as a 5% weight loss—about 10 pounds for most people in the study—reduced the risk of diabetes by 58%. That is truly remarkable.

"It's simple," said Eric Westman, MD, director of Duke's Lifestyle Medicine Program and lead author of the study. "If you cut out the carbohydrates, your blood sugar goes down, and you lose weight, which lowers your blood sugar even further. It's a one-two punch."[15]

COMEDIAN DREW CAREY REVERSES HIS TYPE 2

Most doctors maintain there's no cure for any type of diabetes.

But when a patient becomes free of symptoms and can withdraw all medications, what else can you call it?

One recent high-profile example that diabetes can be reversed is Drew Carey, the 53-year-old host of *The Price Is Right*.

"I'm not diabetic anymore," he recently announced. "I'm completely off medications."

CAREY'S 80-POUND WEIGHT LOSS "MISTAKE"

To reverse his diabetes, Drew lost 80 pounds, going from a size 44 waist to a 34 in about seven months, by performing "lots of cardio" and severely restricting his diet.

It is commonly believed that such weight loss is the only way to improve type 2. But this line of thinking has it backward.

In reality, weight loss is a by-product of normalizing metabolic functions in diabetics. Here's why…

When a diabetic stops consuming the foods and beverages that spike blood sugar and insulin levels, weight loss occurs naturally.

---

[15] Westman, Eric C. (2007). Low-carbohydrate nutrition and metabolism. *American Journal of Clinical Nutrition*, vol. 86, no. 2, 276-284. http://www.ajcn.org/cgi/content/full/86/2/276

INSULIN—THE FAT-STORAGE HORMONE

That's because insulin's main job is to turn all that blood sugar into fat (technically, triglycerides) and store it in the fat cells around your waist, hips, and everywhere else.

By reducing glucose and insulin (by changing the kinds of foods you eat), your metabolism will start burning your stored body fat for fuel. Result? Your body starts to shed pounds automatically.

The real key to losing weight is reversing *insulin resistance*, the condition that forces your body to produce excess insulin (and therefore, excess body fat).

Exercise and dieting will certainly achieve this, but it is the hard (and unnecessary) way.

THE 30-DAY DIABETES CURE SHOWS YOU AN EASIER APPROACH

The problem with "losing weight" is that it's a temporary goal. Most dieters will do (or eat) almost anything to achieve their ideal weight, but usually, these extreme means can't be sustained. That's why 95% of all dieters gain back all the weight they lost—and then some.

The 30-Day Diabetes Cure is different. There are no weird diets or extreme exercise regimens you must force upon yourself.

Instead, it focuses on a diet and lifestyle that you can really "live with" for the rest of your life. Keep reading to learn all about it…

TREATMENTS FOR TYPE 2 AND PREDIABETES ARE ON THE WRONG TRACK

While the majority of conventional physicians believe that managing your blood sugar with drugs and regular glucose monitoring is the most successful treatment for type 2 and prediabetes, I found both to be inferior when compared with diet-and-lifestyle modifications like those highlighted in *The 30-Day Diabetes Cure.*

In my experience, diabetes drugs are unnecessary for a majority of prediabetes and type 2 patients. The only instance in which I even consider drugs for these patients is in emergency situations, and even then I withdraw them as soon as possible. Not only are they unnecessary, but many of these drugs are dangerous—and have been proven so for years.

Vigilant glucose monitoring is also unnecessary and ineffective for most type 2 and prediabetes stations. Clinical studies conclusively show it does *nothing* to prevent diabetic complications. Furthermore, self-monitoring of blood glucose (SMBG) may encourage the same bad diet and poor lifestyle habits that allowed the disease to get a foothold in the first place.

Glucose monitoring is very useful in type 1 patients who take insulin—and occasionally for certain type 2 patients prone to low blood sugar (hypoglycemia), particularly those on sulfonylurea drugs. But in general, type 2 diabetes can be managed effectively with the simple diet and exercise you'll discover in *The 30-Day Diabetes Cure*. Two studies published in the *British Medical Journal* confirm this...

■ The first study (O'Kane, 2008) split a group of newly diagnosed type 2 patients into equal self-monitoring and no-monitoring groups. After 12 months, the diabetes (as measured by hemoglobin A1C testing) was no better in the self-monitoring group.[16]

■ The second study (Gulliford, 2008) divided a separate population of type 2 patients into three groups: no monitoring, moderate monitoring, and intense monitoring. Not only did self-monitoring fail to improve control over diabetes, but it also cost more. More important, monitoring actually decreased the patients' quality of life.[17]

Despite this well-published research, most doctors and the ADA continue to recommend self-monitoring. One has to wonder if the cost of test strips and glucose monitors has anything to do with this.

GLUCOSE-LOWERING DRUGS ARE A MISTAKE

Doctors are fixated on lowering numbers, including glucose levels, triglycerides, cholesterol, or blood pressure, instead of reversing the underlying cause of type 2 and prediabetes, which is insulin resistance. Some insurance companies actually pay doctors bonuses when their diabetic patients drive down their numbers to very low levels.

But this "numbers mentality" leads patients to believe that they can eat whatever they want as long as they just take a pill or inject a little extra insulin to keep their glucose in the normal range. *This is a big mistake.*

Lowering glucose isn't the same as healing diabetes. As you'll read in *The 30-Day Diabetes Cure*, certain foods actually destroy insulin-producing beta cells in the pancreas...cause artery inflammation that leads to heart disease...poison the kidneys...and kill brain cells.

With drugs, you can have ideal "numbers" and yet your diabetes will continue to progress relentlessly.

That's exactly what a shocking study in 2008 proved. Type 2 patients were told to aggressively maintain their hemoglobin A1C (blood sugar) levels at 6.0% or lower. After four years,

---

[16] O'Kane, Maurice J., et al. (2008). Efficacy of self monitoring of blood glucose in patients with newly diagnosed type 2 diabetes (ESMON study): randomised controlled trial. *British Medical Journal,* 336: 1174-1177. http://www.bmj.com/cgi/content/full/336/7654/1174

[17] Gulliford, Martin (2008). Self-monitoring of blood glucose in type 2 diabetes. *British Medical Journal*, 336: 1139-1140. http://www.bmj.com/cgi/content/full/336/7654/1139

these patients suffered significantly more heart attacks and a higher rate of death compared with patients whose levels were between 7.0% and 7.9%.

Many were taking four or five shots of insulin a day. Some were using insulin pumps. Most were monitoring their blood sugar 7 or 8 times daily. The group also took pills to lower their blood sugar, blood pressure, and cholesterol.

In short, they were following their doctor's orders to a tee. But the results were so dismaying that the study had to be canceled early to protect the remaining patients.[18] The medical community was stunned. No one had ever questioned the safety of driving down glucose levels like this. It was always "assumed" to be the right thing to do. Now we know you can have perfect glucose and die from diabetes.

As I said, the real key to healing type 2 and prediabetes is reversing your cells' insulin resistance—not just lowering your blood sugar. And this is incredibly simple to accomplish by simply following *The 30-Day Diabetes Cure* program.

MORE INSULIN ISN'T THE ANSWER, EITHER

Taking drugs to make your pancreas produce more insulin may make your doctor happy (because it brings your glucose levels down), but this is a short-sighted and very dangerous Band-Aid remedy.

A study reported in the March 2010 *New England Journal of Medicine* confirms this. Since doctors assume that "postprandial hyperglycemia" (high blood sugar after eating) is dangerous, researchers proposed lowering it in patients who had prediabetes using a drug called *nateglinide*, which increases insulin secretion. The theory was that lowering postmeal blood sugar with more insulin would decrease the risk of heart disease.

But the results showed just the opposite effect. Not only did nateglinide not reduce the risk of developing full-blown diabetes, but it also failed to reduce the risk of heart disease or "cardiovascular events" (heart attacks). Further, it actually increased the risk of hypoglycemia (low blood sugar), a dangerous condition it its own right.

What's the real solution? Instead of simply supplying your cells with more insulin, they need to be "trained" to become more insulin-sensitive so they can better use your natural insulin—or reduce the amount you need to inject. This reduces your overall "insulin load." This is important because drugs that cause the pancreas to pump out more insulin actually *accelerate* the burning-out of beta cells, triggering type 1 (insulin-dependent) diabetes.

More important, excess insulin in your bloodstream causes widespread inflammation, which is directly linked to metabolic syndrome, heart disease, Alzheimer's, and cancer. In addition,

---

[18] Diabetes Study Partially Halted After Deaths by Gina Kolata; *New York Times*—February 7, 2008

insulin and numerous other diabetes drugs can actually *encourage* weight gain in already overweight diabetics. This can be a real conundrum if your doctor is nagging you to lose weight.

The 30-Day Diabetes Cure includes a number of safe, natural, and easy ways to make your cells more sensitive to insulin. Even if you have type 1, you'll be able to reduce your insulin dose significantly. If you have type 2, you'll be preserving the life of the beta cells in your pancreas by not overworking them.

DRUGS WON'T PROTECT YOU FROM DIABETIC COMPLICATIONS

Doctors routinely see so many horrible diabetes complications that they've come to believe they're inevitable. To many, it's not a matter of "if" but when. In fact, that's why the official treatment for a newly diagnosed type 2 diabetic includes an ACE inhibitor (to control blood pressure and protect the kidneys), a cholesterol-lowering drug (to reduce the risk of heart attack, the leading cause of death in diabetes), and of course, medications that either control blood glucose or enhance insulin production (or both).

But these drugs are rarely effective and do absolutely nothing to reverse the underlying cause of diabetes: insulin resistance in your cells. Yet that's exactly where all the horrible complications of diabetes begin—and no amount of drugs or surgery will stop them. In truth, *no glucose-lowering drug has ever been shown to produce a reliable reduction in diabetic complications*. Neither has aggressive glucose monitoring.

Diabetics aren't dying because we don't know how to lower glucose—they're dying from complications. And they'll keep dying until we heal diabetes at the most fundamental level, using diet and increased physical activity.

In the words of the Cleveland Clinic's Dr. Steve Nissen: "We've got to move beyond a glucose-centric approach.[19] We have 10 classes of drugs to lower blood sugar, (but) we need ways to lower blood sugar that reduce the complications."

Those sentiments are echoed by an overwhelmed family doctor in Logan County, West Virginia (which has the highest rate of diabetes in the entire US): "What happens is, we're throwing medicines at them, but medication is not a cure. We're not getting at the core of diabetes, which is diet and exercise. Some people are taking six, eight pills for their diabetes, checking their sugars four times a day. They just hate it."[20]

In fact, recent research proves that these drugs are not only worthless in fighting diabetes, but actually harmful. The *New England Journal of Medicine (NEJM)* reported in March 2010 on the ACCORD study, which theorized that lowering the high blood pressure of people with diabetes would reduce the risk of cardiovascular disease.

---

[19] *Diabetes Rising* by Dan Hurley; Kaplan Publishing—p. 74

[20] *Diabetes Rising* by Dan Hurley; Kaplan Publishing—p. 84

Half of the 4,773 patients in the study took drugs to lower their systolic pressure (the top number) down to 120, which is considered normal. The other half had a goal of 140, which is higher than normal. Surprisingly (at least to the doctors who assumed it would), the lower blood pressure numbers failed to prevent heart attacks and cardiovascular deaths. And dangerous side effects from the drugs were plentiful, including the toxic load from taking up to three drugs just to lower blood pressure.

The same issue of the *NEJM* reported on yet another failed study to lower blood pressure, this one involving 6,400 type 2 patients trying to lower their systolic blood pressure to 130. The result was a 50% *increase* in the risk of strokes, heart attacks, and death.

Another aspect of the ACCORD study confirms that the current medical obsession with drugs and numbers does nothing to save diabetics from heart attacks. Lowering cholesterol is a common tactic cardiologists have tried—and failed with. Prescribing cholesterol-lowering drugs called statins is the preferred conventional treatment, although these drugs have numerous adverse side effects and little to no evidence proving their ability to prevent heart attack or heart disease.

In this most recent study, doctors wanted to add a triglyceride-cholesterol drug called a *fibrate* to their patients' cocktail of pharmaceuticals, in concert with a statin drug. The results showed that combining the fibrate and a statin drug for diabetic patients did not produce any benefit in lower risk of cardiovascular disease or death as opposed to those taking only one or the other.

Having healthy cholesterol levels and low blood pressure are certainly good for the health of your heart, but tinkering with blood pressure and cholesterol in a patient who already has dysfunctional blood sugar metabolism is not, in my view, the way to treat either the cardiovascular risk or the diabetes. Rather, I've found that once you reverse the insulin resistance with proper diet and lifestyle modifications, cardiovascular risks—including high blood pressure and high triglycerides—resolve themselves. The drugs are unnecessary and counterproductive.

IS THERE ANY HOPE FOR PEOPLE WITH TYPE 1?

The mainstream belief is that type 1 diabetes is an autoimmune disease in which the body's immune system destroys its own insulin-producing beta cells. Once the cells are wiped out, doctors say, they're gone forever and the patient must rely on lifelong insulin injections.

But fascinating new research is questioning this belief. For one thing, type 1 diabetes is rapidly rising right along with type 2. Relatively rare 200 years ago, type 1 is now twice as common among children as it was in the 1980s and five times greater than after World War II. Epidemiologists say the incidence of type 1 diabetes is 1,000% higher than it was 100 years ago.

How can this be true if genetics are responsible? Human genes don't change that rapidly, but our lifestyle and environment certainly have. One emerging theory is that type 1 isn't an autoimmune malfunction at all, but rather the immune system disposing of beta cells that have been damaged in some way—by a virus, environmental toxins, or food chemicals, including alloxan in white flour and bread. (You'll read more about this beta-cell killer on Day 5 of *The 30-Day Diabetes Cure*.)

Research is also disproving the "once they're gone, they're gone" theory about beta cells. Preliminary studies show that certain foods and supplements may indeed regenerate beta cells in the pancreas so they can produce insulin again. Other nutrients have been found to strengthen the remaining beta cells in type 2 diabetics so that they can once again produce insulin naturally.

Finally, simple lifestyle modifications described in *The 30-Day Diabetes Cure* can increase the body's insulin sensitivity, allowing type 1 patients to dramatically reduce their insulin dosage. My type 1 diabetes patient Jay F. is a good example. He was able to cut his dose by 80% by following *The 30-Day Diabetes Cure* (see page 116). Insulin reductions like these allow patients to avoid diabetic complications later in life.

Call me cynical, but I'm not seeing any mainstream curiosity about reviving the strength of beta-cells—or about getting type 1 patients on lower doses of insulin (even though this could greatly improve their outcomes). The global insulin market is currently worth $3 billion and growing at 14% annually. Need I say more?

WHY AREN'T MORE DOCTORS GETTING THE MESSAGE?

Until now, a handful of doctors believed that diet and lifestyle modification *might* improve diabetes, but they had little experience and even less time to educate their patients. Given the amount of time needed for adequate patient education and ongoing support and motivation, the preference for a quick fix involving drugs is far more convenient. Sadly, profit-driven insurance providers have turned physicians into businesspeople.

That's why I wrote *The 30-Day Diabetes Cure*. It empowers you to use education, the most potent medicine on earth, to help you rethink, improve, and even reverse your diagnosis. Step-by-step and day-by-day, you'll read how to heal your diabetic or prediabetic condition…balance your blood sugar…stabilize and rebuild your insulin production…lose the weight that aggravates your condition, without dieting…strengthen your cardiovascular system…protect yourself from diabetic complications…and lengthen your life.

The 30-Day Diabetes Cure has succeeded with my patients and it will help you succeed, too. I've never had a type 2 patient I haven't been able to move completely off medications. *Ever.* Nor have I had a type 1 diabetic for whom I haven't significantly reduced their insulin dose and dramatically improved their outcome. You can do this! In *The 30-Day Diabetes Cure,* you can read case studies of my patients who did it, too.

THE TRUTH IS BEING HIDDEN FROM YOU

Is the public being lied to? Is there a conspiracy to keep you sick? I don't think so, but there are undeniable financial incentives for every player in our entire health-care system…the pharmaceutical industry…insurance providers…food manufacturers…Big Sugar…agribusiness lobbyists…the mainstream media (which depends on advertising from all of the aforementioned)… and just about everybody else who stands to profit from the explosive Diabetes Boom that is currently affecting the global population.

The combined wealth, influence, and sheer clout of these special interests are mind-boggling. So it's not ignorance, or a conspiracy, to deceive, but powerful forces in our society are undeniably in on this deception. Why? Every party involved recognizes the staggering profit potential of the status quo and none of them wants to rock the boat, regardless of how many people have to perish to preserve their bottom lines.

Money has a tendency to trump our more noble motives—like finding the simplest route to health, even if it involves fewer lucrative drugs, procedures, and products, as well as taking some food products off the market. What is the simpler, cheaper, and more effective path to health? This question has been researched again and again and the answer is always the same: basic lifestyle prevention and treatment; in other words, healthy food and more physical activity. Harsh criticism? Rash judgment? Paranoia? I've been accused of all that and more. But one thing I'm *not* is naïve.

MY MEDICAL JOURNEY

I've worked inside the medical industry long enough to witness the warped politics, egotism, corruption, cover-ups, and influence-peddling that guides its policy and practices. While there are many compassionate and devoted people in health care today, the medical system is broken and can crush the spirit of even the most altruistic medical professional.

That's exactly what happened to me early in my clinical career. On my way to becoming a young physician, I worked in several hospital facilities and couldn't help but notice that very little real healing was going on. I also saw the hugely restrictive political red tape that prevented creatively curious doctors from deviating from the official, recipelike treatment protocols that neatly "managed" symptoms but rarely addressed the underlying causes for virtually all of today's chronic and degenerative diseases. A corporate takeover of the medical profession had shifted physicians from their role as healers to a new one: distributors of pharmaceutical drugs. And I wanted no part of that.

SOMETHING WAS MISSING IN MY TRAINING

I didn't want to completely reject conventional medicine. After all, I recognized that its treatments are appropriate in many instances, especially for acute and critical medical care. Yet I had been interested in holistic health all along because I saw the importance of including both mind and body in health care. I stitched together a dual master's degree as both a nurse practitioner and a clinical specialist in psychiatric and mental health nursing. When I passed my certification exams in both areas, I was one of only forty people nationwide who had done so.

After graduation, I went to work at some of the most prestigious hospitals in the world and held clinical faculty positions at three universities. I was in constant company of some of the greatest medical minds. At their urging, I returned to medical school, yet when I looked around, I saw the same problems perpetuated in medical school as in the hospitals. I understood medicine inside and out—but I'd also witnessed the amazing power of the body to heal itself if we just give it a chance.

I'm telling you all this so you'll be reassured that I'm not a fringy medical heretic when I say you're being lied to about diabetes. I've been a licensed clinical practitioner for about 20 years and have treated thousands of patients. My unusual training and background allow me a unique perspective on today's serious health problems—and the solutions Big Medicine isn't telling you about.

I WANTED TO BE A HEALER—NOT A DEALER

What I *did* want was a medical path that would train me in the art of true healing, so I switched my studies to naturopathy. This was no shortcut. Working toward my doctorate required as much time and study as becoming an MD would have. But the two are as different as night and day.

Naturopathy focuses on stimulating the body's inherent ability to heal and repair itself, using a holistic approach and a minimum of surgery and drugs. This is the true tradition of the physician, hailing all the way back to Hippocrates (400 BC), the ancient Greek referred to as "the father of Western medicine" and the first advocate of naturopathic medicine. Besides using a wide variety of natural remedies, naturopaths emphasize nutrition, prevention, and patient education as pathways to body-mind health and well-being.

Naturopathic doctors are some of the most rigorously trained and educated healers in the world. Rather than apply "Band-Aid" treatments for symptoms, we seek to correct the underlying cause of health problems so they can be resolved permanently. In doing so, we address the patient's psychological/emotional state as well as the physical. Our orientation to the healing process is summed up in the oath we take upon graduation:

- First, do no harm—and provide the most effective health care available with the least risk to patients at all times.

- Recognize, respect, and promote the self-healing power of nature inherent in each individual.

- Identify and remove the causes of illness, rather than eliminating or suppressing symptoms.

- Educate, inspire rational hope, and encourage self-responsibility for health.

- Treat the whole person by considering all individual health factors and influences.

- Emphasize the principles of healthy living to promote well-being to prevent diseases in the individual, the community, and our world.

Long ago, physicians took this same oath, but their Hippocratic Oath has been changed several times—especially in the modern era—to accommodate the use of today's drugs (many of which do indeed cause harm) and to de-emphasize the time-honored focus on disease prevention and patient education.

These changes were primarily *economic* considerations. What else might we expect from a pharmaceutical industry that has enormous influence on the curriculum of America's medical schools? Modern medicine, as a result, has become more of a business and less of an art.

WE COULD WIPE OUT TYPE 2 AND PREDIABETES IF WE REALLY WANTED TO

Some experts attribute diabetes to obesity. Others say it's our modern sedentary lifestyle. Still others blame the patients themselves, implying they are lazy and undisciplined. Rarely is responsibility placed where it deserves to be: on the foods you've been taught to crave and believe are a safe part of your diet. What you're *not* being told is how terrible they are for your health and how they constitute a direct causal link to this terrible disease.

The global pandemic of type 2 diabetes and prediabetes is caused *directly* by our modern diet and its highly processed foods. These include high-carbohydrate/low-nutrient junk, overly processed refined foods, and metabolism-distressing ingredients such as high-fructose corn syrup, trans fats, refined vegetable oils, and artificial sweeteners. Factor in hidden allergies to wheat and other substances (which stress and weaken the human immune system) and a catastrophic absence of high-fiber, nutrient-dense whole foods (fresh fruits and vegetables, whole grains and beans, and humanely raised, hormone-free meat, eggs, fish, and dairy products) and you have a perfect recipe for diabetes.

THE DIABETES INDUSTRY IS BIG BUSINESS

If this truth were widely revealed, and if public health officials openly condemned this diabetes-causing diet, the economic repercussions would be devastating for the giant agribusiness corporations that grow the raw materials for these commercial "food products," a term I prefer because much of what's produced doesn't qualify as real food in my book.

The truth would also hit the manufacturers and marketers who stock these products in our supermarkets, the supermarkets themselves, and the media, which thrive on the advertising revenue these products generate. I assure you that unimaginable sums of money are being generated as diabetes develops and spreads.

Were the medical community to point a finger directly at the foods and beverages causing today's tsunami of type 2 and prediabetes in unaware adults and defenseless children, it would trigger a massive cry from the billion-dollar industries involved…and a lobbying barrage more colossal than Washington and other capitals around the world have ever seen.

Placing the blame on obesity, lack of exercise or the patients themselves is a deceitful distraction from the true cause. That the medical and scientific communities are complicit in this deceit—or remain silent—borders on malpractice.

WHO'S PROTECTING THE AMERICAN PUBLIC?

All our food-related government watchdog agencies, which are supposed to be protecting our health, are obstructed by contradictory goals and objectives, as well as by massive special-interest lobbying. This includes the US Department of Agriculture (safety of agricultural products), the Food and Drug Administration (effectiveness and safety of pharmaceutical drugs), the Environmental Protection Agency (environmental quality), and the Federal Trade Commission (quality of broadcast programming and advertising). Literally billions of our tax dollars in the form of federal agriculture subsidies are pumped into price supports for sugar, corn, wheat, soybeans, and feedlot beef—the raw materials from which many diabetes-causing food products are made. Almost nothing goes to small farmers struggling to raise organic fruits, vegetables, and livestock.

US agricultural capacity, which politicians love to boast about, is based on *volume*, not quality. In actual fact, America's bountiful harvests are the result of copious applications of synthetic fertilizers, herbicides, pesticides, growth hormones, antibiotics, and a host of other dubious chemicals that are linked to numerous health problems in our population. Many studies show that these agricultural chemicals depress the body's immune system, compromise the liver (our most important organ for detoxification), and attack the beta cells of the pancreas (which produce insulin). These facts are well known but the scientific community overall remains hauntingly silent. Just one example: 83 active pesticide ingredients known and shown to cause cancer in animals or humans are still in use today.

Cleaning up our agricultural system would result in hundreds of billions of dollars in lost profits for every industry involved. As for the superlative quality of our food and medical systems, both are misconceptions. The US is 33rd out of 195 nations in infant mortality, 47th in life expectancy of 226 countries, and 13th in heart disease mortality. It is the 16th highest in the incidence of breast cancer, ninth in cancer deaths, and we have nearly four times the incidence of diabetes compared with the world average. When it comes to the incidence of preventable diseases, the US is 17th in the world, right behind Portugal, which means it's healthier there than it is here. The one health statistic that we *do* lead every other nation on earth in? Obesity.

HERE'S MY PROMISE TO YOU

Please don't count on the current medical system to solve the problem or find a cure. You could die waiting. You can significantly improve your current condition *right now* without medications, finger-sticking, bariatric surgery, weight-loss dieting, slavish exercise, or a strict food regimen. On *The 30-Day Diabetes Cure*, you'll eat delicious food…shed pounds without trying… and nurture your body back to health. The best news is that this book contains a simple, natural, inexpensive, and proven way out of today's distressing diabetes conundrum.

CHAPTER FOUR

HOW THIS PLAN WORKS

Although the world is full of suffering,
it is also full of the overcoming of it.

HELEN KELLER

TOMORROW, you'll begin *The 30-Day Diabetes Cure*. I hope you've found these introductory chapters helpful in understanding diabetes and what it takes to reverse it. Today, I offer an overview of my 30-day plan so you know exactly what to expect. First, let me briefly explain how I've structured *The 30-Day Diabetes Cure* into three distinct phases…

PHASE I: BLOOD SUGAR "BOOT CAMP"

This is the strictest stage of the plan. During the first 10 days, you're going to go "cold turkey" off all the diabetes-causing foods, beverages, and bad habits that have been making you sick and threatening your life.

For the next 10 days, you won't be consuming any sodas, sugary beverages, fruit juice, candy, or refined carbohydrates (including breakfast cereals, chips, cookies, ice cream, and energy bars). You'll also abstain from bread, rice, potatoes, pasta, whole grains, and baked goods. No beer, wine, or alcohol of any kind. You won't even eat any fruit. And you'll eat no restaurant meals of any kind.

Before you freak out, know that you *will* be eating three regular meals a day, plus two healthy snacks (whether you feel like having them or not!). I want to reassure you that you'll never feel hungry during this initial period—or ever—on *The 30-Day Diabetes Cure*.

You'll be enjoying a satisfying variety of delicious and filling foods, from meat, fish, and poultry to dairy, eggs, veggies, and cheese. Plus, your withdrawal from the diabetes-causing foods will be gradual over the next 10 days and you'll be able to reintroduce many foods (though not all of them) in Phase II.

During Phase I, you'll also relearn an essential skill, one with which you were born: how to distinguish between true hunger and mere appetite, the latter being a psychological desire for certain tastes.

If the cold-turkey approach to quitting certain foods seems harsh, let me explain why my patients and I have found this to be the quickest, most effective way to halt the progression of diabetes and start reversing it:

Cutting back just doesn't work. Study after study shows that gradual withdrawal from cigarette smoking, alcohol dependency, and other drug addictions just doesn't work. The same is true for food addictions—and that's basically what people with diabetes and blood sugar irregularities have developed over the course of their lives. "Cutting back" is like giving a hungry wild cheetah a can of cat food. This only aggravates the animal's hunger, driving it to kill and eat anything it encounters. Your eating habits, along with the particular tastes, appetites, and desires you've developed over a lifetime of consuming food, are not unlike this ravenous animal, and they aren't swiftly changed by gradual withdrawal.

Imagine asking a heroin addict to limit himself to just one injection every 24 hours. Or allowing an alcoholic just one drink a day. Try telling a lifelong smoker she can have just one cigarette every 24 hours. It's impossible to succeed this way because consuming smaller amounts of any troubling substance simply feeds the desire for more of it.

Think about eating just one potato chip. Remember the advertising campaign "Bet you can't eat just one"? I absolutely don't want to set you up for failure—a sure thing with any slow withdrawal method—because it can lead to feelings of guilt, low self-esteem, and "justification" for quitting the program entirely. In the long run, it takes far more willpower to *limit* your consumption of these disease-causing foods every day than to simply say *"absolutely no"* to them.

Your body needs time to recondition. We human beings are creatures of habit. And the older we get, the stronger these habits become—sometimes taking on a life of their own. If you're accustomed to curling up on the couch and munching an after-dinner snack while watching TV, your mind and body will come to expect this night after night. Many of our urges and habits are triggered by our subconscious and we generally obey them without question.

Saying no to the list of diabetes-causing foods for the next 10 days will break one of your enduring habituated patterns. It will also weaken your dependency on (and sometimes even an addiction to) certain strong flavors, whether it's sweet, salty, greasy, gooey, or alcoholic. While it may be challenging for the first few days, these bad patterns will diminish relatively quickly. With determination and commitment during these initial days, you'll find yourself in charge of your subconscious habits and urges, instead of the other way around. And like many of my patients who have worked with this plan, you'll discover that this gives you tremendous confidence to keep moving forward.

Most important, Phase I will change you *internally*. That's because every night, during the eight hours you sleep, your body's biochemistry becomes a clean slate, returning to what we call "baseline." It's as though every morning you're given a new chance. Your goal in Phase I will be to maintain this baseline state by keeping taboo foods out of your system.

You'll break the vicious "carbohydrate craving" cycle. Eating bad carbs creates the desire for more, and by eating more, you continue the cycle over and over, like an endless feedback loop. This isn't just a psychological phenomenon. It's actually very physical. You see, when you eat a food that quickly breaks down into glucose—as all simple carbohydrates do—your pancreas triggers an insulin spike to quickly remove the sugar from your bloodstream. So, first you get a jolt of energy from simple carbs, but this is followed by an equally strong valley of fatigue… and hunger all over again as your bloodstream and brain chemicals actually *crave* more carbohydrates.

Your blood sugar will normalize. Cutting out these bad carbs during Phase I will relax the near-constant demand you've been placing on your pancreas. This means its insulin-producing beta cells can take a much-deserved vacation from being overworked. Quitting simple carbs will also re-sensitize your cells to insulin so they'll need less of it—even if you have type 1 and take insulin injections. If you have type 2, this re-sensitization will start to reverse the insulin resistance in your cells. And that means your doctor can lower your dose of medication.

You'll lose weight without trying. Before Phase I, when you fed your body all that glucose in the form of simple carbs, your body couldn't use it all. Anything extra was turned into fat and stored on your belly and hips. Eliminating bad carbs from your diet will not only halt the fat-storage process, but can reverse it. Without a constant supply of glucose-producing foods, your fat cells will be forced to release their contents back into the bloodstream, where they're reconverted into fuel for energy. That's why, by the end of Phase I, many people on *The 30-Day Diabetes Cure* experience a loss of between two and six pounds. And that's *without dieting*.

You'll be surprised how quickly these 10 days move along. And while the first few days may seem challenging, once you get beyond them, the rest of *The 30-Day Diabetes Cure* is relatively easy. As your food cravings drop away, everything gets a lot easier.

During these first few days, if the going gets tough, I urge you to return to this chapter and re-read the description and benefits of Phase I. It will remind you of the importance of these first 10 days and firm up your resolve.

PHASE II: INSIDE THE BUBBLE

Phase II is a bit like being a newborn in an incubator, where you're relatively safe from temptations and distractions that can undermine your progress.

Once you're able to eliminate your cravings for bad carbs and other diabetes-provoking foods, you'll gradually reintroduce many of the foods you've come to enjoy—but in healthier versions. You'll be able to eat bread and baked goods…pasta…pizza…potatoes…rice…fruit… dessert…and even alcohol in moderation. But no restaurant food just yet.

The goal of Phase II is to re-educate your taste buds so you actually enjoy and *desire* meals and foods that heal your diabetes. With our menu selections, this shouldn't even be a challenge. All meals are based on the flavorful, brilliantly colored Mediterranean diet, perhaps the healthiest way of eating on earth. The emphasis is on plenty of fresh produce, including the most luscious vegetables; tummy-filling whole grains, beans, and legumes; succulent fish and healthy meats; flavorful olive oil and monounsaturated fats; heavenly nuts and fruit; and moderate amounts of fresh eggs and dairy foods.

Phase II will also introduce you to the specific vitamins and supplements that have been shown to be especially helpful for people with blood sugar problems.

Finally, because uncontrolled stress is particularly bad for people with diabetes, you'll discover how to de-stress your nervous system and de-activate the hormones *cortisol* and *adrenaline*, which actually push your blood sugar to dangerously high levels.

You'll also notice an acceleration in your weight loss. By the end of Phase II, most people lose between eight and 15 pounds—again, without even *thinking* about dieting or weight loss. If you're like my other patients who've employed this plan, you'll begin to notice that your clothes fit better. In fact, at this point, many people are able to slip into outfits they haven't been able to wear for years.

But more important, your weight loss is confirmation that you're well on your way to reversing type 2 diabetes and insulin resistance. In addition to losing weight, people who have type 1 should be able to significantly reduce their insulin dosage (with their doctor's permission, of course).

PHASE III: READY FOR THE OUTSIDE WORLD

After 20 days on *The 30-Day Diabetes Cure*, you'll be ready for the real test: the outside world and its relentless enticements to eat and drink as you once did. After spending almost three weeks inside a "bubble" of protection while you learned to replace the foods and beverages that harmed your body with those that can help and heal it, you'll be well prepared to snub the seductions.

During Phase III, you'll learn how to conquer the biggest temptations a person with blood sugar irregularities must face. You'll discover proven strategies for surviving dinner parties, restaurants, travel, gas stations, airports, the food court at the mall—and even fast-food menus. Remember those two daily snacks? They're an integral part of moving into Phase III.

Think of this as your "advanced training." You'll gain valuable insights into the subtle ways some people sabotage their progress so you can avoid these pitfalls altogether. You'll learn how to identify where to find friendly support for your new mission. You'll read about special nutritional supplements that can help elevate you to the next level of natural glucose management and possibly even support and repair your damaged beta cells. And you'll see how easy it can be to add more lean muscle to your physique, which will help your body utilize insulin much more efficiently.

MEET THE NEW "YOU!"

In just 30 short days, you're going to transform your mind, your body, and your biochemistry. You'll go from being sick, feeling tired all the time, and relying on multiple medications... to being a "younger," stronger, leaner, healthier, and more energetic human being. How will you change? Let me count the ways...

1. Right off the bat, starting with Day 1, this program begins to reverse your cells' insulin resistance, the root cause of type 2 diabetes.

2. You'll discover a wide variety of delicious foods and nonstrenuous physical activities that actually increase your cells' sensitivity to insulin.

3. Your pancreas won't be flogged into producing as much insulin—and this alone will protect the health and longevity of your beta cells, as well as your entire body.

4. This improvement naturally leads to weight loss as your cells begin to empty out their stored fat, using it for energy.

5. Less sugary glucose in your arteries means they won't be so inflamed (the number-one way heart disease develops). And by consuming more antioxidant-rich foods and supplements, you'll begin to heal the damage that past inflammation has caused. Result? In addition to healing your diabetes and insulin resistance, you'll also be reversing the process of heart disease...Alzheimer's...and quite possibly cancer at the same time.

6. Less fat in your bloodstream will make your blood platelets less sticky, which can dramatically improve your circulation. At this point, more oxygen-rich blood and nutrients are reaching the tiny capillaries in your eyes, your brain, and your extremities. All of this greatly reduces the underlying problems that lead to the most horrific complications of diabetes— vision loss, dementia, and Alzheimer's, plus the horrible amputations that are so common when insulin and glucose are out of control.

7. Better circulation and nutrition also means more energy gets delivered to all parts of your body. As a result, you'll feel better...have more energy...and find you're more lighthearted because the "happiness neurotransmitters" in your brain will be getting fed.

Bingo! In a relatively short time, your metabolism will be acting "normal" again, just as long as you don't go back to the crazy foods and lifestyle that triggered your disease in the first place. It's that simple and straightforward.

AND IT REALLY WORKS!

Day by day—in a simple, systematic way—you'll remove the diabetes-causing substances and habits that threaten your life and happiness. And, one by one, you'll replace them with the life-affirming foods and behaviors that can repair, regenerate, and revitalize your entire being from head to toe.

By the end of my program, you may not be completely free of diabetes, but you *will* be well on your way and absolutely grounded in the Diabetes Healing Lifestyle that can conquer type 2 and reverse insulin resistance, while normalizing your blood sugar and hormone balance.

Those of you with type 1 should find your need for supplemental insulin significantly reduced as your body becomes better able to utilize insulin. Best of all, your risk of nasty diabetic complications will be dramatically reduced.

WHAT IF YOU SLIP UP?

I've planned for that, too. We're only human, after all, and sometimes we fall back into old habits. If this happens to you, you'll quickly recognize you're in trouble by the junky stuff you're eating again…by the tired, half-sick way you feel…and by the pounds and inches creeping back on your body.

Should the slip occur, just go back to Phase I and start with the first day. It will be easier this time, because you've already followed my plan once. Stay there as long as you like, but at least until you get things back under control.

Keep in close touch with your doctor. If you fall off the wagon for a lengthy period, you may need help with medications temporarily until you can regain your balance. But keep in mind that you will never, *ever* be able to return to the lifestyle that upset your blood chemistry in the first place and damaged the beta cells in your pancreas as a result. *The 30-Day Diabetes Cure* is not a magic bullet that allows you to go back to a life of junk food, sodas, and rich desserts. That path will always lead to diabetes and other serious health complications.

More than anything, *The 30-Day Diabetes Cure* is a lifestyle, not a temporary fix. As they say at Alcoholics Anonymous: "It works if you work it." So work it, friends. I have every confidence you can.

MAKE YOUR DOCTOR YOUR PARTNER IN THIS

I strongly urge you to seek your doctor's help and support in implementing this program, especially if you're on any medication. *Never discontinue any medicines without your doctor's approval.* If you're self-administering insulin, your blood sugar reading will be your best guide as to the dose you need. But always advise your physician of your progress.

Many doctors are skeptical of the power of natural healing, nutrition, and lifestyle modifications, so be sure to explain everything you're attempting on *The 30-Day Diabetes Cure* to your physician. Your success could open his or her mind and perhaps even trigger a significant change in the way your doctor treats diabetes as a result. (Wouldn't that be nice?)

Occasionally, you'll encounter a physician whose beliefs are so rigid that he/she refuses to entertain *any* unconventional therapies. If this describes your doctor, you may want to reconsider whether this clinician is right for you.

Always remember: Your doctor works for you—not the other way around. If your physician isn't supportive and cooperative, find one who is. Modern medicine is changing rapidly, so it shouldn't be difficult to locate a physician or health practitioner who is willing to incorporate new ideas, as long as they aren't dangerous (or nutty).

In fact, the reverse is often true. Many doctors are *excited* when their patients make a commitment to getting well using steps like the ones in my plan. The truth is, physicians just don't see that many patients who want to try. Imagine how depressing it is to try to save the lives of patients who won't lift a finger to save themselves. In many cases, doctors have to fight just to get a patient to take his or her medications. No wonder they get so discouraged.

YOU'LL BE A HERO TO EVERYONE AROUND YOU

But you're not that kind of patient. You're going to be a "diabetes warrior." You're going to fight for your health as if your life depends on it (because it does!). You're going to turn your condition around, starting tomorrow on Day 1 of *The 30-Day Diabetes Cure*. You're going to inspire your doctor and your friends by your example. You're going to be the poster child for self-healing. Are you smiling at the prospect?

You're also going to declare your independence from the greedy corporations that run the food, insurance, and advertising industries, as well as our corrupt medical system. And in doing so, you're going to help *change the world.*

You've already read in chapter one about the numerous studies that prove the effectiveness and superiority of simple lifestyle modifications over drug therapy. As I've said before, the deck is stacked against you. Everyone will be pushing diabetes drugs on you, including TV ads, the ADA, your local pharmacy, and, most likely, your doctor.

Corporations—especially drug companies and food manufacturers—are counting on Americans to take the lazy way out. They don't believe we're strong enough to take real responsibility for ourselves. They've watched us go soft in just two generations, and they don't believe we've got the grit to resist their junky foods, insipid television programs, heavy-handed politics, and their sneaky undermining of democracy and our individual freedoms. This is your opportunity to prove them wrong.

THIS IS ALSO YOUR CHANCE TO TAKE BACK YOUR POWER

Diabetes isn't a contagious virus you catch. It isn't a genetic aberration (except in the case of type 1, and new research is beginning to cast doubt on this theory). And it isn't some unpredictable accident, like a car crash or falling off a ladder. Rather, 95% of all diabetes is something we give to ourselves. It doesn't begin in your blood or pancreas. Diabetes begins in your mind. And that's also where the real cure resides.

There is no doctor, drug, or treatment that has more power over this disease than you do. Saving your life requires *changing* your life. It means taking the next step up the stairway of evolved thinking and discovering a smarter, stronger, happier, and healthier you. It's like the line in the Bob Dylan song: "He not busy being born is busy dying." You're never too old to get better. Now, just one more thing before we get started…

ARE YOU STILL SMOKING?

It's a question I have to ask, especially if you've read this far already and you or a loved one has been diagnosed with diabetes, insulin resistance, or metabolic syndrome, putting you on the fast track toward this deadly disease and all its complications.

If you have somehow missed the last 30 years of clinical studies and medical research and public service media campaigns and new laws protecting nonsmokers' rights…and you continue to smoke, I'm just not sure we can help you heal your diabetes—unless you quit now.

That's because I can hardly expect you to be able to make the kind of commitment that healing your diabetes and restoring your birthright of good health and longevity will require by following *The 30-Day Diabetes Cure*…if you insist on negating that effort every time you puff on a cigarette.

Quite frankly, with every cigarette you smoke, you are shutting the door on any chance of healing your diabetes because diabetes increases your risk of heart disease by some 400%…and if you smoke, you're already there.

Now is the time to take matters in hand. If you are serious about healing your diabetes, then you have to be serious about your good health, and the absolute first thing you have to do is commit to quitting smoking.

It's not easy. I'll be the first to say that quitting smoking is not easy. You're battling a serious chemical dependency that is insidiously entwined with routine, ritual and lifestyle. If you smoke, then your friends are probably smokers, as is your spouse. Your parents probably smoked when you were growing up. If you have children who are teenagers or young adults, they smoke. Your coworkers smoke, and you join them outside, no matter the weather, losing valuable time at work while you're out there.

Your car stinks, your house stinks, your furniture and your clothing and your hair smell like an old ashtray. You have tried to quit, maybe more than once, and maybe you were temporarily successful. (The American Cancer Society says 70% of smokers want to quit, and 40% have tried.) You may have gained weight when you quit, and started again to slim down. You may have felt like the odd man out around your friends and family and found it impossible to be a non-smoker around them.

Quit now for immediate benefits. Within 20 minutes of your last cigarette, your blood pressure and your pulse rate will go down, and circulation to your hands and feet will improve. Within 24 hours, your heart begins to repair itself. In another 24 hours, your nerves will begin to repair themselves. In a couple of weeks your lung power will improve, your ability to take a walk around the block will improve…and your potential life span will have increased dramatically.

Unfortunately, nicotine withdrawal is more than unpleasant; it's almost impossible to withstand. According to the American Cancer Society, less than 10% of smokers are able to quit without some kind of assistance. Your dependence on this drug—and its connection to dozens of social triggers that prompt you to keep smoking—ensures the cigarette manufacturers a lifelong customer base (though those individual customers have a shorter life span than nonsmokers).

Quit today, and you will feel irritable and impatient. You may be hostile or anxious. You'll have headaches and difficulty concentrating; you may feel depressed or have trouble sleeping. Your heart rate may go down, but your appetite will go up, and your metabolism is going to take a while to recover its ability to naturally burn energy before it turns into fat.

You'll want to smoke every time the phone rings…every time you have a cup of coffee… every time you drink a beer…every time you watch television, or get in the car, or finish a meal or run into a buddy at work or out and about. And you won't get much support from your co-smokers, either.

Yes, you can. Healing your diabetes is as much about changing your lifestyle as it is about rebuilding your health. It's about learning how your food choices impact your body's natural process. It's about understanding the ways in which our consumer culture, our advertising-driven media, and our profit-inspired medical system all work *against you* in your quest for health and well-being.

If you're going to take *The 30-Day Diabetes Cure* challenge, then the first thing you need to do is make the commitment to free yourself from the chains that hold you back from a healthy and balanced life. The honest truth is, there's no room in this plan—or in any life lived to the fullest—for risky and self-defeating behaviors that sabotage your own best efforts, whether or not you are aware of them.

If you are ready to do *whatever it takes* to get back to a natural life of harmony and emotional balance, eating the foods that support your good health, enjoying nights of restful sleep and physically active days, looking forward to a spry old age of enjoying your grandchildren…then be prepared to kick the cigarette habit along with the junk-food habit, the soda habit, the overeating habit, the couch-potato habit…

Build a support system. I strongly urge you to get the support you need to make your transition from smoker to nonsmoker easier. There are "stop smoking" helplines, Web sites, support groups and counselors everywhere you turn, and you will find trained facilitators who can help you with your questions, your fears, your withdrawal symptoms, your cravings, and your commitment.

You're going to need the help of your family and your friends, and you'll find you will need to make changes in the way you spend your time with them until you are confident you can be around them without cigarettes. You'll also have to change every social activity that included smoking while you are working on quitting, so the gatherings and get-togethers with other smokers will be off-limits for a while too.

A plan for stress. You'll need to address your stress levels—not only the added agitation that comes from nicotine withdrawal but also your everyday stress that contributes to your urge to smoke…which ultimately helps calm you down or deal with stress. Take care to avoid situations that are going to aggravate your stress level while you are quitting.

We offer several stress-busting options in *The 30-Day Diabetes Cure*, especially between Days 15 and 20. Take a peek at those suggestions and get started now on reducing your stress levels. Any kind of exercise, including walking, yoga, water-walking, spinning classes, and strength-training, will keep you occupied and diverted, as well as give you an outlet for the excess agitation and anxiety you may be feeling. Join a gym and you'll have plenty of nonsmoking companionship and social interaction as well.

Coping with sleep disorders and depression—both side effects of nicotine withdrawal—are also addressed in *The 30-Day Diabetes Cure*, and in a nutshell are best treated with a healthy diet, the right supplements, and physical activity.

In fact, everything that we recommend in this plan for healing your diabetes fits in perfectly with accepted methods for quitting smoking and coping with nicotine withdrawal. If your doctor is willing to be on board with you for the next 30 days to help you quit smoking and beat your diabetes at the same time, then you have the entire plan at your fingertips.

Get the help you need. Only you can decide if your addiction to nicotine is so severe that—even with all the willpower, motivation, and determination you can muster up—you need extra help. While going cold turkey gets the nicotine out of your system in a matter of days, making it the fastest method toward freedom, the withdrawal symptoms can be brutal, and if your health is further compromised by advanced diabetes, obesity, or heart disease, you may not have the stamina for it.

Talk to your doctor about nicotine replacement therapy, in the form of a patch, gum, lozenges, inhaler, or nasal spray. These treatments all contain nicotine, but none of the other toxic chemicals found in cigarettes and cigarette smoke. The dosage tapers off as you use them over time, allowing your body to have a gradual withdrawal from nicotine if you follow the proper protocol. While there is a danger of continuing addiction, if you stick with the program and hold on to your original commitment and determination, these methods are usually successful.

There are also prescription drugs, including antidepressants and nicotine receptor inhibitors, that can be taken under a doctor's supervision. Like all drugs, these will create other side effects and disrupt your metabolism; if you can avoid going this route, or have the wherewithal to limit your exposure to these medications to a short, pre-arranged duration for quitting smoking, you will be better off.

Hypnosis has offered some success to help people wean themselves not just from cigarettes, but also the lifestyle habits and social triggers that are entwined with smoking. Find a certified hypnotherapist in your area and be sure to ask for references so you can judge the therapist's success rate for yourself.

You can also try acupuncture for nicotine addiction. Because acupuncture works toward balancing the energy in your body, your entire metabolism becomes involved in moving you from addiction to health. Many courts now mandate acupuncture for drug addicts because it's known to be successful in treatment of withdrawal symptoms and cravings. Research at the University of Oslo in Norway found that acupuncture treatment was successful in reducing the desire to smoke for up to five years after the initial treatment.

Quit now...quit for life. Whatever method you choose, know that making the decision now to quit smoking is the single most powerful step you can take toward healing your diabetes and living an active life of health and well-being.

SECTION TWO

THE 30-DAY DIABETES CURE PLAN

PHASE I:

Blood Sugar "Boot Camp"

Days 1 to 10

Character cannot be developed in ease and quiet.
Only through experience of trial and suffering can the soul
be strengthened, ambition inspired, and success achieved.

HELEN KELLER

(-)

DAY 1: BREAK AWAY FROM SWEET FOOD

Denial ain't just a river in Egypt.

MARK TWAIN

ANTI-HEALER: Is a "sweet tooth" worth suffering and dying for? *Hardly.* Breaking this habit is crucial for reversing your diabetes and saving your life. The good news is: It only takes a few days to break its deadly grip…

SOME HISTORIANS believe that the fall of the Roman Empire was hastened by lead contamination. It was the toxic metal the Romans used in everything from plumbing pipes, paints, and spermicides to wine preservatives, eating utensils, face powders, and rouge.[21] Some theorize that exposure to so much lead caused widespread poisoning, which slowly but surely eroded their physical and mental health and brought the empire to its knees. Scientists today acknowledge the toxic effects of lead on the brain, which can indeed make one insane. I believe *sugar poisoning* is the 21st-century equivalent that could very well cause modern Western culture to crumble. If you've read the dreadful diabetes statistics stated in the Introduction to this book, you know that it isn't unreasonable to conclude this.

SUGAR IS POISON IN THE AMOUNTS WE CONSUME TODAY

Americans consume, on average, 170 pounds of sugar *per person* per year, according to the USDA. That's roughly a half pound every single day. Compare that with 100 years ago, when the average sugar consumption was just four pounds per person *per year.*[22]

There can be no doubt that this overconsumption of sugar and sweeteners has led the way to the explosion of diabetes in Western cultures. In fact, sugar is directly responsible for the staggering number of people suffering from severe health problems caused by diabetes. There are patients who require dangerous multiple medications, constant monitoring and frequent invasive medical care because they suffer horrific complications, a miserable quality of life and, eventually, premature death. And that's not to mention the tremendous financial burden these medical

---

[21] http://www.epa.gov/aboutepa/history/topics/perspect/lead.html

[22] http://ezinearticles.com/?Not-So-Sweet---The-Average-American-Consumes-150-170-Pounds-of-Sugar-Each-Year&id=2252026

problems place on the world economy. Last year alone over $400 billion was spent on diabetes treatments.

SUGAR IS THE MOST SICKENING FOOD ON EARTH

There is absolutely no chance of reversing your diabetes or getting off medications until you break this deadly addiction. So for the first 10 days of *The 30-Day Diabetes Cure* (Phase I of my diabetes-reversing plan), you're going to take a healing break from sugar in its many forms, be it candy, dessert, added sweeteners such as brown sugar, table sugar, and honey, or processed foods containing high-fructose corn syrup or other sweeteners (even so-called "diet sweeteners"). On this first day, I want you to remember—if not memorize—these important points…

- Sugar damages your arteries, which causes nerve damage, tissue death, gangrene, and amputation.

- Sugar is the leading cause of heart disease.

- Sugar will steal your eyesight.

- Sugar is devastating to your hormone balance and metabolism.

- Sugar adds to your weight and girth.

- Sugar triggers dangerous inflammation throughout your entire body.

- Sugar represents a severe health risk. It leads directly to diabetes, cardiovascular problems, and cancer.

TAKING A "SUGAR BREAK" WILL SAVE YOUR LIFE!

I won't sugarcoat the truth: If you have a serious sweet tooth, taking a break from sugary desserts and snacks will be challenging. But it's absolutely essential—and entirely possible. Thousands of other people with stronger cravings for sweets than you have succeeded. So you can too. (As you'll soon see, *The 30-Day Diabetes Cure* includes plenty of clever tricks and ingenious strategies that will help make this easier.)

What's your motivation? Your life is at stake. Your future happiness hangs in the balance. If you want to glimpse the misery and suffering that lie ahead for the average diabetic, please re-read my Special Report, *Dodging Diabetes Complications*, that accompanied this book. I assure you, breaking your addiction to sweets will be a walk in the park compared to going blind…having your limbs amputated…suffering a heart attack…or receiving a cancer diagnosis. Besides…

YOU ONLY HAVE TO DO THIS FOR 10 DAYS

That's usually all it takes to break sugar's hold on you—and to learn to love other deliciously satisfying foods that can *heal* your diabetes, instead of making it worse. Giving up sugar and sweets for a short time won't be as painful as you imagine. But if you don't believe you can make it 10 days without sugar, I urge you to stash this book away right now and don't retrieve it until you're really serious about reversing or at least improving your condition.

And if you're one of those people who think: "Life without sweets just isn't worth living," then please return this book for a refund immediately—because unless you are determined to break sugar's stranglehold on you, your future life certainly *won't* be worth living.

COLD TURKEY IS THE FAST LANE TO SUCCESS

You might be wondering: "Why can't I just cut back on my consumption of sweets slowly?" Because it's distressing, painful, counterproductive, and almost always ends in failure. Gradual withdrawal of (or "cutting down" on) any addictive substance—from Camels and Coors to cocaine—simply doesn't work. Plenty of research proves it. And people waste a lot of valuable time trying (and repeatedly failing) with this approach because they still have one foot in the river of "de Nile." To my knowledge, there is not one single addiction-breaking program that successfully uses the "cutting back" approach.

The point is: If you crave sugary dessert foods to the point where you can't give them up for 10 days, you have a serious dependence on them. The only successful solution to this problem is to quit them. If you can do this, you'll emerge a changed person. You won't need to eat doughnuts for breakfast and a vending machine snack cake to quell the mid-afternoon slump. You won't be that person who must have a bowl of ice cream every night in front of the TV.

Now you see why diabetes medications are so popular, don't you? They offer the illusion that you can continue to eat all the sweets you want as long as you use glucose-lowering drugs to pump up your insulin or reduce your blood sugar. Sounds like the perfect plan, right? Wrong. Drugs won't stop the progression of diabetes or protect you from its horrific complications. Study after study confirms this. I urge you to go back and read the Special Report that accompanied this book, *Dodging Diabetes Complications,* so you can see the scientific proof.

UNDERSTANDING THE POWER OF SUGAR

There's no doubt that sugar can have a powerful hold on some people. A famous study involving rats showed that sugar was even more addictive than cocaine. When rats were offered the choice between cocaine and sugar water, more than 90% of them chose the sugar! In addition, they were more motivated to work harder for a sugary reward than for the cocaine.[23] We all know how powerfully addictive cocaine is—could sugar actually be stronger? In my mind, there's no question.

And then there's the sugar–cancer link. In 1924, German scientist Otto Warburg was awarded the Nobel Prize for discovering that cancer cells use glucose as their primary fuel. Subsequent research shows that when cancer develops, blood sugar that should be used by the body for normal functions gets hijacked by cancer cells. This generates excess lactic acid, causing overwhelming fatigue in patients and a welcoming environment in which cancer cells multiply and form tumors. When you have cancer, 95% of your glucose gets diverted to it, instead of to your healthy cells. This deprives the body of the nutrition, and so cancer patients die from malnutrition. Is it worth it?

MY PATIENTS THANK ME FOR THIS "TOUGH LOVE"

Quitting sugar-laden foods is the first step in allowing your body and mind to break the carbohydrate-craving cycle. (I even want you to restrict fruit during Phase I in order to move your blood sugar to baseline.) But don't worry: You'll be reintroducing fresh fruit and healthful sweets into your diet after this initial 10-day period. Here's what you're going to accomplish with this approach…

- We're changing your eating habits and rewiring your brain. Eating sugar leads to craving more sugar (known as "carbohydrate craving"). So abstaining from it temporarily will almost magically disrupt your sugar cravings—often as quickly as within 72 hours.

- Your internal metabolism will begin to change as well. Your need for insulin will be reduced, and the insulin your body does require will be used far more efficiently. You'll be clearing your system of one of the most health-destroying substances.

- As you push on, day by day, something miraculous will happen. The absence of all these sugary foods will begin to normalize your blood glucose. Your pancreas will say "Ah! I can relax" from the relentless drive to produce more and more insulin to process all that sugar— and your overtaxed beta-cells will be able to take a well-deserved break.

- When you stop eating sugary products, your body's leptin response will come back online. (Leptin, as you'll recall, is the hormone that tells your brain when you've eaten enough and also commands your metabolism to burn stored body fat when it needs fuel instead of signaling "It's snack time again!") As a result, you'll begin to lose weight without trying.

---

[23] Appleton, Nancy, MD. *Lick the Sugar Habit*. Penguin Group (USA). 1988.

YOU'LL EXPERIENCE IMMEDIATE BENEFITS

During these first 10 days, you'll also learn to discern the difference between appetite and hunger. (Once we flush all the excess sugar from your system, the distinction will become much clearer to you.) *Hunger*, you see, is a genuine physiological need for nourishment. *Appetite* is a desire or craving for a specific food. Appetite has more to do with your brain than your stomach (plus all those advertisements and appetite triggers that surround us daily). As long as you're ruled by your appetite, you'll never be able to reverse your diabetes.

Believe it or not, your craving for sweets will actually weaken. You read correctly: Not only will you lose your constant desire for sugary foods, but when you do take a bite of something overly sweet, you may not even like it, because your taste buds will have become more sensitized to the delicate sugars in real foods.

Your body will begin to regulate its sugar intake on its own because after this Phase I period, it will know when "enough is enough." This doesn't mean you won't be eating anything sweet for the rest of your life. You can and will—but you'll just be more moderate about it. There's a bounty of natural sugars in natural foods that are satisfying and won't produce abnormal weight gain or out-of-control blood sugar. You'll be re-introducing them—or getting acquainted with them all over again—in Phase II of *The 30-Day Diabetes Cure*.

TIPS FOR CONQUERING YOUR CRAVINGS NOW

Here are some tips my patients successfully employ when they get the yearning for something sweet…

Hydrate often. Drink a large glass of water, a cup of hot herbal tea, a hot coffee, or a chilled glass of plain fizzy water (club soda or seltzer) instead of reaching for sweets. Make sure there's no sugar added, but a tiny bit of stevia and SlimSweet® (see page 75) are okay.

Go nuts. A small handful of mixed nuts (without dried fruit) is a satisfying between-meals snack. The protein in nuts will perk up your brain, instead of triggering a crash the way candy does. Even better, nuts contain healthful monounsaturated fats that help heal diabetes (more about this on Day 11). Just be sure the nuts you munch are unsalted and dry-roasted. Go easy on them, though; nuts contain a lot of calories, so a little goes a long way.

Choose cheese. In Europe, people like to finish a meal with a sampling of cheese instead of a sweet dessert. Choose stronger-flavored artisan cheeses because you won't need a big chunk. A portion about the size of your pinky finger should be plenty. (Cheese is a high-calorie food, too.)

Eat protein instead. Withdrawing from sugar can make you feel tired, unfocused, or headachy. Having a little protein will stabilize your blood sugar in a healthy way. Try half a hard-boiled egg, a quarter cup of chicken or tuna, a few raw nuts, a piece of cheese the size of your pinky, or a quarter cup of chickpeas with a little olive oil. Half a cup of plain low-fat yogurt or cottage cheese will fit the bill. So will a tablespoon of natural peanut butter with celery sticks.

Crunch raw veggies. Always keep a small baggie of fresh-cut vegetables with you. Celery sticks, radishes, carrots, and bell pepper strips satisfy best. There's something about the crunching that satisfies. And if you pay close attention, these veggies are loaded with delicate natural sugars. The problem is, your taste buds need the time to readjust. Coming off of a diet loaded with candy and sweets is like leaving a loud rock concert and not being able to hear your partner whisper "I love you" in your ear.

Gargle and brush. It's good dental hygiene, and it's a slick trick for thwarting sugar cravings. This usually is all it takes to dull the "I need sugar!" impulse. Try it, and while you're at it, floss.

Cut back on caffeine. During this period of sugar withdrawal, caffeine in coffee and tea can manipulate your blood sugar levels for the worse, making you feel like you want sugar. Switching to decaf temporarily will help.

Never skip a meal. Not eating three regular meals is like starving a wild tiger. It's going to eat anything it can get its claws on—and you're no different. When your hunger is raging, you grab the first thing in sight. And in our junk-food world, that's usually the nearest vending machine or snack cart. You'll learn more about this in the days ahead. But for now, eat! Keep that tiger of yours behind bars.

Sip some hot soup. There's something about a cup of soup that takes the edge off of hunger. And the majority of soups are good for you. When you have the urge for something sweet, turn to soup. Microwave for a minute or so and sip it slowly. It will satisfy your appetite and relax you at the same time. Be sure to get low-sodium versions!

What do you really need? Very often, the craving for a sweet treat is really an emotional need for something that's missing from your day—or your life. Maybe you're just bored…or tense… or anxious…or angry…or lonely (or all of the above). Sugar has druglike effects on brain chemistry, so something sweet is usually comforting. But the relief is only temporary. Like all mind-altering drugs, you need to keep taking it to feel the effect. Of course, this won't change your circumstances or problems—and constant eating increases your weight, lowers your self-esteem, weakens your willpower, and puts off until "tomorrow" addressing the source of your distress. Stop eating to make yourself feel better—and change what's really making you feel bad.

In an emergency. If you have a strong dependence on sweets and this temporary abstinence is unbearable, here's an "escape hatch" that can prevent you from completely breaking down and scuttling the entire plan: If your cravings are irresistible, allow yourself a single Lifesaver®, piece of hard candy, or a dark chocolate Hershey's Kiss®.

Whichever you choose, be sure to suck on it slowly and savor all of this sweetness until it has completely dissolved. Strictly limit yourself to just one—and only on those occasions when you just can't make it any other way.

BEWARE OF ALL THOSE "HIDDEN" SUGARS

In addition to the 170 pounds of sugar the average American eats every year, we also ingest another 83 pounds of sweeteners that are added to our foods. Food manufacturers do this because refining and processing food (to make it last on supermarket shelves indefinitely) destroys most of its natural flavor. So to compensate, they add loads of sweeteners, sodium and "flavor-enhancing" additives to make their products palatable. The problem is that this also makes them very unhealthy.

So, on this "giving up sweets day," I also want you to develop an eagle eye for the sweeteners that food manufacturers sneak into their products. (You may need to splurge on a magnifying glass, because these guys intentionally keep the type small on their ingredient lists and disguise the sweeteners they use with exotic names.)

As many as 60% of all processed foods contain high-fructose corn syrup (HFCS), which is why today you'll also start to become an expert on reading labels. (We'll get into more HFCS specifics on Day 3. For now: If you see a product that contains it, drop it like a hot potato.)

Food manufacturers add sugar to just about every processed food imaginable—even foods that don't taste especially sweet, including ketchup, mayonnaise, canned soups, spaghetti sauce, salad dressings, frozen dinners, commercial peanut butter, seasoned potato chips, sports drinks, bottled tea, and so-called "energy" bars.

In order to back off from sugar right now, you may want to call a truce on eating virtually all prepared foods. I say "virtually" because some prepared foods—such as canned tuna, beans, and tomatoes that contain no added sugar—are healthful whole foods, which are an integral part of my 30-day diabetes-reversal plan. From this day forward, read the label on anything you're thinking about eating, from a bag of frozen veggies to a jar of peanut butter.

NEVER EAT "DIABETIC" FOOD PRODUCTS

A quick word here about the deluge of products marketed to diabetics. Go into any drugstore and you'll see shelves of "diabetic" candy and "sugar-free" snack and dessert products. Don't be fooled. These food products are usually sweetened with "sugar alcohols" such as *xylitol*, *mannitol*, and *sorbitol*—or one of the other artificial sweeteners we'll discuss in a moment.

Some of these artificial sugars are derived from plants, while others are manufactured in the lab from various sugar and starch molecules. Though they're not as sweet as table sugar, these artificial sweeteners still shoot into your bloodstream almost as quickly. They have serious downsides, as you'll soon read. And if you've ever had chronic gas, bloating, diarrhea, or intestinal upsets after eating one of these products, check to see if it contained one of these odd sugars, because they produce unpleasant gastric side effects. But even worse: They raise your blood sugar and keep you in a cycle of wanting/needing "fast carbs" for energy.

While diabetic candy and snacks may seem like a clever solution, the larger issue is that these "treats" continue to promote a pattern of eating sweet snack foods that are lacking the diabetes-healing nutrients you'll get in whole, nutritious foods. We want to break this habit in Phase I and move you toward a diet that can reverse—or at least dramatically improve—your condition.

NEVER UNDERESTIMATE "BIG SUGAR'S" INFLUENCE

The American public is slowly becoming aware of the horrible health toll that consuming excessive sugar exerts on our health and that of our children—and manufacturers are beginning to run scared. In 2009, 62 food and beverage manufacturers spent a mind-boggling $56 million to lobby Congress, seeking government favors and protection for their products. That's a nearly 300% increase over the year before!

Furthermore, they are beginning to churn out so-called "healthful" products such as energy drinks and vitamin water to keep us hooked on a steady supply of sugar and sugarlike substances. But these "sugar-free" products are loaded with highly refined chemical concoctions—not just sugar alcohols, but HFCS and weird laboratory-manufactured sugar-derived molecules with natural-sounding names that are anything but.

And because these giant food companies are so powerful, they're able to receive FDA approval for them. But, generally speaking, the FDA is more concerned with the interests of these food companies than the consumers it's supposed to protect. It would take an entire book to expose the FDA's links to the corporate food lobby and the evidence that these lab-constructed sweeteners are in fact harmful to your health. To save time, I'll merely point out which sweeteners you should reject and which are fine to use in moderation.

Remember, the "diabetes industry" would have you believe it's impossible to eat anything without some kind of sugar added. Why else would there be such a market for artificial sweeteners? And I'm not just talking about the dangerous chemical sweeteners added to "diet" soft drinks (more about this on Day 3).

SWEETENERS: MAKING GOOD CHOICES

During the Day 1 phase, there are two sweeteners you may use very occasionally to sweeten your coffee and tea…

Stevia. *Stevia rebaudiana* is a member of the sunflower family and native to South and Central America, where it's commonly known as "sweet leaf" or "sugar leaf." Stevia extract is 300 times sweeter than table sugar, yet contains zero calories. Because stevia has a negligible effect on blood glucose, it's an ideal natural sweetener to use in moderation as you begin to control your carb cravings. Stevia is also recommended for people being treated for obesity and high blood pressure.

Widely used as a sweetener in Japan, stevia has been banned in the US as a food ingredient since the early 1990s (at the request of NutraSweet®, which is now owned by Monsanto), although it is legally sold as a supplement. Rebiana is a trade name for a sweetener containing mainly *steviol glycoside rebaudioside*. Truvia™ is the brand name of a zero-calorie stevia sweetener marketed by Cargill and developed jointly with the Coca-Cola Company, but it's not true stevia. Instead it's been processed and modified using rebiana (a stevia component) and a sugar alcohol called *erythritol*. Avoid these imposters and stick with the real thing. In December 2008 the USDA permitted certain stevia-based sweeteners to be used as food additives (no doubt because the food conglomerate Cargill is behind this). When shopping, experiment until you find a stevia product you like. Some brands can have a bitter or licorice-like aftertaste at high concentrations.

SlimSweet®. Made from a Chinese fruit called *lo-han*, SlimSweet® has less than one carb and zero calories. It's chemical-free and it's a low-glycemic food that has a thermogenic effect, which means it promotes fat burning (rather than fat storage, like most sweeteners). It's about 15 times sweeter than table sugar but won't raise your blood sugar. If your local health food store doesn't carry it, you can order it online.

WHAT ABOUT "FAKE SUGARS"?

I don't recommend artificial sweeteners in "diet" drinks and "sugar-free" food products because they confuse your body's ability to know when it's full. Even though they're marketed as diet aids, these products actually *cause* weight gain, in direct opposition to their stated purpose. Artificial sweeteners don't trigger your body's "I'm full" response because they bypass the leptin response, and thus you end up eating more calories.

The outcome is that fake sugar in any form can increase the amount of calories you take in. In the US, consumption of artificially sweetened foods and drinks has increased exponentially over the past 25 years—and obesity and diabetes right along with it. Some research has even linked artificial sweeteners to depression, memory loss, fatigue, migraines, and seizures.[24]

---

[24] Suzy Cohen, R.Ph., *The 24-Hour Pharmacist* (New York: Collins, 2007), 92

The history behind fake sugars should be enough to make you cringe: Aspartame (marketed as Equal®, NutraSweet®, AminoSweet®, and Canderel®) got its start as a Pentagon biochemical warfare agent. Today it's nearly ubiquitous, appearing in more than 5,000 so-called diet foods, including gum, cereal, soft drinks, table-top sweeteners, jams—even over-the-counter medications.

It's shocking that more than two-thirds of adults in the US and about 40% of kids use aspartame, whether as NutraSweet® or Canderel®. Research already points to aspartame-produced adverse effects including Parkinson's-like symptoms, headaches, mood swings, memory loss, and seizures.[25]

From where I sit, there's a serious lack of long-term studies questioning the safety of the following artificial sweeteners. Their danger as carcinogens and links to various cancers are being ignored, downplayed, or purposely suppressed by their manufacturers and the FDA. For your health, steer clear of any product that contains the following…

- Saccharine (Sweet'N Low®, SugarTwin®)

- Aspartame (Equal®, NutraSweet®, AminoSweet®)

- Sucralose (Splenda®)

- Acesulfame-K (Sunette®, Sweet One®)

- Tagatose (Naturlose™)

- High-fructose corn syrup, corn syrup, or fructose as an additive to any food (on Day 3 we'll talk about HFCS in detail and why you should avoid it).

- Agave syrup. While successfully marketed as a health food, agave syrup actually is so highly processed that it's essentially a high-fructose syrup just like corn syrup, with the same harmful effects on your blood sugar.

To receive free Diabetes Healing Recipes, please visit our Web site, *www.myhealingkitchen.com.*

TAKE ACTION TODAY: Break your dependence on sweets by taking a 10-day break from them starting now. These include white cane sugar, white beet sugar, corn syrup, honey, molasses, pancake syrup (real maple syrup as well as the commercially produced syrups), and brown sugar. Eating a little extra protein and three regularly spaced meals (plus two healthful snacks in between) will weaken your craving for sweets considerably. Nutritious, balanced meals filled with protein, fresh whole fruits and vegetables, and good fats such as olive oil will satisfy hunger and provide your body with the energy it needs.

---

[25] https://www.health.harvard.edu/healthbeat/HEALTHbeat_033005.htm#art1

EXTRA CREDIT: Plan on how you'll break free from sodas (including diet!), fruit drinks, fruit juice, and alcoholic beverages as well (Day 3).

(+)

DAY 2: ADD CINNAMON FOR LOWER BLOOD SUGAR

I've failed over and over and over again in my life, and that is why I succeeded.

MICHAEL JORDAN

HEALER: **This common spice is Mother Nature's glucose reducer. Eat a little every day to lower your blood sugar, improve insulin sensitivity, and reduce inflammation.**

HERE'S A DELICIOUS, heavenly scented way to lower your blood sugar: Just add a sprinkle of cinnamon to your coffee, yogurt, or baked chicken.

Researchers at the USDA have found that cinnamon speeds the conversion of glucose into energy, quickly moving excess blood sugar out of your bloodstream and into cells where it's needed. The magic's in a compound called MHCP (*methylhydroxy chalcone polymer*), which actually stimulates insulin receptors the same way your own insulin does.

If you think it sounds too good to be true, consider the rice pudding study published in the *American Journal of Clinical Nutrition*. Scientists added cinnamon to rice pudding and found those who ate it had a significantly lower rise in blood sugar after eating compared with participants who ate pudding without cinnamon.

ONE-HALF TEASPOON IS ALL IT TAKES

The US Agricultural Research Service says less than half a teaspoon of cinnamon daily reduces blood sugar levels in people with type 2 diabetes. Remember, we're talking about a yummy spice here, not an expensive pharmaceutical. And there are other health benefits as well…

Antioxidant-rich cinnamon also helps block the formation of damaging free radicals, which cause body-wide inflammation leading to heart disease, dementia, and cancer. Antioxidants are what make it such a powerful anti-inflammatory. In fact, a study conducted by the National Institute of Health found that cinnamon, cloves, and allspice have more antioxidant *phenols* per weight than blueberries, one of the most powerful antioxidants in nature.

If you have chronic high blood sugar, your arteries, tissues, and nerves are in a near-constant state of inflammation. But cinnamon actually inhibits the release of *arachidonic acid*, the highly inflammatory fatty acid that contributes to the buildup of plaques in blood vessels and leads to cardiovascular disease, heart attack, and stroke, as well as arthritis, Alzheimer's, and other serious conditions.

SPICE UP HEART HEALTH

Heart disease is a looming threat to every diabetic (heart attack is the cause of death in 75% of all diabetes-related fatalities), but, incredibly, a little daily cinnamon can protect you! Not only does it lower blood sugar, but it also reduces your cholesterol and triglyceride levels (two other serious risk factors for heart attack). Research published in *Diabetes Care* magazine found that people with type 2 diabetes who ate one gram (a quarter teaspoon) to three grams of cinnamon daily reduced their…

- Fasting blood sugar levels by as much as 29%

- Triglycerides by 30%

- LDL cholesterol by 27%

- Total cholesterol by 26%

That's a big return for such a small investment! Dutch scientists reported that participants who consumed three grams of cinnamon per day (less than a teaspoon) lowered their fasting blood sugar 300% better than those who didn't. To discover other Diabetes Healing Superfoods, visit our Web site, *www.myhealingkitchen.com.*

GET CINNAMON HAPPY TODAY

Once you start using cinnamon, you'll wonder how you ever lived without it. Treat yourself to a fresh bottle of ground cinnamon and use a teaspoon daily for best results. Consider these approaches…

1. Dust onto yogurt for breakfast or a snack.

2. Sprinkle on oatmeal, barley, lentils, or split peas.

3. Blend a cup of cooked brown rice with some yogurt and cinnamon (and a little stevia if you like). Heat and enjoy for breakfast or dessert.

4. Add a spoonful to the ground coffee in your coffeepot. Your kitchen will be filled with a delicious aroma and your coffee with the exotic flavors of Mexico.

5. Easier yet, sprinkle it directly into your brewed coffee or tea.

6. Add it to smoothies made with soy milk or yogurt.

7. Sprinkle on cooked sweet potatoes, squash, or pumpkin. A half cup of canned pumpkin (no sugar added) with cinnamon and a couple tablespoons of cream tastes delightful!

8. Bake chicken in a cup of yogurt and a can of chopped tomatoes with a teaspoon of cinnamon for a cinnamon-based curry with incredible flavor.

TAKE ACTION TODAY: Use a teaspoon of cinnamon every day to quickly bring your blood sugar metabolism into balance.

EXTRA CREDIT: Try using cinnamon's high-antioxidant friends—cloves and allspice—in all the same ways you use cinnamon. While their potentially beneficial effects on blood sugar aren't clear, their powerful effects on total body health certainly are.

CASE STUDY: TIM

"On Dr. Ripich's plan, I've lost 26 pounds without even trying!"

When Tim first came to my office, he weighed 222 pounds. When I told him he was prediabetic, it hit him like a ton of bricks. At first, he dismissed the lab findings—even though his A1C was 7.5 and his blood pressure was 162/96. Instead of seeing this as an opportunity to change his life, he viewed *The 30-Day Diabetes Cure* as just another obstacle.

Case Study: Tim	Before	After
Weight	222	196
A1C	7.5	5.6
Blood Pressure	162/96	128/82
Triglycerides	287	132
Meds	Metformin	Nothing

At each exam, he'd complain about having to eat better and schedule time for walking. But, like most of my patients, he noticed improvements right away. The pounds came off more easily than he expected after only a couple of weeks—and he actually began enjoying the eating plan. Fairly soon he decided he could never go back to his old eating habits. After 3 months, he had lost 26 pounds and his blood pressure had returned to normal. After 6 months, his A1C was a normal 5.6.

(-)

DAY 3: ELIMINATE SODAS AND SUGARY DRINKS

We are living in a world today where lemonade is made from artificial flavors and furniture polish is made from real lemons.

ALFRED E. NEWMAN

ANTI-HEALER: **Sodas cause big health problems for people with diabetes. They make your blood sugar go crazy. And the high-fructose corn syrup in them causes you to overeat without realizing it—so you gain weight day after day.**

ELIMINATING SODAS, soft drinks, and fruit juices—and all sugary drinks—is one of the single most important ways you can normalize your blood sugar and then get off your medications. Quitting all this sugar water will dramatically reduce the glucose load on your body, lower your blood sugar levels, and allow your body to better utilize insulin (either your own or your dose) immediately.

Sodas and sugary beverages (even "diet" drinks, and I'll get to that in a moment) are nasty for everyone's health, but they're especially devastating for people with blood sugar problems. So today you're going to put a stop to this.

Exactly what are you eliminating today? All sweetened beverages, including carbonated sodas (the number-one source of calories in the US diet)…"sports" and "energy" drinks… sweetened coffees and teas…fruit drinks, including those made from 100% juice…and every beverage that contains high-fructose corn syrup (HFCS).

THE SCOURGE OF HFCS

Food and beverage manufacturers once used cane sugar (sucrose) to add sweetness to their beverages, but today 55% of sweeteners are made from corn syrup in the form of HFCS. In the 1970s, the soft drink industry turned to corn syrup when they discovered HFCS was 20% sweeter than sugar—and a lot cheaper.

It may have been good for their bottom line, but it's been absolutely terrible for the health of their customers. Here are two reasons HFCS is so damaging…

First, your body actually metabolizes HFCS differently than sugar. The entire burden of processing it falls on your liver, which is already overtaxed because of the myriad chemicals in our food supply. In addition, HFCS converts to fat more readily,[26] making those extra pounds pile up even faster, while elevating the level of triglyceride fats in your bloodstream (a leading cause of heart attacks and heart disease).

Second, research shows that your body doesn't register the calories in HFCS, so it doesn't add to the satiety signal (which tells your body that you've had enough to eat or drink). That's because HFCS interferes with *leptin*, a hormone that relays the "I'm full!" message to your brain. As a result, consuming beverages containing HFCS causes you to consume even more calories.

HFCS IS MAKING US FAT

A 2010 study performed at Princeton University found that rats fed water sweetened with HFCS gained significantly more weight than those that drank water sweetened with ordinary table sugar—even though the calorie intake was exactly the same. (The HFCS concentration used was similar to that found in the sugary drinks Americans gulp by the gallons.)

And the Princeton rats weren't just getting fatter. They were becoming outright obese, with abnormally large fat pockets in their abdomens and high levels of triglyceride fats in their bloodstreams. The same thing happens in humans.

High triglycerides are bad news for your heart. When they circulate in your blood instead of being put to use for energy, they clog up your arteries, impede blood circulation, and force your heart to work harder (which eventually leads to high blood pressure and heart failure).

Worse yet, many of the highly processed, low-fat foods that people eat in order to lose weight are often the ones highest in HFCS. These foods may contain less fat, but because extra sweeteners are substituted in its place, these foods have the same amount of calories—or more.

LOSE A POUND A WEEK WITHOUT EVEN TRYING

It's hard to believe that Americans drink 56 gallons of soft drinks per person per year.[27] And research shows that drinking sodas increases your risk of obesity by a staggering 60%.[28] On the flip side, researchers have found that eliminating just one soft drink per day results in one pound

---

[26] http://well.blogs.nytimes.com/2008/07/24/does-fructose-make-you-fatter/

[27] http://articles.mercola.com/sites/articles/archive/2005/09/29/liquid-candy-the-rise-of-soft-drinks-in-america.aspx

[28] http://articles.mercola.com/sites/articles/archive/2005/09/29/liquid-candy-the-rise-of-soft-drinks-in-america.aspx

lost per week. And that's without changing your diet or lifestyle in any other way. That totals up to 48 lost pounds per year without you ever breaking a sweat. Remember, that's just from cutting out one daily soda—and you're going to give up *all* sugary drinks entirely. Imagine the results!

WHY ELIMINATE 100% FRUIT JUICE TOO?

Even 100% fruit juice spikes your blood sugar because of its natural fructose content. Normally, the fiber portion of the whole fruit slows the conversion of fructose into glucose. But with the fiber gone, drinking the fruit's juice has the same effect on your blood sugar as drinking a soda.

Of course, natural fruit juice contains vitamins, antioxidants, and phytochemicals that are good for your health (which is why you'll reintroduce them in Phase II). But until we get your blood sugar down to baseline, I want you to abstain from juice.

HOW SODAS DESTROY YOUR HEALTH

Cutting out sodas and sweetened beverages will improve your blood sugar and general health almost immediately. That's because these supersweet drinks are really harmful. Here's how…

They immediately spike your glucose levels. This sudden rise in blood sugar triggers your body's insulin response. Insulin converts any glucose you don't immediately burn as fuel into fat for storage in fat cells. When glucose and insulin levels are chronically elevated (and this is precisely what happens when you drink sugary beverages), these cells eventually grow resistant to insulin's efforts, so your pancreas is forced to pump out still more insulin to get the job done. Not only does this drench your cells with insulin, causing a toxic overdose, but eventually your pancreas wears out and can't produce any insulin at all. When this occurs, you are officially a type 1 diabetic.

They make you fat. As insulin transforms excess blood sugar into fat, your body usually stores it in the belly and buttocks areas. Fat cells in these regions act more like glands, secreting enzymes that are highly inflammatory. This inflammation damages blood vessels, tissues, and organs, which leads to serious complications such as heart disease and cancer. Some of the nation's top obesity researchers at institutions like Stanford, Harvard, and Yale have pronounced sodas and other sweetened drinks the leading cause of obesity today. Harvard's famous Nurses' Health Study found that women who drank sugary beverages such as soda or fruit punch increased their risk of weight gain and diabetes by a staggering 50%.

They age you faster. Elevated levels of sugar and insulin in your bloodstream produce inflammatory waste products called advanced glycation end products (AGEs), which accelerate the aging of all tissues in the body. On the skin, they're seen as "age spots" and wrinkles—but this accelerated aging also occurs in organs. People with diabetes frequently appear 15 to 20 years older than their chronological age because biologically they are. But it isn't diabetes that's causing AGEs to flourish. Rather, it's chronically high glucose levels caused by one factor: too much sugar.

They weaken your bones. Sodas contain *phosphoric acid*, which leaches minerals from bones and leads to osteoporosis. This acid also inhibits your body's ability to absorb manganese. Low levels of this trace mineral significantly weaken the stabilizing ligaments that support joints, making them unstable and subject to increased risk of osteoarthritis, dislocation, and injury.

Diet sodas are just as bad. Instead of helping you lose weight, diet sodas actually cause weight gain by boosting insulin production, leading to excessively high insulin in your blood, which triggers greater fat accumulation and even more cravings for sugar. The science against these artificial sweeteners is extremely disturbing (even though many diet drinks are recommended by the American Diabetes Association!)…

- According to a study at University of Texas-San Antonio, people who drank one diet soda daily were 65% more likely to be overweight than those who drank none. Drinking two or more diet sodas a day boosted the risk of obesity even higher.

- A 2009 study published in *Diabetes Care* found that drinking diet soda every day increases the risk of metabolic syndrome (another way of saying "prediabetes") by 36% and the risk of developing type 2 diabetes by as much as 67%.

- Researchers at Purdue University discovered that consuming saccharin (Sweet'N Low®) actually contributes to weight gain. The FDA won't permit saccharin's use as a food additive because it's linked to bladder cancer. Apparently adding it to soft drinks is somehow different (yet I certainly don't understand their rationale).

- Scientists at Duke University found that the sucralose in Splenda® increases the likelihood of obesity, while destroying many beneficial intestinal bacteria (known as probiotics).

- Aspartame, the sweetener in NutraSweet®, Equal®, and Sugar Twin®, has been linked to serious adverse effects, including a higher risk of cancer. When aspartame is broken down in the body, the neurotoxin (brain poison) methanol is produced, causing a range of neurological symptoms, from headaches to seizures. Aspartame, by the way, is being rebranded as AminoSweet®, perhaps with the idea that uninformed consumers will think this carcinogenic chemical is a new "health food."

SODA MANUFACTURERS ARE WELL AWARE OF ALL THIS

Coca-Cola and the US federal government recently entered into a ludicrous partnership with the National Heart, Blood and Lung Institute to promote heart health in women…by encouraging them to drink Diet Coke! Decorating the cans with little hearts and using an ultrathin supermodel spokesperson indicates the height of hypocrisy and widespread propaganda the public is being subjected to.

WHY YOU NEED TO READ LABELS CAREFULLY

Remember that magnifying glass I suggested you buy on Day 1 to start examining the tiny print of food labels? If you haven't yet gotten one, please buy one now, and I'll tell you why…

Americans consume nearly as much HFCS as table sugar, not only because it's in virtually every sweetened drink in the supermarket, but also because food processors add it to almost every processed convenience food.

Would it surprise you to know that HFCS is in Thomas' English Muffins, Campbell's Vegetable Soup, Stove Top Stuffing, Sara Lee Heart Healthy Whole Grain Bread and Special K cereal? (I don't mean to pick on Special K; virtually *every* breakfast cereal on the market contains it.)

HFCS is also included in a vast array of everyday processed foods, including ketchup, tomato sauce, salad dressing, deli coleslaw, crackers, cottage cheese with fruit—and even cough syrups. From pickles to relish, applesauce to baked beans and yogurt, HFCS is everywhere.[29] Why? Because food manufacturers are keyed in to the fact that most Americans have a serious sweet tooth—and they know foods that taste sweet (actually "oversweet") sell.

TAKE YOUR MAGNIFYING GLASS SHOPPING

By examining food labels closely, you'll also begin to notice the mystifying variety of "camouflage words" used to hide the presence of added sweeteners, including corn syrup, molasses, sucrose, dextrose, lactose, juice concentrate, glucose, maltose, fructose, maple syrup, corn sweetener, natural sweeteners and, of course, high-fructose corn syrup.[30]

But you can save yourself the trouble by heeding this rule of thumb: The vast majority of food products that bear a label contain sugar. (Yes, there are some exceptions—and later I'll share my list of nutritious prepared foods that you can feel free to enjoy.)

ARE THERE ANY "GOOD SWEETENERS"?

Let me also answer a question that many of my patients ask: Is there a significant difference among such "natural" sweeteners as molasses and honey? The answer is yes. These do contain

---

[29] http://www.accidentalhedonist.com/index.php/2005/06/09/foods_and_products_containing_high_fruct

[30] http://www.laplaza.org/health/dwc/nadp/mtg3.htm

nutrients and important minerals, but—aside from HFCS's special horrors—your body responds to all sweeteners in the same way: by spiking your blood sugar and calling for more insulin to clear it from your bloodstream.

TAKE A MINI-BREAK FROM ALCOHOL

Everything you've read and heard about moderate alcohol consumption being good for your health is correct. A drink or two helps lower blood pressure, protects against heart disease and destresses your nervous system. Numerous studies confirm its place in a healthful diet—even if you have diabetes. (By the way, I define "moderate" as up to two drinks per day for men and no more than one for women.)

But I'm going to ask you to abstain from any alcohol for Phase I of *The 30-Day Diabetes Cure* because alcohol is high in calories and sugars—and we want to get your blood sugar down to baseline.

Taking a short break from alcohol will accomplish two things. First, it will help make dramatic reductions in your glucose levels. If you're currently on medication, this will lead to a significant reduction in the dose you take. Second, it will reveal any hidden dependency you may have.

Moderation is key to healthful alcohol consumption, and it's just not possible to reverse diabetes or prediabetes if you're overconsuming. If you experience difficulty abstaining from alcohol for these first 10 days, it could be a sign that you have a dependency (and your blood sugar problems could be a direct result). This is a good opportunity to get help if you do have a problem.

If you have been drinking too much, cutting back on your alcohol consumption (provided you don't have an outright dependency) will produce some immediate health benefits. You'll lose weight, improve your blood pressure, and feel better overall. You'll be able to manage your blood sugar more easily and you might even experience a surge in sexual desire. You'll think more clearly, your mood will brighten, and your relationships could improve. Long-term, you'll lower your risk of cancer, stroke, liver disease, and Alzheimer's. You'll be adding precious years to your life. And you'll dramatically reduce your chances of diabetic complications such as vision loss, kidney failure, and limb amputation.

THE PROBLEMS WITH TOO MUCH ALCOHOL

Even moderate amounts of alcohol can cause your blood sugar to rise, a condition that makes diabetes symptoms worse. But drinking even more alcohol can make your blood sugar plummet (hypoglycemia). If you're taking diabetes medications that already moderate your blood sugar, you can quickly become hypoglycemic, suffering a sudden swing to such low blood sugar that you might become dizzy, sleepy, or disoriented. You could confuse this with being drunk, but you won't get the right treatment if you're suffering from a hypoglycemic episode rather than excessive alcohol consumption.

Alcohol prevents fat burning. One of the benefits of changing your diet and lifestyle is that you lose weight. But alcohol consumption may work against this, according to the *Journal of the American Medical Association*. Swiss researchers found that alcohol in the bloodstream slows fat metabolism by more than 30%. If you're in the habit of enjoying chips or pretzels with your drink, you're adding even more empty calories.

In addition, when you drink alcohol, your liver goes into overdrive trying to clear it from your bloodstream, leaving glucose to be converted not into energy, but body fat. Alcohol also reduces the amount of enzymes that break down triglyceride fats—and even encouraging the production of more triglycerides. So you end up with a liver that's so overtaxed by removing alcohol from your blood that it can't pay attention to your cholesterol levels. Your LDL cholesterol and triglycerides go up, increasing your risk for heart disease and added fat storage. (They don't call it a "beer belly" for nothing.)

Alcohol adds empty calories. Still need convincing? Alcohol, which is chemically similar to fat, has about seven calories per gram. Giving up sugary drinks and desserts will help you cut calories, but if you're still sipping two or more cocktails, beers, or glasses of wine daily, you won't make much headway. Incidentally, the sugar that beer is made from (*maltose*) has a higher glycemic index (GI) than white bread. After fermentation, sugars known as *maltodextrins* are left behind. They too have a high GI score and cause an insulin response that leads to fat storage in your abdomen. All alcohol contains calories that get stored as fat, period. What other foods and beverages make your blood sugar problems worse? Find out at *www.myhealingkitchen.com*.

COMING TOMORROW: DIABETES-FRIENDLY BEVERAGES

Tomorrow, I'll provide you with a list of beverages that can actually help and heal your blood sugar, as well as improve your overall health. Until then, slake your thirst with good ole water…iced or hot tea/coffee (if you must have it sweetened, use a tiny bit of stevia)…sparkling water or seltzer with a wedge of lemon/lime…or low-fat milk. That should hold you for the next 24 hours.

TAKE ACTION NOW: Eliminate all sugary beverages, including sodas, "sports" and "energy" drinks, sweetened coffees and teas, and fruit drinks, including those made from 100% juice. Also take a break from alcohol for the next 10 days (you'll be able to reintroduce moderate alcohol consumption after this initial period).

EXTRA CREDIT: Eliminate all products that contain HFCS—not just drinks but also packaged foods. Remember: Use your magnifying glass to scrutinize food labels.

(+)

DAY 4: DRINK THESE HEALING BEVERAGES INSTEAD

It is never too late to be what you might have been.

GEORGE ELIOT

HEALER: **These Diabetes Healing Beverages provide beneficial nutrients while slaking your thirst—but without upsetting your glucose levels and increasing your weight. In fact, they'll help you shed pounds…**

DIABETES CAUSES DEHYDRATION, a dangerous health condition that can lead to shock and death. When glucose isn't metabolized properly, the process of excreting it from the body requires extra fluid. If you're not adequately hydrated, this fluid is pulled from the tissues in your body. This is why excessive thirst and frequent urination are symptoms of impending or existing diabetes.

Unless you're replenishing your body's fluids by drinking extra liquids, you can cause a deficiency of essential electrolytes. According to the Mayo Clinic, the symptoms of dehydration include dry or sticky mouth, a decrease in urine, urine becoming concentrated and dark yellow, the absence of tears, sunken eyes, vomiting, diarrhea, and lethargy—or simply feeling "thirsty" most of the time. So how will you stay hydrated now that you've given up sodas, soft drinks, and fruit juice?

It's easy. The Diabetes Friends Action Network advises that you drink at least 64 ounces of water or other liquids every day. This doesn't include soda or diet soda, fruity drinks, fruit juice or punch, sweetened coffee or tea, or alcoholic beverages. These drinks don't hydrate your tissues and cells, and they trigger a host of blood sugar problems.

GOOD OLE WATER IS STILL BEST

Drinking plenty of water is still tops when it comes to staying hydrated without adding to your health troubles or weight. Get into the habit of carrying a bottle with you everywhere you go, and sip from it frequently. Be sure to avoid plastic containers, though—especially hardened

BPA plastic. New studies are confirming older research, which links plastic to hormone irregularities. So use glass or stainless steel bottles for your portable water supply, and don't drink from plastic cups or bottles. (To be safe, don't store or microwave food in plastic containers or covered with plastic wrap, either.)

As a reminder, some people like to fill a 32-ounce glass bottle with water or some healthful substitute (see our suggestions on page 95) first thing in the morning and keep it on the kitchen counter or their desk at work. If you're uncertain about the quality of your municipal tap water or your water pipes, it's wise to purchase a good-quality water filter to avoid dangerous chemicals.

Here's a tip for making sure you get enough water when you're out: Always order water in restaurants and drink a glass *before* your meal; it'll keep you hydrated *and* help curb your appetite. A slice or two of lemon gives it some flavor and offers a multitude of added benefits, from balancing stomach acids to getting more vitamin C.

TEA PROTECTS AGAINST DIABETES

Tea, whether black or green, is especially good for people with diabetes. Research reported in the *Journal of Agricultural and Food Chemistry* found that tea lowers blood sugar and inhibits the development of diabetic cataracts.

- A five-year study in the UK involving 17,000 participants discovered that those who drank three or more cups of tea (or coffee) per day were at a significantly lower risk for developing diabetes than those who did not drink tea.

- Other studies show that green tea also helps stabilize blood sugar and, especially important for people with diabetes who struggle with weight issues, produces a thermogenic effect, which stimulates the metabolism and helps to burn calories at a faster rate.

- Green tea also has been shown to improve kidney, liver, and pancreatic function—an essential benefit for people with diabetes. It also alleviates arthritis, protects the skin and eyes from disease, and improves gastrointestinal function. In fact, this deliciously multipurpose beverage has also been used to manage allergies, prevent bacterial and viral infections, and treat a variety of other diseases that stem from inflammation (including diabetes and cancer), as well as improve psychological health.

- The primary healing compound in tea is ECGC (Epigallocatechin gallate). Researchers at the University of Minnesota School of Public Health tested the benefits of ECGC in more than 35,000 women. A mere two cups of tea per day reduced their risk of colorectal, esophageal, stomach, and mouth cancers by 30%—and they were 60% less likely to get bladder cancer as well.

And according to a Chinese study reported in 2009 in the *Journal of Food Science*, the same compounds that protect against cancer also reduce blood sugar spikes after eating (your doctor calls this postprandial hyperglycemia) by inhibiting an enzyme called alpha-glucosidase. Black tea performed even better than green tea in their research.

Clever marketing has given Americans a wide range of choices in drinks called "tea," although few of them bear any resemblance to the nutritious traditional beverage we're talking about. Iced tea in a pretty bottle with added fruit "flavor" isn't an energy boost; it's a sugar rush.

BEWARE OF IMPOSTERS

To get the maximum healing benefits, drink tea that's brewed from the leaf or twigs of the plant. Look for true Japanese green tea, which is readily available in health food stores and Asian markets. Rich, fragrant black teas like oolong and other varieties of Japanese tea such as *matcha*, *sencha*, and *gyokuro* all contain more ECGC benefits than Chinese tea (even if it's decaf).

Steep your tea for three to 10 minutes in piping-hot water, but never boil the tea itself or you'll destroy its nutritional value. Drink within one hour of brewing for maximum benefits. One to three cups of tea per day provides plenty of diabetes-healing benefits, while also triggering liver enzymes that detoxify your body of accumulated poisons.

GET BACK TO BASICS WITH REAL COFFEE

The caffeine in coffee is a known stimulant, and some small studies have shown a rise in blood sugar levels immediately after participants were given caffeine tablets. But brewed coffee— black, not loaded with cream, sugar, and flavorings—is actually highly beneficial for people with diabetes.

- Coffee contains magnesium, polyphenols, and a substance called *quinides*, all of which have been found to help regulate blood sugar levels and insulin production. Dutch researchers also discovered compounds in coffee that aid in the metabolism of sugar in the body.

- Multiple studies by Australian researchers reported in a recent article published in the *Archives of Internal Medicine* show that drinking regular or decaf coffee can significantly lower the risk of developing diabetes. And research done at University of California-San Diego with people with prediabetes—whose levels of blood sugar were above normal but not high enough to be defined as diabetes—found the coffee drinkers had a 60% lower risk of developing diabetes compared with those who never drank coffee. According to the researchers, coffee has a "striking protective effect," and not just against developing diabetes.

- Researchers in Finland note that people with diabetes who drink five to six cups of coffee a day have a 30% lower risk of dying from heart disease—and a 36% lower risk of dying from stroke compared with people with diabetes who didn't drink coffee.

However, if you think coffee should taste like a candy cane or apple pie with a huge dollop of whipped cream on top, you're not reaping coffee's health benefits. Instead, you're drinking a dessert that's loaded with over 300 calories, including 43 grams of sugar (not to mention that $4 to $5 price tag and a throwaway cup).

A smarter, healthier (and cheaper) solution is to get yourself a simple, drip-style coffee-maker and brew a pot of coffee at home. Buy a sturdy thermos carafe (glass-lined stainless steel is best) and tote your java to work if you want. Skip the high-calorie additives and the nondairy, chemical-laden "creamers." Instead, add soy milk or a small amount of low-fat milk plus some no-cal stevia[31] if you prefer it sweetened.

If you're feeling more adventurous, try a French-press carafe or a traditional Italian stove-top espresso pot. Experiment with different types of roasts and blends from various coffee-producing countries. Just stay away from those unnatural flavorings like raspberry and caramel because they're usually sugar-based—and don't belong in a good cuppa joe anyway. For an extra zing with healing benefits, remember to sprinkle your grounds or coffee with a little cinnamon. Cinnamon has been shown to reduce blood sugar levels, as you learned on Day 2.

WHAT ABOUT FRESH-SQUEEZED JUICE?

You might think that fresh-squeezed organic fruit and vegetable juices would be acceptable because they provide a wealth of vitamins, minerals, antioxidants, and other supernutritious com-pounds. But as I mentioned on Day 3, these juices must be off-limits for people with diabetes and prediabetes during Phase I because they contain too many calories and quickly elevate blood sugar. This is because they've had their fiber removed—and it's fiber that slows the breakdown of carbohydrates into blood sugar. The more fiber a carb has, the slower its transformation. This results in lower glucose levels and less insulin required for its storage. (You'll learn more about this important distinction in the days ahead.)

Two exceptions to the juice rule for people with diabetes are unsweetened pomegranate juice, which has been diluted by water or fizzy mineral water, and low-sodium tomato juice or V-8 vegetable juice. All other juices and juice drinks should be avoided because they'll play havoc with your glucose levels.

---

[31] For more information on stevia (Stevia rebaudiana), see page 75.

10 DIABETES-FRIENDLY BEVERAGES

These 10 suggestions will help you widen your thirst-quenching horizon, reduce your soda habit, and satisfy your taste buds and thirst. Since you probably won't find these in any vending machine or convenience store, carry them with you in a small thermos so they stay cool. For more free Diabetes Healing Beverages, visit our Web site at *www.myhealingkitchen.com.*

1. **Accessorized water.** Plain water too boring? Add slices of your favorite fruits and veggies—lemons, oranges, watermelon, cucumber, mint, or limes—to a pitcher of ice-cold water for a refreshing and flavorful drink. Carry your own supply with you wherever you go (use a glass bottle or stainless steel container to keep your beverage safe from plastics and chemical leaching).

2. **Soda spritzer.** If the idea of going off soda cold turkey is too scary, break your soda habit by diluting your favorite soft drink with ½ to ⅔ sparkling water. Eventually you'll graduate to just a splash of soda in your sparkling water, and then you'll wonder why you should even bother with it.

3. **Chilled green or black tea.** Both are loaded with antioxidants to fight free radicals, as well as other nutrients. Sweeten with a little no-cal stevia and lemon and/or ginger.

4. **Iced ginger or herbal tea.** Sweeten with a little no-cal stevia and/or unsweetened pomegranate juice to taste.

5. **Low-fat milk.** The calcium in dairy products not only strengthens your bones, but studies show that it also helps you lose weight by burning extra calories. Or, just buy whey protein powder and add it to water. Researchers from University of Sweden and University of Copenhagen have discovered that when whey protein (a by-product of the cheese-making process) is added to a high-carb meal, insulin production is increased between 35% and 57%, helping to manage that flood of glucose into the system.

6. **Iced coffee.** But that doesn't mean a 16-ounce Starbucks Iced Caffe Mocha with Whipped Cream (330 calories)! Instead, brew strong black coffee for its healing antioxidant and caffeine benefits. Mix with a splash of milk and pour over ice.

7. **Fruit spritzer.** Mix ¼ unsweetened pomegranate or blueberry juice with ¾ sparkling water. (Be sure to check the sodium content in mineral waters, though; you want as little added sodium as possible because it's a blood-pressure risk.)

8. **No-cal lemonade.** Squeeze fresh lemons into water or mineral water; sweeten with a little no-cal stevia.

9. **Soy milk.** Be sure to check the sugar content of prepared soy milk, and choose the lowest you can find. (I think unsweetened soy milk is delicious!) Soy protein powder (again, read the labels to avoid high sugar content) can be added to water for a tasty and nutritious drink.

10. **Unsweetened fruit juice smoothies.** In Phase II, when we reintroduce small amounts of whole fruit back into your diet, you can enjoy this treat any time of day: Mix a few frozen berries with unsweetened yogurt and just a splash of apple or orange juice in the blender. (You'll discover other Diabetes Healing Beverages by visiting *www.myhealingkitchen.com*).

TAKE ACTION TODAY: Replace sodas and other sugary beverages with these diabetes-friendly alternatives. Breaking the soda habit is easier when you substitute these for sweetened drinks. You'll find your craving for sodas will drop away in a matter of days.

EXTRA CREDIT: If you can drink 64 ounces of pure water every day for the next week, you get extra credit *and* a gold star!

CASE STUDY: RON

"I was amazed how fast I lost 10 pounds!"

Ron is an estate lawyer who helps people get ready for what happens after they die. It never occurred to him, despite his enormous belly, that he might have a deadly problem himself. When he came to me, he had a dangerously high A1C, high blood pressure, elevated triglycerides, and was seriously overweight. Yet, he lost 10 pounds on his first week on *The 30-Day Diabetes Cure* without even trying to lose weight. He made real progress. His energy improved and his mental clarity helped him in his work. Since then he's lost 34 more—and his A1C is normal again. As of this writing, he's making great progress toward getting off all his meds.

Case Study: Ron	Before	After
Weight	268	224
A1C	8.2	5.4
Blood Pressure	162/92	128/82
Triglycerides	202	142
Meds	Aceon	Aceon (much lower dose)

DAY 5: ELIMINATE ALL "FAST CARBS"

The breakfast slimes, angel food cake, doughnuts and coffee, white bread and gravy cannot build an enduring nation.

MARTIN H. FISCHER

ANTI-HEALER: **Eating white bread—and all other products made of processed, refined grains—spikes your glucose levels as quickly as eating table sugar with a spoon. Cutting fast carbs out of your diet will significantly improve and start reversing your blood sugar problems.**

ONE OF THE SINGLE most important things you can do to *quickly* lower your blood sugar and reduce your weight is to stop eating bread, baked goods, and other "fast carb" foods made from refined wheat and other grains. This includes bagels, muffins, pancakes and waffles, flour tortillas, breadsticks, pizza crust, noodles and pasta, white "minute" rice, dinner rolls, instant mashed potatoes, burger buns, flatbread, crackers, cookies, and chips.

"Oh, no!" you might gasp. "I *love* all those foods. I thought you said this wasn't a 'diet,' Dr. Ripich. You promised there wouldn't be any *deprivation*!"

THIS *ISN'T* A "DIET"

"Dieting" means abstaining from high-calorie foods or excessively large portions until you reach your goal, with the idea that you can somehow return to your old eating habits once you've reached your goal. This is why 95% of all diets fail. And I'm not going to let you set yourself up for this type of failure.

Instead of dieting, you'll be making important lifestyle changes—with the emphasis on *life*—because the foods you're giving up on *The 30-Day Diabetes Cure* are quite literally "killers" to you. You won't be returning to eating like you once did (and believe me when I say: *You won't want to*). This doesn't mean you won't occasionally enjoy a small portion of fast carbs in the future but not until Phase II. And let me explain why…

IT TAKES TIME TO BREAK ANY HABIT

Over the course of your life, you've developed a strong *appetite* for "fast carb" foods, such as bread, cookies, and chips, all of which enter your bloodstream very quickly and spike your blood sugar. But "appetite" is merely a conditioned (learned) yearning—a *habit*—which is something quite different from genuine hunger. You may be thinking, "Life is going to be so miserable without these yummy foods," but that's just your habit speaking.

Every time you've eaten these foods in the past, your appetite (your habitual desire) for them has been reinforced: They taste good…the advertising is so appealing…and, hey! they're so cheap and readily available. In fact, they're everywhere, all the time, wherever you go. So in order to weaken that habit, you've got to abstain for a short time. This isn't impossible, I promise. In fact, I've never had a patient who hasn't been able to do this for the first 10 days of my program.

Yes, the first two or three days will be the toughest, while your body chemistry starts to adjust. But after that, it gets much easier. After a mere three to 10 days or so, your craving for these foods will be greatly diminished, if not all but gone. Many of my patients lose their desire for these fast carbs *completely*—and that's when their blood sugar really starts to normalize and their pounds melt off.

THE SECRET OF THEIR SUCCESS

How is this possible? Do they have superhuman willpower? Not at all. These patients are ordinary people just like you who've lived with powerful carbohydrate cravings all their lives. Yet they've been able to let go of their appetite for them because they've substituted "brain power" for willpower.

You see, willpower says, "No." And guess what happens when you try to resist strong desire? Most people rebel because no one likes to be denied. Brain power, on the other hand, uses *knowledge* to de-energize a craving. The secret of my patients' success is that they've developed the ability to recognize an "appetite" when they feel it arising. Instead of acting unconsciously or habitually, they use *awareness* to notice what's going on in their mind. They're able to recognize when their habituated appetite is being stimulated by a picture, memory, or seeing the actual food itself, rather than having a genuine hunger for nourishment and sustenance.

HERE'S HOW IT WORKS

For example, you see a doughnut. You remember how good the last one tasted: the sweet sugary glazing…the rich, fatty "doughiness" when you chewed it…the satisfaction as you swallowed it down with a splash of sweet, hot coffee. Yum!

But now, these memory-trigger sensations are entering your conscious mind before you impulsively act. You're not blindly ordering the doughnut without realizing what you're doing. You're watching all this unfold. You now have *awareness* of the process that used to occur unconsciously over and over. And what gave you this new awareness? Your knowledge of the *consequences* and your commitment to fighting for your health and life. It's much easier to stop eating certain foods when you know exactly how they are harming you. Once you step out of the shadows of ignorance and denial, it's difficult to continue the habit that you know is slowly, surely killing you.

"But what about cigarette smokers, alcoholics, and drug users?" you might wonder. Their cravings aren't mere habits; they're powerful physical and chemical addictions, much different than what you are experiencing. And yes, even dependencies such as those can be (and are) broken by developing awareness and realizing the harmful consequences of these actions. So, what's so bad about white bread, breakfast foods, snacks, and desserts?

They instantly raise your blood sugar. Your body responds to the fast carbs in white-flour foods such as bread and pasta as if you just ate pure sugar. Your glucose spikes up, the insulin response is triggered, and fatty triglycerides are formed and stored around your belly. A steady diet of toast, breakfast cereal, waffles, pancakes, sandwich bread, burger buns, dinner rolls, breadsticks, bagels, crackers, cookies, and cake makes your cells *resistant* to all the insulin that keeps getting pumped out to handle the glucose until your pancreas burns out from overproduction.

Insulin resistance (prediabetes) turns into type 2 diabetes and suddenly you're taking medications that make you feel really lousy (not to mention their cost). Unless you change your eating habits, the next thing you know you've got type 1 and you're injecting yourself with insulin several times a day. Now your risk for a sudden heart attack or stroke has skyrocketed. You're in danger of going blind…having your digits and limbs amputated one by one…and developing Alzheimer's. Believe me, it's hard to enjoy doughnuts day after day when you're really aware of how much they're harming you.

They trigger inflammation. Fast carbs create inflammatory proteins called *cytokines*, which regulate the body's inflammation response. More inflammation is the last thing you want in your body because it raises your risk of practically every serious chronic and degenerative disease, including diabetes. Inflammation makes your joints and muscles painfully sore. It causes your arteries to clog up with plaque. It destroys brain cells. And it raises your risk of all cancers. Sure, you can pretend to ignore all of this as you chomp on your morning bagel. But that won't stop the inflammation one bit.

They're loaded with damaging fats. Most processed foods, including buns, rolls, breakfast cereal, soft breads, crackers, and chips, contain refined vegetable oils, such as soy, corn, cottonseed, or canola, which are high in omega-6 fatty acids. They often contain trans fats (labeled as "hydrogenated oil" or "vegetable shortening"). Omega-6s deplete omega-3 essential fatty acids—

which are anti-inflammatory—resulting in higher inflammation throughout the body (more about this on Day 11).

With commercial baked goods such as burger buns, snack cakes, and dinner rolls, you're getting a double-whammy: a spike in glucose from the fast carbs and more inflammation due to the excessive omega-6 content. Too much omega-6 also elevates your levels of triglycerides and cholesterols…increases insulin resistance…impairs normal cellular repair…and raises your risk of diabetic complications.

Although there has been some progress by food manufacturers, trans fats—the unhealthiest fats ever invented—are still present in baked goods, crackers, and snack foods, and are also frequently used to deep-fry restaurant foods such as French fries, fried chicken, fish and chips, and most fast food.

Trans fats raise LDL (bad) cholesterol levels, lower HDL (good) cholesterol, and are directly responsible for arterial plaque and heart disease. A study of 80,000 women published in the *American Journal of Clinical Nutrition* found that increasing the intake of trans fats by only 5% results in a 37% increase in the risk of heart disease—for which people with diabetes already have a higher risk. So before you take a bite, ask yourself: Is it worth it?

They lack fiber. When you're fighting diabetes, fiber is your best ally. High-fiber carbohydrates (such as beans and vegetables) contain fewer calories because the fiber component isn't digested. Fiber is the *roughage* component of vegetables, fruits, whole grains, and beans that give these foods their bulk. Because the ratio of calories-to-volume is so high, you can eat until you're full without gaining weight—in fact, you find yourself *losing* pounds steadily by eating these foods. For example, an apple is more filling than a half cup of apple juice that contains about the same calories. (In the days ahead, you'll learn much more about fiber and how to use it to reverse your blood sugar problems.)

Refined carbs, such as bread products, are the black sheep of the carbohydrate family. Because they've had their bulk and fiber removed, they're a more concentrated source of calories. And since their volume has been reduced by processing, it's easy to eat more of them before your stomach tells your brain: "I'm full." That's just one reason they're so fattening: We simply eat more than we should.

A bigger problem results when many of these refined carbs are combined with other high-calorie ingredients, as in the case of bakery goods. When white flour is mixed with eggs, oil, milk, and sweeteners, its calorie content jumps, but its volume (the amount it takes to fill your stomach) increases only slightly. The sugar combined with the refined flour carbs also triggers an instant spike in your glucose levels. As you now know, this signals the release of insulin, which unfortunately facilitates the rapid conversion of carbohydrates into fatty triglycerides.

They may trigger hidden allergies. Bread products are loaded with gluten, a compound found in wheat, rye, oats, and barley, which can be difficult to digest and cause inflammation of the intestines. A full-blown allergic reaction to gluten is called *celiac disease*. Doctors are beginning to realize that millions of Americans may have an undiagnosed sensitivity to or outright intolerance for gluten. Symptoms include fatigue, weakness and general achiness, abdominal bloating, and chronic diarrhea. Gluten intolerance has also been linked to osteoporosis, anemia, cancer, lupus, multiple sclerosis, and other autoimmune diseases as well as psychiatric and neurological conditions such as depression, migraines, and schizophrenia, according to the *New England Journal of Medicine*.

You may not even suspect you have gluten intolerance until you start paying attention to how you feel after eating gluten foods. Eliminating these foods is the first step to improving your health and well-being, especially if you suffer from an already debilitating disease like diabetes.

They take the place of nutritious healing foods. If you're consuming a lot of bread-based foods, you're eating fewer of the Diabetes Healing Superfoods (which you'll soon be able to recognize after Day 10). Remember: You always have the choice. The next time you reach for a piece of toast, a thick sandwich, a plate of pasta, a dinner roll, a cupcake or brownie, a Danish or morning muffin, ask yourself: "What could I be eating instead that would help *heal* my diabetes and blood sugar problems?"

In the days and weeks ahead, you'll discover many answers to this important question. You'll be learning about the delicious, supernutritious foods that are proven to lower your blood sugar…reduce your inflammation…help you lose weight naturally…slash your triglycerides, cholesterol, and blood pressure…give you more energy…perk up your moods…improve your general health…and lengthen your life.

WHITE FLOUR IS POISON TO YOUR PANCREAS

When we talk about bread and flour products, we are talking about the highly refined flour that most commercially processed baked goods are made with. This flour starts its life as wheat, a whole grain, but in the refining process, the nutritious bran and wheat germ are removed to give the flour a finer texture and longer shelf life. In order to make it a more appealing white color instead of its natural brown, a known toxin called chlorine gas is added to bleach it. When chlorine gas comes into contact with wheat, it forms a by-product called *alloxan*, a substance that actually damages the pancreas by destroying the beta-cells that make insulin.

Scientists are well aware of the dangers of alloxan. They actually use it to induce diabetes in lab animals because they know that it will destroy the insulin-producing function of the pancreas and allow high blood sugar to get out of control. If you eat white flour products, you are ingesting this toxic substance and harming your pancreas. What can protect you from this insidious poison lurking in so many common foods? Two things…

First, if you ever needed more of an incentive to stop eating white flour products, I hope you've gotten it with the awareness that white flour is literally poisoning your pancreas.

Second, take 400 IU of vitamin E (mixed natural *tocopherols*) every day. Scientists use it to protect their lab animals from the dangers of alloxan, and since this powerful antioxidant has a host of other protective benefits, we think it's a good way for you to start reversing the damage alloxan can cause as well.

MUST YOU GIVE UP BREAD FOREVER? *NO!*

Are there any safe options? Of course. Unbleached whole grain flour, almond flour, rice flour, and quinoa flour are perfectly fine for cooking and baking, but I am going to wait until later in the plan to reintroduce grains, so you're sure to know the difference between the good and the bad. After Phase I, you'll be able to eat bread and other baked goods again—although probably not the kind you've grown accustomed to. Trust me on this: You'll be able to satisfy your appetite for bread and it won't make your blood sugar problems or diabetes worse. Quite the opposite: These delicious baked goods will actually be healing you! If you're still unsure what *not* to eat, here is a list of what to avoid:

TOP 10 WORST DIABETES-CAUSING "FAST CARB" FOODS

1. White bread, toast, bagels, English muffins, breadsticks
2. Fruit juice, soda, energy drinks, and all sweetened beverages
3. Waffles, pancakes, French toast
4. Pastries, coffee cake, muffins, doughnuts, cupcakes, cake
5. Jams and jellies, especially those with added sugar or sweeteners; fruit pies
6. Boxed breakfast cereals
7. "Instant" hot cereals, including instant oatmeal
8. Tortillas; corn or white flour
9. Large portions of home fries, hash browns, and other potato dishes
10. White "minute" rice

Other foods to avoid, because they are high in sugar or other sweeteners, dangerous oils and/or processed flours (and low in fiber and nutrients): snack cakes, energy bars, marshmallows, candy, flavored gelatin and pudding, commercially flavored and sweetened yogurt, potato chips, corn chips, pretzels, crackers, desserts, cookies, cake, ice cream, pie, commercially made sweet breads and pastries.

HOW TO TELL A FAST CARB FROM A SLOW CARB

Fast carbs. Slow carbs. Good carbs. Bad carbs. Simple carbs. Complex carbs. Maybe you've heard all these terms tossed around, but maybe you aren't sure what they mean—or how to tell one from the other. So let's clear the air…

The issue is the *speed* at which your body is able to break down any food into energy-providing sugar in your bloodstream.

Fast carbs are highly refined grain products that have a simple, short chain of natural sugar molecules that convert *quickly* into glucose in your bloodstream. Fast carbs are also called "simple carbs" because of their simple chain of molecules.

Slow carbs contain fiber and other components that *slow down* the food's conversion to glucose in your bloodstream. Slow carbs have a more complicated molecular chain, which is why they're also called "complex carbs."

USING THE GLYCEMIC INDEX

Fast carbs rank very high on the glycemic index (GI), a system devised to determine how fast or slow a food enters the bloodstream and raises your blood sugar level. In general, foods with a high glycemic index are fast carbs and should be avoided.

Another way to determine whether a food is a fast carb is its glycemic load (GL), which not only gives its GI rating, but also tells how much carbohydrate is actually in the food. Here's where the science can get a little confusing because a food might have a high GI number but actually a small amount of actual carbohydrate in relation to its fiber (which slows it down).

That means that some whole foods, like carrots or potatoes (which are high in fiber), might have a high GI number but a low GL ranking. The GL reveals the true impact a food has on your glucose metabolism.

YOUR BODY NEEDS CARBS!

Carbohydrates are your body's main source of energy. Your goal is not to eliminate carbs—far from it. What you want is a carbohydrate that will enter your bloodstream *slowly* so it won't trigger an overproduction of insulin.

But let's not turn eating into a science project; that'll kill not only your motivation but also your enjoyment faster than a raspberry Danish hits your bloodstream. The easiest way to choose a slow carb over a fast carb is to *always choose a whole food* rather than one that has been commercially refined and processed.

In Phase II, when we reintroduce fruit as well as whole grains, you'll find this process a lot easier. In the meantime, you are going to be loading up on fresh vegetables and meals made with beans for that good slow-carb energy, as well as plenty of nutritious protein foods, such as grass-fed beef, organic milk and dairy products, and free-range eggs. And here's a bonus: In the next 10 days or so, you can expect to lose between 8 and 13 pounds while you are eating slow carbs!

CARBO CRAVING IS ALSO A PHYSICAL-BIOCHEMICAL PHENOMENON

"Carbohydrate craving" is a very *biological* phenomenon, too. As you've already learned, when you eat a fast carb food, your body breaks it down into glucose very quickly. This sudden spike in blood sugar triggers a surge of insulin which, if it's functioning properly, pulls the glucose out of your bloodstream.

Because glucose is the main fuel for your body and brain, this quick exit causes a sudden drop in your energy level. Deprived of fuel, your brain feels foggy and your body feels tired. You may have the urge to nap so your brain can consolidate the neurochemicals required for clear thinking and concentration.

But what happens if you can't take a snooze because you're at work or behind the wheel in traffic? Your brain will call for more glucose in the form of carbohydrates. In short, you're hungry again—for a very specific kind of food. You want a candy bar. Or chips. Or a soda. And you *really* want them. That's a biological carbohydrate craving. Continually satisfying this powerful urge upsets your body's basic metabolic functions and leads to permanent damage in the form of diabetes. Breaking this vicious cycle is absolutely essential to restoring your body's healthy management of glucose.

BREAKING THESE CRAVINGS IS RELATIVELY EASY

All you do is reach for a "slow carb" food instead of a fast carb. Crunch a raw carrot instead of a candy bar. Bite into an apple rather than a cupcake. Substitute sipping a cup of green tea for slurping a soda. Your brain will get its glucose in a slow, steady supply. And your insulin won't be aroused because it won't need to deal with a big barrage of blood sugar.

But your mind might be thinking, "Hey, I really wanted a candy bar" or "This doesn't taste as good as a mouthful of chips." That's because it's easy to become habituated to certain flavors and foods. The good news is that it simply takes time to break an old habit and establish a new one—usually 21 to 30 days (and that's why most drug and alcohol rehabilitation programs last for 28 days).

If powerful addictions like drugs and alcohol can be reversed in such a short time, curing your body's craving for carbohydrates is a cinch. Just follow these daily steps and your success will be assured.

TAKE ACTION TODAY: Stop eating fast carbs right now. Tomorrow, you'll begin to substitute diabetes-healing foods. For today, have eggs for breakfast with yogurt mid-morning; vegetable soup and a big salad for lunch; and lean protein with plenty of vegetables for dinner. In the days ahead you'll learn more about specific foods that can heal your diabetes. Your immediate goal is to get through today without eating any fast-carb foods.

EXTRA CREDIT: Go through your pantry, cupboards, and fridge and give away any fast-carb foods to someone who doesn't have diabetes, blood sugar irregularities, or a weight problem (if you can find one!).

DAY 6: DIABETES-HEALING BREAKFASTS

Never work before breakfast; if you have to
work before breakfast, eat your breakfast first.

JOSH BILLINGS

HEALER: **These diabetes-healing breakfasts are the perfect way to start your day. Here's how to eat your way to better blood sugar…**

BACK WHEN EARLY MORNING meant the start of back-breaking labor on the farm or at the factory, breakfast was the most important meal of the day—the one that "broke the fast" of a long night's sleep and fueled your tank with energy for the hard day to come.

Most of us don't toil long days in fields or factories anymore, but we still face stressful, energy-draining days juggling 21st-century pressures including commuting, work deadlines, complex family challenges, and an overscheduled calendar. There are children and elderly parents to care for, financial insecurities to overcome, and personal needs to look after too.

Living life and controlling diabetes is challenging enough when your energy level is less than abundant. And that's why breakfast is so important. You already know how rundown and mentally "fogged" you feel on mornings when you skimp on breakfast (or bypass it completely). Without a nourishing breakfast, your blood sugar drops and you experience powerful mid-morning cravings for the wrong foods, such as sugary muffins, flavored coffees, and whatever snacky foods.

THE MOST IMPORTANT MEAL OF THE DAY

Ask an overweight person if he or she eats breakfast, and the answer is usually no. Ask a fit, trim, healthy person and you'll virtually always hear an enthusiastic "yes!" For people with blood sugar problems (especially), breakfast is the most important meal of the day. That's because it's important to stabilize your blood sugar and get your body's metabolic engine revved up as soon as possible after waking. But you have to be careful about the kind of fuel you pump into your tank in the morning…

THE IDEAL BREAKFAST FOR DIABETES—OR PREDIABETES

During Phase I of *The 30-Day Diabetes Cure*, I want you to build your breakfast around lean-and-clean protein like free-range chicken eggs, low-fat yogurt, or other healthful dairy foods. Nuts, seeds, and certain soy foods are also good choices. These should comprise the majority of your meal. After Day 10, we'll add small amounts of fruit plus whole grains such as slow-cooked oatmeal and whole-grain bread. For now, I want to keep it basic. Remember: It's always easier to *add* good foods to your diet rather than to fight your cravings for the bad ones. Here are some specific tips that will help get your day off to a roaring start…

Protein for strength and stable blood sugar. Your entire body—organs, brain, and immune system included—needs protein for healthy function. People who don't eat enough eventually feel weak and lethargic and can experience slow wound healing (a big risk for people with diabetes, who already have compromised circulation), hair loss, skin rashes, brittle nails, muscle loss, heart problems, depression, and anxiety. Breakfast protein also stabilizes blood sugar, slowing the rush of glucose from any carbs you eat and keeping blood sugar from spiking too high or dropping too low.

Make the centerpiece of your breakfast lean-and-clean protein like free-range chicken eggs, low-fat or full-fat yogurt, and milk. Nut butters (peanut, almond, and sesame) are also good choices. Meats and fish also provide essential protein: Choose small portions of lean chicken breast, Canadian bacon, or turkey sausage or even a piece of salmon or other fish, part of the traditional Asian breakfast. Avoid low-grade processed meats, such as greasy sausage and bacon. They're high in fat and sodium and loaded with chemical additives and preservatives (including nitrates and nitrites), which are known carcinogens.

Unprocessed soy foods are a fine option too, but avoid soy-based meat substitutes such as "soy bacon." They're highly processed with lots of additives. Soy is also a known hormone disrupter that can accelerate some hormone-driven cancers. Many questions remain about these types of *processed* soy products. No need to be confused. It's best to enjoy soy as it has traditionally been consumed in Asia: either as soybeans themselves (Japanese edamame) or in the healing fermented foods such as tempeh and miso. Occasional use of soy milk and soy protein powder (without added sugars, of course) is okay as long as it is not a large portion of your diet.

Egg-cellent eggs. In the grocery, look for eggs labeled "omega-3 fortified," produced by hens allowed to range free and fed grasses and wild herbs that are rich in omega-3 essential fatty acids. These eggs have three to six times the omega-3s of other grocery eggs, and omega-3s are definitely essential for both cardiovascular and mental health.

■ Eggs have been much maligned over the past few decades, accused of causing high cholesterol, clogged arteries, and heart disease. But researchers have long suspected the exact opposite is true, and new studies prove it. As reported in the *International Journal of Cardiology* in 2005, participants who ate two eggs a day for six weeks showed no increase in total cholesterol, no increase in LDL (bad) cholesterol, and no narrowing of the arteries.

- Eggs are also a weight-loss dream, too. Two extra-large eggs contain just 160 calories and 14 grams of protein. In fact, researchers at St. Louis University found that people who ate eggs instead of a bagel (with equal calories) for breakfast ate fewer total calories at both lunch and dinner. The egg eaters lost 65% more weight than the bagel eaters.

- Eggs are also a great source of the vision-protecting compounds lutein and zeaxanthin, carotenoids that are especially vital for people with diabetes whose sight can suffer. Risk of cataracts and macular degeneration are both significantly lower in people who eat eggs regularly.

- As a bonus, your new diabetes-healing breakfast might help you remember where you put the remote control. Eggs are an excellent source of choline, essential for proper brain development and function, including memory.

Butter's back. A little butter in the omelet pan makes for a heavenly breakfast, but remember when we were told that butter was bad and margarine was better? We now know that hydrogenated vegetable oils (trans fats) like those found in many margarines are extremely damaging, and researchers are beginning to prove that the saturated fat in butter is a far better choice. According to a 2009 article in the *Journal of American Dietetic Association*, saturated fat seems to provide protection *against* weight gain.

Haven't we been told repeatedly to stay on low-fat diets to prevent obesity and cardiovascular disease? Well, Danish researchers who studied the links between eating different foods and their effect on waist size (which at certain measurements is a "red alert" for increased risk of heart disease, cancer, insulin resistance, and diabetes) found that women who ate more butter and high-fat dairy products gained *less* weight around the middle than those whose diets were lower in saturated fat. Those who ate more red meat also had smaller waistlines.

The secret to reaping these benefits is portion control. Go easy on the butter and other high-calorie, saturated-fat foods like dairy products and red meat. Moderate consumption of good fats will protect you. Overindulgence will work against your goals.

Yay for yogurt. Talk about a living food. Protein-rich yogurt is naturally fermented milk that offers a wealth of health benefits, starting with the stabilization and reduction of glucose levels. In addition, according to a study published in *Natural News*, fermented foods such as yogurt have a lower glycemic index (GI) than unfermented food because they convert sugar into lactic acid, thus bypassing the glucose-insulin cycle.

The secret is in yogurt's beneficial bacteria (called *probiotics*), added to milk and kept warm until the lactose (milk sugar) turns to lactic acid and ferments, providing an ideal environment for the good bacteria to multiply. That makes eating yogurt like sending in the cavalry to reinforce the beneficial bacteria in your gastrointestinal tract, where infections are fought and the immune system is kept strong. These beneficial bugs also keep the "bad-guy" bacteria (such as *E. coli*, *salmonella, listeria, Campylobacter,* and *clostridium perfringens*, which cause food poisoning and other health problems) from overwhelming your body.

For the very best results, choose yogurt made of milk from organically raised, grass-fed cows or goats. Absolutely avoid yogurt that has any added sugar or fake sugar (read labels carefully). Yogurts that contain fruit, cereal, cookie bits, or other flavorings are loaded with health-robbing sugars, chemicals, and unpronounceable additives. Most grocery-store yogurts bear little resemblance to the ancient healing food that's been eaten throughout the world for millennia for longevity and health, but some now stock varieties of plain, unsweetened Greek yogurt, a dreamy, thick concoction containing the live bacterial cultures that confer such remarkable healing properties. Again, read all labels to ensure no added sugar. Your local health food store is another source for this living food. Better yet, learn to make your own and save a bundle.

The calcium in yogurt is great for weight loss. A study published in the *International Journal of Obesity* found that obese men and women who ate three six-ounce servings of fat-free yogurt daily while on a reduced-calorie diet lost 22% more weight and shed 80% more abdominal fat than those who ate the same number of calories but got just one serving of dairy products. The yogurt eaters lost an impressive 61% more body fat than the non-yogurt group.

Got milk (and cheese)? You should, because research published in 2005 in the *American Journal of Clinical Nutrition* found that eating a diet high in calcium foods boosts the metabolic burn-rate of body fat. Women from 18 to 30 years old with normal weights were put on either a high-calcium or a low-calcium meal plan for a full year. The high-calcium women took in 1,000 mg to 1,400 mg per day from food sources, while the low-calcium group got less than 800 mg daily. Results? The high-calcium group burned fat at 20 times the rate of the low-calcium group! This is a true testament to calcium's fat-burning power.

For maximum benefit, choose protein-rich milk and ricotta and cottage cheeses made of milk from organically raised grass-fed cows or goats. You'll reap the benefits of extra omega-3s while you enjoy a high-calcium food that boosts the metabolic burn-rate of body fat.

Complex carbs for sustained energy. Whole grains open up a new world of breakfast options. And starting on Day 12—just six days from now, when your blood sugar is back in balance— you'll be adding whole grains (and fresh fruit!) to your morning meal. After abstaining from them (as well as sugary foods and fast carbs for 12 days) you should be experiencing a dramatic but safe lowering of your blood sugar levels. This could permit your doctor to reduce your glucose-lowering medication (or withdraw it entirely!)—or if you're type 1, greatly reduce your insulin dosage.

START THE DAY OFF RIGHT!

Still not sure how to break the bad-breakfast habit? Give yourself extra time in the morning by waking up a little earlier than usual. (This may require "calling it an evening" no later than 10 p.m.) Prize this morning respite as "me time" and savor it by sipping a hot cup of tea or fresh-brewed coffee. Or sit quietly, meditating on just being in the present moment—or planning your day.

Be sure your kitchen is neat, clean, and well-organized when you wake up. Remember: "Healing takes planning; illness just happens." Here are a few suggestions for a healthful, protein-centric breakfast…

Veggie scramble. Warm some butter or pure olive oil in a skillet and sauté chopped onions, garlic, tomatoes, broccoli, asparagus and/or green peppers—whatever you like or have on hand. Then whisk a couple of omega-3 eggs in a bowl and pour over the vegetables. Add a tablespoon of plain yogurt so the eggs stay soft—and a bit of grated cheddar if you like—folding no more than three times (no stirring!) to keep the eggs fluffy. Option: Sauté the veggies first and set aside. Pour the whisked eggs and yogurt into a mildly hot pan. Add the veggies and cheese and fold over into a perfect omelet.

Go Mexican. Warm some canned vegetarian refried beans or black beans with melted cheese and tomatoes. Enjoy with a dollop of salsa.

Asian-inspiration. Have miso soup or scrambled tofu with veggies. Also enjoy a small dish of edamame (boiled green soybeans) with your tofu.

Grass-fed morning. One of my patients eats three ounces of (high in omega-3s) ground grass-fed beef for breakfast about once a week. She sautés the meat with onions, garlic, and fresh oregano—and sometimes adds canned or fresh tomatoes.

If you can't manage to cook in the morning, try these "quickies"…

Make the veggie egg scramble the night before, cool, and refrigerate. The next day, heat for a minute in the microwave and enjoy.

Protein power. Cook and peel a few hard-boiled eggs. Keep them covered in the fridge and in the morning enjoy one with a piece of parmesan cheese the size of your little finger.

Yogurt with chopped nuts and sprinkled with cinnamon.

Celery sticks with almond butter.

Chopped almonds in ricotta cheese. Add a shake of unsweetened cocoa powder and/or cinnamon.

TAKE ACTION TODAY: Eat a protein-rich breakfast every day, replacing "fast carb" breakfasts (toast, waffles, pancakes, etc.) with these diabetes-friendly foods. Combining protein and good fats will provide sustained energy while helping to heal your diabetes. On Day 12, you'll add nutritious whole grains and fresh fruit to your healing breakfast for even more options.

EXTRA CREDIT: Make your own yogurt. Here's how…

HOMEMADE YOGURT

Making your own yogurt is easy, saves money, and you can use grass-fed cow's milk to boost the omega-3s. Ensure all utensils and bowls are extremely clean—any microbes can interfere with the yogurt's bacterial growth. It takes a little practice to make great homemade yogurt, but it's worth the effort.

1. Heat four cups organic 2% or whole milk in a saucepan to 170–180 degrees F.
2. Cool milk to 108–112 degrees F.
3. Add starter, either packaged (see the facing page) or a few dollops of a high-quality plain, whole-milk yogurt.
4. Put in fermentation container (see below).
5. Let sit 4 to 8 hours.
6. Spoon into a glass bowl or glass jars and refrigerate.

FERMENTATION METHODS

Thermos Method: Once milk has cooled and starter has been added, place the mixture in an exquisitely clean quart-sized thermos. Wrap in a kitchen towel and set in a warm place. When yogurt is done, transfer to a glass jar or plastic container and store.

Cooler Method: This method works well for bigger batches. For a double batch, boil two quarts of water and place the water in two jars. Place the yogurt mixture in two quart-sized glass jars and nestle them in a small picnic cooler with the hot water. Make sure the yogurt is right up against the hot water. Cover jars with towels and close the cooler. When yogurt is done, place the jars in the fridge and cool.

STARTERS

There are numerous strains and combinations of bacteria that can be used to make yogurt. We tried a few and they were all very similar in texture and taste. They had a tart bite and were creamier and softer than store-bought brands but still sturdy enough to use in a sauce or dip. The addition of milk powder actually seemed to mellow out the flavor without thickening the product very much. Experiment with your own recipes. Once you've created a yogurt you like, you can use it to start your next batch. Here are some other starters to try…

- Yogourmet Freeze Dried Yogurt Starter®. This premixed starter has the strains bulgaricus, thermopiles, and acidophilus as well as skim milk powder and ascorbic acid.

- Two tablespoons acidophilus and ½ cup store-bought Greek yogurt. This is a simple, no-fuss recipe that is extra affordable.

- ½ cup previous batch of acidophilus-based yogurt and ¼ cup milk powder. Milk powder mellows out the sourness.

For richer, thicker Greek-style yogurt: To make a thicker Greek yogurt, drain the finished yogurt in a muslin cloth or coffee filter over a bowl for two hours. The bowl will capture the probiotic-rich liquid, which you can drink. Scrape the Greek yogurt from the cloth or filter and refrigerate for up to a week. (For more Diabetes Healing Recipes, visit *www.myhealingkitchen.com.*)

CASE STUDY: JAY

"I've reduced my insulin by 80%…and feel so much more energetic!"

Jay is a cancer survivor and lost a kidney. In the process, the tumor damaged his pancreas and he got type 1 diabetes. He took insulin for nearly 10 years without anybody telling him about the power of a good diet. His doctors allowed him to eat crazy foods as long as he took his shots. He believed the lie that insulin is harmless and would take care of everything. But for those 10 years, Jay felt "sick." He was just so happy to have escaped cancer that it seemed like an acceptable trade-off. So, he'd eat with friends, entertain guests at dinner, but he'd retire after an hour or two to sleep. That's what all his diabetic friends did. And after all, he had dodged the cancer bullet.

Case Study: Jay	Before	After
Weight	158	146
A1C	8.3	6.0
Blood Pressure	146/84	118/78
Triglycerides	304	148
Meds	Ultralente: 65 units per day	Ultralente: 12 units per day

Imagine the disconnect when he came to see me! I explained that insulin wasn't a "cure-all" and that he was still in trouble. He needed 65 units of Lente and still all that regular insulin! Despite an A1C of 8.3, this was totally fine with his endocrinologists.

Today, Jay has completely revised his lifestyle with the *The 30-Day Diabetes Cure*. He doesn't nap anymore. He goes to the gym and doesn't eat a crazy meal afterward. And despite all of his self-destructive behavior condoned by the conventional doctors, he turned things around. Even after years of high sugars, he was able to significantly reduce his insulin and lose 12 pounds with a healthy diet.

DAY 7: ELIMINATE FAST-FOOD LUNCHES

Let me tell you the secret that has led me to my goal.
My strength lies solely in my tenacity.

LOUIS PASTEUR

ANTI-HEALER: **Fast-food meals and snacks are unhealthy choices for everyone—and especially people with diabetes. They make you fat and increase your risk of developing serious diabetic complications. Substitute these healthier choices today…**

WHEN YOU EAT French fries or chips and a soda with your lunch, you're pumping a massive dose of fast carbs into your bloodstream and weakening the power of your insulin. Result? Elevated blood sugar. Weight gain. Chronic inflammation. Insulin resistance. Prediabetes leading to type 2 diabetes. Elevated risk of complications, including heart attack, stroke, blindness, and limb amputation.

IS IT WORTH IT?

Even though the big fast-food chains *pretend* to be introducing less destructive lunch menus, the three most popular menu items have remained constant over decades: hamburger, fries, and a soda. You may suspect that fast food is one of the main causes of today's diabetes and obesity epidemics—and you're right. Here's why…

Fast food wrecks your blood sugar. We've already discussed the dangers of fast carbs, sodas, breads, buns, and baked goods. The same holds true for the massive serving of French fries and the football-sized baked potatoes loaded with imitation cheese sauce, sour cream, bacon bits, and fake butter. The fast-food industry has been highly successful at turning the humble potato into a high GI, high-fat, high-calorie, low-nutrient fat bomb that raises your blood sugar, your calorie intake, and your risk of cardiovascular disease and diabetes *without* any of the health benefits you'd find in a small baked potato with a sensible pat of butter.

Fast food is brimming with bad fats. You'll learn a lot more about the difference between good and bad fats later in this book, but here's some advance information:

The bad fats that the fast-food industry uses prolifically (such as polyunsaturated vegetable oils made from corn, soybean, safflower, sunflower, and canola), plus the trans fats in shortening and margarine, are *extremely* damaging to your health. Trans fats raise LDL bad cholesterol levels, lower HDL good cholesterol, and lead to the buildup of arterial plaque and heart disease (the number one killer of people with diabetes).

These unhealthy oils raise triglyceride and cholesterol levels, increase insulin resistance, impair cellular repair, and amplify your risk of diabetic complications. The average fast-food lunch is extremely high in these dangerous fats. A Big Mac has 29 grams of fat and a large order of fries has another 25 grams. Contrast that to the one gram of fat in a turkey sandwich on whole wheat bread. Kind of a no-brainer, isn't it?

Fast food is high in calories. And that means weight gain. All fats are high in calories—about nine calories per gram, or more than twice the amount of calories in carbohydrates or protein. (When measuring at home, figure about 120 calories per tablespoon of any oil.) That big juicy burger with all the trimmings contains 540 calories, and more than half of them come from the fat alone. French fries have another 500 calories. Add the 310 in a large soda and you've topped 1,000 calories for a *single meal*. That's more than half the total calories the average person should eat in an entire day!

Guidelines for maintaining a healthy weight recommend getting no more than 1,500 to 2,000 calories per day (the low end for women, the high end for men), and even less if you're overweight and trying to shed some pounds and inches. It's easy to see how quickly fast food can get you in big trouble.

Fast food is full of salt. That Big Mac also has over 1,000 milligrams (mg) of sodium, the fries another 350. The American Heart Association recommends a daily salt intake of *less* than one teaspoon (2,300 mg) to minimize your risk of hypertension, stroke, and heart disease. The typical fast-food lunch contains more than half that. (More than 75% of the salt we consume daily comes *not* from the saltshaker, but from hidden sodium in prepared and processed foods.)

Read the labels on any soup can, box of stuffing mix, bottle of salad dressing, jar of spaghetti sauce, bag of chips, or frozen dinner and you'll be shocked at how much sodium is in there: Campbell's Chicken Noodle Soup: 890 mg, 37% of your suggested daily requirement; Ragu Spaghetti Sauce: 540 mg, 22% of your suggested daily requirement; Marie Callender's Frozen Chicken Pot Pie: 857 mg, 36% of your suggested daily requirement.

Why is there so much salt in fast food and processed foods? Simple. Salt masks the inferior taste of poor-quality food. And we've been conditioned to add salt to every meal in order to "bring out its flavor." But good-quality food already has flavor of its own, yet we can't get those delicate sugars and unique tastes because we're so used to all that salt.

But here's the kicker: Too much sodium in the bloodstream elevates your chances for a sudden stroke or heart attack—and people with diabetes are *already* at higher risk of these because of their blood sugar and insulin imbalance. That's the main reason one of the first prescriptions your doctor may give you when you're diagnosed with diabetes is blood-pressure medication.

Do you want to take this drug for the rest of your life? Or would you rather just lower your salt intake? Stay away from fast foods and processed foods and you'll accomplish this goal far more successfully (and with the added benefit of actually *healing* your diabetes and high-blood pressure), instead of merely "managing" it with medicine.

Fast food is poor-quality food. If all these calorie and sodium numbers aren't scary enough, understand the meat in your fast-food burger comes from industrialized factory-feedlot operations. This ground beef is often an amalgamation of edible meat and scrap trimmings from various feedlot sources—one burger can come from literally hundreds of animals. Highly susceptible to dangerous *E. coli* and *salmonella* bacteria (not to mention the very real possibility of mad cow disease), the animals that produce these meat products are routinely treated with antibiotics and growth hormones. Some feedlot operations have even started injecting their ground beef with *ammonia* to keep it bacteria-free. It's easy to see why many foreign countries forbid the importation of US beef.

Setting aside both the environmental devastation wreaked by these "factory beef" operations (feedlot waste products are the number-one source of greenhouse gas emissions) *and* the thorny question of the heartless, inhumane treatment of these animals, what about the actual nutritional quality of this meat?

According to the *Journal of Animal Science*, grain-fed beef from factory feedlots contains 300% more fat than grass-fed cattle. The high amount of beneficial omega-3 fatty acids found in pasture-raised beef (in amounts that rival some fish varieties) is practically nonexistent in feedlot cattle. And vital nutrients such as vitamin B and vitamin E—plus essential minerals like calcium, magnesium, and potassium—are greatly depleted in feedlot beef. No wonder red meat has gotten such a bad rap in medical and nutritional circles. But it isn't red meat per se that's bad for you (properly raised, it's actually a very healthful food), it's the quality that really counts. And isn't that true about all food?

THE HIGH COST OF CHEAP FOOD

Sure, grabbing a fast-food lunch is convenient—and it's certainly cheap. If you're pressed for time (and who isn't these days?), the idea of cruising through a drive-up window or stopping for a quick bite with coworkers can be irresistible. But who wants a lunch that's going to make you feel bad, look bad, have bad blood sugar, and shorten your life? *Not you!*

The truth is, that 99-cent burger is way more expensive when you factor in paying for the medical care it ultimately necessitates, not to mention the environmental cleanup and waste disposal for all the packaging. And what about the damage agribusiness does to our farm economy?

The old saying "There's no such thing as a free (or cheap) lunch" is absolutely true. You see, *you* pay all the hidden costs in the form of taxes and higher insurance premiums. Our federal government doles out generous farm subsidies to agribusiness corporations that produce enormous quantities of meat, milk, and sugar…to corporations that grow mile after mile of soybeans and wheat for feeding cattle (whose natural food is *grass*)…and to corn growers whose crops are turned into high-fructose corn syrup and corn oil. They may call it a "farm" subsidy, but you can be sure all those mega-dollars are *not* going to small family farmers struggling to raise high-quality organic food.

Furthermore, your city and state tax dollars pay to dispose of all the packaging that fast food is wrapped in at your local landfill. And your taxes pay for the heart attack and stroke patients without health insurance who show up at the emergency room of your town's hospitals.

These agribusiness subsidies and hidden taxes permit fast-food corporations to charge artificially low prices that don't reflect the actual costs of their products. That $5 lunch might seem like a good deal at first glance. But when you look closer, you're really paying a lot more— *especially* if it gives you diabetes or heart disease.

BUT I *CRAVE* FAST FOOD!

It's true. Many people actually have powerful cravings for fast food. Some scientists have even shown that it's physically addictive. But the *real* reason fast food is so appealing to the masses is that it combines three flavors our brains are programmed to feast upon: fat, sugar, and salt.

You see, back in the days when our ancestors were constantly foraging for food, calories were in short supply. And locating salt, a mineral our bodies need for essential functions, was extremely difficult (except for those who lived near the sea). In fact, salt was so rare it was used as money for a period of history.

Back in those days, survival also meant seeking out foods with the highest caloric content. As a result, we developed a strong taste for sweet and fatty foods. When early humans happened upon a bramble of wild berries or killed an animal, they gorged themselves because the next meal was uncertain.

Thus, our brains became hardwired for sweets, fats, and salt—and this programming stays with us today. Just for a moment, visualize the last gas station or convenience store you were in—remember rack after rack of sweet, salty, fatty snacks and other packaged foods? Today we're literally surrounded by an abundance of cheap, fatty, high-calorie foods. Ironically, the "survival programming" that's been hardwired into our brains over tens of thousands of years could now be the cause our extinction—unless we commit ourselves to outsmarting it. And that's what *The 30-Day Diabetes Cure* is all about.

IT'S A MINEFIELD OUT THERE!

Promise yourself right now that you'll say "no" to fast food for lunch. In fact, now's the time to say "no" to dining out *entirely* until after Day 22. I assure you the next few weeks will be easier *without* restaurant food. One-third of the total calories in the American diet comes from restaurant food, with fast food accounting for about 10% or more. In fact, nearly 20% of Americans are hard-core "fast foodies," meaning they eat convenience or fast food an average of five or more times a week. You definitely don't want to be one of these statistics.

That's why "there's no place like home" when it comes to lunch. You're much better off in a controlled environment—your own kitchen—so you can be certain you're eating the healing foods that will stabilize your blood sugar, help you lose weight, and keep you from being tempted by familiar greasy fast-food aromas that we've grown up with.

In a couple weeks, when you're more educated about my Diabetes Healing Diet—and you've broken the hold these destructive foods have on you—you'll be able to go out for lunch, have dinner with friends, and even enjoy a party or a pot-luck with confidence and know-how.

In fact, if you can conquer the desire for a fast-food lunch today, you've eliminated one of the biggest stumbling blocks to healing your diabetes. So the question now is: What do you eat instead?

What's it like to step outside the lunch "box" and rethink the whole midday meal concept? What are your options when you say no to the ubiquitous fast-food industry and all their seductive ads and "value menus"? Where do you turn when you say no to the office peer pressure and ask yourself: "What kind of lunch is going to make me healthier, slimmer, sharper, more productive on the job, and feeling better about myself?" Suddenly, a new world of lunch possibilities opens up!

THE SMARTEST SOURCE FOR LUNCH IS *HOME*

Of course, when you're rushing out of the house in the morning on your way to work, the last thing on your mind is "What am I going to have for lunch?" But if you're trying to balance your blood sugar or lose weight (or both), eating a good, safe Diabetes Healing Lunch can make a huge difference in how you feel all afternoon long. Not to mention your long-term health. Here are a few tips that to help you get started…

Brown-bag it. Your most healthful (and frugal) strategy is to bring your food with you. That way you're *certain* of what you're getting. Even so-called "healthy" lunch places like the salad bar or deli at your natural foods grocery harbor foods that contain too much salt, sugar, and disguised fast carbs.

Your homemade Diabetes-Healing Lunch can be quick and easy if you're pinched for time. All you need are a few small containers and little time to pack them the night before to make sure your lunch will contain foods you *know* will heal your body, instead of hurting it. Perhaps some celery sticks stuffed with cream cheese or almond butter. Sliced grilled chicken or steak from last night's dinner. A real salad. Chopped veggies, which you can eat raw or steam in the office microwave. Or a little bit of everything above. (I told you there would be no deprivation on my eating plan!)

You might have a baggie of mixed nuts, maybe a slice of tasty artisan cheese and a hard-boiled egg. How about some yogurt or ricotta cheese? After Day 12, you can include a piece of fruit…or have a one-bowl meal of brown rice mixed with vegetables and some rotisserie chicken…a whole-grain pita pocket stuffed with chopped veggies, hard-boiled egg, and crumbled feta or goat cheese…a whole-grain tortilla wrapped around whatever's left from last night's dinner with some fresh tomatoes and grated cheese inside. (Mmm! Warm it up and you have one satisfying lunch.) The variety is endless as well as delicious. Most important, you'll be healing your diabetes with every delicious bite.

Pack it yourself for portion control. One of the primary advantages of bringing your lunch from home is your control over your portion sizes. Restaurant food is notorious for too-big-to-finish servings, and yet we somehow manage to force ourselves. We finish it because we're paying for it, and because wasting food is just not in our genetic makeup.

And let's not forget the entire concept of "supersizing," which started in the mid-1990s and has led to a complete and utter distortion of appropriate meal sizes. This profit-motivated "up-sell" strategy has been so successful that it's everywhere these days. In fact, we don't even know what a normal portion is anymore.

Researchers at the University of Minnesota examined the effects of different meal portion sizes on energy intake. Participants were given a prepackaged box lunch every day at work for two months in either small or large sizes. They were told they could eat as much or as little as they wanted. The small lunch was a very satisfying 767 calories, the large one a hefty 1,528 calories.

It turned out that those who got the bigger lunch consistently ate nearly 300 calories more than those given the smaller lunch. And, not surprisingly, those who ate more also gained weight: on average, two pounds in just the two months alone. That's 12 pounds a year, and you can do the math on that rate of weight gain over just a few years! This is a perfect example of how today's supersized portions work against our better judgment.

Be prepared. Home is where the most diabetes-friendly foods come from—*if* you're an informed shopper. So today I'm going to suggest a wide variety of easy and satisfying take-to-work lunches you can put together in a snap. The trick is setting up things in advance to save precious time, especially on busy mornings. Once you learn how to stock your fridge and pantry, half the battle is won. And when you start preparing Diabetes-Healing Dinners regularly, making your lunch out of creatively inspired leftovers won't take any time at all. Let's look at what you want to ensure you include in the typical Diabetes-Healing Lunch…

VEGGIES RULE!

The more ways you can fit vegetables, cooked or raw, into your noontime meal, the better you'll feel later in the afternoon and the *faster you'll reverse your diabetes or prediabetes*. Vegetables are the ultimate "good carbs," and here's the best news: You can literally eat as much of them as you want without gaining weight or upsetting your blood sugar.

Fresh in salads or lightly steamed, veggies are loaded with phytonutrients, antioxidants, vitamins, and minerals. They're the centerpiece of my Diabetes-Healing Diet—and they travel well. You can even buy carrots and other vegetables already peeled and sliced in small packages, for mornings when prep time is limited. Sliced carrots, sweet bell peppers (red, yellow, and green), and cucumbers are easy to carry along anywhere. Just rinse, toss in a container or baggie, and you're ready to go. Try a light sprinkle of sea salt on peeled cucumber. Add peanut butter or low-fat cream cheese to your celery sticks for a nutritious treat. (The protein will slow the breakdown of the carbohydrates even further—and satisfy your hunger longer.)

Chopped broccoli and cauliflower contain abundant antioxidants and the anti-inflammatory chemical *sulforaphane*. (Remember: Inflammation always makes diabetes worse.) Make these cruciferous vegetables the centerpiece of a salad or raw veggie medley—or steam them and splash with a tablespoon of extra-virgin olive oil. In a few more days, you'll be adding them to a container of brown rice you cooked the night before (or make a bigger batch on the weekend and portion it out for lunches and dinners during the week).

When lunchtime rolls around, place the vegetables in a glass bowl and add a piece of leftover salmon, skinless organic chicken breast, or turkey sausage. Cover with a piece of paper towel or wax paper and microwave for about one minute. (Never microwave in plastic containers or with plastic wrap; it is highly carcinogenic!) Result: perfectly steamed vegetables with high-quality protein. This is an ideal Diabetes-Healing Lunch, something you'll look forward to all morning. Add a pat of butter or a drizzle of olive oil and you're good to go.

PROTEIN KEEPS YOU GOING

You need protein at lunch—just like you do at breakfast—to maintain the strength and stamina to get through the tasks of your day with energy and vitality. You don't need a lot of it, though, and you certainly don't need a quarter-pound slab of poor-quality ground beef from questionable sources. Here are my choices for the best sources of protein for a midday meal…

- Chicken and turkey can be added to salads. After Day 12, these can be chopped and mixed with brown rice. You'll also be able to use whole-grain bread for a sandwich—but you can also skip the bread entirely and enjoy thin slices of chicken or turkey wrapped in lettuce leaves. (Be sure you're eating real meat, though, and not processed and prepared "lunch meat." We'll talk about the dangers of the additives in heavily processed meats in a few days. Meanwhile, a quick look at the lunch meat labels should be enough to convince you to steer clear!)

- Beans are a terrific protein source and ideal for people with diabetes because they're a low-calorie, high-fiber choice. Buy canned, unsalted, organic beans like garbanzos, kidney beans, white beans or favas; rinse them thoroughly and drain before adding to salads or chopped vegetables. Easier yet, rinse, drain and heat a half cup of beans in the microwave. Toss gently with a half tablespoon of extra-virgin olive oil and shake in a few herbs. You'll never miss that noontime burger. Buy refried beans (be sure to choose organic and fat-free varieties to avoid the unhealthy oils) to make a perfect south-of-the border lunch with chopped tomatoes and grated cheddar cheese. Just skip the chips!

- Wild salmon, either fresh or canned, is loaded with omega-3 essential fatty acids, an important anti-inflammatory compound. (Most canned salmon is wild Alaskan salmon, making it a convenient choice for a healthful lunch.) Canned salmon can be made into a number of delicious dishes, including salmon patties, salmon loaf, or salmon salad—all of which work perfectly as yummy lunchtime choices.

- Hard-boiled eggs are a supereasy lunch food. Peel and eat them out of hand, or make an easy and nutritious egg salad with onion, celery, cilantro, plus a little olive oil and vinegar. Or chop them up with vegetables and leafy greens. Eggs from free-range, pasture-fed hens are naturally high in omega-3 and other nutrients. Lots of people are keeping hens today in places you might not expect—even the city and suburbs. Check around for a source of ultra-fresh eggs. (You might make a few new friends in the hunt.)

- Don't forget yogurt. This go-to food can be eaten for breakfast, lunch, as a refreshing snack, or even dessert. Mixed with nuts (in a few days you can add berries or whole-grain granola), yogurt is a terrific lunch option. Just remember to buy live-culture yogurt that's unsweetened and unflavored. After Day 12, mix in your fresh fruit. Completely avoid sugary grocery-store yogurts loaded with fruit mixes and other add-ins such as cookie bits or cereals. Even worse are the yogurts with artificial sweeteners (remember our discussion of the dangers of artificial sweeteners in Day 1?).

ADD A DIABETES-HEALING BEVERAGE

What to drink instead of that habitual soda? Return to Day 4 if you need a reminder of healthy drink options. In a nutshell, enjoy tap water or mineral water with a squeeze of lemon. Have tea—green or black tea, hot or iced—or brewed coffee, with a little stevia for sweetness if you must. Or just enjoy a glass of ice-cold low-fat milk! Remember to avoid all sodas, fruit juices, and sweet teas. The taboo list also includes flavored coffee drinks, flavored milk shakes and drinks, processed protein drinks and commercial smoothies, yogurt drinks, and juice blends (they're all high in sugars and calories).

DIABETES-HEALING MEALS BEGIN WITH SMART SHOPPING

Here's another old saying that's absolutely true: "If you don't buy it, you can't eat it." Improving your eating habits begins with shopping smarter. Check out these pointers…

Never shop hungry. Plan your shopping trip in advance, making sure you eat a healthy meal before you go. You'll be in much better shape to resist temptation along the way. (And the "supermarketeers" have plenty of psychological tricks up their sleeves!)

Shop from a list. Make a meal plan of menus for an entire week that's built around Diabetes Healing Superfoods. Shop strictly from your list to avoid "impulse purchases." (This is also an excellent way to reduce your weekly food bills.)

Stick to the perimeter. That's where you'll find fresh produce and the dairy case, plus the meat and fish. "Trouble foods" are stocked in the interior aisles, with the worst and often most expensive foods at eye-level (or wherever your kids can reach them). Brace yourself for the sale items stocked on the outside ends of each aisle. These are high-traffic areas and temptation is almost always lurking there.

KNOWLEDGE IS POWER

More people die from ignorance every year than from any other cause. Diabetes, like so many other chronic and degenerative diseases, is completely preventable and reversible when you make informed, intelligent choices about what you put in your mouth. With the exception of type 1, diabetes is virtually *always* a result of poor eating and self-care. But all that's changing now for you. Even though you're still in the first week of *The 30-Day Diabetes Cure* plan, you're already starting to turn the ship around: Your diabetes and blood sugar problems are now in reversal!

These seemingly small steps you're taking are having a big effect. Keep going. Don't let anything slow the momentum you're building by making better food choices. If you slip, I'm here to catch you. Just get back up, dust yourself off, and return to the foods that are healing your diabetes.

TAKE ACTION NOW: Sit down and plan a week's worth of Diabetes-Healing Lunches, based on the information you just learned. (You can add brown rice, sandwiches, and other whole-grain bread products after Day 12, but avoid them for now.) Just like breakfast, structure your midday meals around vegetables and protein—they will stabilize your blood sugar and control your hunger.

Next, create a shopping list from your lunch menus and head for the supermarket. Don't forget to eat a good Diabetes-Healing Meal before you leave the house. Finally, spend a little time each evening preparing the next day's lunch, so you can grab it and go.

EXTRA CREDIT: Make a commitment to pack your lunch each night for a week to get yourself into the habit. Don't go to bed without your lunch being ready to go for the next morning.

DAY 8: ADD DIABETES-HEALING SNACKS

Did you ever stop to taste a carrot? Not just eat it, but taste it?
You can't taste the beauty and energy of the earth in a Twinkie.

ASTRID ALAUDA

HEALER: **Munching the right snacks between meals will help you balance your blood sugar, lose weight, heal your diabetes, and reduce your risk of serious complications. Here's how…**

IT'S A FACT: Snacking is good for you, and even more so if you've got prediabetes or diabetes. Between-meal eating keeps your energy balanced, which means your blood sugar will remain stable. You see, when you don't eat between meals, you're likely to experience roller-coaster blood sugar, which will trigger hunger-induced lows followed by peaks from eating sugary snacks and fast carbs.

GOOD SNACKS VS. BAD SNACKS

It all comes down to one question: *What* are you snacking on? The answer can make all the difference between a midday blood-sugar bomb and a healing helper that keeps your energy and your glucose levels stable.

You've already learned the harm that sugary food products and fast carbs (such as chips, cakes, doughnuts, and crackers) have on your blood sugar. So I'm not going to go into too much detail about the "bad" snacks. You're already savvy enough to know what most of them are. So today I'm going to teach you about the good stuff: the diabetes-friendly snacks that will keep your blood sugar on an even keel, control your hunger, and peel off the excess pounds without you even thinking about dieting.

THE PERFECT SNACK

Here's what you want in a snack: It should contain between 100 and 150 calories…include a slow-carb food coupled with either fat or protein…and relatively high in fiber content. In a moment, I'll give you some specific examples.

Snacking is absolutely vital, because it helps you stay one step ahead of your hunger. That's why I want you to make sure you snack twice a day—even if you aren't hungry. Remember my example of the ravenous tiger? That's your hunger when it gets out of control. It's such an irresistible drive that willpower can't contain it. Once your stomach starts growling and your brain screams for food, you'll gobble whatever's handy. And that's usually junk that will upset your blood sugar and set your progress back.

When it comes to healthful snack options in our daily environment, there are few to none. So your best strategy is to "pack your snacks" from home and keep them close at hand at work and when you're traveling. My most successful patients wouldn't dream of leaving the house without two essentials: a bottle of water and a baggie or container of healthy snacks. Here are some examples…

Fiber plus healthy fat plus protein. Fresh veggies or fresh fruit (in just a few more days you'll be able to add it to your diet) plus cheese equals great snacking. Try sliced apples with a pinky-sized piece of sharp cheddar…celery sticks with cream cheese or peanut butter…pears and bleu cheese…or raw broccoli with goat cheese. These fiber-plus-fat combos are endless and so are the nutritional benefits. Just remember that fruits and veggies are the ultimate slow-carb foods because they break down into blood sugar slowly thanks to all that fiber. The result is that you receive a steady-sustained supply of energy. The protein and good fats digest even more slowly, so you feel full sooner and hunger is abated for longer. In addition, a protein snack will perk up your brain and mental functions.

Dipping permitted. Have you tried making your own hummus? It's easy as opening a can, and this yummy dip brings together several diabetes-healing foods: chickpeas, olive oil, and the sesame-seed "butter" called *tahini,* along with lemon juice and garlic. Yogurt also makes a perfect base for a dip—add herbs, a dash of hot sauce, and some curry powder (all of which are beneficial for diabetes and healthy blood sugar). Another satisfying dip can be made by seeding and dicing cucumbers, then stirring them into yogurt with fresh chopped mint and cracked pepper. These dips are perfect with raw carrot sticks, bell peppers, celery and/or radishes (called *crudités* in gourmet circles).

Sweet surprise. Once you get into Phase II of *The 30-Day Diabetes Cure,* you'll be allowed to nibble a small square of high-quality dark chocolate (containing at least 75% to 85% cocoa solids). This type of dark chocolate is quite healthful in small amounts (about 150 calories) due to the cacao bean's antioxidants, called *polyphenols.* In Italian research reported in the September 2008 *Journal of Nutrition,* a group of healthy people were given a daily dose of either white or dark chocolate and measured their blood sugar. The dark chocolate group showed 10% greater insulin sensitivity and 45% less insulin resistance than the white chocolate group, thanks to the higher concentration of polyphenols.[32]

Go nuts. Eat them out of hand or in nut butters…sprinkle them on a salad…or add them to yogurt. No matter how you enjoy them, nuts are a quick, nutritious snack that's rich in healthful monounsaturated fats, antioxidants, vitamins, and minerals that reduce the risk of diabetes and keep it under control. They're also high in protein (ounce for ounce, nearly as much as lean meat!) and have a low glycemic index (GI). A small handful of nuts will do the trick, especially if you don't want them one by one. Don't actually "go nuts" with nuts, though, because they are high in calories, so "a little dab will do ya," as the old Brylcreem® commercial used to say.

Nuts help control glucose levels and improve your body's response to insulin. A Harvard study of 83,000 women found that those who frequently ate peanuts, almonds, walnuts, pecans, pistachios, cashews, macadamia, hazelnuts, Brazil nuts, or pine nuts reduced their risk of developing diabetes by an amazing 27% compared with those who rarely ate them. Those who ate at least two tablespoons of peanut butter (always choose natural peanut butter with no additives or extra sodium) more than five times a week were 20% less likely to develop type 2 diabetes or cardiovascular disease than those who didn't. As a bonus: The women who ate nuts tended to lose weight as well.

Almonds are especially good at keeping blood sugar levels under control. According to a study published in the *Journal of Nutrition*, their high antioxidant content helps neutralize free radicals caused by chronically high glucose levels. And a study published in the medical journal *Metabolism* reported that almonds not only have a low GI, but actually help lower the GI of the entire meal eaten. They're also rich in the antioxidant vitamin E.

Try almonds lightly toasted and sprinkled on yogurt, or buy natural almond butter and spread it on celery sticks. Whole-grain bread or sliced apples (after Day 12) are delectable snacks when spread with a little almond butter. Have a few almonds between breakfast and lunch to keep your energy and blood sugar stable.

Eating almonds and other nuts can actually help you lose weight. A study published in the *International Journal of Obesity and Related Metabolic Disorders* found those who ate almonds in a low-calorie diet for six months reduced their weight by 11% and their waistlines by 9%. Plus, 96% of those in the study who had type 1 diabetes were able to reduce their medication. A similar Spanish study involving 8,865 adults found that people who ate nuts at least twice weekly were 31% less likely to gain weight than those who seldom ate nuts.

More health benefits: The monounsaturated fats in almonds also help lower LDL cholesterol and reduce the risk for cardiovascular disease. According to a study published in the *British Journal of Nutrition*, eating almonds instead of other fats reduced LDL by 8% to 12%.

---

[32] http://jn.nutrition.org/cgi/content/abstract/138/9/1671

Walnuts are a great snack choice too because they are exceptionally high in omega-3 essential fatty acids—and have the lowest ratio of omega-6 to omega-3 of any nut (4.2 to 1). Numerous studies show that a diet rich in omega-3s helps prevent the blood clotting and plaque buildup that can lead to atherosclerosis. And omega-3s also improve the ratio of HDL cholesterol to LDL cholesterol, while reducing inflammation. Walnuts and apples are a classic combo eaten by hand or mixed into yogurt with a generous sprinkle of cinnamon—and it's a fantastically healthful snack…

■ In a study published in *Diabetes Care*, eating walnuts was linked to a significant increase in the ratio of HDL to total cholesterol and a 10% reduction in LDL.

■ A Spanish study involving high-cholesterol adults found those who ate walnuts drove down their total cholesterol by 4.4% to 7.4% and their LDL by 6.4% to 10%. A quarter cup of walnuts provides an astonishing 90.8% of your daily omega-3 needs.

■ Eating antioxidant-rich nuts also lowers your risk for coronary heart disease that often results from having diabetes. According to a study published in the *British Journal of Nutrition*, walnuts, pecans, and chestnuts are also exceptionally high in antioxidants.

■ Another study published in the research journal *Phytochemistry* identified 16 different antioxidant polyphenols in walnuts they describe as "remarkable."

■ Four large studies, including the Adventist Health Study, Iowa Women's Study, the Nurses' Health Study, and the Physicians' Study, found that those who ate nuts at least four times a week lowered their risk for coronary heart disease by an amazing 37%.[33]

And don't overlook peanuts. Although technically a legume, peanuts contain *oleic acid*, the same healthy fat found in olive oil. Peanuts are high in vitamin E and a great source of antioxidants. A study published in the journal *Food Chemistry* found that peanuts contain high concentrations of the antioxidant polyphenol *p-coumaric acid*. Slow roasting (170 degrees F for 20 minutes) can increase the levels by 22%.[34]

Peanuts are also high in *resveratrol*, an antioxidant found in red grapes and red wine and linked to the "French Paradox," which maintains that eating a diet high in certain fats, the way the French do, can actually benefit your heart. According to a study published in the *Journal of Agricultural and Food Chemistry*, resveratrol improves blood flow to the brain by as much as 30%, significantly reducing the risk of stroke.

---

[33] Talcott S, Passeretti S, Duncan C, Gorbet W. Polyphenolic content and sensory properties of normal and high oleic acid peanuts. Food Chemistry 2005 May;90(3):379-388. 2005. http://www.sciencedirect.com/science/article/pii/S0308814604003280

[34] http://pubs.acs.org/doi/abs/10.1021/jf990737b

MORE TIPS FOR ENJOYING NUTS

- Stay away from packaged nuts and nut mixes that have sugar or salt added. The sugar and fruit will spike your blood sugar and the extra salt is bad for blood pressure. Buy peanut or other nut butters without anything else added (you should be a well-practiced food label reader by now).

- Avoid packaged, premade trail mix that includes added candy or dried fruit. Dried fruit is high in sugar and you should avoid it until Day 12. After that, be sure to limit yourself to one or two dried apricots or date pieces, sliced and mixed into yogurt, or a spoonful of raisins or dried cranberries. Make sure the dried fruit has no added sweeteners.

- Like so many foods exposed to high heat, packaged roasted nuts lose some of their nutritional potency. It's best to buy organically grown raw nuts, lightly toasting them in a dry fry pan over very low heat (or in your oven). Keep nuts in a tightly sealed glass jar in the refrigerator to prevent their natural oils from going rancid.

- Remember that nuts are high in fat—and fat is high in calories. While this fat is good for you in so many ways, too many nuts will add excess calories and increase your weight. Eaten too abundantly, nuts can also overpower your desire to eat low-calorie vegetables and other diabetes-healing selections. Keep nut snacking to a small handful or no more than two tablespoons of nut butter daily.

MORE HEALING (AND LIP-SMACKING!) SNACK OPTIONS

Popcorn is a bona fide whole grain that's loaded with fiber—it's all the junk added to popcorn that makes it a poor choice unless you pop your own. First, reject microwave popcorn. It's bathed in toxic chemicals, artificial flavors, and excess salt. Movie theatre popcorn is also off-limits due to its high omega-6 oils and salt content. Buy your own popcorn (organic is best) and pop it in an inexpensive air popper. Two tablespoons of melted butter or extra-virgin olive oil on a large bowl of popcorn is a sufficient snack for two to four people, so be careful not to overdo it. Pack some in a sealed container and take to work for a snack. In place of salt, add chili powder, garlic powder, dry mustard, cinnamon, or herbs like basil or oregano.

Turkey. A piece of thinly sliced turkey rolled up around a slim stalk of cheese makes a fine protein boost midafternoon.

Other suggestions. Other savory snacks to keep your blood sugar stable while providing a bounty of healing nutrients include: a few canned sardines in olive oil (or a forkful or two of canned salmon) with a smear of cream cheese (after Day 12, you can eat these on whole-grain crackers). A midday hard-boiled egg. Half a cup of yogurt. Cottage cheese with cinnamon. Peanut butter on celery stalk. Warmed vegetarian refried beans from a can as a dip for raw veggies. Let your imagination run wild!

"BUT THOSE AREN'T THE SNACK FOODS I'M USED TO!"

That's right. The snacks of your past—whether sweet or salty, crispy or creamy—are among your worst enemies. They're loaded with empty calories…increase your weight…spike your blood sugar…cause widespread inflammation…add to your risk of other serious diseases…and distract you from eating nourishing foods that can help heal your diabetes. The vast majority of snacks we're faced with every day are precisely the foods that have helped create today's epidemic of obesity and diabetes in the first place. Take a pass on these items…

Assume that virtually every snack food in a bag or packaging or stocked in a vending machine, convenience store, or snack-food aisle at the grocery has high-fructose corn syrup or other added sweeteners, plus trans fats, polyunsaturated vegetable oils like soybean or canola, refined white flour, excessive salt, and myriad chemicals used as preservatives, stabilizers, dough conditioners, artificial colors, and artificial flavors. And don't forget the high calorie count.

DON'T BE FOOLED BY "ENERGY BARS"

Junky snacks can masquerade as "health food." Most so-called energy bars (including granola bars) are high in processed soy products (much harder for the body to metabolize than traditional soy foods such as miso and tempeh, and possible hormone disrupters to boot), as well as sweeteners and refined carbohydrates such as rice "crisps" and highly concentrated fruit syrups. Read labels carefully.

"Yogurt-covered" raisins and dried banana chips are sweeter than candy. Rice cakes may be low in calories, but they're really just another refined and processed fast carb. Cheese-flavored or spice-flavored "puffs" are nothing more than damaging fats filled with air, fake colors, and added flavors. "Natural" potato chips are potatoes minus their healing fiber that have been fried in polyunsaturated oils and salted for maximum fulfillment. Even innocent-sounding "whole-grain" pretzels and crackers turn into a rush of sugar in your blood.

And those cute little "100-calorie" cookie packs? Portion control is helpful, but it's still 100 calories of cookies—made of sugar, white flour, artificial flavors, and chemicals instead of 100 calories of fiber, vitamins, antioxidants, and protein.

AVOID HFCS LIKE THE PLAGUE!

Let's not forget the most popular sugar substitute: high-fructose corn syrup (HFCS), the sweetener of choice in soft drinks and snack foods.

Dr. Robert Lustig, Professor of Pediatrics in the Division of Endocrinology at the University of California, San Francisco, has discovered a number of subtle differences from regular cane sugar in the way our bodies respond to HFCS. Chief among them is that HFCS calories are stored immediately as fat in a much higher ratio than plain old sugar. Nearly one-third of HFCS calories don't even line up to be converted into energy—they move directly into fat storage.

HFCS is used in many common processed snack foods, even those that don't taste sweet (such as spicy, flavored chips and crackers). It also creates a range of waste products for your liver to process that ordinary sugar does not. The resulting toxin buildup includes uric acid, which pushes up blood pressure and causes gout, a painful inflammatory condition.

THE TOP 10 DIABETES-FRIENDLY SNACK SUBSTITUTIONS

Instead of...	Choose...
Chips	Air-popped popcorn (with a little olive oil and grated parmesan cheese)
Soda pop	Half a cup 100% pomegranate juice with half a cup or more sparkling water
Cookies	Apple slices and five walnut halves (you'll be able to enjoy fruit on Day 12)
Candy bar	Four prunes and four almonds
Ice cream	Yogurt with berries, chopped nuts and cinnamon
Granola bar	Tablespoon peanut butter, plus raisins on whole-grain slice, cut into quarters
Nachos	Potato skins with diced spinach or broccoli slices, onion and a bit of cheese, baked until crisp
Milk shake	Smoothie with plain yogurt, berries, and flaxseed
Popsicle	10 tart fresh cherries

To discover other yummy Diabetes Healing Snacks, visit *www.myhealingkitchen.com.*

TAKE ACTION TODAY: Clear all damaging snack foods out of your kitchen and stock up on my Diabetes-Healing Super Snacks described above. Prepare the next day's snack supply the night before so you can just grab it and go. Always have a healthful snack supply with you at all times so you're never caught off-guard.

EXTRA CREDIT: If you can toss all the bad snack foods in your house without taking a last bite, you've more than earned your extra credit

---

CASE STUDY: FENTON

"I was just so happy. I called everyone and told them: 'My diabetes is all gone!'"

Fenton prided himself on being fit. He exercised regularly, did Pilates…the last thing he would have imagined was that he had type 2 diabetes. But with an A1C of 7.1, there was no denying it.

Case Study: Fenton	Before	After
Weight	164	145
A1C	7.1	5.2
Blood Pressure	126/80	128/82
Triglycerides	187	112
Meds	–	–

His diet was the cause. Fenton believed he could eat anything because he exercised regularly—and that was his downfall. Most doctors would have started him a glucose-lowering drug, but I felt Fenton could turn things around with the simple dietary changes outlined in *The 30-Day Diabetes Cure*. And he came through with flying colors!

Not only did he reverse his diabetes, but he also lost close to 20 pounds simply by eating healthier.

DAY 9: ELIMINATE JUNKY PROTEIN

Red meat is not bad for you. Now blue-green meat, that's bad for you!

TOMMY SMOTHERS

ANTI-HEALER: **Processed meats like bacon, bologna and hot dogs are high in calories, fats, salt, and cancer-causing preservatives like sodium nitrite. Farmed fish are loaded with toxins. These inferior sources of protein are also deficient in the diabetes-healing nutrients. Choose from these better protein sources instead...**

A GOOD WAY to keep your blood sugar levels stable, your muscles strong, and your mind sharp is to increase the amount of animal protein meat you consume. But this only works if this protein is from high-quality sources. When shopping, keep this little phrase in mind: *Protein good; preservatives bad.*

GOOD PROTEIN VS BAD PROTEIN

You may not be aware that there are two kinds of animal protein available to you. There are animal products (beef, pork, poultry, eggs, and dairy) generated from huge factory feedlot operations, which are then manufactured into a variety of "meat products" laced with chemicals, hormones, antibiotics, and carcinogenic preservatives. Farmed fish are included in this junky protein category because they're raised in overpopulated corrals and fed artificial grains and antibiotics, while living in waters concentrated with waste products and parasites.

Make no mistake: These animal products are not good for your health and have been linked to numerous medical problems. Some nutritionists suggest that you give up animal products entirely and eat only plant-based foods. I don't agree with this line of thinking. Yes, it's fine to become a vegetarian if that's your choice. Perhaps you're philosophically or spiritually opposed to killing and eating animals or their products. No problem. You certainly can live a healthy life without meat. This choice is entirely personal, and the arguments for and against eating meat can be debated forever. But no one should be able to impose their dietary philosophy on you.

There are absolutely no valid scientific studies showing that consuming animal protein is bad for your health. Quite the opposite: We humans are omnivores, and the way our digestive system functions is proof of this. My main concern is that if you choose to eat animal products, you pick those of the highest quality so they don't make you ill or shorten your life.

There are only two main dangers associated with eating animal protein: consuming too much of it and eating nutritionally inferior products. Today I'm going to help you distinguish healthful animal protein from the kind that actually contributes to disease.

THE GOOD STUFF

There are ranch-style operations where cattle, dairy cows, bison, pigs, and poultry are allowed to roam and graze on grassy pastures all day and fed organic grains to supplement their diet. This is humane animal husbandry. The meat and food products of these animals (milk, cheese, eggs, etc.) are hormone-free, devoid of antibiotics, and prepared for market without chemical additives. Wild seafood from ocean waters and even well-maintained ponds contains "clean" protein and essential fatty acids that are good for your heart.

More grocery stores now offer these naturally raised products. Just ask the butcher to get you what you want. Most fresh fish and seafood are labeled "wild" or "farmed" if you look carefully.

JUNKY MEATS ARE BAD FOR YOU

Highly processed meats such as bacon, sausage, jerky, and "lunch meats" are heavily preserved so they can move across the country by train or truck and then sit in your grocery refrigerator case for months on end. The preservatives sodium nitrite and sodium nitrate are widely used in the meat industry to create "breakfast meats" and "lunch meats." The meats in canned soups, jarred sauces, and frozen dinners are also subject to these chemical treatments, as are those served in school lunch programs and other institutional settings like convention centers, sports arenas, hospitals, senior centers, and prisons.

Nitrates and nitrites turn meat—which is usually a brownish grey—an appealing bright red color so it looks much fresher than it really is. These chemicals also possess antimicrobial properties, and hence their function as a preservative. But these chemicals convert into *nitrosamines,* which are carcinogenic in the human body. A seven-year study of almost 200,000 people by Dr. Ute Nöthlings at the University of Hawaii showed those who ate the most processed meats, such as hot dogs and bologna, had a 67% higher risk of pancreatic cancer than those who ate few or no such products.[35] A diabetic already has a malfunctioning pancreas, and these foods clearly weaken it more. So my advice is to avoid them.

DOUBLE DANGERS OF PROCESSED MEAT

If these meat products are so harmful, why are they permitted to permeate our food supply? Never underestimate the power of Big Food—it is not a friend of people with diabetics. Several vivid examples…

- High-fructose corn syrup is the main ingredient in almost all sodas and many packaged foods. It is known to interfere with leptin and insulin metabolism, yet manufacturers continue using it—and government agencies, plus the scientific community in general, avert their attention.

- Trans fats are now universally recognized as health-damaging, but the food industry is still dragging its feet on eliminating them entirely from our food supply.

- Margarine continues to be promoted as a "healthy" alternative to butter (especially now that it's fortified with omega-3 fatty acids), even when the science clearly shows the opposite is true.

- Growth hormones and antibiotics are still widely used by meat producers, although they are known to damage the human immune system and foster antibiotic-resistant strains of bacteria.

So don't expect any acquiescence from the packaged-meat industry on the dangers of chemicals, hormones, and preservatives used widely in animal products. It's up to *you* to know the difference between good and bad meat products—and to make your purchasing choices accordingly.

MORE REASONS TO AVOID PROCESSED MEATS

They're loaded with sodium. Sodium is an essential nutrient in very small doses. About one 2,300-mg teaspoon equals the recommended daily allowance, although far less—250 mg to 500 mg—is perfectly adequate for your body's needs.

You should keep your sodium consumption at the low end if you have diabetes, which already puts you at risk for high blood pressure. Sodium increases your danger for hypertension, heart disease, and kidney stones, among other painful conditions.

That means stay away from processed meats. Bacon contains over 100 mg sodium per slice, breakfast sausages up to 200 mg each, and hot dogs over 600 mg. Most Americans eat well over

---

[35] http://www.ncbi.nlm.nih.gov/pubmed/10695593

a teaspoon per day, much of it hidden in convenience foods such as processed meats, snack foods, canned soups and sauces, meals-in-a-box, frozen dinners, and fast food.

They're high in calories. Diabetics need to watch their weight and that's another good reason to cut out processed meats. A plain hot dog has about 240 calories. Add the bun, ketchup, mustard, mayo, and perhaps chili or cheese—plus the soda and chips that often accompany hot dogs—and you're staring at a caloric hand grenade. You already began eliminating these junk-food lunches from your diet on Day 7. If you need more encouragement, take a gander at the fat/calorie content of these meat-centric menu items from The 1,000+ Calorie Fast Food list…

- Carl's Jr. Double Six Dollar Burger: 1,520 calories

- Hardee's Monster Thickburger: 1,420 calories

- Hardee's Double Bacon Cheese Thickburger: 1,270 calories

- Hardee's Double Thickburger: 1,250 calories

- Burger King TRIPLE WHOPPER Sandwich with Cheese: 1,230 calories

- Hardee's Big Country Breakfast Platter, Breaded Pork Chop: 1,220 calories

These numbers are especially alarming because a healthy calorie allowance for the entire day is approximately 1,500 to 2,000 calories (more if you exercise). That means each of the above meals provides almost all your daily calories in a single meal! If you haven't already, I urge you to get these meats out of your diet as fast as you can.

SWITCH TO LEAN, CLEAN, "GREEN" PROTEIN

Now that you've removed the bad junk, let's add the good stuff…

Don't be afraid to eat meat. Forget about meat's "bad reputation" because it contains saturated fats.

- Danish researchers found that among their subjects, those who ate more saturated fat, especially in butter and high-fat dairy products, actually gained less weight around their midsections than those eating low-fat diets. The same was true of participants who ate more red meat: Their waist measurements were smaller than those who ate less.[36]

- A study from Georgetown University demonstrated that chronic stress along with a high-fat, high-sugar diet—the equivalent of a fast-food or junk-food diet—causes belly fat. And your waist size is strongly linked to an increased risk for heart disease, cancer, insulin resistance,

---

[36] Stender, Steen, et al. (1995) The Influence of Trans Fatty Acids on Health: A Report from The Danish Nutrition Council, Clinical Science 88(4):3 75-392 http://findarticles.com/p/articles/mi_m0887/is_n4_v14/ai_16896763/

and diabetes. Red meat per se is not the problem. Leading a hectic life and eating too many calories and too much sugar is.[37]

It's not the meat, it's the quality. Studies attempting to link poor health to a diet high in saturated fats from animal sources rarely, if ever, mention the source of that meat. I believe that most of the clinical data indicating that red meat consumption is linked to heart disease and cancer has more to do with the *quality* of the meat products, and not red meat consumption per se. There's a big difference between a can of Spam® and a pasture-raised sirloin.

Scientists at Harvard Medical School and Simmons College in Boston examined 10 years' worth of dietary data from 70,000 women, aged 38 to 63. They found that the group eating a diet emphasizing fruit, vegetables, beans, fish, poultry, and whole grains had far less risk of developing diabetes. Their research also showed that those who ate a typical American diet heavy in meat products, sweets, desserts, and other fast carbs had a 26% increased risk of developing diabetes *per meal*—and an astonishing 52% higher risk if they ate some type of meat with every meal. Hot dogs raised the risk of diabetes by double-digits: 43% *per serving* and bacon by 49%.

Another overlooked factor in these red meat studies is that people who consume lots of meat products tend to eat fewer fruits, vegetables, and whole grains. So it's hard to tell which causes these diseases: eating meat or *not* eating fruits and vegetables.

On the other hand, there are many studies that focus exclusively on grass-fed, naturally raised cattle and bison and free-range chickens. All find that these provide excellent sources of high-quality protein that's lower in overall fat (and thus calories), higher in good fats, and less likely to spread dangerous bacteria that thrive in crowded feedlot conditions.

Grass-fed beef is lower in calories. One of the many advantages of grass-fed beef over its industrialized grain-fed factory feedlot counterpart is its lower calorie count. You might be thinking: "Meat is meat. How can one piece of beef have fewer calories than another?"

The secret is in the amount of fat, which has more than twice the calories (9 calories per gram) as protein or carbohydrates (4 calories per gram). The more fat you eat, the more calories you take on. Lean grass-fed beef and bison have just a few more calories than chicken (about 200 calories per cup), but the same amount of meat in a fast-food hamburger, which comes from cattle deliberately fattened up in an industrialized feedlot, is twice as high in calories (about 400 calories per cup).

Naturally raised meats contain good fats. Grass-fed beef is also high in omega-3s, an essential fatty acid (EFA) that lowers inflammation and is beneficial for cardiovascular health, proper blood sugar metabolism (essential for treating diabetes or avoiding it altogether), and reducing cancer risk. Your brain also benefits from omega-3s: People with a diet high in omega-3s are

---

[37] http://www.nature.com/nm/journal/v13/n7/abs/nm1611.html

less likely to fall victim to depression, schizophrenia, attention deficit disorder, and Alzheimer's disease. Pasture-raised cattle are two to four times higher in omega-3s compared with grain-fed beef. You'll read more about omega-3s in Day 11.

How do grass-fed animals get so much of the good omega-3 fat? Some 60% of the fatty acids in grass are omega-3s, which accounts for the high level in grass-fed beef. And when cattle are taken from the pasture to the feedlot to eat a diet of omega-6 corn and other grains, the cattle's beneficial EFA plummets. And the longer they stay on the feedlot, the lower their omega-3 drops.

Other healthful fats. *Conjugated linoleic acid* (CLA) is another healthy fat with multiple health benefits, including a powerful defense against cancer backed up by lots of science. Researchers from Ohio State University found that diabetics who added CLA to their diets had a lower body mass as well as lower blood sugar levels. Grass-fed cattle produce meat and dairy products containing up to *500% times more CLA* than animals on grain diets.

Here's great news for gourmets: French cheese has twice as much CLA as American-made cheese from grain-fed cows, which is not surprising when you consider European dairy animals are strictly pasture raised. This certainly could be one explanation for why the French have such a low incidence of cancer, even though their diet is high in fat (and they smoke cigarettes like crazy).

But you needn't go to France or eat fancy cheese to get this benefit. Buy American grass-fed beef and dairy products, which are available at farmers' markets, health food stores, some natural food chain grocery stores, and online sources. You'll immediately reap the benefits of this superior protein source.

Other benefits of grass-fed beef. The meat from grass-fed cattle is 400% higher in the antioxidant vitamin E than grain-fed beef. (It's even higher than that of feedlot cattle, which have been fed vitamin E supplements!) Vitamin E is highly protective against free radicals and their oxidative damage to cartilage, blood vessels, and pancreas cells. According to many studies, vitamin E appears to be most effective for human health when obtained from a whole food rather than a supplement, making grass-fed beef and dairy products an ideal source.

Grass-fed beef is also rich in beta-carotene, the B vitamins *thiamin* and *riboflavin*, plus the minerals calcium, magnesium, and potassium, all of which are essential nutrients for optimum health. B vitamins help with nerve damage, although many diabetics are low in this important complex.

Grass-fed animals are healthier. Here's another important benefit to eating naturally raised meat products. Grass-fed beef is far less likely to transmit infectious bacteria such as *E. coli* than factory feedlot beef, particularly when the final feedlot product has been mashed together from countless different meat sources, a common practice in meat manufacturing.

Grass-fed cattle eat a natural diet in natural surroundings: pasture grass rich in omega-3 fats and CLA plus wild herbs that bestow numerous health benefits. This keeps the overall bacteria count much lower than it is in the crowded, filthy feedlots. In a 1998 study published in *Science*, feedlot cattle were found to harbor *6.3 million* cells of *E.coli* per gram of meat, whereas grass-fed cattle had only 20,000.

WHAT'S WRONG WITH FARM-RAISED FISH?

Fish is a fantastic source of protein. Just as grass-fed beef is healthier than its factory feedlot grain-fed counterpart, the same is true for wild versus farm-raised seafood. Farmed fish don't flourish in a natural environment as wild varieties do, and their nutritional value is lower as a result...

- Farmed fish are 35% fattier overall than their wild cousins because they swim around all day in a little circle, becoming the sea world equivalent of "couch potatoes."

- Farm-raised seafood contains about 35% less omega-3 oils than their wild counterparts.

- Farmed fish are up to 14% higher in inflammatory omega-6 fatty acids. Chronic low-grade inflammation is linked to insulin resistance. (I'll tell you more about the omega-3/omega-6 ratio on Day 11.)

And there are other important reasons for avoiding farm-raised fish. Researchers from Indiana University found that farmed salmon contained high levels of *polybrominated diphenyl ether* (PBDE) compounds, thought to be contaminated from their feed. PBDEs, used as a flame-retardant additive in electronics and foam-based furniture, are endocrine disrupters that negatively affect reproduction. University of New Hampshire researchers are also finding that PBDEs may be a factor in the increase in obesity because they are fat-soluble and disrupt insulin sensitivity.

Farmed salmon also contain *dioxin*, a known human carcinogen implicated in cardiovascular disease and diabetes. According to the Midwest Center for Environmental Science and Public Policy, farmed salmon contains between 3 and 10 times as much dioxin as wild salmon.

SMARTER FISH SELECTIONS

Cold-water fish tend to be the healthiest, although some larger ocean varieties are contaminated with mercury (residue generated by the acid rain created by coal emissions). High levels of mercury have been linked to brain disorders, so pregnant women, nursing mothers, young children, and women who might become pregnant should avoid swordfish, shark, and king mackerel—and limit their consumption of other large fish, including albacore tuna and large grouper.

I think this is good advice for everyone to follow. Mercury has been linked to Alzheimer's, one of the scariest medical conditions of our time. (And since Alzheimer's is a serious complication of diabetes, anything you can do to lower your risk is a wise strategy.) Since mercury levels accumulate in the brain and other fatty tissues in your body, it's smart to avoid these fish. (See the list on page 143.)

THE TOP 10 OMEGA-3–RICH FISH

So what fish should you eat? These cold-water species contain the highest levels of omega-3s and have low levels of contaminants. Here are the leaders of the pack…

1. Wild Pacific salmon (fresh or canned)

2. Scallops

3. Sardines

4. Anchovies

5. Tuna

6. Pacific Halibut

7. Mackerel (not King)

8. Herring

9. Rainbow trout

10. Pacific oysters

For maximum health benefits, you should consider eating two or three servings of omega-3 fish weekly, while avoiding all farmed fish. Ironically (and tragically), their healing gifts are causing the depletion of many omega-3 fish. Worldwide demand has placed them in peril due to overfishing. The Monterey Bay Aquarium posts a "Seafood Watch" alert on its Web site that serves as an updated list of endangered fish. By refusing to purchase these species, you won't be contributing to the problem—and will be doing your part to help them make a comeback. To see which fish are currently on the list, go to *www.montereybayaquarium.org*.

Smaller fish, such as sardines and anchovies, are fine to eat. Their omega-3 content is remarkably high—and because they have a shorter life span, their fat doesn't accumulate mercury residues. Other good choices are domestic shrimp (stay away from Asian or Chinese imports!), mussels, squid, domestic crab, mahi-mahi (because it reproduces abundantly and grows fast), and abalone (farmed or ocean-harvested are okay).

FISH TO AVOID

Avoid these fish varieties because they are either mercury-contaminated or under threat of extinction:

1. Bluefin tuna

2. Chilean sea bass (aka Patagonian toothfish) grouper

3. Monkfish

4. Orange roughy

5. Atlantic salmon

Several Web sites maintain lists of fish that are safe to eat, as well as those to avoid. You can also visit *www.greenamerica.org* for current listings compiled from a number of well-respected sources.

TAKE ACTION TODAY: Stop eating processed meats such as cold cuts, pepperoni, and commercial sausages. Also avoid fish, beef, poultry, eggs, and dairy that aren't raised in healthy, natural environments. Make the switch today. You won't believe how much better these naturally raised foods taste, and you'll be positively impacting your health.

EXTRA CREDIT: Because most of us never get a glimpse behind the scenes at how inhumanely feedlot cattle are treated, an undercover agent took a temporary job at one of these operations and shot some video footage, which he posted on YouTube at *http://www.youtube.com/watch?v=CrxvxewC-gA*. WARNING: This video contains extremely disturbing images, so view it at your own discretion.

DAY 10: ADD DIABETES-HEALING VEGETABLES

Every patient carries her or his own doctor inside.

ALBERT SCHWEITZER

HEALER: **High in fiber and healing nutrients, low-calorie vegetables keep your blood sugar in balance, help you lose weight, and nourish every cell in your body.**

WHEN IT COMES TO Diabetes Healing Superfoods, fresh vegetables top the list. They're loaded with vitamins, minerals, antioxidants, and fiber, plus other phytonutrients that have overwhelmingly positive effects on your blood sugar, your metabolism, and your cardiac health—making them a virtually unbeatable healing food.

How do vegetables work so much healing magic? For one thing, they're incredibly low in calories, meaning you can eat your fill without gaining weight. And because they're rich in all-important fiber, they slow down the digestive process so glucose is metabolized slowly. That means they provide your bloodstream with a steady supply of energy, instead of spiking it up and down like a roller coaster. On top of that, they're loaded with roughage that scoops up cholesterol, fats, toxins, and waste products and escorts them out of your body.

Making vegetables the main focus of your meals helps you lose weight without "trying," lowers insulin resistance, and allows your pancreas to catch its breath.

THE WEIGHT-LOSS CONNECTION

Many vegetables also have high water content—cucumbers, celery, and tomatoes come to mind—which helps hydrate your cells and fill your stomach with their volume. Eat all the vegetables you want. They'll fill you up and trigger your "I'm full" hormone, signaling your brain to stop eating. This metabolic message tells you when to push the plate away, but it's often bypassed by overconsuming sweetened and processed foods, much to the detriment of your waistline and your health.

Veggies are so jam-packed with vitamins, minerals, phytonutrients, and antioxidants that I can unequivocally say they're one of my favorite diabetes-healing foods.

WHY, EXACTLY, DO DIABETICS NEED VEGETABLES?

Nutritionists and dieticians (and mom, of course) often remind us to eat our vegetables, but most of us have only a vague understanding of why they're so good for us. Here are some specifics…

Heart and circulation health. Cruciferous vegetables, including broccoli, cabbage, cauliflower, bok choy, and broccoli sprouts, are all high in *sulforaphane*, which plays a major role in healing blood vessels harmed by inflammation. If you have diabetes, you already know that too much glucose in the bloodstream eventually damages and constricts blood vessels, triggering serious circulation problems in the feet, lower legs, and hands.

In fact, people with diabetes are also nearly 500% more likely to develop cardiovascular diseases such as heart attack or stroke. But according to the Mayo Clinic, sulforaphane encourages the production of enzymes that reduce the damage to blood vessels caused by high blood sugar, thus helping to minimize the devastating effects of diabetes. And UK researchers publishing in the journal *Diabetes* wrote that sulforaphane in broccoli and other cruciferous veggies not only helps boost the immune system and support the liver's job of detoxifying your body, but also protects against oxidative stress.[38]

Oxidative stress is a term for the damage done to cells, tissues, and blood vessels by reactive oxygen species (ROS) molecules, which include free radicals. Sulforaphane combats oxidative stress by activating a certain protein in the body called *nrf2,* which is able to switch on genes that actually increase the body's production of its own antioxidants and detoxifying enzymes. In lab tests, sulforaphane was found to double the activation of the protein nrf2 and reduce ROS molecules by an astonishing 73%. All this from enjoying a serving of broccoli or its cruciferous cousins! (Be sure to try broccoli sprouts, too. They contain even higher sulforaphane concentrations.)

Here's more good news for your heart. Folic acid (also known as folate) is one of the B vitamins that are so helpful in preventing blood vessel damage, thereby reducing the risk of heart attack and stroke. In a study of more than 150,000 women, those who consumed folic acid (found in romaine lettuce, spinach, asparagus, cauliflower, and beans) significantly decreased their risk of high blood pressure and cardiovascular disease that can develop as a result. Both complications are quite common among people with diabetes.

---

[38] http://www.mayoclinic.com/health/diabetes/DS01121/DSECTION=complications

Protection with vitamins. Just one cup of broccoli delivers about 116 mg of vitamin C, almost twice the recommended daily amount for adults. Bell peppers, mustard greens, zucchini, celery, asparagus, fennel, parsley—and of course many fruits—are all powerful sources of vitamin C.

According to the Linus Pauling Institute, even small amounts of vitamin C can protect against the damage done by free radicals and ROS that results from metabolic irregularities, as well as exposure to pollution and toxins (damage that can lead to directly to diabetes, cardiovascular disease and/or stroke).[39]

Vitamins protect your eyesight. Your body uses beta-carotene to make vitamin A, another powerful antioxidant that's particularly protective of your vision. This is a condition people with diabetes must be especially on guard for, since damage to the retina (retinopathy) is one of the serious consequences of diabetes. Besides broccoli, sweet potatoes, carrots, kale, and spinach are all bountiful sources of beta-carotene.

Another important eye-protector is the antioxidant *lutein*, a carotenoid your body coverts into *zeaxanthin*. Lutein not only neutralizes oxidative damage done by free radicals and helps prevent atherosclerosis, but it also improves eye health, according to a study published by the *Journal of the Science of Food and Agriculture*. This is good news for people with diabetes, who are at much greater risk for developing not only vision-destroying retinopathy but also cataracts and macular degeneration. Leafy greens such as romaine lettuce, kale, and spinach are excellent sources.

Minerals help, too. Broccoli, romaine lettuce, onions, and tomatoes are good sources of the trace mineral chromium, used to manufacture glucose tolerance factor (GTF), which helps break down blood sugar. Chromium drives down your blood sugar, cholesterol, and triglyceride fats, which greatly reduces your risk of cardiovascular disease. Chromium aids in the metabolism of glucose by actually resensitizing the insulin receptors on the surface of every cell. Many Americans are chromium-deficient thanks to a diet of refined carbohydrates such as white sugar and white flour. These foods are not only low in chromium but they also deplete it from your body.

Romaine lettuce (a great alternative to bread for wrapping around sandwich ingredients) is high in manganese, a mineral that helps you metabolize fats and carbohydrates. Manganese is also essential for good blood sugar management. And it's a component of *manganese superoxide dismutase* (Mn-SOD), the antioxidant that neutralizes free radicals and repairs the damage they cause. Manganese also helps protect against the oxidation of LDL cholesterol, preventing the buildup of plaques in your arteries, which is the major cause of heart attack and stroke. Other leafy greens are also loaded with manganese, among them mustard greens, kale, and chard, as well as spinach, garlic, and green beans.

---

[39] http://www.medicinenet.com/script/main/art.asp?articlekey=41765

Fill up on greens and you'll never be manganese-deficient, which up to 37% of Americans are these days because of eating all those fast-carb refined foods, according to researchers at the University of Maryland. Curiously, some research has found that people with diabetes have much lower levels of manganese than normal, but it's not known whether this is a cause or an effect of diabetes. And it really doesn't matter; what *is* important is that you up your intake.

Romaine lettuce, by the way, is also very high in vitamin K, which prevents arterial plaque and may also improve insulin resistance. In a recent three-year study published in *Diabetes Care*, researchers found that vitamin K decreased insulin resistance in men over 60.

BUY LOCALLY GROWN

Agribusiness lettuce and other vegetables—even when labeled as organic—are often transported over long distances, sometimes halfway around the world. They're washed with chlorine and may be treated with other chemicals to prolong shelf life. While these practices may benefit industrial growers, they don't do much for your health. Choosing locally grown produce from your local farmers' market is better for your health *and* your local economy. The veggies and other locally grown goodies you buy will not only taste better but also be healthier for you because they're far fresher. Make sure they're 100% organically raised. If you want to take ultimate control, grow your own!

TOP 10 WAYS TO ENJOY VEGETABLES

1. **Salads all mixed up.** Start with romaine or red and green leaf lettuce. Grate in carrots, chopped cucumbers, and bell peppers. Toss in a few nuts and seeds (lightly toasted pine nuts, pumpkin seeds, almonds, or walnuts are delicious and add beneficial fats, protein, and other nutrients) as well as a quarter cup crumbled feta, goat, or bleu cheese. Slice in a hard-boiled egg. Whisk a tablespoon of extra-virgin olive oil with a few drops of balsamic vinegar or lemon juice. (Add some Dijon mustard if you're feeling wild.) You've just made a perfect dressing. Avoid bottled dressings altogether—they include unhealthy polyunsaturated oils such as canola or safflower, along with sugar and artificial flavorings.

2. **Ride the (micro)wave.** Lightly steam finely chopped vegetables such as broccoli or Brussels sprouts by placing them in a glass dish with a little water, covering with a paper towel, and heating for one to two minutes. Pour off the water and add a tablespoon of extra-virgin olive oil or butter. Your veggies will be perfectly *al dente*: crunchy, bright green, and delicious.

3. **Try a one-bowl meal.** Add steamed veggies to brown rice (after Day 12, of course), toss in some chopped cooked chicken breast or salmon, a tablespoon of olive oil, a dash of soy, and your favorite spice mix. Enjoy!

4. **Snack on raw veggies.** As I recommended on Day 8, keep sliced carrots, celery, bell peppers, broccoli, and other veggies on hand for a quick snack. Spread celery with peanut butter or low-fat cream cheese. Dip broccoli in hummus. Plain yogurt with minced garlic and other spices also makes a great dip.

5. **Pick a pita pocket.** Whole-wheat pita bread (which we'll add to your diet in just two days) can turn a healthy salad into a hearty sandwich. Toss a variety of finely chopped vegetables and lettuce with a slivered hard-boiled egg or any leftover cooked meat you might have, such as roasted chicken or fish. Add a spoonful of hummus, garlic-flavored yogurt, or a splash of extra-virgin olive oil along with your favorite seasonings. Now tuck into half a pita pocket for a salad you can eat with your hands.

6. **Juice it.** A high-quality juicer can turn a whole crisper drawer of fresh vegetables into a nutritious meal-in-a-glass. Tomatoes, carrots, lettuce, spinach, cucumbers—even parsley and celery (which can reduce high blood pressure)—can be juiced together for a high-vitamin, low-calorie midday boost in a glass. Experiment to find a recipe that works for you. Just remember to go for variety every time. Straight carrot juice, for instance, will be very high in natural sugars and could overwhelm your bloodstream. But you can add carrot and sweet raw beets to juiced greens and other veggies for sweetness and flavor.

7. **Step up and sauté.** Lightly sauté chopped leafy greens such as spinach, kale, and collard greens in olive oil and garlic over low heat. Serve over brown rice (after Day 12). Or use light olive oil (not extra virgin) or peanut oil, sesame oil, or coconut oil to sauté the vegetables. Toss in a few tofu cubes, shrimp, or strips of skinless chicken breast and dress with a splash or two of low-sodium *tamari* (wheat-free soy sauce).

8. **Do the mash.** Cube a small potato along with cauliflower and/or turnip slices and steam in the microwave or in a stove-top steamer. If you're feeling bold, add minced garlic or Japanese *wasabi* (the green Asian horseradish served with sushi). When soft, add some butter and mash with a fork. Serve alongside baked chicken or a small piece of grass-fed steak. Yum!

9. **Make slaw.** Shredded carrots and broccoli stems, purple and green cabbage, even zucchini, all make excellent additions to salads or mixed up on their own without any lettuce at all. Whisk yogurt with herbs for dressing. Or combine extra-virgin olive oil with rice wine or cider vinegar and toss to blend.

10. **Experiment. Discover. Be adventurous.** Vegetables are enormously versatile—they can be baked, broiled, steamed, sautéed, or just chomped raw. They're the ideal accompaniment to just about everything: meat, fish, brown rice and other whole grains, and beans. Enjoy them the way they do in Asia and the Mediterranean countries—as the star of the plate, with animal protein in the supporting role. (Get more Diabetes Healing Recipes at *www.myhealingkitchen.com*.)

TAKE ACTION TODAY: Make a point to eat vegetables several times a day—the more frequently, the better. Challenge yourself to consume at least three to five servings. The more you eat, the better your blood sugar and general health will be. Don't be afraid to eat your fill; their high-volume, generous fiber content and low-calorie roughage will more than satisfy your hunger without increasing your weight. In fact, you'll actually shed pounds without dieting.

EXTRA CREDIT: Challenge yourself to discover new ways to include vegetables for breakfast, i.e., vegetable omelettes…veggie and egg burritos…Eggs Benedict with spinach and salmon. Search cookbooks and the Internet and dare to be creative.

PHASE II:

Inside the Bubble

Days 11 to 20

Have patience with all things, but chiefly have patience with yourself.
Do not lose courage in considering your own imperfections
but instantly set about remedying them—every day begin the task anew.

SAINT FRANCIS DE SALES

(-)

DAY 11: ELIMINATE BAD FATS AND OILS

Health is the thing that makes you feel that now is the best time of the year.

FRANKLIN PIERCE ADAMS

ANTI-HEALER: **Most processed vegetable oils are highly inflammatory, which leads to serious complications of your diabetes, including heart disease and other diseases.**

FAT IS AN ESSENTIAL COMPONENT of a healthy diet. It's a nutrient that should constitute 30% of your total daily calories. Fat is necessary for hormone production, healthy bones and skin, and for regulating all your bodily functions. Fat helps you absorb nutrients and even protects the organs inside your body.

Not only that, but fat also serves the important purpose of telling your brain when you've eaten enough. That's because it's a natural "appetite regulator" that stimulates *leptin*, a helpful hormone that keeps you from overeating by sending the "I'm full" signal. It's the fat in your meals that satisfies your hunger (called *satiety*). Even lean steak fills you up, while you could devour bags of "low-fat" cookies or a pint of Ben & Jerry's.

This is why low-fat and fat-free diets simply don't work, and why people usually *gain* weight when they dramatically lower their fat intake. When fat is lacking, your brain doesn't know when you've eaten enough. In the meantime, you've plowed through way more calories than you should—piling on extra pounds.

Excess carbohydrate consumption, not fat, is the real villain of the typical American diet. This may sound strange, but *food fat does not make body fat.* We think of insulin as the hormone that carries glucose to cells, but it's also the hormone responsible for body fat storage. Eating fat doesn't raise blood glucose or insulin levels. Because fats do not elicit an insulin response, they cannot be stored as body fat.

On the other hand, shortly after a carb-rich meal, the glucose in your bloodstream rises fast, so the pancreas releases insulin. Insulin takes glucose out of the bloodstream by converting it to glycogen, which is stored in the liver and in muscles. Then it converts the excess glucose into body fat.

DON'T TRUST THE "AUTHORITIES"

Despite this, the ADA and AMA continue to recommend a low-fat diet for people with diabetes and heart disease. Proper diet and prudent lifestyle modifications (another way of saying physical activity) have been proven—by the Centers for Disease Control and many others—to be vastly superior to potent drug treatments for reversing both medical conditions. Yet mainstream medicine keeps singing the same old medication-centric song.

They are like the naked Emperor in the folktale "The Emperor's New Clothes" who can't see that he is undressed in public. They are unfazed by the statistics showing that drug therapy hasn't succeeded one bit to contain diabetes, arthritis, or heart disease—and in the case of drugs like Avandia and Vioxx, they deliberately hide news about the dangers of these drugs.

SUBSTITUTING CARBS FOR FAT

Read the labels closely on fat-free and low-fat food products and you'll discover they are quite high in sweeteners and refined carbs as substitutes for the missing fats. In most cases, high-fructose corn syrup is added in copious amounts to make up for the satisfying, creamy texture that fats provide.

As I mentioned before, HFCS does not stimulate insulin secretion or leptin production, which regulate your sense of fullness. The irony is that these low-fat products end up containing as many—and often, *far more*—calories than the full-fat versions. And they make you eat more because you never feel satisfied. We've been brainwashed into believing that "fat makes us fat," when in reality it's sweeteners and refined carbs that are doing the dirty work. Fat is really your friend, but only if you're eating the *right* fats, because the wrong fats can get you into big trouble.

FATS THAT HURT; FATS THAT HEAL

You read on Day 9 that natural, beneficial saturated fats abound in responsibly raised meat, eggs, and dairy products. There are also good fats in vegetables, nuts, and seeds. Let's look at the different kinds of fats so we know what we're talking about…

Saturated fats are highly stable and unlikely to become oxidized, or rancid. They are solid or semi-solid at room temperature and are excellent for cooking. Your body manufactures saturated fats from carbohydrates and they are also found in animal fats and tropical oils such as palm and coconut. They provide nutrients for growth, hormones, and energy, and also provide elasticity for cell membranes. We need saturated fats to metabolize the essential fatty acids (EFA) that the body cannot produce.

Monounsaturated fats tend to be liquid at room temperature and solidify in the fridge. They are stable, too, and don't go rancid easily. The common food sources for monounsaturated fats are olives, almonds, avocados, pecans, cashews, and other nuts. These oils are associated with lower levels of inflammation, heart disease and cancer, and longer life spans.

Polyunsaturated fats are the most unstable and are very susceptible to becoming rancid, so they must be treated with great care. Rancidity releases free radical molecules into the system that attack artery linings and cell menbranes, rob the body of antioxidants, and weaken the immune system. This is why these fats are associated with chronic disease. Polyunsaturated oils come from soy, corn, safflower, cottonseed, and canola. Because of instability, they are highly processed and therefore these oils should be avoided. Unfortunately, they are present in most baked goods, processed foods, and salad dressings. They should make up no more than 4% of your calories and should come directly from food such as grains, nuts, green vegetables, and fish—not processed commercial vegetable oils.

Trans fats are the worst fat for your health. They are factory-created by injecting hydrogen into vegetable oil (also called hydrogenated vegetable oil and vegetable shortening), good for junk-food manufacturers but terrible for you.

Trans fats are used in place of butter in most commercial baked goods, and also for frying in fast-food joints. You might still have a can of this stuff under the name of Crisco® sitting in your kitchen cupboard…or in your fridge in the form of margarine or another butter substitute. These manufactured fats allow products to sit in shipping containers and semi-trucks for months, until they finally arrive at your grocery…months later. This is called "shelf life" but it's no life for you.

Trans fats are the worst because they are known to increase triglycerides and inflammation, directly increasing your risk of diabetes as well as heart disease, cancer, and arthritis. I hope you've already eliminated them from your diet, because they're nothing but bad for your health.

WHICH FATS ARE HEALING FATS?

Although fats can be grouped into different categories, they all have some levels of essential fatty acids, fats the human body requires but can't produce on its own, so they need to be ingested from food. The two most important are omega-6s and omega-3s. And like all nutrients—vitamins, minerals, antioxidants, carbohydrates, protein—omega-6s and omega-3s are supposed to work in harmony with each other and with every system in your body.

Thousands of years ago, when humans ate foods in their natural form—long before our food was processed in industrial factories—our diet of whole foods naturally consisted of two parts omega-6s to one part omega-3s (a ratio of 2 to 1). Scientists and nutritionists generally agree that's the ideal balance for optimal health, as well as for minimizing internal inflammation.

Omega-6s are good—and bad. One of the roles of omega-6 is to respond to injury or cell damage by activating the immune system and creating helpful inflammation. When you get a scratch on your skin, for instance, the redness and swelling you see is part of the healing process. It's actually a complex protective mechanism that increases blood flow to the damaged area in an attempt to purge the invading substance and heal the tissues.

But chronic internal inflammation—which occurs when your blood vessels are constantly irritated by an ongoing flood of sugar and the insulin that's trying to process it—does exactly the opposite. Rather than *helping* the immune system return you to health, chronic inflammation *completely overwhelms your body's innate healing instincts*. It starts you on the path to a host of serious medical conditions.

High levels of omega-6 fats overstimulate the inflammation response, prompting the body to churn out hormone-like substances called eicosanoids, which *cause* inflammation. People who cook with refined vegetable oils like sunflower, safflower, canola, and corn oils are getting whopping amounts of omega-6s. They are also found in most processed foods like breads and other commercial baked goods, as well as being hidden in literally hundreds of packaged foods like sauces and soups.

Processed foods contain these manufactured polyunsaturated fats that make up the bulk of the average diet. Instead of a healthful 2:1 ratio, *our intake is closer to 20:1*…some nutritionists suspect it's closer to 50:1. In fact, some scientists believe the overwhelmingly out-of-balance amount of omega-6s we consume today is one of the main reasons for the dramatic increase in inflammation-driven medical conditions such as diabetes, heart disease, Alzheimer's, and arthritis.

Eat more omega-3 and less omega-6. Not only do we eat too many omega-6 foods, but most Americans definitely do not eat enough foods high in omega-3s, which play a completely different role. One of their chief advantages is this: Whereas omega-6 is pro-inflammatory, omega-3 fat is *anti-inflammatory*.

Omega-3 deficiency is a heavily researched field, and scientists now know that dozens of medical conditions and serious illnesses have omega-3 deficiency as a component, including heart disease, high blood pressure, cancer, depression and, of course, diabetes. Combine your overexposure to omega-6s in a diet high in processed foods with the low intake of omega-3s and you have a recipe for a major health disaster.

Rich sources of beneficial omega-3 fats include wild Alaskan salmon and sardines, as well as flax and other seeds, and nuts such as walnuts and pecans. Avocados are a good source, too. You'll also recall that eggs from hens that feed on grass are a good source of omega-3s…as are beef, milk, and cheese from grass-fed cattle.

Omega-3s have so many benefits specific to people with diabetes that it's one of the few supplements I think you should be taking daily. In the meantime, let's start getting rid of all these bad fats—not just in the packaged and processed foods, which I hope you've already purged from your shopping list—but also in oils you may use for cooking at home.

Here's one more consideration when selecting your omega-3–rich fats: Omega-3 fatty acids consist of *docosahexaenoic acid* (DHA) plus *eicosapentaenoic* acid (EPA). DHA is an essential nutrient for optimal neuronal functioning (learning ability, mental development—teens who get high levels of DHA/EPA have higher grades) and vision. DHA plus EPA together help with prevention and management of cardiovascular disease as well as other chronic disorders.

The plant-derived omega-3 fatty acid is known as *alphalinolenic acid* (ALA). DHA/EPA are absent from plant food sources rich in ALA (such as flax and walnuts). Since the metabolic conversion of ALA to DHA/EPA is limited in humans, the best way of providing DHA/EPA is through direct consumption. Americans don't usually eat enough fish to get the right amount of DHA/EPA, so a safe fish oil supplement is a good alternative. For more detailed information on these important components of omega-3s, go to *http://dhaomega3.org*.

THE TOP 10 OMEGA-6 FOODS TO AVOID

- Refined, polyunsaturated vegetable oils you use in cooking: canola, safflower, sunflower, corn, and soybean

- Farmed fish and factory feedlot beef, dairy, and poultry

- Microwave popcorn with butter "flavoring"

- All fast foods, especially the deep-fried ones

- Most commercial salad dressings and dips

- Most granola bars and processed snacks, including chips and crackers

- Commercial baked goods and mixes for coffee cakes, cookies, brownies, etc.

- Mayonnaise

- Most veggie burgers

- Tub margarines, butter substitutes, and butter "blends"

If you avoid all those packaged foods, will you get enough omega-6s? Absolutely. Like omega-3s, omega-6 fats are naturally present in beef, poultry, and eggs—though the ideal ratio is found only in the grass-fed or free-range options, *not* from the factory feedlot product. Avocados, nuts, and seeds are also excellent sources of good, balanced omega-6s. These naturally occurring whole foods have just the right ratio of omega-6 to omega-3 fats. Plus, when you use oil made from avocado, walnuts, or sesame seeds for salads and cooking, you'll reap the same benefits of the whole foods.

IT'S NOT JUST ABOUT THE OMEGAS

Fact: All the highly processed and manipulated oils bear no resemblance to natural foods once they land in your body. Eating soybeans is not the same as eating a spoonful of soybean oil. Enjoying corn on the cob is not the same as adding corn oil to pancake batter. And canola? It's a manipulated plant product that started life as the lowly rapeseed plant, a relative of the mustard family. Rapeseed oil has known toxicity issues, and canola was developed to address this, although whether manufacturers have succeeded in creating a nontoxic version long-term waits to be seen. Don't even think about using canola for frying. Studies are beginning to explore a link between the high lung cancer rates in Chinese women and their use of canola oil for high-heat wok cooking.

Unlike corn, safflower, canola, soy, and sunflower, which require extensive processing and heat treatment to create and process the oils, naturally oil-rich foods like olives, nuts, and coconut require very little processing—and no heat—to produce flavorful oils that are perfect for salads and low-heat cooking. Look for the expeller-pressed or cold-pressed varieties.

SOURCES OF GOOD FATS FOR EATING AND COOKING

- Grass-fed beef and dairy products, poultry and eggs

- Wild Alaskan salmon, sardines

- Fish oil and krill oil supplements

- Avocados and avocado oil (for salads)

- Nuts and seeds (flax, sesame)

- Walnut and flax oil for salads

- Extra-virgin olive oil for salads and very low-heat cooking

- Sesame and peanut oil for cooking

- Coconut oil for cooking

- Dark green leafy vegetables

WHAT MAKES THE GOOD FATS SO GOOD?

Beneficial fats such as omega-3s are Diabetes Superfoods, thanks to their ability to protect your heart and blood vessels from the risks of cardiovascular disease, a serious complication often stemming from diabetes. Foods high in good fats—wild Alaskan salmon and the monounsaturated fats in extra-virgin olive oil, avocados, and nuts—also lower your cholesterol, prevent obesity and insulin resistance, and reduce dangerous inflammation, all essential for healing your diabetes.

Lower triglyceride fats and better cholesterol numbers. High triglycerides contribute to metabolic syndrome, a combination of conditions that increase the risk for diabetes, stroke, and cardiovascular disease. In a six-month study of overweight adults published in the journal *Nutrition*, those who ate fish high in omega-3s were able to drop their triglyceride levels by almost 7%.[40]

Omega-3 fats also improve the ratio of good cholesterol to bad, making blood less likely to clot and preventing damage done to your blood cholesterol. In a three-year study published in the *American Journal of Clinical Nutrition*, which looked at postmenopausal women with diabetes, those who ate omega-3-rich salmon at least twice a week reduced their risk for atherosclerosis (clogged arteries) by an astounding 60%.

Control your weight. The EPA in omega-3s stimulates the secretion of leptin, a vital hormone that helps regulate your appetite, food intake, body weight, and metabolism—essential in reversing diabetes.

Prevent cardiovascular disease. Wild salmon and krill oil are both rich in antioxidants that help prevent and even reverse the damage free radicals do to blood vessels. The antioxidants (and the pink color) in wild salmon and krill come from the phytochemical *astaxanthin*. According to a joint Korean and Japanese study published in the *Journal of Agricultural and Food Chemistry*, astaxanthin helps protect cells in blood vessels from the damaging effects of high glucose levels.

A study of 5,000 women with type 2 diabetes conducted over 16 years found that those eating five servings weekly of omega-3–rich fish such as salmon reduced their risk for cardiovascular disease by an amazing 64%! Those who ate fish two to four times a week reduced their risk by 36%. And even those eating fish just one to three times a month were able to reduce their risk by 30%.

Protect against stroke. Stroke is another dangerous complication for people with diabetes. A study published in the journal *Stroke* found that those who ate cold-water fish such as wild salmon one to three times a month reduced their risk of stroke by 9%. Eating fish once a week reduced the risk by 13%. Eating fish two to four times weekly for supper reduced the risk by 18%, and those who ate fish five or more times a week reduced their risk for stroke by an astonishing 31%.

---

[40] http://www.ajcn.org/cgi/content/abstract/90/6/1566

Vitamin D and insulin. A Belgian study linked a deficiency in vitamin D to insulin resistance and the development of diabetes. Researchers from Boston University discovered that eating just a 3.5-ounce serving of wild salmon provides *147% of your daily D* requirement. Fortunately, most canned salmon is wild salmon, making it convenient to incorporate into your diet.

A word about supplements. Purified fish oil and omega-3 supplements are increasingly popular because they avoid the toxicity of marine life. While boosting dietary omega-3 is extremely beneficial for people with diabetes, there's one problem with taking fish oil supplements. *They work too well!* If you're taking any blood sugar medications, the superior blood sugar stabilizing effects of omega-3 supplements can easily interact with your medications and cause serious problems.

That's why I advised you at the very beginning of *The 30-Day Diabetes Cure*—and want to reinforce now—that it's essential to stay in close contact with your physician while you're making these lifestyle and dietary changes. Now would be a very good time to have your glucose levels rechecked. You and your doctor will be surprised—and I think delighted—with the results.

More omega-3 options. Sometimes it seems as though the world is divided into people who love to eat fish and those who don't. You're in luck, though, because there are plenty of other options. Flaxseeds (including ground flaxseed and flax oil), hemp seeds and hempseed oil, walnuts, pumpkin seeds, Brazil nuts, sesame seeds, avocados, and dark leafy green vegetables (kale, spinach, purslane, mustard greens, chard, and collards) all are good sources of omega-3s. These foods can be readily incorporated into your daily diet, especially in the form of salads. Sprinkle toasted pumpkin seeds on a leafy green salad. Slice avocados into the salad bowl too, or mash them into guacamole with lemon juice and garlic. Walnuts are delicious eaten alone as a snack or crumbled into yogurt.

Coconut oil is highly beneficial for people with diabetes, especially for cooking. As a "medium chain fatty acid," it's easier for the body to use it immediately as an energy source, instead of the "long chain" of refined vegetable oils. As a healthy fat, coconut oil slows the digestive process, ensuring that foods converted into glucose enter the bloodstream at a slow and steady rate. High in saturated, polyunsaturated, and monounsaturated fatty acids that are heart-healthy, coconut oil is also loaded with beneficial polyphenols, vitamins, and minerals, including iron.

There's one more extremely important "good fat" that you'll want to enjoy every day …

EXTRA-VIRGIN OLIVE OIL

Where to begin singing the praises of olive oil? A diet rich in olive oil has enhanced the health of Mediterranean peoples for thousands of years, and it's not surprising that this healing way of eating relies heavily on olives and olive oil. The health benefits are clear for any person eating this traditional diet: a greatly reduced incidence of the chronic health problems that plague the globe, including heart disease, obesity, and diabetes. Monounsaturated fats are especially important for diabetics because these fats help control glucose levels, minimize weight gain, and lower high cholesterol that can lead to cardiovascular disease.

Olive oil is rich in *polyphenol antioxidants*, which give the golden elixir its astringency and help prevent oxidative damage to cells by free radicals. A Greek study published in the *Journal of Agriculture and Food Chemistry* found that the antioxidants in olive oil helped lower LDL cholesterol and blood pressure, mitigating the risk of diabetes and cardiovascular disease.

How does fat help diabetes? New research finds that a diet *rich* in monounsaturated fats like olive oil is far more effective in controlling diabetes than the approach once pushed by nutritionists: that diabetics should eat a low-fat/low-carb diet. Their assumption was that fewer fats would prevent heart damage and fewer carbs would help avoid swings in blood sugar. But a study published in the journal of the German Diabetes Association found that glucose levels *were lower in people who ate monounsaturated fats* than in those who avoided all fats. They also found that the monounsaturated fats present in olive oil helped lower LDL (bad) cholesterol, kept triglyceride fats in check, and increased HDL (good) cholesterol.

What about weight gain? Similarly, researchers in Spain concluded that a calorie-controlled diet rich in monounsaturated fats such as olive oil did not cause weight gain among diabetics. They also found that eating olive oil was more realistic and pleasing than eating a strict low-fat diet. Now that's a piece of research we can all support!

A little goes a long way. Just like all fats, olive oil is high in calories (about 120 per tablespoon), so I advise moderation. Just one tablespoon of extra-virgin olive oil daily is enough to get all its benefits without overdoing it. In fact, all the good fats need only be eaten in small amounts to have a positive impact on your health. Six or seven walnut halves, a four-ounce piece of baked salmon, a drizzle of olive oil on your salad—this is all it takes to make a big difference in your blood sugar, your risks, and your overall health.

A little burn drives down inflammation. A compound in olive oil called *oleocanthal* actually reduces inflammation. The more oleocanthal present, the greater its anti-inflammatory capability. Taste a little of your extra-virgin olive oil to see if it stings the back of your throat. The stronger the sting, the greater the anti-inflammatory effects.

How to best enjoy olive oil. Select the highest-quality olive oil you can afford. Extra-virgin olive oil has the most antioxidants and anti-inflammatories, and is best when it's unfiltered, cold-pressed, and packaged in dark glass bottles. Avoid heating olive oil beyond the very low temps necessary for light sautéing—high heat damages delicate antioxidants. Cook with more heat-tolerant "good fats" like coconut oil and peanut oil to preserve the exceptional diabetes healing properties of good fats.

TAKE ACTION TODAY: Quitting processed and commercially prepared convenience foods is the first step in reducing your overexposure to these damaging fats. Next, you'll want to

eliminate the following oils from your own kitchen and table: corn, canola, safflower, sunflower, soybean, vegetable shortening, hydrogenated oils, and margarine products. Include a wide variety of good fats in your daily diet, both in the foods you eat and the fats you cook with. There are plenty of delicious options, and all provide essential nutrients for healing your diabetes while lowering your risks for further complications.

EXTRA CREDIT: Search out bottles of bad oils in your pantry and toss them into the trash today. You could even try cooking without oils! It's easy to sauté in chicken or vegetable stock.

CASE STUDY: BETSY

"The 30-Day Diabetes Cure changed my life.
I was prediabetic and now I'm not."

Case Study: Betsy	Before	After
Weight	Unknown	30-pound weight loss
A1C	7.4	5.6
Blood Pressure	124/82	128/82
Triglycerides	208	47
Meds	-	-

Betsy was about as low as a person could be—sick, demoralized, stressed out, and overweight. The one thing in her life that she still clung to was tennis, and it was quickly getting out of her reach. Then Betsy got her minor miracle. She got sick with the flu and her factory-style doctor couldn't see her for over a week. She called me at the end of her rope, in tears. "Can you see me?" "Of course," I answered.

When I saw Betsy it was clear that her "cold" was a minor problem. You see, our bodies don't have language, our bodies don't have words, and yet they talk to us in the language of symptoms. I insisted we start with a complete understanding of her health and ordered labs. The diagnosis was clear: Betsy needed to change because her A1C and triglycerides were really high. She wept. Fortunately, Betsy was able to hear that she could turn this around with *The 30-Day Diabetes Cure*.

The wheel turned for Betsy the same way it can for all of us. We didn't measure her success in pounds lost, so much as points lost off her A1C. Now, nearly a year later, her A1C is normal and she states proudly that she lost 30 pounds.

DAY 12: ADD WHOLE GRAINS AND FRUIT

Though no one can go back and make a brand-new start,
anyone can start from now and make a brand-new ending.

CARL BARD

HEALER: **You're off and running with Phase II now—and it's time to celebrate your success by adding "comforting" whole grains and fruit into your everyday routine!**

DIDN'T I ASSURE YOU that Phase I of *The 30-Day Diabetes Cure* would pass quickly? How are you feeling? How're your blood sugar levels? Your energy? Your mental and emotional states? I hope your answer is "Great!"

You've made some essential changes during Phase I that should be paying off already. By now, your diet is focused on the top Diabetes Healing Superfoods, and you've eliminated the diabetes-causing foods and drinks that have been upsetting your blood sugar and weight. Bravo! Let's take a few moments to look back over the past 11 days and chart your progress…

CELEBRATE WITH A SANDWICH!

You've proven that you're perfectly capable of making important, health-saving lifestyle changes in order to beat this disease and take back your independence from Big Medicine. Not only that, but by eliminating fast carbs from your diet, you're on your way to completely conquering the carbohydrate cravings that caused your glucose-insulin imbalance. Now that it's safe to carefully reintroduce more carbs into your meals, how about a sandwich to celebrate?

You won't be returning to lifeless white bread. Or even a fresh-baked, crusty French baguette. The bread and baked goods you can now enjoy are those made with hearty whole grains bursting with nutty, chewy flavor and loaded with fiber. You'll find these healthy whole-grain carbs are every bit as "comforting" as their refined cousins, but they won't disrupt your blood sugar. Instead, their fiber content actually slows the breakdown of carbohydrates into glucose, so you get a steady energy release instead of a sudden spike and drop.

Just be careful when you shop. Food marketers are always trying to make a fast buck from uninformed consumers, and when they call their bread "whole wheat," it's a scam. Whole-wheat flour is highly refined and may have brown dye added to make it look healthy. I assure you it *isn't*. The only way to be certain you're getting the entire grain of wheat—including all its fiber and nutrients—is to buy products labeled "whole grain."

More good news: You can enjoy a little butter on your whole-grain toast in the morning. As we learned yesterday, fat slows the absorption of whole-grain carbohydrates even more.

Today's an important day. Starting now, you can enjoy a wider variety of satisfying and delicious foods, beginning with whole grains and fresh fruit. I asked you to abstain from both during Phase I in order to get your blood sugar back to baseline and to break your carbohydrate-craving cycle. If you've been true to my plan, you've not doubt succeeded on both counts.

Before you began *The 30-Day Diabetes Cure*, you probably thought whole-wheat bread was the same as whole grain. Now you know better. You'll learn something new about fruit today too. So let's explain how to work whole grains and fruit back into your diet, but in healthier versions.

WHOLE GRAINS ARE DIABETES FIGHTERS

Whole-grain foods (see Top 10 list on page 170) are true "diabetes fighters" because they're packed with fiber, which slows digestion and sends a steady flow of glucose to your bloodstream at a rate your metabolism can handle. This is precisely how you'll control and eventually reverse your type 2 or prediabetes diagnosis: by having *balanced* blood sugar, instead of the peaks (hyperglycemia) and valleys (hypoglycemia) caused by a glucose rush from fast carbs. The natural fiber in whole foods is essential for controlling your blood sugar. And when it comes to fiber content, nothing beats whole grains. Here's proof …

According to a study published in the *Archives of Internal Medicine*, people who ate the most dietary fiber lowered their risk of developing diabetes by 27%—primarily due to whole-grain fiber from wheat, oats, rye, barley, and brown rice. Scientists at the German Institute of Human Nutrition analyzed the food choices of 25,000 people for nearly 10 years to discover this, and also found that eating high-fiber fruits and vegetables alone was *not enough* to reduce the risk.

The best thing about whole-grain fiber is that it works quickly to stabilize blood sugar imbalances. Another team of German researchers, in a study reported in *Diabetes Care*, added bread enriched with 31 grams of grain fiber to the diet of diabetics. And after just three days, patients' insulin sensitivity improved by 10%. That's a quick return for a short-term switch!

Whole grains work their magic by helping cells reverse their resistance to insulin. That's because whole grains digest slowly, requiring less insulin, which helps prevent the toxic build-up of glucose (and excessive insulin) in your bloodstream. As you already know, the more responsive (sensitive) your cells are to insulin, the better able they are to metabolize glucose and the less likely you are to develop full-blown diabetes. By improving cell sensitivity to insulin, you can also *reverse* your diabetes, and that's just what we've been doing over the past 11 days. Plus, this approach is vastly superior to the results you get with drugs that artificially lower your glucose. Healing diabetes involves achieving the right balance of blood sugar to insulin so your entire endocrine system works in harmony, just the way it was designed to. Drugs can't mimic, or force, that kind of balance.

COMFORTING CARBS MAKE YOU FEEL GOOD

Whole grains are nature's most healing "comfort foods." They're warm, chewy, tasty, and filling, providing lots of pleasure and satisfaction without the empty calories of processed fast carbs. These slow carbs are most beneficial when eaten *moderately* and *consistently*. Italian researchers noted in *Diabetes Care* in 1991 that while diets high in carbohydrates throw blood sugar and metabolism into chaos, the problem is easily resolved (especially for people with diabetes) when those carbs are rich in dietary fiber. You'll reap the benefits long after mealtime is over, too. Researchers at the Creighton Diabetes Center in Nebraska found that when people ate a breakfast cereal made with fiber-rich barley, their rise in blood sugar after eating was 600% *lower* than when they ate oatmeal—already one of the best slow carbs you can eat. That's because barley is particularly high in a type of fiber called *beta-glucan* that's uniquely effective at slowing down digestion.

The point here is that eating a *variety* of whole grains is important, but portions matter too. Because of their roughage, whole grains help you feel "full" much faster than refined carbs like commercial breakfast cereals. This means you won't need a large serving to satisfy your hunger; many of my patients find that a half-cup serving of any whole grain is plenty. Some start with even less. But bite for bite, whole grains provide more nutrients and fiber—with fewer calories—than any other food group. Are you starting to see how grains play such an essential part in controlling your glucose levels and your weight simultaneously?

ENJOY WHOLE GRAINS FOR BREAKFAST

Fiber makes weight loss easier and, at the same time, lowers insulin resistance, allowing your own natural insulin to do its job better. So as your blood sugar drops, so does your weight—and this can help you reduce or even eliminate medications. There's a lot of exciting research on whole grains…

- In a UCLA study that allowed obese men to eat as much food as they wanted as long as most of it came from high-fiber fruits, vegetables, and whole grains, the guys lowered their blood sugar levels by 7%, cholesterol by an average 20%, and their blood pressure dropped too. They also walked for up to an hour daily.[41]

- According to a 10-year Harvard Medical School study of 75,000 women, 97% of the women who ate whole-grain foods avoided diabetes entirely.[42]

- A similar eight-year project by the Black Women's Health Study of 59,000 African-American women (an ethnic group twice as likely as white women to develop diabetes) confirmed the power of whole grains. Those eating whole grains such as wheat, oats, barley, rye, wild rice, and brown rice prevented dangerous swings in their blood sugar, thus effectively and dramatically reducing their risk of diabetes.[43]

- You can reduce your diabetes risk by 40% just by replacing a few fast carbs with slow carbs like whole grains, a Harvard study showed. That means substituting whole-grain bread instead of white bread, brown rice over white rice, and slow-cooked oatmeal (or any of the Top 10 Diabetes-healing Whole Grains listed on page 170) over any boxed ready-to-eat breakfast cereal.

BEGINNING YOUR WHOLE-GRAIN ODYSSEY

Whole-grain hot cereals. Slow-cooked real oatmeal (look for varieties labeled as "steel-cut oats" and "old-fashioned oats"), wheat berries, or, if you're gluten-sensitive or are just looking for a change, brown rice, barley, or buckwheat all make excellent breakfast choices. You might want to try what I do at home: Prepare a large batch on the weekend and store it in the fridge so you can quickly scoop out and heat a portion in the microwave on weekday mornings. One of my patients even places his half-cup portions into small bowls, sprinkles them with cinnamon, and pops them into the fridge so he doesn't have to think at all in the morning! If you like, add toppings like fresh berries, nuts, flax, a few raisins, or unsweetened yogurt (both soy yogurt and dairy yogurt have beneficial probiotics).

Choose whole grains and hot cereals that have slow cooking times (20 to 40 minutes). Avoid all instant or quick-cooking hot cereals. They've been processed to within an inch of their lives and offer no more fiber than white bread. Many packaged instant hot cereals also contain added sweeteners and artificial flavorings. *Yuck.*

Don't forget the cinnamon. Remember Day 2, when I explained cinnamon's extraordinary glucose-lowering benefits? Less than half a teaspoon daily significantly reduces blood sugar levels in people with type 2 diabetes, according to a study conducted by the US Agricultural Research Service. Cinnamon works by stimulating the insulin receptors on cells, improving your body's response to insulin. So be sure to sprinkle some on whatever whole-grain cereal you're enjoying!

---

[41] http://www.college.ucla.edu/news/03/barnard.html

[42] http://www.hsph.harvard.edu/nutritionsource/more/type-2-diabetes/

[43] http://www.bu.edu/bwhs/

Whole-grain breads and homemade granola. Toasted whole-grain bread topped with natural almond butter provides protein, complex carbs, and good fats in a single serving. Homemade granola (when *you* control the ingredients) is delicious eaten with yogurt and fresh fruit. There are abundant sources for recipes. Just remember: Use a small amount of good fats including coconut oil, olive oil, or even butter. Skip any sweet ingredients that are more candy-like than nutritious. A few raisins or a little honey/molasses to sweeten a large batch of granola is just fine.

How do I bake without sugar or white flour? A home-baked muffin made with buttermilk and bananas, pumpkin, or zucchini is a good occasional treat as long as you use whole-grain flours, eliminate the sugar, and include real butter or olive oil instead of shortening. Applesauce is a perfect substitute in any recipe calling for vegetable oil, which you're avoiding because of its "bad fat" omega-6 content. As a bonus, applesauce provides sweetness and extra moistness without adding sugar or extra oils. You can also add a few raisins for sweetness. As for flour, there's a world of whole-grain flours to discover. Start by looking for Bob's Red Mill brand at your grocery (or online). This company offers high-quality flours made from whole oats, garbanzo beans, and even black beans! You can quickly make your own brown rice flour by whizzing some brown rice in a coffee grinder. Same for oat flour. Don't be afraid to experiment. If you suspect that you're allergic or sensitive to wheat, look to gluten-free cookbooks. Because gluten-intolerant people can't eat wheat, these cookbooks offer a wide range of substitutes that fit perfectly with my plan.

Pasta? **Yes, pasta!** Some manufacturers have gotten smart—they've heard our message about fast carbs and responded by transforming white-flour pasta into diabetes-healing whole-grain selections. A good example is Racconto® whole-grain pasta, offered both in health food stores and mainstream groceries. Their "8 Whole Grain" series of pastas is made from whole grains including rye, barley, brown rice, buckwheat, kamut, spelt, and millet. Two ounces of their pasta contains just 190 calories and is delicious. This is comfort food I highly recommend! If your local store doesn't carry this brand, order it online. For more healthy pasta recipes, go to *www. myhealingkitchen.com.*

Eat real food. Remember to eat foods as close to their natural state as possible. Slow-cooked, old-fashioned oatmeal is a much better choice than a store-bought oat bran muffin, which includes refined flour, lots of vegetable oil, and way too much sugar or other sweeteners. Slow-cooked whole oatmeal, on the other hand, is one of nature's perfect Diabetes-Healing Super-foods. It's hearty, satisfying, loaded with healing nutrients, and chock full of fiber, which slows the release of glucose in your bloodstream requiring less insulin and providing a steady flow of energy all morning long. Top it off with some fresh berries, yogurt, ground flaxseed, and cinnamon, and you'll have the perfect Diabetes-Healing Breakfast.

What about fiber powders and mixes? I'm a big fan of eating whole foods so you can reap the benefits of all their nutrients—good fats and vitamins, minerals and antioxidants, proteins and carbs. Doesn't that make more sense than gulping down isolated supplements? I feel the same way about fiber. When eaten in foods such as whole grain, veggies and fruit, it produces a natural, synergistic effect in the body. Instead of opening up a jar of fiber supplement that works on your intestines, I prefer you eat foods naturally high in fiber. This way, you get the benefits of lower blood pressure, reduced blood sugar, effortless weight loss, plus added nutrients that come with. Tastes better, works better, and *is* better!

TOP 10 DIABETES-HEALING WHOLE GRAINS

Whole grains at any meal—brown rice, a hearty mushroom-barley soup, and whole-grain breads—are easy to incorporate into your daily diet and make eating a lot more enjoyable. Enjoy old favorites such as oats, barley, and brown rice every day. But don't hesitate to experiment with new whole-grain foods. The variety of whole grains is phenomenal, making this a way of eating you can stay with for life. Try cooking up a large batch of whole grains and freezing it in individual portions for later use. To discover a wealth of free Diabetes-Healing Recipes, visit *www. myhealingkitchen.com.*

1. Rye
2. Barley
3. Quinoa
4. Spelt
5. Whole wheat
6. Corn
7. Buckwheat
8. Oats
9. Brown Rice
10. Millet

WHAT IS A WHOLE GRAIN?

Whole grains are living foods and therefore have a limited shelf life. That's because they contain oils, fats, and vitamins that go rancid (the result of the oxidation process that "spoils" any living food). To extend the shelf life of these foods, manufacturers remove the living elements of these foods, rendering them lifeless. This may be good for their profit margins, but it's terrible for human health because these refined foods are devoid of nutrition and life force. To overcome this, manufacturers "fortified" refined foods with synthetic vitamins, but this is a far cry from their normal state.

In a classic research study, researchers fed rats a diet of white bread exclusively. The experiment ended when all the rats died from starvation and malnutrition, proving that refined foods can't sustain life, let alone optimal health.

Complex carbohydrates such as whole grains haven't had the life force removed from them by the refining process, which strips away nutritious parts of the *whole* in whole grains. Whole grains can be viewed as rooms in a house, each with a different function. For example…

The bran, or outer coating of a whole grain, is like the walls and roof of a house—the protective layer that defends the inside from environmental assault. When you eat whole grain with its bran, you get loads of fiber and more than 60% of the grain's minerals. And just as the bran protects the plant material inside, it protects your cells with its generous quantity of micronutrients.

The germ is the part of a whole grain that would sprout, given the right conditions (which isn't good for storage purposes). The germ is packed with B vitamins, vitamin E, and health-giving micronutrients. Like a child in our house, it wants to be fed (that's what the endosperm does). A note about the germ: Most refined grains including white flour have not only had the bran stripped away, but the germ as well!

The endosperm is like the pantry in our whole-grain house, filled with starchy calories to feed the hungry young germ. This endosperm portion of the whole grain is nutritious when eaten along with the bran and the germ, as nature intended. But eaten alone—as it is in fast-carb foods such as white bread—it acts like sugar in your bloodstream, offering negligible nutrition and a lot of calories.

FEELIN' FINE WITH FRUIT

You're also going to welcome fruit back into your diet today. Most fruits are high in fructose, a simple fast-carb sugar that can cause a rush of blood glucose. This is why I eliminated them during Phase I. Fruit juice can cause even bigger problems because it's been separated from its fiber (the same fiber that slows fruit juice conversion into blood sugar). Now that you're ready to return fruit to your diet, it's important to know the best ways to enjoy fruit so you can benefit from its many advantages.

No doubt about it, fruit is best when it's eaten in a whole, natural state. An apple with a piece of cheese after lunch is an ideal snack. Taking the time to peel an orange after dinner and enjoying it slowly, perhaps with a handful of nuts, is a time-honored tradition in many cultures.

Put down that peeler. A large part of fruit's most beneficial antioxidants lie in its skin (plus 87% more anticancer phytochemicals), so eat the peel on everything from apples to peaches, pears to kiwi. Kiwi? It's worth trying: Compounds in kiwi ward off infections like *E. coli* and *staphylococcus*.[44] Not to mention the skin has loads of extra fiber.

---

[44] http://www.womenshealthmag.com/nutrition/why-eat-fruit-peels?page=4

Go easy on the juice. During Phase II, you'll still avoid drinking juice regularly (although it's fine occasionally and when watered down with seltzer), but you'll continue to completely avoid juice "drinks," which are merely highly concentrated sources of sugar. Restrict your consumption of pure 100% juice to three-ounce portions a couple times weekly. Ideally, you'll be eating whole fruit and saving juice for special occasions. For a special treat, fresh-squeeze the juice yourself, trying a medium-size grapefruit or two large oranges. Hand-press so plenty of pulp remains.

Other forms of fruit to avoid? Reject jams and jellies—except those made with *zero* added sweeteners and other ingredients. Many "all-fruit" brands use grape or apple juice as sweeteners, and these are also off-limits. Commercially canned and jarred fruits have virtually no nutritional value—they've been peeled and heated and are often packed in sugary syrups. "Fruity" desserts like pies, fruit-flavored yogurt, fruit sauces, and fruit syrups should also be avoided because of their high added sugar as well as additives, chemicals, and fillers.

Dried fruit is particularly problematic due to its concentrated natural sugar content, as well as the added sugars, oils, flavorings, and chemicals that manufacturers often add. A couple of pieces of naturally dried fruit are fine, though—think raisins or chopped prunes, apricots, or dates added to yogurt or oatmeal. Just remember: *Moderation!*

Mix and match. One more thing to remember about fruit: It's best to consume a protein or fat with it to slow the conversion of fructose into blood glucose. That means pairing fresh fruit with a companion food such as peanut or almond butter, a handful of nuts, or a small chunk of artisan cheese. This makes a terrific midday snack. And don't forget yogurt. It's a great accompaniment to a handful of fresh (or thawed frozen) blueberries or raspberries in a bowl.

WHAT'S SO GREAT ABOUT FRESH FRUIT?

Let me count the ways: It contains lots of fiber for glucose management and toxin removal. Fruit is loaded with nutritious antioxidants for neutralizing free radical damage and for healing inflammation. It's also one of nature's best sources of *phytonutrients* (plant chemicals that lower cholesterol and promote healthy blood vessels, heart, and brain cells). What more could you ask for? Well, there *is* more…

Fresh fruit is sweet and delicious, as well as readily available in every supermarket in America. Purchase organically grown whenever you can—especially berries, apples, and other fruits—because when they're conventionally raised, they contain high levels of pesticides. Organic frozen berries are an excellent option. Stock your freezer when they're in season and at their lowest price. If you have a local farmers' market or access to a pesticide-free orchard or berry patch, you'll be getting the cleanest, freshest fruit available.

Any fresh fruit (I especially love berries!) makes an excellent addition to a breakfast, snack, or a dessert bowl of yogurt with chopped nuts, cinnamon, and a sprinkling of ground flaxseed.

An apple or banana makes an easy diabetes-healing midday snack when eaten with a little peanut butter or cheddar cheese. Fresh pears are delectable with soft, pungent cheeses like bleu and gorgonzola. Fruit is also a sweet treat when added to a smoothie: Just a little juice or soy milk, some yogurt, and a handful of berries and you're good to go!

HANDY FRUIT TIPS

While most fresh fruits are beneficial, there are a few that are particularly noteworthy. Here's a round-up...

Berries and cherries. Loaded with healing power, berries and cherries are one of nature's richest sources of anthocyanins, a group of antioxidant flavonoids with exceptional anti-inflammatory properties. Blueberries, blackberries, raspberries, strawberries, and cherries top the list of fruits that can actually relieve pain and lower your risk for diabetic complications by reducing inflammation.

Thanks to their vivid pigment, richly colored berries have the highest anthocyanin content and deliver a knockout punch to those devilish free radical molecules that damage your organs and accelerate the aging process. A mere half cup of berries has more antioxidant activity than five servings of broccoli, a powerful healer in its own right.

The widely publicized "French paradox" reminds us that the anthocyanins in red wine (and grapes) contribute to a healthy cardiovascular system. And according to research done at the Linus Pauling Institute, anthocyanins in the pigment of bilberries (European blueberries) have long been used for improving vision and treating circulatory disorders, two health issues of particular interest to people with diabetes.[45]

Cranberries and strawberries. These little gems are incredibly rich in another antioxidant flavonoid called *quercetin*, which also produces strong anti-inflammatory effects—as does the flavonoid content of the humble strawberry. Researchers at the Harvard University School of Public Health discovered that strawberries drive down levels of C-reactive protein (CRP), a blood marker for inflammation that's strongly predictive of a host of degenerative diseases. The Harvard scientists found that women who ate just 16 or more fresh or frozen strawberries per week lowered CRP levels by 14%![46]

POMEGRANATE POWER

With every rule it seems there's usually an exception, and here's mine. The one juice people with diabetes should definitely make room for in the refrigerator is unsweetened pomegranate

---

[45] http://lpi.oregonstate.edu/ss01/anthocyanin.html

[46] http://www.jacn.org/cgi/content/abstract/26/4/303

juice (best enjoyed diluted with some tap or mineral water). Pomegranate juice has tons of benefits that stem from that rich, dark color, evidence of their powerful antioxidant anthocyanins.

What exactly do antioxidants do? They fight *oxidation,* a natural part of the respiration process. Oxidation causes metal to rust and fresh meat and produce to turn brown and spoil. It also can damage your blood vessels. In fact, oxidized LDL cholesterol clogs arteries, leading to heart disease and stroke. Damaged blood vessels in the eyes cause retinopathy and in the kidney they cause kidney disease. In the feet they cause neuropathy, infections, and gangrene, leading to amputation. Additionally, too many oxidized cells can damage your DNA and cause cancer. What causes oxidation in the blood? High blood sugar. The remedy? Antioxidants along with a diet that naturally lowers your blood sugar.

Israeli researchers in the Lipid Research Laboratory at the Rambam Medical Center in Haifa gave two ounces of pomegranate juice per day for three months to a group of people with diabetes, and then measured changes in oxidation before, during, and after the experiment. They found that pomegranate juice reduced LDL oxidation by 39% and reduced TBARS (specific oxidants that particularly target arteries and veins) by 56%! Not only that, they observed a 141% *increase* in the powerful antioxidant glutathione. Glutathione is a very important nutrient. It helps your liver remove toxins from the bloodstream—and in today's toxin-crazy world, your liver needs all the help it can get. You can boost your body's natural glutathione levels by eating foods rich in this powerful antioxidant, but if your diet has been lacking whole foods—or you have a degenerative disease—it's likely your stores of cellular glutathione are low.

According to scientists at the National College of Naturopathic Medicine in Portland, Oregon, hospitalized patients with cancer, AIDS, and other serious diseases routinely show depleted levels of glutathione, underscoring its necessity for maintaining intracellular health. So, by all means, keep that unsweetened pomegranate juice handy and enjoy two to four ounces (that's half a cup, maximum) mixed with some sparkling water for a healthful spritzer!

MY FAVORITE TOP 10 "IN A HURRY" BREAKFASTS

1. **Oatmeal topped with nuts and fruit.** Prepare steel-cut or old-fashioned oats in quantity over the weekend, so a daily portion is ready to be warmed on weekday mornings. Add yogurt, skim milk (or soy milk), and top with your favorite fruit, chopped walnuts and a teaspoon of cinnamon. For a "pumpkin pie" effect—plus a big dose of antioxidants and extra fiber—mix a can of organic pumpkin into your weekly oatmeal preparation.

2. **Quickie burrito.** Scramble eggs with sliced onions and peppers. Add mashed black beans, a bit of your favorite cheese, and spicy salsa. Roll it all up in a nonfat, whole-grain tortilla. Grab it and go!

3. **Cottage cheese with fresh fruit.** Sprinkle a cup of 1% cottage cheese with cinnamon and top with chopped almonds, fresh fruit, and ground flaxseed.

4. **Lox and bagel.** Toast half a whole-grain bagel, spread lightly with low-fat cream cheese or soft goat cheese, sprinkle on a few capers for a salty note, and top with smoked wild salmon, tomato, and onion slices. Squeeze a few drops of lemon juice on the fish if you like. Heavenly!

5. **Fresh berries and yogurt.** This is my all-time favorite. Fill a bowl with fresh, organic strawberries, blueberries, and blackberries. Gently mix in one-half cup of unsweetened organic plain yogurt or vanilla soy yogurt, and top with three or four teaspoons of ground flaxseed. (Don't forget the cinnamon!) This lasts me till lunchtime.

6. **Power smoothie.** Toss fresh berries and any other fruit into a blender with either organic yogurt, soy milk, soft tofu, and/or a little pomegranate juice. Add protein powder or spirulina, plus a few teaspoons of ground flaxseed. (Recipe below.)

7. **Hard-boiled eggs and cheese.** A European tradition. Keep a few peeled hard-boiled eggs in the fridge for mornings when you're really squeezed for time. Grab an egg, a hunk of hard artisan cheese about the size of your thumb, and an apple or banana and enjoy them on your way to work. The protein should last you until your mid-morning snack.

8. **Whole-grain cereal.** If you rely on a packaged breakfast cereal, make sure it's truly made from whole grains, including bran—and with no added sugars (Uncle Sam® cereal has been around for more than 100 years and still offers a wholesome product). Splash on some low-fat milk or soy milk—or a couple spoons of yogurt—and top with fruit. Sprinkle on some cinnamon, plus a tablespoon of ground flaxseed to boost its fiber content even further.

9. **Bircher-muesli.** This is a terrific breakfast that you can prep the night before. Soak a bowl of dry muesli (available at your supermarket) in low-fat milk or unsweetened soy milk in the fridge the night before. The grains and dried fruit in the muesli will soften and be ready to eat the next morning. All you'll need is a spoon.

10. **Turkey on whole grain.** Breakfast sandwiches can take many healthful shapes. Don't discount lean protein like turkey breast or chicken breast, layered onto whole-grain bread and topped with sliced tomato and avocado and a few leaves of romaine. Cut and enjoy the first half before you leave the house, the rest on your way to work or for a mid-morning snack.

DIABETES-HEALING "POWER SMOOTHIE"

Serves: 2 to 3
Prep. Time: 10 minutes

This "in a hurry" breakfast smoothie is packed with protein, fiber, and nutrition. It's naturally sweet, but don't let the flavor fool you: It's a Diabetes-Healing Superfoods powerhouse. Your smoothie whips up in minutes and is easily transported in a thermos bottle, so you can sip it during your commute or later in the morning.

INGREDIENTS:

2 cups either strawberries, blueberries, blackberries, or raspberries (in any combination, fresh or frozen)

1 cup plain, unsweetened yogurt with live cultures (low-fat dairy or soy)

2 tablespoons whey protein powder or spirulina powder

1 cup unsweetened soy milk or unsweetened cherry or pomegranate juice

1 to 2 tablespoons ground flaxseed

A few ice cubes (omit if you use frozen berries)

INSTRUCTIONS:

Place all ingredients in a blender and blend until smooth. Drink immediately or transfer to a thermos bottle for easy transport. Even easier: Make a bigger batch and freeze in ice cube trays. Transfer frozen "smoothie cubes" to a Ziploc bag and store in the freezer. When needed, pop a few cubes into the blender, add juice or soy milk, and you're good to go!

NUTRITION FACTS: *Calories 449.5, Total Fat 14.3 g, Sat. Fat 3.1 g, Cholesterol 15 mg, Sodium 348 mg, Carbs 68 g, Fiber 15 g, Sugars 21 g, Protein 32 g*

TAKE ACTION TODAY: Give yourself a big pat on the back for making it through Phase I without junk food, sodas, processed food products, and alcohol. Now it's time to incorporate more Diabetes-Healing Superfoods into your diet, including delicious whole grains and fresh fruit. Life is good—and the healing is easy!

EXTRA CREDIT: Sit down tonight and draw up one week's worth of breakfast menus. Create a shopping list and add it to your regular one.

DAY 13: CLIMB OFF THAT COUCH!

*Those who think they have no time for bodily exercise
will sooner or later have to find time for illness.*

EDWARD STANLEY

ANTI-HEALER: **For the person with diabetes, being a couch potato means more weight, more medications, more illness, and more risk of serious complications. Here's the surest way to reverse this trend and get "more" out of life...**

THE OLD ADAGE "When you stop moving, you start dying" is absolutely true. Bad things begin to happen to your body and brain when you stop being physically active. And this is especially true for people with diabetes and prediabetes.

REGULAR MOVEMENT ENERGIZES YOUR HEALTH

Our bodies are designed to be in motion—that's when they work best. Physical activity is the key to unlocking optimal health and longevity because it's the driving force that powers all metabolic functions. Activity burns calories so you don't gain weight. It moves wastes and toxins out of your body. It thins your blood. And it pumps life-giving oxygen and nutrients to all your organs, including the most essential one: your brain.

I know of no other single endeavor that can come close to generating the positive benefits of being physically active. It keeps your muscles toned and strong, makes your heart pump more efficiently, strengthens your immune system, helps flush away excess cholesterol, maintains your trim profile, bestows self-confidence, fights frailty, and discourages cancer. Study after study shows that being active brightens a person's mood, boosts intelligence, improves memory, and makes you feel more fully "alive." In short, physical activity is a true anti-aging, anti-diabetes elixir.

NOT MOVING PRODUCES THE OPPOSITE EFFECTS

Inactivity, on the other hand, creates a stagnant environment inside you, and that's when health problems can easily develop. A body that's active is like a mountain stream that's constantly flowing: The water is always fresh and pure because movement oxygenates it and pathogens don't have a chance to establish themselves. But inactivity produces stagnant conditions, like a land-locked pond where algae overgrowth depletes the oxygen, pests and insects breed, fish die, and the water becomes putrid and full of disease.

When water doesn't move, it definitely dies. And the same is true for the human body—especially if you have blood sugar irregularities because they multiply health problems very quickly. Here's how being a slug-bug shortens your life…

Glucose inefficiency. Remember, in a healthy metabolism, the carbs you eat are converted into glucose for immediate use as energy. Any glucose you don't burn immediately is stored for later use in your cells and liver in the form of fat. The hormone insulin oversees the conversion of glucose into fats (called triglycerides) and then unlocks the pathways on your cells so these fats can enter for storage.

If you're not sufficiently active to burn off that excess glucose, blood sugar levels become constantly elevated, your cells begin to resist insulin's effect so that greater amounts of insulin are required, and you wind up with type 2 diabetes. Without physical activity (which naturally keeps your cells sensitive to insulin), the insulin-producing beta-cells in your pancreas eventually wear out from exhaustion. At this point, you have full-blown type 1 diabetes and will need insulin injections for the rest of your life. This degenerative progression can take many years to unfold—sometimes 10 or even as long as 20 years. (In its early stages, type 2 diabetes can be symptom-free: Up to 33% of people with diabetes don't even know they have this "silent disease." But some 20% of those with early, undiagnosed diabetes already have retinopathy, a vision-robbing condition that can lead to blindness.)

During this undetected "stealth period," your body can suffer serious damage without you even realizing it. Yet chronically elevated levels of glucose and insulin in your bloodstream damage your arteries, accelerate the aging of tissues, organs, and skin (making you look much older than your years), and shorten your life by an average of two decades. Regular physical activity can help prevent this, but few people, doctors included, have been properly educated about its remarkable healing power.

Poor circulation. Circulation means movement of the blood. It's important because blood carries life-giving nutrients and oxygen to every part of the body—and healthy circulation provides the push. When an organ is deprived of these vital elements, or its supply is diminished, it becomes malnourished and sick. This is one of the most important causes underlying many of the serious complications that result from diabetes. It happens this way…

Your blood is made up of tiny disc-shaped cells called platelets, red blood cells or corpuscles that carry an x-shaped molecule called hemoglobin, upon which two oxygen molecules ride. This is how oxygen travels through your body and nourishes it. When there's excessive sugar in the bloodstream, glucose molecules kick the oxygen molecules out of their seats and take their place. In effect, they hijack the blood cell and ruin its oxygen-carrying capacity. By measuring what percentage of hemoglobin has become "sugared" this way, we can tell how high your blood sugar has been over the last 120 days—that is the meaning of the hemoglobin A1C test. Diabetes is called a "wasting disease" for this very reason, because it forces your body to switch to alternative metabolic pathways, and as a result the body wastes away.

COMPLICATIONS...

When blood cells can't nourish distant parts of the body, such as toes and lower limbs, the eyes and the brain, they begin to die. In the case of fingers, toes, and lower limbs, gangrene sets in and amputation is required. When the eyes are deprived, vision loss and blindness occur. And when the brain doesn't get a sufficient supply, dementia and Alzheimer's often result. Poor circulation also can cause intense, chronic leg pain known as neuropathy. If avoiding these problems isn't enough to get you moving, keep reading…

Heart disease. Excess glucose also makes blood platelets sticky, which leads to a thick, sluggish circulation. Slow-moving blood is responsible for a host of serious (and often life-threatening) cardiovascular problems. Sticky blood cells are more likely to clump together and adhere to artery walls, causing plaque buildup and blockages that trigger chest pain (angina), heart attack, and stroke. Thick blood is also more likely to clot. This is why people with diabetes have a stunning 400% higher risk of cardiovascular disease than non-diabetics.

When insulin becomes ineffective, it takes longer to convert glucose into fat for storage. Instead, the fats (triglycerides) hang around in your bloodstream and flood your liver. The liver then emits particles that move this fat into your arteries and smaller blood vessels. It's not so much the carbs themselves that cause heart disease, but rather the body's inability to properly process the blood fats that result from all that circulating blood sugar.

Physical activity helps reverse all this by thinning the blood and speeding its flow. It also allows more oxygen and nutrients to reach distant limbs and nourish vital organs. In addition, besides making your cells more sensitive to insulin, physical activity also burns up excess blood sugar and stored fats, which facilitates weight loss.

Dangerous inflammation. Too much glucose flowing through your bloodstream is highly inflammatory. This is a bad situation because inflammation has been revealed as the causative factor underlying most of today's serious chronic and degenerative ills. The widely respected physician Mark Hyman, MD, author of the book *Ultra-Metabolism* and former medical director of the world-famous Canyon Ranch health resort, gets right to the point when he says, "All the diseases that kill us in our society are related to refined carbohydrates and sugars—cancer, heart disease, obesity, diabetes, stroke and Alzheimer's."[47] In every instance, people with diabetes or other blood sugar problems have a much higher incidence of these diseases.

Inflammation results when high blood sugar generates a barrage of free radical molecules that inflame and damage delicate tissue such as artery linings. Plaque is created when cholesterol and other blood fats try to patch up this damage, because these plaques are the main cause of artery blockages, chest pain, heart attack, and stroke.

There's a cancer connection as well. When you have too many free radicals in your body, they can overwhelm the antioxidants defending your DNA, damaging its genetic blueprint. This triggers cellular malfunctions, which cause tumor growths and cancer. But performing physical activity and eating a diet of antioxidant-rich foods can prevent and even reverse inflammation and the health problems it causes.

Unhealthy weight gain. Too many sugary calories and fast carbs—and a lack of physical activity to quickly burn it off—can lead to rapid weight gain. And that extra body weight makes diabetes much worse. But it's a vicious cycle that can be broken. Studies clearly show that people with an "apple shape"—who carry weight around their midsections—have a far greater risk of developing insulin resistance and, eventually, diabetes.

An expanding waistline (not just weight itself, but where it is deposited) is now viewed as the single most important factor in the development of diabetes. In 2008, the International Obesity Task Force discovered that 60% of diabetes cases worldwide were due to this type of fat accumulation. (In Europe and North America the figure was closer to 90%!)

Because the connection between belly fat and diabetes is so strong, doctors invented a new term, "diabesity," to describe it. To medical professionals, it's a dead giveaway that diabetes is silently developing. Belly fat is clear visual evidence of a malfunctioning metabolism and a blood profile that's loaded with risk. With all the frightening health consequences at stake, you have to wonder why so many people continue to eat junky foods and skip exercise.

DON'T BLAME YOUR LACK OF WILLPOWER

It may come as a shock to learn that your body is genetically programmed to hoard calories and store them in the form of body fat. This was nature's way of protecting us from starvation back in the early days of human development. But our ancient programming to conserve energy and calories has another dangerous aspect. It creates a kind of natural aversion to physical activity, which is why a lot of people say they "hate to exercise." Here's the explanation…

---

[47] Hyman, Mark. *Ultra-Metabolism*. New York: Atria, 2008.

Tens of thousands of years ago, daily life was an arduous struggle. People wandered all day in search of food, hunting from sun up till sundown, often chasing wounded game for miles. And because there was no guarantee they'd land that animal and be able to eat it, early humans expended up to 2,000 calories or more per day in search of food—often more energy than the calories they ultimately ingested. This "deficit eating" was the rule of the day, and death from starvation or malnutrition was quite common.

In this scenario, calories were scarce and therefore precious, so energy had to be conserved. Wasting calories for frivolous activity could cost you your life, so people rested whenever possible (although because they had to be vigilant against many dangers, this didn't often happen). Sleeping through the night was rarely possible and people lived on the brink of exhaustion.

Flash forward: Over the course of human development, this urge to conserve energy became part of our genetic makeup and remains with us today. Maybe it shouldn't surprise us that conserving energy is the underlying principle behind our labor-saving devices—from the escalator to the automobile to the thermostat. And while it's true that physical activity often feels good, resting usually feels better.

THE MODERN PREDICAMENT WE FACE

Why am I taking the time to tell you all this? Because I want you to understand the powerful forces you must overcome to get yourself into motion. Today we find ourselves in a double-whammy situation. We're still genetically programmed to eat our fill (which we do, at almost every meal) and our bodies continue to store as many of those calories as it possibly can (even though the next meal is guaranteed in our culture). Most of us take every opportunity we can to rest—gym memberships and home treadmills aside. We've become creatures of comfort as well, with most of us no longer facing hard physical labor day after day. Bottom line? The genetic forces that worked in favor of our ancestors' survival when food was scarce are now working against us. And with deadly consequences.

While we can't change our genetic programming, we can *outsmart* it. And that's the secret of our success with *The 30-Day Diabetes Cure*. In addition to changing the way you think about food (and changing the way you eat), it's time to change your attitude about physical activity so it becomes something you like and *want* to do, instead of something you must force upon yourself.

START WALKING TODAY!

Walking is the easiest way to rescue yourself from the dangers of a sedentary life. Nothing is easier. Walking helps you manage your weight, lowers your glucose levels naturally, controls blood pressure, and decreases your risk of heart attack. It also boosts your "good" cholesterol, lowers your risk of stroke, and protects against hip fracture.

Need more reasons to start walking? How about less stress, improved sleep, stronger muscles and bones, elevated moods, and a better sex life—all worthy of pursuing on their own but especially vital if you want to increase your life span and the quality of your life by healing your diabetes.

AND YOU'LL LIVE LONGER

Yes, walking will literally increase your life span. The National Center for Chronic Disease Prevention and Health completed an eight-year study of nearly 3,000 adults with diabetes to uncover the long-term impact of physical activity—specifically, walking—on death from diabetes, heart disease, and all other causes.[48] This is what they found...

- Walking lengthened the life of diabetics regardless of age, sex, race, body mass index, length of time since diagnosis, and presence of complications or limitations.

- In addition, walking just two hours a week (that's less than 20 minutes a day) lowered the death rate from all causes by 39%. Walking three to four hours a week reduced mortality from all causes by 54%. Wow! This isn't running two miles, or lifting weights, or taking aerobic exercise classes. Simply walking around your neighborhood, a park, the mall, or a local track every day means a person with diabetes can live a longer, healthier, and happier life.

- Here's even more evidence: The Diabetes Prevention Program showed that walking 120 to 150 minutes per week and losing just 7% of your body weight (12 to 15 pounds) can reduce your risk of diabetes by 58%. Time to put on those walkin' shoes and step out!

WHY IS WALKING SO HEALING FOR DIABETES?

In addition to helping you shed extra pounds, walking actually increases the number of insulin receptors on your cells. Insulin, as you know, helps blood sugar move into cells, where it's needed to produce energy. And because physical activity has this amazing benefit of helping your body use insulin more efficiently, you might even be able to reduce the amount of medication you take—another reason to keep your doctor clued in on your progress.

Walking and other moderate exercise should be a standard prescription not only to treat but also prevent diabetes, but many doctors (and their patients) find it easier to rely on prescriptions than to make an exercise commitment. In less than two weeks on *The 30-Day Diabetes Cure*, you've already experienced the health-shifting power of changing the way you eat. Now it's time to really show your stuff by understanding how far just a few minutes of daily walking can go to reverse your diabetes. Here are a few tips...

---

[48] http://www.jacn.org/cgi/content/abstract/26/4/303

WALK WITH YOUR OWN STYLE

Start with a stroll. If you're not used to exercise, walk slowly for the first three to five minutes. This prepares your heart, circulation, and muscles for their new activity, sending the message that says, "We're starting to move." This is the best way to avoid shin pain and foot discomfort.

After a few minutes of gentle strolling you can pick up the pace for another five to 15 minutes until you feel a little sweat emerging. Slow down again for your last five minutes to let your body relax and cool off. That's really all there is to it!

Set your personal pace. This isn't an Olympic event—it's just a pleasant walk, a break from work and stress, a little time outside after sitting at your desk or being cooped up inside for hours. It does take practice to find your personal walking speed, so it's important to start with a slow pace and gradually increase it so you're walking slightly faster than normal for you (but without any discomfort). If you can talk out loud without becoming out of breath and maintain that for 15 to 20 minutes, you've hit just the right pace. Remember, this isn't about speed. A faster speed puts stress on your knees and we don't want that until they become stronger. If your knees do get sore or swell after a walking session, rest with an ice pack on them for a few minutes—and next time, don't walk as fast or for as long.

Watch your stride. More important than your speed is the length of your stride and how much you swing your arms. This is how you turn a walking rhythm into your own diabetes-healing dance. To make your walk more brisk, swing your arms with your stride—a longer stride will stretch out those long muscles and get your heart pumping.

Time or distance? A time goal usually works better for beginners than shooting for a certain distance. You'll always be successful within your allotted time frame, whether you need to walk a little more slowly, combine periods of brisk and slow walking, or even add a few rest breaks to breathe deeply and get the oxygen flowing.

Once you begin your commitment to walking, you can start out with as little as 10 minutes and then gradually extend that to 30 minutes. You don't need to walk any longer, because 30 minutes is the life-saving, diabetes-healing magic number. My patients who start walking often love it so much they forget about time (and please don't worry if this happens to you). It's not bad for you to walk longer and farther; just make sure your feet and legs feel comfortable throughout your walk.

How much is enough? A mere 30 minutes, three or four days a week is your basic goal. Plus, you don't even have to do your 30 minutes all at once! You can accumulate exercise throughout the day. Three short walks of 10 minutes give you the same health benefits as a single 30-minute walk. That's just a quick stroll in the morning on your way to work or school, another at lunch time, and one more when you get home. If that sounds easy, that's because it is: Walking is the simplest and most effective form of life-saving exercise you can incorporate into your daily life.

What's most important, though, is to make a habit of walking at least every other day. Once you begin to enjoy your walks, you can walk five or six days a week. When you exercise regularly, your body learns a new skill, so you steadily become stronger, more capable—and more motivated to continue your newfound habit.

Ask the pros. If you haven't exercised for a while and have questions about what's safe for you, ask a person who has experience with exercise and diabetes. Your local Diabetes Foundation office, health-care providers, or fitness professionals are all good sources for referrals and information. And remember that you're not alone: Most people who now exercise regularly say they needed information and reassurance when they started. But the most important thing is that they started, and that's what you can do for yourself by beginning today. Make a commitment now to developing this new habit. You'll be losing weight, improving your blood sugar, and lowering your triglycerides and "bad" cholesterol without drugs.

ARE YOU STILL ON THE COUCH?

If you're still not motivated, read this: Another study of sedentary women showed that short bouts of brisk walking (three 10-minute walks per day) brought similar improvements in fitness and were at least as effective in decreasing body fat as one 30-minute walk per day. That's a pretty easy way to start to reverse your diabetes.

Does the idea of doing even three 10-minute walks a day seem out of reach? You're in luck! New research out of Harvard shows that if you don't want to walk for a long time, you can walk in quick spurts, then slow down and then walk quickly again. Also known as interval-walking, this approach dramatically improves triglyceride levels even better than cardio or aerobics. How long do you have to walk fast? You can start improving your metabolism with just 45-second bursts! The deadly combination of high triglycerides, low HDL, and central obesity occurs in 80% of people with type 2 diabetes. But the Centers for Disease Control found that more sustained vigorous walking is *not* as beneficial for people with type 2 diabetes as these quick intervals. Just make sure you breathe a little harder and get that little bead of sweat on your forehead after a few intervals.

You can thumb your nose at those buffed-up weightlifters and treadmill junkies, because you could live longer than they do with just 30 minutes a day…or 10 minutes three times a day… or 45-second interval walking. Coupled with eating the right foods and losing weight, healing diabetes is as easy as stepping outdoors.

Where should you walk? Maybe you feel completely ready to start walking right this minute but you can't think of a good place to go. Let's say your neighborhood has bad sidewalks, no street lamps or no park. Maybe you don't feel safe outdoors alone, even in the daytime. Or your urban sidewalks are so busy you can't set a comfortable pace. That can really put a damper on your enthusiasm. A study published in the *Annals of Internal Medicine* shows that simply having a good environment may mitigate the risk of type 2 diabetes because it creates a community of active people. In a nutshell: Finding a place with safe sidewalks, parks, and attractive public green spaces can help you reverse this disease.

If you live in an unsuitable neighborhood, make it your personal challenge to find a nearby park, walking track, or safer neighborhood that you can use for your walking territory. Sometimes local schools will let you use the athletic field. Contact your city council representative and advocate for a new park, an improved lot, or a public greenbelt. The research on the importance of regular walking is on your side. You deserve it. And your life depends on it.

Listen up. Many of my patients enliven their walks by listening to music or audio books on their iPods. Music puts rhythm in your stride and makes the time pass quickly. Listening to an audio book allows you to improve your mind while you're healing your body.

Find a buddy. Studies show that people who walk with a buddy are more consistent and stick with it longer. That's because it's more difficult to excuse yourself when another person is counting on you.

TAKE ACTION TODAY: Step out of your home or office for a 10-minute walk today. Scope out your surroundings by car to determine the path you take. Maybe you'll just walk around the block. Remember the Nike slogan "Just do it" if your mind starts churning out excuses. There is tremendous power in breaking your inertia. Don't think about tomorrow or the next day. Just take it "one day at a time."

EXTRA CREDIT: Find a walking buddy and decide on a regular time and place that you'll walk together.

CASE STUDY: ROY

"I've lost more than 150 pounds by walking to my mailbox!"

Roy was so big that I couldn't determine his actual weight because my office scale stops at 350. He was out of shape, had no stamina, and felt ashamed about how he looked. His life was pure misery. After less than a year on *The 30-Day Diabetes Cure*, his weight came down to below 200 pounds (lower than it was in high school). He never thought he'd be able to become physically fit. But I convinced him to start by just walking to his mailbox every day. In no time, he was walking farther and eventually started riding his bike and exercising. You should see his before and after pictures! Helping him make such dramatic improvements gives me great joy.

Case Study: Roy	Before	After
Weight	350+	199
A1C	7.4	5.6
Blood Pressure	132/88	128/82
Triglycerides	287	132
Meds	Metformin	Nothing

DAY 14: EAT MORE BEANS

Beans, beans, good for the heart...

CHILDREN'S RHYME

HEALER: **Beans are the *perfect* food for people with diabetes because they regulate blood sugar and improve your body's insulin response. And you can eat your fill without gaining weight. In fact, the more you eat, the more weight you'll lose!**

BEANS ARE the world's most powerful Diabetes-Healing Superfood. No other single food packs the diabetes-reversing power that they do. Beans are extremely low in calories, high in protein, packed with fiber, and versatile enough to be enjoyed at every meal of the day. And man, are they inexpensive. Now *that's* a superfood!

Because beans are so effective at lowering blood sugar and helping you lose weight (without even trying!), I want you to include them in your daily diet, starting today. Add them to soups, serve them as side dishes, and toss them into salads. The more often you eat them, the faster your blood sugar will normalize and your diabetes will reverse. I promise!

THE HEALING POWER OF BEANS

Beans' bountiful fiber comes in two varieties, and both help trigger reversal of diabetes and other blood sugar irregularities. Here's how...

Super-high in fiber. On Day 12, I told you about the remarkable healing attributes of fiber in whole grains. Today I'll share the details about bean fiber, because knowledge is power, and the more clearly you understand the power of beans, the more likely you are to start eating them regularly.

Fiber is the indigestible part of plant foods, commonly called *roughage*. Because it isn't digested, it has no calories and yet keeps you feeling full because it's bulky and literally "fills you up." Fiber is the ultimate weight-loss food: You could stuff yourself with fiber (not that I recommend it) and not gain a pound. And because high-fiber foods contain so few calories, they actually make weight loss easy—without dieting or ever feeling hungry. Understand that beans contain two types of fiber, insoluble and soluble, in perfect balance for healing diabetes.

Insoluble fiber is the roughage that fills you up without many calories, making weight loss easy. This action is essential for people with diabetes because shedding weight lowers insulin resistance and allows your natural insulin to do its job better. (If you have type 1, decreasing your body's insulin resistance usually allows you to lower your dosage of synthetic insulin.) Losing weight via a fiber-rich diet also helps drive down high blood sugar, which can reduce or even eliminate your need for medications. Because insoluble fiber soaks up water, it softens stools, relieves constipation, hemorrhoids, and diverticulosis, removes fats and cholesterol, and cleans the intestine walls on its way out of your body.

This roughage component of fiber also reduces your body's use of insulin by slowing the rate at which you absorb carbohydrates (an action that also prevents surges in blood sugar). By contrast, a diet of sugary, fast-carb, low-fiber foods creates a chronic demand for insulin. Over time, the pancreas's ability to manufacture insulin weakens, and more glucose stays in the bloodstream. The resulting condition, known as insulin resistance (or prediabetes), is the most common cause of type 2 diabetes.

Soluble fiber in beans and other foods (your morning oatmeal is loaded with it) produces several extraordinary benefits for people with diabetes. This type of fiber turns into a sticky gel in your body that delays the emptying of your stomach (helping you feel full longer), slows down your digestion of sugars and starches, and controls blood sugar spikes in the process. Soluble fiber's "magic gel" is beneficial in so many ways. Like a sponge, it soaks up cholesterol, triglycerides, and other blood fats and escorts them to the colon so they can exit the body before they have a chance to clog up your arteries. By decreasing the level of blood fats, soluble fiber also reduces your risk of heart disease, the main complication of diabetes. Plus, some studies even show that fiber helps reduce the risk of certain cancers—especially colon cancer—by speeding the removal of toxic wastes from the body.

Packed with pectin. Another big bean benefit is their high pectin content. Pectin is yet another type of fiber that helps sensitize your cells to insulin. It actually helps insulin uptake by producing extra insulin receptors on cells. (No drug is able to achieve this!) These additional insulin receptors are like extra "doorways" that make it easier for insulin to move out of your bloodstream and into your cells. Boosting insulin receptors on cells is one of the keys to reversing diabetes naturally. Plus, pectin reduces your risk of heart disease by lowering cholesterol levels.

Stashed with resistant starch. "Starch" is the most essential fuel for the human body. It's the component of carbohydrates that metabolizes into glucose as the body digests it. All plant foods contain starch. But as you recall from our fast carb/slow carb discussion on Day 5, not all starches digest at the same rate. The fast-carb starch in cold breakfast cereals and white-flour baked goods moves into your bloodstream as rapidly as pure table sugar, because it's quickly broken down into glucose in the small intestine and released immediately.

"Resistant starches," on the other hand, literally resist digestion. These include beans, barley, brown rice (and even white potatoes, especially after they've cooled a bit). Resistant starch foods bypass breakdown in the small intestine and are thus broken down at a slower rate. As a result, they cause a far slower and lower rise in blood sugar and insulin—and, incredibly, less fat storage after you eat them. In fact, some resistant starch is *never* turned into glucose at all.

Burn off more body fat. People who eat resistant starches such as beans burn more body fat, which is crucial for weight loss and controlling diabetes. An Australian study found that people eating meals that included a mere 5% of resistant starch (a small amount of beans would do the trick) increased the rate at which their bodies burned fat by an amazing 23%.[49] And this effect lasted for 24 hours afterward!

THE AMAZING HEALTH BENEFITS OF BEANS

Eating resistant starch foods, including every type of bean imaginable, produces some other surprising health benefits as well, including…

- Improves insulin sensitivity, whether you're using your body's own insulin or injecting it. Either way, this is an important way eating beans helps heal your diabetes.

- Improves glucose tolerance the following day (also known as the "second meal effect"). Research confirms this sustained, slow-absorption effect even a day after you eat resistant starch foods.

- Produces more satiety (the feeling of "fullness") with less food. An obvious and welcome benefit when you're trying to control your weight!

- Blocks your body's ability to burn carbs and prevents the liver from using carbs as fuel. Instead, your body burns stored body fat and recently eaten fat.

- Shuts down hunger hormones. Animal studies show that resistant starch prompts the body to churn out more leptin, the "I'm full!" hormone. Eating a meal that includes resistant starches like beans triggers a hormonal response to shut off hunger. Result? You end up eating less. Research shows you don't reap this benefit from other sources of fiber.

- Lowers cholesterol and triglyceride levels. Who wouldn't welcome this as an alternative to drugs?

- Promotes helpful bacteria, while suppressing bad bacteria and their toxic by-products. Great for your immunity!

- Encourages bowel regularity and discourages constipation.

---

[49] http://www.nutritionandmetabolism.com/content/1/1/8

> **More surprises:** Normally, refined-flour pasta is off-limits to people with diabetes. But here's a simple cooking trick that puts it back on the menu: When prepared *al dente* ("slightly firm"), the starch molecules are so tightly packed that just 50% of it is rapidly digested! Additionally, when some cooked starches, such as potatoes and rice, are allowed to cool before eating, some of their starch takes longer to digest. This means pasta and potatoes are not completely off-limits anymore.

■ Produces the protective compound called *butyrate*, which helps shield you from colon cancer.

THE WORLD'S #1 ANTI-DIABETES FOOD

When it comes to resistant starch, beans top the list by far. Along with non-starchy vegetables, they have one of the lowest glycemic ratings of all the slow carbs. Although the type of bean and its preparation method affect the amount of resistant starch available to you (canned beans contain less than reconstituting your own), the starch in beans is evenly divided between slowly digested starch and resistant starch.

This makes them the perfect food for people with diabetes or those who want to lose weight—or both! But what about the "gas" they produce for some people? Enzyme products such as Bean-o® increase the digestibility of beans and can reduce their gassiness. If gas is a problem for you, try starting with a quarter-cup serving of beans sprinkled with Bean-o and work your way up to half-cup portions several times a day. Given time, many people find they're digesting beans without any gas at all.

As an added benefit, beans are loaded with beneficial antioxidants. The pigments that give berries their bright colors also occur in the bean's "skin," thanks to *anthocyanins*. Anthocyanins help control blood sugar and limit the damage diabetes causes to blood and arteries. And black beans contain levels that rival that of berries!

TO OUTSMART DIABETES, USE YOUR BEAN...

■ People with type 2 diabetes who boost their consumption of high-fiber foods actually improve their blood sugar to the point where they can reduce their drug doses, according to a study published in the *New England Journal of Medicine*. During the research, participants ate 24 grams of dietary fiber from food every day for six weeks. (If that sounds like a lot, you'll get this much fiber from a mere one-cup serving of beans.) Over the next six weeks, patients doubled their fiber consumption by increasing the amount of high-fiber foods they ate. At the end of the 12 weeks, they had dramatic blood sugar improvements (and in their cholesterol levels too).[50]

- High-fiber foods are so powerful they can defeat a genetic tendency toward diabetes. "It appears that adult-onset diabetes is largely preventable," says JoAnn Manson, MD, an endocrinologist at Brigham and Women's Hospital in Boston. "This is one case where heredity is not destiny."

Her study examined 6,000 adults for eight years and was reported in *The American Journal of Clinical Nutrition*. It focused on several known risks for heart disease, a serious danger for people with diabetes. Dr. Manson's study found that people who eat more high-fiber foods are likely to have a lower body mass index (BMI), lower blood pressure, and less homocysteine—all major risk factors for heart attack and stroke.

- An active lifestyle and fiber-rich diet can greatly lower a genetic susceptibility to diabetes, according to research presented to the American Diabetes Association (ADA). Scientists at the National Institute of Diabetes and Digestive and Kidney Diseases discovered that the rate of diabetes among Mexican Pima Indians—who eat a traditional diet of low-fat unprocessed beans and corn tortillas—is 85% lower than that of Pima Indians living in Arizona, who tend to favor a higher-calorie, low-fiber Western-style diet. The Arizona Pimas have the highest diabetes rate in the world, with a stunning 50% of tribe members between the ages of 30 and 64 suffering from type 2.

"Our results show that having a genetic predisposition to the disease doesn't mean that you'll develop type 2 diabetes," says Leslie Schultz, a nutritional biochemist with the University of Wisconsin in Milwaukee, who worked on the study. "If you can control your lifestyle, you can control, to a large extent, whether or not you develop the disease."

- Women who eat a high-sugar, low-fiber diet, including soft drinks, white bread, white rice and mashed potatoes, are nearly 400% more likely to get diabetes than women who eat high-fiber foods. That's the conclusion of a six-year study reported in the *Journal of the American Medical Association*, reinforcing the importance of eating fiber for people with all forms of diabetes.

- Overweight Latino children (a population with a much greater incidence of being diabetic than the general US population) lowered their risk for type 2 diabetes, lost weight, and showed significant improvements in their insulin response. How'd they do it? In a recent study conducted by researchers at the University of Southern California, the kids substituted a half-cup of beans for one daily soda. Amazing!

- People with type 1 diabetes were able to reduce their dosage of injectable insulin by 44% by adding beans to an already healthy diet. This exciting conclusion comes from Dr. James Anderson, one of the early research pioneers on the health benefits of fiber. And people with

---

[50] http://content.nejm.org/cgi/content/short/342/19/1392

type 2 also benefited greatly. Eating beans not only reduced the need for insulin and other diabetic medications, but in some cases all but eliminated the need for supplemental insulin!

WHY YOU CAN'T ALWAYS TRUST CONVENTIONAL MEDICINE

Despite these impressive scientific studies about fiber, the ADA and a majority of physicians continue to underrecommend the amount of dietary fiber a person with diabetes should consume. Their suggestion—a meager 24 grams—is ridiculously inadequate. Every healthy adult needs at least *twice* that amount to prevent and reverse medical conditions such as hypertension, cardiovascular disease, obesity, and cancer, among others. And people with diabetes would benefit from even more.

Yet the average American consumes a scant 14 grams of dietary fiber a day—even *less* than the amount doctors are recommending. If you're eating a 2,500-calorie diet, you need a minimum of 35 to 40 grams of fiber every single day. And if you have diabetes, you should push this amount even higher. How do you do it? Just follow the eating plan in this book and go to *www. myhealingkitchen.com* for free Diabetes-Healing Recipes, plus helpful information about preparing delicious high-fiber meals.

The SAD bottom line: This is another clear example of how you can follow your doctor's orders religiously, take every drop of medication prescribed, eat the official ADA-recommended diabetes diet (which isn't very different than the Standard American Diet, appropriately abbreviated as SAD) and still succumb to this disease and its horrible complications. Not so on *The 30-Day Diabetes Cure.* I don't want any of my patients taking diabetes medications or using excessive insulin for the rest of their lives, because I know this will ruin their quality of life and subtract about 20 years from their longevity. I want to see type 2 people off medications *entirely*. In the case of injectable insulin, following this plan can lower your dosage to a minimum amount. This is the *only* way to kick this disease out of your life, improve the way you feel day by day, and live to see your grandkids grow up!

THE MORE YOU EAT, THE MORE YOU'LL HEAL,
"... SO EAT SOME BEANS AT EVERY MEAL!"

That's the last line of a little ditty that every kid knew (at least when I was growing up) which began: "Beans, beans: Good for your heart..." As you've just read, beans *are* good for your heart—but they're even better for your blood sugar. The more you eat, the more you'll heal. So, starting today, I want you to eat some beans at every meal. You won't need a heaping portion. A half-cup serving two or three times per day is perfect.

You already know that this relatively small amount of beans will produce enormous benefits. Besides reversing your diabetes, beans will help you lose weight, improve your health, keep you strong (they're a great source of protein), and save you money because they're so inexpensive. Now that's a food that really delivers the goods!

MAKE FRIENDS WITH BEANS

Beans are members of the legume family, which includes lentils, split peas, string beans, and all dry beans. Black beans (20 grams of fiber per cup!) and red kidney beans top the list for total fiber and resistant starches. Lentils and chickpeas (garbanzo beans) rate very low on the glycemic index, making them stars of the legume family in terms of stabilizing blood sugars.

My suggestion: Start with your old favorites and then investigate the more exotic types you're not familiar with. There are more than 13,000 varieties of beans to choose from, so this could become quite an adventure! Here are some of my favorites…

■   Adzuki beans, black beans, black-eyed peas, fava beans (also called broad beans), butter beans, calico beans, cannellini beans, chickpeas (also called garbanzos), edamame (green soybeans), Great Northern beans, Italian beans, kidney beans, lentils, lima beans, mung beans, navy beans, pinto beans, soybeans, split peas, white beans

HOW DO I LOVE THEM? LET ME COUNT THE WAYS…

Whether it's a three-bean salad, baked beans, bean fritters, refried beans, bean soup, or bean dip, beans lend themselves to endless menu possibilities. Try these suggestions from *www.myheal ingkitchen.com* for starters…

Beans with beef. Sauté ground grass-fed beef or bison with chopped onions, garlic, mushrooms, and a can of crushed tomatoes. Toss with cooked white beans and finish with chopped fresh basil.

Curried classic. Make a spicy lentil and green bean curry with low-fat coconut milk, curry paste, onion, garlic, and fresh minced ginger. Experiment with different flavors by adding Kaffir lime leaves. Add cooked chicken breast for even more protein.

Vegetarian burgers. For an easy bean burger, cook black beans with minced onion, garlic, and chipotle peppers. Stir in some corn kernels and form into patties. Sauté or bake until crispy on the outside. Serve with a spread made of adobo (the sauce that canned chipotles come in), non-fat yogurt, and chopped cilantro. Serve on a genuine whole-grain bun.

Garbanzo flour crepes. These thin pancakes are super easy! Just mix equal parts of garbanzo flour and water (added slowly and whisked until lumps are gone) and then cook in small batches in a lightly oiled nonstick pan. Add chopped fresh herbs such as rosemary, chives, or basil to the batter and fill with a scrambled egg, turkey bacon, and cheese for a heavenly breakfast, lunch, or dinner. Or mix a teaspoon of cinnamon into the batter, cook, and fill with nonfat yogurt and fresh fruit.

Dip in. Add a new bean dip to your repertoire by pureeing cooked fava beans or butter beans with nonfat yogurt, nonfat cottage cheese, and roasted garlic. Stir in chopped cooked spinach, pine nuts, and low-fat feta. Heat in the oven until bubbling hot and serve with fresh veggies.

Black beans for breakfast. Traditional Mexican breakfasts incorporate beans—and there's no reason you can't do the same. Open a can of refried black beans, microwave a half-cup portion, and enjoy with scrambled eggs, with or without a small corn tortilla or one made from genuine whole-grain (Ezekiel makes a great one!). Or sauté some tomatoes and onions in butter, add them to a serving of beans, and melt a little grated cheddar cheese on top. (Discover more free Diabetes Healing Recipes at *www.myhealingkitchen.com*.)

TAKE ACTION NOW: Start eating beans at every meal. This simple act will help you lose weight, improve your overall health, and most of all, help you get diabetes out of your life!

EXTRA CREDIT: If you have no beans in the house currently, head to the store and pick up six cans of various beans (or bean soups). Make sure the sodium level is no more than 300 mg to 400 mg. Use some of the suggestions above to include them in your very next meal.

OTHER RESISTANT-STARCH SUPERSTARS

Bananas (slightly green)
Resistant starch content: 6 g per banana
Serving suggestions:

- Slice and mix with yogurt and oatmeal for breakfast.

- Dip in yogurt and roll in chopped nuts before freezing for a snack or dessert.

- Dice and toss with lemon juice, salt, sugar, and onion to make tangy banana chutney.

Potatoes and Yams
Resistant starch content: 4 g per half cup
Serving suggestions:

- Serve cold potato salad tossed with olive oil and herbs as a side dish.

- Add chilled, chunked skin-on red potatoes to a salad.

- Puree sautéed yams, onion, and carrots to create a soup.

Barley
Resistant starch content: 3 g per half cup
Serving suggestions:

- Sprinkle onto garden salads.

- Mix into tuna, chicken, or tofu salad.

- Add to chilled lentil salad.

Brown Rice
Resistant starch content: 3 g per half cup
Serving suggestions:

- Order sushi with brown rice.

- Mix cooked brown rice with milk, raisins, and cinnamon for breakfast.

- Add to chilled marinated cucumbers as a side dish.

Corn
Resistant starch content: 2 g per half cup
Serving suggestions:

- Add to a taco salad, burrito, or quesadilla.

- Sprinkle into salsa or vegetarian refried beans.

- Make fresh corn relish with red bell pepper and onion.

(-)

DAY 15: REDUCE STRESS

Worrying is like a rocking chair,
it gives you something to do,
but it doesn't get you anywhere.

AUTHOR UNKNOWN

ANTI-HEALER: **Because uncontrolled stress upsets your entire hormonal system—including your glucose metabolism—today you're going to get a handle on it to help heal your diabetes…**

WHEN JAPANESE RESEARCHERS examined blood sugar levels in diabetics immediately after a large earthquake, they discovered that the stress had pushed up their blood glucose significantly. Levels were highest of all in those who lost property and family members.

How does stress affect your blood sugar? Badly, say researchers. Because stress is a stimulant, it causes sugar to be released into your bloodstream and triggers hormones that upset glucose levels. Plus, being stressed increases the likelihood that you won't eat properly or exercise.

HIGH STRESS EQUALS HIGHER BLOOD SUGAR

Researchers now place stress on par with smoking in terms of risk for heart disease, heart attacks, and irregular heartbeat rhythms. People with diabetes are already at risk for heart disease, giving you yet another reason to get a handle on your stress. Uncontrolled stress also boosts your blood sugar because it's the job of the stress hormones (adrenaline, epinephrine, and cortisol) to ensure you have enough energy (in the form of blood sugar) to fuel the "fight-or-flight response." By pumping out stress hormones in the blood sugar during an urgent situation, such as a mugging, you're able to act fast and survive.

But a steady diet of lower-level, chronic daily stress causes your body to churn out *cortisol*, the "worry hormone," which in turn spikes your blood sugar and triggers unconscious eating patterns. If you have an angry boss or troubled relationship, chances are they're making your blood sugar issues worse. This type of stress is simply awful news for blood sugar control. In fact, constantly living in a stressful state literally can wear you out. Researchers at Tel Aviv University in

197

Israel studied a large group of healthy professionals to evaluate the consequences of work stress on their health. Their results should be a red flag to anyone with diabetes. They discovered that people with the highest level of burnout during the five-year study were 84% more likely to get a diagnosis for diabetes. Dr. Samuel Melamed, who directed the research, explained that burnout interferes with the body's ability to metabolize blood sugar properly.

STRESS TRIGGERS BAD HABITS

Living with diabetes is stressful enough, involving a state of heightened alert about what to eat, whether you're making the right health decisions, and being fearful about how you'll manage food choices at the next company function or family dinner. Add this to any minor or even major emergency and your sugar can skyrocket.

Then there are all those conscious and unconscious responses to stress: skipping meals or overeating…snacking on unhealthy foods…eating more sweets and processed foods…not getting sufficient sleep…drinking extra alcohol…or turning to tranquilizers or recreational drugs. They're all particularly dangerous when you have a blood sugar imbalance.

Many of us have been living with chronic stress for so long that we're not even aware of the "background anxiety" in our lives. Highly adaptable, we humans continue to adjust to whatever's in front of us—working longer hours, overscheduling our lives and those of our children, letting ourselves be swept up in frenzy of overstimulation. Today you'll start to address this threat to your well-being.

WHICH STRESS FACTORS CAN YOU CONTROL?

You really *are* in charge of more stress-provoking situations than you might think. In fact, feeling out of control is the underlying basis for most stress. Here are some easy ways to address this problem…

Take stock. Even if you're not a list-maker by nature, now's a good time to write down everything that stresses you out, including anything that causes you worry, fear, anxiety, nervousness, or tension. If your first response to this is "I don't have time for this!" then make "lack of time" number one on your list. The truth is, identifying the stressors in your life is non-negotiable. If you can't make time for this important exercise, that's proof enough that your stress level is at an unhealthy high. Bonus: While you're working through this process, you might actually find some stressors you can eliminate right away.

Stop watching so much news. It's not an overstatement to say most news outlets follow the "If it bleeds, it leads" playbook. And yes, I'll admit there are more crisis situations in our world than we'd prefer. But if you keep your TV on with a constant stream of bad-news programming, your stress levels will definitely rise. Find a calm news channel and watch an hour to catch up. Or get the news in your local paper while you take a nice hot bath. Or read it online, but don't dwell on bad news. If a particular issue is upsetting you, take action—write, contribute, or volunteer. Just don't let a flood of bad news wreck your health.

Sort it out. Once you've identified your stress sources, determine which ones you can immediately address. Work toward eliminating some. Do you really need to take the bus the last five blocks home—or could you exit earlier and release some of your after-work tension with a short walk? Some stressors just require a new method. (Yes, your kids actually *can* help with dinner, rotating assignments like setting the table or unloading the dishwasher. In the process, you'll be helping them organize their lives too.)

Limit your drive time. Cooperate with other parents to carpool, so you're not driving every single day. Bundle your driving errands for one day a week if possible: Shop, pick up the cleaning, and buy groceries on the same day. Plan appointments for car maintenance, doctor visits, and other must-do's with plenty of off-days in between, so you're not feeling rushed all the time. Once in a while you need to stay home and regroup. Do it as often as possible. Remember, this is *your* life, and it's filled with choices.

Unclutter your life. Sort your mail and "to-do" list into three piles: Must Do Now, Do Later, and Forget About. Recycle the Forget Abouts immediately. Then open and organize your Do Later pile. If "now" means now, sit down and take care of it immediately: bills, phone calls, forms to be filled out, etc. Procrastination creates extra background stress. Believe it or not, actually dealing with tasks as they pop up is much less stressful than letting them accumulate in your psyche or on your desk.

Learn to say no. As in, "Sorry, I just can't make those cookies for the bake sale." Or, "I'd love to see you for lunch, but I can't make it this week—let's make a date for next month." Or, "While I appreciate your cause, I simply can't volunteer right now." Saying no and not overly obligating yourself is saying *yes* to your health and peace of mind. Remember, healing your diabetes is your top priority now, more vital than being the perfect mom or wife...dad or husband...friend...or employee. (Without good health, you can't be any of those in the long run anyway.)

Make some "me time." Taking care of your health requires making time just for yourself. That means taking the time to cook and eat well...exercise properly...get enough sleep...lose yourself in a hobby...study quietly...and just relax. If you're thinking, "Yeah right, who has time for that?" it's another signal that you're overscheduled and overstressed. If you don't make time to nurture yourself now, when will you do it? Remember Jim's friend Sally (from the Foreword) who died of lung cancer because she put off giving up cigarettes until "later"?

ARE STRESS-PROVOKING PEOPLE MAKING YOU SICK?

Your doctor. Seeing your doctor is enormously important, but if you find your doctor visits stressful and less than satisfying, ask yourself these questions: Am I getting enough personal care and attention? Am I arguing with my doctor over my decision to control my blood sugar with diet and exercise, instead of medication? Are my appointments with "whichever doctor is available" instead of one person who gets to know me and works with me as I progress? Do I have to wait a long time before my consultation or exam?

If any of these issues are causing you anxiety, it may be time to start researching alternatives and following through. Join a diabetes support group and ask members about their doctors. Is someone raving about theirs? Interview that doctor and see how you feel in his/her presence. Search your community for properly credentialed alternative physicians, such as naturopaths or certified nurse practitioners (your local health food store may have a newspaper or magazine devoted to alternative health and this is a good resource). Many doctors who include alternative modalities in their practice are also open to managing diabetes just as we're doing now. Interview potential candidates until you find one who will serve your needs. Remember, you're paying your doctor and he/she works for you. If you're not getting the care you want, find another doctor.

Creditors. Financial problems are one of the biggest stressors, and these days it's rare to find any working person who doesn't carry this burden. It's easy to feel panicky and fearful about your financial security, but this just amps up your stress levels. Pull together your financial information and get some professional advice. Most cities have free financial counseling centers or offer support via state offices, community colleges, and other noncommercial endeavors. Letting anxiety burn like a flaming torch is not helping you heal. Address your financial woes with maturity and commitment so you can weather these uncertain times with grace. Steer clear of hucksters promising "credit relief"—they've descended on vulnerable homeowners and credit card debtors like vultures on wounded prey.

Family members and coworkers. Parent and sibling disagreements can endure for decades. Negative coworkers can make your workday miserable. Navigating difficult romantic relationships and life partnerships can generate constant stress. Even some friendships become burdensome. Occasionally, stressful entanglements can be eased by simply becoming less available, but for others a swift, clean break is preferred. In general, committed relationships that have become stressful can benefit from the guidance of a professional counselor. If this sounds like your situation, don't put it off. Remember: You need calm strength to heal your diabetes. Ask a therapist for advice in steering you toward independence and *away* from problems that are unsolvable.

It's also worth considering this: Close relationships are always affected when someone has a chronic illness. Your personal health challenges may be making life more difficult for those around you. Be compassionate, empathetic and open-minded. Make time for conversations in which you invite others to describe how your health situation has affected *them*. Listen attentively and avoid the temptation to be defensive. Many times, just inviting honest dialogue has a profound healing effect and actually brings people closer.

GET A GOOD NIGHT'S SLEEP!

A good night's sleep usually will reduce the physical damage caused by stress. But few people today are getting the recommended eight hours required for this repair. And people with diabetes are particularly vulnerable when they don't get enough sleep. We'll talk about this in more detail later on Day 19, but for now, pay attention to your sleep habits.

- Researchers have found that sleep deprivation actually increases insulin resistance. In a study published in the *Archives of Internal Medicine*, scientists reported that women who slept only five hours a night were 250% more likely to have diabetes, compared with those who got seven or eight hours.

- In a study of healthy young men who slept just four hours a night for six nights in a row, researchers found insulin and blood sugar levels that mirrored those of metabolic syndrome (prediabetes).

There are many steps you can take to increase the odds of getting a good night's sleep. Limit caffeinated coffee and tea consumption to one or two cups before noon—and none after that. Well before bedtime, turn off the TV, dim household lights, and put on some quiet music. Change your clothes and prepare for bed earlier than usual so your body gets all the cues to relax. Avoid suspenseful or action-packed movies, and don't watch or read the day's news at night. Instead, read a quieting book, write in your journal, or simply sit and meditate (see below). Creating an atmosphere of calm relaxation will diminish your stress and encourage a good night's sleep.

YOUR STRESS-RELIEF TOOL KIT

You'll never be able to eliminate all the stress from your life, but you *can* relieve it. Here are some of the best ways to de-stress your nervous system and reverse the harm it wreaks on your health…

Meditate. One of the best ways to unwind and renew your calm vitality is to "check out" for a few minutes with meditation. In addition to immediately relaxing you, meditation lowers your heart rate and blood pressure, reduces the adrenaline and cortisol in your bloodstream, and sharpens your mental functions and creativity.

Consider meditation a "time out" from your problems, worries, fears, and racing thoughts. (Don't worry—they'll be there when you return.) Schedule an uninterrupted period of 10 to 20 minutes daily and create a comfortable place to sit without distractions. Close your eyes and bring your focus to the rhythm of your breathing, mentally counting each out-breath until you reach 10 (when you get to 10, start over). When your mind wanders (and will it ever!), gently return it to focusing on your breathing and begin counting again. Don't turn this into another achievement project. The whole idea of counting is simply to distract your chatty, cognitive mind, which exists in the past and the future. The point of meditation is to be in the present moment, the *now*. As your mind quiets, your body will begin to relax.

You may find that in this peaceful mind-state, solutions to problems simply bubble up un-requested. A meditation break helps you face the rest of the day with a feeling of harmony and balance, and this sense of relaxation will extend throughout your day. Sleep may also come more easily if you meditate just before bedtime.

Regular meditation produces profound benefits on the body and brain. As Deepak Chopra reports in his book *Ageless Body, Ageless Mind*,

> "We now know that meditation may actually reshape the brain, modify our responses to daily situations and train the mind.… In terms of aging, the most significant conclusion (about meditation) is that the hormonal imbalance associated with stress—and known to speed up the aging process—is reversed. This in turn slows or even reverses the aging process, as measured by various biological changes associated with growing old. From my experience with studies on people using Transcendental Meditation, it has been established that long-term meditators can have a biological age between five to 12 years *younger* than their chronological age."

In short, science has proven that meditation turns back the clock!

Exercise. Are you someone who just can't sit still? Try meditating in motion. Some people find it easy to lose themselves in physical activities that involve repetitive movements, such as walking, running, swimming, or cycling. To enter a meditative state during exercise, simply focus on your breathing or the rhythm of the movement itself. In no time, your mind will still and you'll enter the eternal present. Try this today on your walk.

Spend time outdoors. Fresh air, green foliage, and the peaceful natural world are all powerful healers. In fact, researchers have discovered that hospital patients whose windows looked out onto nature healed better (and faster) than those whose view was a brick wall.[51] Today's hospitals are being designed with these principles in mind. You can take advantage of nature's destressing effect by walking outside in the park, down a tree-lined street, or just by leaving your home for your own green backyard or garden.

Relaxation. Relaxation reduces the wear and tear that daily life can exert on your body and your mind. By consciously focusing your concentration on relaxing, you can lower your blood pressure and heart rate, boost your immune function, reduce muscle tension, alleviate chronic pain,

---

[51] http://www.emagazine.com/archive/3863

and increase blood flow to your muscles. Mayo Clinic doctors recommend these three relaxation techniques…

Autogenic relaxation. This technique uses a word, phrase, suggestion, or mental image to help you relax and let go of muscle tension. In a comfortable position, repeat any of these phrases to yourself over and over: "I am perfectly relaxed…I am living in harmony and balance…I am healing my diabetes by becoming more and more relaxed." Imagine a peaceful visual setting and then focus your concentration on your breathing.

Progressive muscle relaxation. This focuses your awareness on different muscles, tensing each one for a few seconds and then relaxing it, keeping your awareness on your body instead of allowing your mind to wander. Start by flexing your toes for 10 to 20 seconds, then release. Next, move to your ankles…then your calf muscles…then your knees…and so on. Move progressively up to your scalp, focusing on as many individual muscles as you can.

Visualization. This involves taking an "internal journey" to a peaceful imaginary place, engaging as many of your senses as you can. Visualize a beautiful scene, such as a sunny beach or verdant flower garden. Create the scene with as much detail as you can, and place yourself in the scene. Feel the warm sun on your back, smell the flowers, hear the surf rolling in. It's a mini-vacation in your mind.

Relaxation takes practice. While your body shifts from "go-go-go" to "stop-and-rest-a-while," you'll find your mind wandering and you may notice all sorts of twitches in your muscles and itches on your skin. Relaxing well and deeply is a learned skill, but don't let it turn into a stressful accomplishment. Just take your time, breathe slowly and deeply, and give yourself a much-needed break. You'll soon reap the rewards.

Biofeedback. If you need support in learning to relax, locate a biofeedback therapist. Research psychiatrists at the Medical University of Ohio in Toledo divided diabetes patients into two groups, with one receiving biofeedback and relaxation training and the other getting educational information about the disease. People in the biofeedback group reduced their blood sugar by a remarkable 11%, while the blood sugars of those in the education group actually *increased*. Conclusion? "Patients with type 2 diabetes could significantly improve blood sugar control through the use of biofeedback and relaxation training," said the researchers.[52]

Biofeedback's easy and actually fun. You're hooked up to a monitor that senses stress in your body through skin temperature or muscle tension. A beep or flashing light notifies you when you're stressed. By modifying your breathing and calming yourself, you teach your body how to turn off the signal. After mastering this technique, you can replicate it in real-life situations.

Prayer. The calming effects of prayer rival those of meditation, relaxation, and biofeedback. Praying for healing assistance and forgiving your enemies really works, and plenty of unbiased

---

[52] http://care.diabetesjournals.org/content/28/9/2145.abstract

scientific studies prove it. What's important is that you remember to pray when you need it most—and this requires you to notice when you're stressed.

If you belong to an established religion—or even if you don't but feel drawn toward one—go to church, temple, mosque, or ashram and seek help from its spiritual director. You needn't adhere to a religion's tenets to reap the benefits of contemplating your problems in the context of the greater spiritual universe.

Counseling. To keep stress, depression, and anxiety from overtaking your life, consider seeking help from a trained therapist who specializes in mental health issues. Be wary of those who want to write you a prescription without taking the time to offer you other options. Studies show that antidepressants are *rarely* effective. (More about this on Day 17.) Talking with a therapist to gain perspective and control over stressful issues can help you keep a grip on your core problems without resorting to drugs.

TAKE ACTION TODAY: Reduce or eliminate as many stress-producing factors in your life as you can. Commit to getting a good night's sleep. Neutralize stress with an effective stress-management technique that's best suited to your personality and temperament.

EXTRA CREDIT: Put down this book and close your eyes. Breathe deeply and rhythmically, counting your "out breaths" until you reach 10. Keep going if you feel relaxed. Congratulations! You've just had your first healing meditation session!

DAY 16: ADD VITAMINS

A vitamin is a substance that makes you ill if you don't eat it.

ALBERT SZENT-GYORGYI

HEALER: Give your health a super-boost with a high-quality multivitamin. And add vitamin D because it prevents diabetes from worsening—and actually *improves* blood sugar better than the leading medication. Here's the story…

WHY TAKE VITAMINS when you're already eating high-quality whole foods that are naturally loaded with nutrition? Simple. Because even when you're eating the best diet, having diabetes increases your need for certain nutrients—and getting the amount you need isn't always possible with food alone.

As you work through my 30-day plan (you're more than halfway home already!), it's essential you get maximum nutritional support. One of the best ways to achieve this is by supplementing your diet with a high-quality multivitamin. Consider it a nutritional "insurance policy" that covers you with a regular supply of critical nutrients for extra demands that having diabetes places on your body. Here's how to locate a reliable product…

QUALITY IS KEY

Enter any local big-box discount store, pharmacy, grocery, natural foods store, or neighborhood market and you're confronted with shelf after shelf of nutritional supplements. How can you possibly know what to take, what might work, and which products are worth the money? Vitamins and supplements are a huge industry, and your ignorance is what some unscrupulous manufacturers count on. In fact, independent analyses of common supplements often find that many (if not most) products don't contain the raw materials or the amounts that the labels claim, rendering them ineffective at best—and harmful at worst.

How can this happen? Because no government agency regulates the quality of nutritional supplements and quite often the raw materials are imported from countries shielded from the reach of potential lawsuits by jilted consumers. In the US, anyone with enough money can start a supplement company because there are no requirements and few regulations. With millions of Americans seeking to self-treat themselves with supplements, there's plenty of temptation to profit from their pain and disability (and lack of knowledge) by producing cheap, inferior products.

And the cheaper the raw materials they use, the greater their profits. Surprisingly, quality-control safeguards and supplement testing/analysis actually cost *more* than the raw materials that go into supplements. Companies that choose the cheapest materials for their products are very likely to ignore quality-control procedures and product testing.

HOW CAN YOU PROTECT YOURSELF?

Look for the GMP seal. This signifies that the company follows Good Manufacturing Practices (GMP). These voluntary standards describe exactly how supplement manufacturers should receive and handle raw materials, produce supplements, check for safety, and track problems and consumer complaints. Quality supplement manufacturers adhere to GMPs to distinguish themselves from disreputable companies. Compliance is monitored and graded by third-party audits to help ensure that the manufacturer is conforming to these guidelines. If you don't see this seal, don't buy the supplements.

There are other organizations that also monitor the quality of manufactured products. When shopping, look for "approval" seals from these third-party organizations…

- USP-DSVP - The US Pharmacopoeia Dietary Supplement Verification Program

- NSF - An international dietary supplements certification program

- NNFA - The National Natural Foods Association, an industry group

- GHSA - The Good Housekeeping Seal of Approval

Don't cheat your health with cheap supplements. We're all trying to save money these days, but your health and diabetes healing are too important to scrimp on. No matter how inexpensive a brand is, it's not a bargain if it doesn't help you. Does this mean you should buy the most expensive supplements? No way. A high price tag isn't a reliable indicator of quality, although very low cost *is* a dead giveaway that a product is of inferior quality.

Steer clear of store brands. They're usually priced well below brand-name supplements because they're made of inferior raw materials. While store brands of basic food staples is an acceptable way to stretch your dollar, when it comes to vitamins and supplements, you definitely get what you pay for. Plus, paying half-price for a product that does your body no good not only wastes your money; it cheats your health. You're better off finding a brand you can trust. How? Several independent organizations regularly test nutritional supplements:

Consumer Reports (*www.consumerreports.org*) is a nonprofit, independent organization that tests and evaluates a wide range of consumer products, including nutritional supplements. A few years ago, they tested 12 brands of joint supplements that supposedly improved arthritis symptoms. Three of them failed the exam, and *Consumer Reports* published the names of these inferior products. In fact, they're the only group that lists product failures along with those that pass. A one-year subscription to *Consumer Reports* gives you access to thousands of current and past evaluations. For just $29, it's a tremendous bargain—and a smart investment.

Consumer Labs (*www.consumerlab.com*) is another independent testing organization, though it's a for-profit corporation. A 12-month membership costs $29.95. They test and evaluate vitamins and supplements exclusively.

GO FOR A GOOD MULTI

There are definitely some nutritional supplements that are especially beneficial for people with diabetes and blood sugar issues. (I'll discuss these on Day 28; I'm waiting because I want to give your new diet and exercise routine the chance to do the job by itself.) Starting today, I want you to begin taking a high-quality multivitamin that will boost your daily intake of essential nutrients.

I don't recommend the vast majority of one-a-day multis you find in the drugstore because their nutrient levels are based on the Recommended Daily Allowances (RDA), which are the official nutritional guidelines used by the USDA and FDA. These are *minimal* levels designed to prevent their nutritional deficiency diseases based upon the old Minimum Daily Requirement (MDR) thinking. This criterion is a bit ludicrous. For example, the RDA for vitamin C is a scant 75 to 90 mg—the dose required to prevent scurvy, a potentially fatal disease that afflicted British sailors in the 1700s.

Your chances of coming down with scurvy these days is about the same as being attacked by sharks in Indiana. But your prospects of coming down with heart disease are far greater, and numerous studies have shown that vitamin C doses higher than the RDA actually lower this risk. (The famous Nurses' Health Study involving more than 85,000 women over 16 years is just one of these studies.) My point is that the RDA system is antiquated because it's based on nutrient doses that prevent deficiency diseases, not chronic diseases. Rather than basing your purchasing decisions on *minimal* levels, you should be looking for *optimal* amounts.

With literally dozens (if not hundreds) of individual vitamins, minerals, and other nutrients to consider, there simply isn't enough space here to list the optimal levels for each one. Besides, this would require a tedious label-reading undertaking on your part every time you shopped. So let me save you the time by listing a few general guidelines to follow when shopping for a multivitamin…

Are the ingredients absorbable? Just as important as the nutrient levels are the *form* the ingredients' nutrients come in. For example, many companies boast high levels of magnesium but use forms of magnesium your body can't absorb. It looks great on the label but actually does you no good. Look for supplements—like the ones I will recommend in a moment—that are from natural, absorbable sources of vitamins and minerals.

The one pill myth. Natural, absorbable forms of vitamins and minerals take up a lot of space inside a pill. So don't be surprised when the label says, "Six capsules provide…." (The multivitamin I take suggests this, so I simply take three in the morning and three before bedtime.)

Quality will cost. To get a supplement made from top-quality raw materials that is highly absorbable and that will make positive improvements in your health, you're going to have to pay a premium price. But since your good health is your most prized possession, it's worth it, right?

Get good advice. Big Pharma isn't the only industry capitalizing on consumer confusion about health. Many supplement companies make products that are highly questionable—and they invest plenty on "educating" the clerks in health food stores about the benefits of their products. Remember: Most of these clerks are there to sell you products (and often the ones with the biggest profit margins, which are usually of the lowest quality). Your best defense is to educate yourself before you go shopping.

Avoid supplement gimmicks. Two of the most popular gimmicks today are liquid multivitamins and "whole food" vitamins. Liquid vitamins are a marketing ploy strategy. They don't provide better absorption, nor are they worth the high price. The "whole food vitamins" concept is also a scam. Here, manufacturers inoculate a batch of bacteria to break it down into vitamins. I'm all in favor of fermented foods, but when it comes to total nutritional support they're no substitute for a high-quality multivitamin.

Physician-sold supplements. Beware of nutritional products available only in a doctor's office. This strategy leverages the enormous influence doctors have over their patients—and their reward is usually a big mark-up. If your health-care provider is selling you some product that's not available without a "prescription" or special professional advice—or it can't be found anywhere else—that's just hogwash. The same goes for multilevel marketing schemes. I've never found a single multivitamin product that was so special that it required a closed network of buyers. In fact, there are so many middlemen profiting at each one of these "multilevels" that the price is jacked up sky-high (which usually means the actual cost of the product is dirt cheap and low quality). And what about the products bearing the name of "celebrity doctors"? In almost every case, the doctor merely licenses his name to a third-party formulator and has very little to say about the product or what it contains.

My favorite products. Having said all that, here are some suggestions for multivitamin brands that I know and like, starting with the multivitamin made by Pure Encapsulations called Nutrient 950. (If you are over 50, I suggest you take their UltraNutrient.) Solgar is a manufacturer that's been around for a long time and I have come to trust their products. Another company that makes an excellent line of supplement products (including a good-quality multi) is Thorne. But do your own research by consulting with Consumer Reports and Consumer Labs. Make sure you shop around for the best prices.

WHY YOU NEED EXTRA VITAMIN D

One nutrient that all multivitamins score low on is vitamin D (known as the "sunshine vitamin," because our body manufactures it when solar rays hit our skin), so this is one individual nutrient I want you to take in addition to your multi. In my opinion, it is the most important, yet highly underrated, nutrient you can take today—especially if you have diabetes.

The epidemic of vitamin D deficiency in America and other Western cultures today is a major reason why we are experiencing such poor health. In fact, it is the leading nutritional deficiency in our nation: Up to 90% of all Americans aren't getting enough vitamin D. Numerous studies suggest this deficiency is directly linked to our soaring rates of diabetes, types 1 *and* 2...

- Finnish men and women with higher blood levels of vitamin D had a 40% lower risk of developing type 2 diabetes than those who had less vitamin D, according to a study published in the October 2007 issue of *Diabetes Care*. This was the conclusion from researchers who spent 17 years following a population of 4,000 people in Finland. Studies also show that infants who get the highest levels of vitamin D (through sun exposure or supplements) develop 80% less type 2 diabetes as adults.

- Vitamin D appears to prevent or delay the onset of diabetes. And in people who already have diabetes it reduces complications such as heart disease, according to research published in *Diabetes Educator* in 2009 by scientists at Loyola University.

- Women who took at least 800 IU (international units) of vitamin D and 1,200 mg of calcium each day had a 33% lower risk of developing type 2 diabetes compared with those taking less. That's another conclusion from the Nurses' Health Study just mentioned, which provided the most powerful evidence linking type 2 and vitamin D.

VITAMIN D ACTUALLY *IMPROVES* DIABETES

A report appearing in the June 2009 issue of *Nutrition Research Review* involving several clinical studies shows that vitamin D actually improves insulin sensitivity. In fact, *vitamin D might be all that some people with mild type 2 need to improve their condition.* Here's more good news...

- Insulin-resistant women significantly decreased their risk of developing diabetes simply by taking more vitamin D. Research published in the *British Journal of Nutrition* in 2010 looked at a group of Asian women who had all been diagnosed with insulin resistance, a precursor to full-blown diabetes. The women were randomly assigned to take either 4,000 IU of vitamin D or a placebo. After six months, insulin resistance in the vitamin D group dramatically decreased, along with their fasting insulin levels.

■ Researchers reported in the *American Journal of Clinical Nutrition* in May 2004 that vitamin D improves insulin sensitivity by up to 60%! Those are better results than metformin (Glucophage) achieves (and it's the leading diabetes drug prescribed today)! A 1998 study published in the *New England Journal of Medicine* showed that metformin lowers blood sugar by a meager 13%.

IT LESSENS DIABETIC COMPLICATIONS...TOO

British researchers recently reviewed 28 different studies of naturally occurring (meaning it came from sunshine) vitamin D levels in almost 100,000 people. They found that higher levels of vitamin D translated into a 33% reduction of cardiovascular disease, 55% reduction in type 2 diabetes, and 51% reduction in metabolic syndrome.

WHY ARE WE SO DEFICIENT IN THIS IMPORTANT VITAMIN?

The reason is because we are not spending enough time outdoors anymore—and because doctors and health experts have turned us into "solar scaredy-cats," making us afraid of going out in the sun unless we slather ourselves with sunscreen and don ridiculously wide-brim hats. Most people are living in the shadows because of popular but wrong-headed health advice that says sunshine causes skin cancer. In addition, we're being discouraged from eating organ meats (such as calf's liver) and animal fats, dairy foods, and eggs—foods all naturally high in vitamin D.

THE TOP 10 VITAMIN D FOODS

1. Liver and other organ meats
2. Wild salmon (not farm-raised)
3. Shrimp
4. Cod
5. Anchovies
6. Fish oil
7. Eggs
8. Milk (fortified)

9.   Red, yellow, and orange fruits and vegetables

10. Dark-green, leafy vegetables

DOCTORS HAVE BEEN WRONG ABOUT SKIN CANCER

This is bad advice for everyone, but especially for people with diabetes, for whom vitamin D has been proven to be beneficial. There's no getting around the fact that sunshine is our primary source of vitamin D. Your body produces it when the sun's ultraviolet (UV) rays penetrate the skin, with lighter skin producing more vitamin D than darker skin.

It's no coincidence that equatorial countries receiving copious amounts of sunshine, such as Cuba, Peru and Bermuda, have some of the lowest rates of type 1 diabetes on earth. Indeed, an analysis of 52 nations shows that those closest to the equator have the lowest incidence. And even within the US, there's a huge difference in the rates of type 2 between northern states and southern, sunny states.

Vitamin D actually *protects* against many cancers, including skin cancer. Studies show that people with the lowest levels of vitamin D actually have *higher* rates of the skin cancer melanoma and other cancers. Plus, being deficient in vitamin D *increases* the risk of death from all causes. Sunscreen not only blocks the sun but also blocks your body from making health-giving D (and some of sunscreen's ingredients have been found to be carcinogenic).

BECOME A SUN-WORSHIPER

Sunbathing for 10 to 15 minutes a day in the summer is actually good medicine. Lying in the sun feels good because it *is* good for you. Solar rays nurture all of life, and we humans are no exception. Scientists have yet to identify the many ways that sunshine helps heal us, but when I'm ill, I like to recuperate in the sun's warmth and fresh air. Sun exposure was a popular therapy for tuberculosis before the advent of the TB vaccination. It's now believed that patients got well because of increased blood levels of healing vitamin D.

Until we understand more about the sun's beneficial effects on health and healing, we should do as our ancestors did and expose our skin to the sun instead of hiding from it. Take care not to burn because sunburn generates free radicals and *is* linked to skin cancer. But don't wear sunscreen unless you know you'll have an extended stay in the sun—sunscreens block vitamin D production by 95%.

Minimize your exposure during peak midday hours when the sun is at its strongest (11 am to 3 pm). Take a short walk in the morning or late afternoon when the sun is less intense than midday, with arms and legs uncovered, to soak up as much sunshine as you can.

SHOULD YOU TAKE A VITAMIN D SUPPLEMENT?

Given that 90% of Americans are thought to be deficient, the answer is yes. Getting 100% of your vitamin D requirements from food sources is nearly impossible (though I recommend you eat generously of these foods for their other nutritional benefits). Additionally, sunbathing isn't realistic during the winter months in the Northern Hemisphere, when the sun is low in the sky and gray is the color of most days.

FOLLOW THESE SUPPLEMENT TIPS:

The ideal form. Purchase only high-quality brands of vitamin D3 (*cholecalciferol*). This is the same form of D that our skin produces from sunlight. Good old cod liver oil works just as well. Avoid vitamin D2 (*ergocalciferol*), because it is inferior and potentially harmful.

The right dose. Take a minimum of 1,000 to 2,000 IU of vitamin D3 on days when you can't expose your body to sunshine. African-Americans, who have higher cancer rates and lower blood levels of vitamin D, should double this dose. The skin of African-Americans does not seem to convert UV rays into vitamin D efficiently, which causes chronic deficiency, particularly among those living in Western countries. This may help explain why African-Americans generally have a higher incidence of many cancers and in more aggressive forms.

Attention, seniors. Your body's ability to produce vitamin D declines with age. A 70-year-old's skin makes about a quarter of the D that it manufactured from the sun's rays when you were in your 20s. Seniors should take 2,000 to 3,000 IU daily.

Children need it, too. Michael Holick, MD, PhD, perhaps the world's preeminent expert on vitamin D, cites no fewer than 74 studies showing that giving vitamin D supplements to children reduces their risk of developing type 1 diabetes. Word to the wise.

TAKE ACTION: Begin taking a high-quality multivitamin every day. Also start taking vitamin D daily in the doses recommended above. Don't be afraid to let the sun shine on your bare skin every day if possible, so your body can naturally make its own vitamin D. Eat more vitamin D-rich foods as well.

EXTRA CREDIT: If it's sunny outside where you are, get out right now, strip down, and soak up some D!

(-)

DAY 17: ELIMINATE DEPRESSION

Hope is the thing with feathers
That perches in the soul
And sings the tune without the words
And never stops at all.

EMILY DICKINSON

ANTI-HEALER: Diabetes and depression often go hand in hand. Follow these tips to roll back your "diabetes blues"—or to prevent them entirely…

HERE'S A DEPRESSING STATISTIC: The incidence of depression among people with diabetes is 400% higher than in the general population. According to the ADA, up to 20% of people with diabetes are clinically depressed. Plus, more than 20% of people with type 1 currently are taking antidepressant medication.

Diabetes can be depressing. It's easy to see why. Diabetes is a difficult medical condition to live with. Type 2 patients are told to constantly monitor their glucose levels, watch their diets, exercise more, and lose weight. This relentless demand for self-monitoring and self-control takes a serious toll on mental health. Many live in constant fear of heart disease and other imminent complications. There's the energy-draining discomfort of physical symptoms and the difficulties of overcoming them (not to mention side effects from those drugs, too). Then there's the sense of not having control over your body or your life. Who wouldn't be depressed?

The sad fact is that people who have diabetes *and* depression often forget to test themselves, take their medication on time (if at all), exercise, or eat at regular intervals. And as depression becomes more severe, they're likely to give up their treatment regimen entirely.

Brain chemical imbalances. Depression can be traced to a chemical imbalance that affects not only how you face your day but also how you think about yourself and your world. *Serotonin*, the neurotransmitter (brain chemical) responsible for good moods, feelings of confidence, security, relaxation, calmness, and emotional balance is usually involved. Low levels of it can affect your sleep patterns and concentration…your interest in work and daily activities…your relationships and family life…even your sex drive.

Decreased serotonin plays a key role in the development of depression as well as anxiety, fatigue, insomnia, low self-esteem, low levels of concentration, plus a host of illnesses that stem from chronic depression. In a way, this diagnosis is less about your low moods than it is about a "depression" of your serotonin levels.

In addition, symptoms of depression or brain-chemistry imbalance can include such eating disorders as anorexia (undereating), overeating that leads to excessive weight gain, and bulimia (routine bingeing and purging). Women with type 1 especially can develop these. The most common, *diabulimia*, involves intentionally reducing your insulin dose in order to lose weight (even though this causes frequent urination, thirst, exhaustion, plus other symptoms of uncontrolled diabetes). One study discovered that as many as 30% of young women with diabetes were engaging in this dangerous practice, despite the fact that it increases their risk of death by 300%.

THE LINK BETWEEN DIABETES AND DEPRESSION

The pharmaceutical approach to depression (including antidepressants such as Prozac and Paxil) attempts to concentrate your existing serotonin in an effort to boost its effectiveness. What these drugs *don't* do is increase your brain's levels of serotonin. In fact, some studies show they may actually *reduce* your natural serotonin levels over long-term use.

Certain foods, on the other hand, play a major role in maintaining brain chemistry, and can actually help your brain make enough serotonin so that you feel better and more emotionally stable, even in the face of discomfort or crisis. I'll describe some specific "mood foods" in a moment, but first, it's important to understand that brain chemistry works on the same principles as the rest of your body's chemical makeup. When functioning normally, your entire body is like a finely tuned race car. Every engine part relies on all the others in a delicate dance of cooperation and synergy. If an air hose has a slight blockage, over time the entire engine will suffer from a lack of adequate circulation. And if there's a malfunction in your blood sugar chemistry, it's quite likely that a brain chemistry imbalance will follow.

When you have a lack of the proper nutritional components to support the conversion of one chemical to another in the brain, you end up with a chronic imbalance in your brain chemistry as well as the rest of your metabolism. Result? Debilitating disease *and* serious depression.

Here's another twist to that concept: Depression is one of the indicators of the possibility of *developing* diabetes, meaning a scientific correlation between mental/emotional health and blood-sugar metabolism is apparent—but the depression may actually come first. In a 2004 study at Johns Hopkins that tracked more than 11,000 middle-aged adults over six years who initially were *not* diabetic, scientists found that symptoms of depression actually predicted a later diagnosis of type 2 diabetes. And a Kaiser-Permanente study of almost 1,700 people found that those with diabetes were more likely to have been treated for depression within the six months before their diabetes diagnosis and that 84% of diabetics reported having "depressive episodes" earlier in their lives.[53]

THE DIET-DEPRESSION CONNECTION

Poor diet can predict a risk for depression and other mental illnesses in the same way it does for heart disease. That's what a study published in the *British Journal of Psychiatry* found. Another research project reported in the *American Journal of Psychiatry* analyzed the dietary habits of more than 1,000 women, ranking them according to their psychological symptoms.[54] The women whose diets mirrored my 30-day plan—high in vegetables and fruit, meat and fish, and whole grains—showed a correspondingly lower incidence of depression and anxiety. Women who had a higher incidence of depression and anxiety partook of a diet of fried foods, fast-carb refined grain products, sugary foods, and beer—the very same eating habits I've been urging you to abandon in order to heal your diabetes.

Foods that depress your serotonin. Since you began *The 30-Day Diabetes Cure*, I've been encouraging you to abandon the foods that caused your blood-sugar imbalance: sugar and sweets, sodas, fast carbs, high-fructose corn syrup, trans fats, and refined vegetable oils with excessive omega-6 fatty acids and not enough omega-3s. Why? Because these foods encourage rampant inflammation, damage blood vessels, create dysfunction in your blood-sugar metabolism, increase your risk of heart disease and stroke, kidney failure, blindness, and limb amputation, and shorten your life span. These same foods also depress your serotonin levels and can trigger depression.

Other factors that deplete serotonin. Equally harmful to serotonin are chronic stress…excessive use of stimulants such as caffeine…alcohol and other drugs of abuse…cigarette smoking… and insufficient sleep. Depressed levels of serotonin in turn continue to disrupt sleep (because serotonin is required to create *melatonin*, the sleep hormone). And of course, lack of sleep can cause you to be even more depressed, more stressed, and to gain weight through overeating.

That's how low serotonin triggers junk-food binges. In an effort to relieve stress and comfort your brain, you begin to crave fast carbs to stimulate a serotonin rush. Unfortunately, this only makes you feel good for a short time before your blood sugar plunges again. Like a junk-food junkie, you keep coming back, trying to "self-medicate" with fast carbs and creating even more serotonin spikes.

---

[53] http://bjp.rcpsych.org/cgi/content/full/184/5/404

[54] http://ajp.psychiatryonline.org/cgi/content/abstract/167/3/305

FOODS THAT RAISE YOUR SEROTONIN—AND YOUR SPIRITS

Follow the nutritional advice outlined in *The 30-Day Diabetes Cure* and you'll be choosing foods that boost your serotonin levels naturally to help stave off both depression *and* your recurring cravings for junky foods.

Foods that contain the amino acid *tryptophan* (including turkey, which is why you feel like dozing off after Thanksgiving dinner) are especially good for elevating serotonin levels in the brain. Tryptophan is not produced by your body—you get it strictly from food sources. Serotonin production is also supported by B vitamins, calcium, magnesium, omega-3 essential fatty acids, plus the essential fatty acid omega-6 (when taken in the right proportion to omega-3).

Where do you find these serotonin-supporting substances? Besides that Thanksgiving turkey, these vitamins, minerals, amino acids, and essential fats are found in naturally raised meats, eggs, fish, and dairy products—plus whole grains, leafy green vegetables, soy foods, nuts, and seeds. All of these are staples of my 30-day eating plan. Stick with the foods I've been recommending and you'll be healing your diabetes by balancing your blood sugar metabolism. In addition, you'll be improving your brain chemistry and your moods will brighten as a result. Your sleeping patterns will improve. You'll feel calmer and less anxious. And your ability to cope when faced with stress will surprise you.

Keep walking, too. Numerous studies also show that regular physical activity elevates serotonin levels enough to prevent and chase away mild depression. In fact, scientists now know that exercise works just as well as antidepressants! In the days ahead, you'll also learn specific ways to destress your nervous system. Often, this dramatically improves depression and sleep problems.

SUPPLEMENTS THAT HELP

Tryptophan. A 1992 study reported in the *International Journal of Neuroscience* confirms that tryptophan can stimulate the proper function of serotonin in the brain, thus alleviating mild depression. (Many antidepressant drugs work to increase the amount of serotonin in the brain, usually by preventing the serotonin from being depleted.) Tryptophan actually increases serotonin levels, and has the advantage of doing it without the adverse side effects associated with antidepressant drugs. Tryptophan should be taken on an empty stomach so it won't compete with other amino acids for absorption. I recommend taking vitamin C and a B-complex supplement along with tryptophan to facilitate the formation of serotonin. The FDA banned tryptophan from the market in 1989, but it is now back on the market. The recommended dose is 500 to 1,000 mg taken at bedtime because it also helps induce sleep.

5-HTP. Serotonin is made from the amino acid *5-hydroxytryptophan* (5-HTP), which itself is made from tryptophan. As you've just read, not getting enough tryptophan can cause depression.

And while eating tryptophan-rich foods is often helpful, some people occasionally need supplemental help. In this case, I've also found 5-HTP to be very helpful. More than 25 clinical studies comparing 5-HTP and selective serotonin reuptake inhibitor (SSRI) antidepressants showed that this supplement is just as effective—and sometimes even better. Other studies show that 5-HTP helps induce sleep and limit appetite as well as improving mood by increasing serotonin. Look for a quality product and follow directions on the label.

Folic acid. Studies show that people are more likely to be depressed when they have low blood levels of B vitamins—particularly B6, B12, and folic acid—or high blood levels of the protein *homocysteine* (which, interestingly, signals the presence of inflammation and a deficiency in those three B vitamins). Coincidentally, these people are also less likely to feel better after taking antidepressants. Having a high homocysteine level actually doubles a woman's risk of developing depression. But there's good news: The higher your level of homocysteine, the more likely folic acid will work for you.

In a study that compared the effects of taking an SSRI antidepressant along with either a placebo or with folic acid, 61% of patients improved with the placebo combination, while 93% improved by adding folic acid. Three other studies showed that patients treated with folic acid improved their Hamilton Rating scores (a standardized measure of depression symptoms) by more than 50% after 10 weeks compared with those taking antidepressants.[55]

Fish oil. Numerous studies show the omega-3 fatty acids in fish oil (particularly its EPA, or *eicosapentaenoic acid*) are beneficial for mild depression. In fact, EPA seems to be a natural antidepressant, and that's confirmed by six double-blind clinical trials that showed significant improvement with fish oil. If you're not already taking fish oil every day, I urge you to start, and especially if you're feeling depressed.

Shop for a product that contains 500 mg DHA/EPA (300 mg DHA and 200 mg EPA). Take one or two capsules daily. Larger doses of fish oil can decrease the effectiveness of some glucose-lowering drugs and cause your blood sugar to rise, so always talk to your doctor before starting a new supplement. Use fish oil with caution if you're on the blood sugar-lowering medications glipizide (Glucotrol and Glucotrol XL), glyburide (Micronase or DiaBeta), Glucophage (Metformin), or insulin. Excessive omega-3 supplementation may increase your need for these medications.

TAKE ACTION TODAY: If you're feeling unhappy or "blue" for no explainable reason, try one of these remedies today. Sometimes simply talking to an understanding friend or journaling is very helpful. Life is too short to not experience joy *most* of the time. Affirm your commitment to be happy *and* healthy.

EXTRA CREDIT: Walking outside boosts your serotonin, too. Right now, put on a comfy pair of shoes and go wandering, walking around the block, the neighborhood, or your city.

---

[55] http://www.ncbi.nlm.nih.gov/pubmed/15671130

CASE STUDY: CECILLE

"I never thought I'd get off all those medications—but I did!"

Cecille was sick and sad most of the time. She had fibromyalgia, diabetes, chronic fatigue, and was catching every bug that went around. She was also on antidepressants (which is very common for diabetics). Her whole life was controlled by her symptoms and her medications. She tried exercise. She tried the Atkins Diet. Nothing seemed to help her.

Case Study: Cecille	Before	After
Weight	158	134
A1C	7.2	5.6
Blood Pressure	122/72	124/72
Triglycerides	156	78
Meds	Lexapro, Ambien, Amitriptyline, Lipitor	None

Even though Cecille was relatively thin, I put her on *The 30-Day Diabetes Cure.* (This isn't a diet; it's about healthy eating.) Her life turned around in just three months. Her craving for sugar stopped. Best of all, she was able to get off all her meds. Today, she's completely drug-free and naturally happy. (In fact, she's usually the life of the party!) She has an amazing social life—and knows how and what to eat, so "party foods" never upset her blood sugar.

DAY 18: ADD YOGA

Blessed are the flexible, for they shall not be bent out of shape.

AUTHOR UNKNOWN

HEALER: **Yoga is an excellent way to help heal your diabetes. It offers both physical and emotional benefits by providing gentle physical activity at a calming, meditative pace.**

IT'S TIME TO UNPLUG. It's time to relax. It's time to focus your energy on healing not only your body but also your mind and your heart. It's time for some "time out." To remember to breathe deeply. To release your hold on all the problems of the world. And to bring your entire self back to a state of natural balance and harmony. It's time to heal.

YOGA FOR YOUR HEALTH

Yoga is a gentle "mindful movement" practice that's tailor-made for people with diabetes—both for its positive physical effects, as well as for superior stress relief. As a physical exercise, yoga offers muscle toning, flexibility, and cardiovascular benefits at a calm, gentle, no-impact pace, making it ideal for people with chronic illness. Various movements and postures (called *asanas*) serve to stimulate different organs, including your liver, kidneys, and adrenal glands, which results in more effective natural detoxification within your body.

Yoga movements also stimulate the *vagus nerve*, which extends from your brainstem all the way down to your abdomen, carrying vital information to and from the brain. The vagus nerve is responsible for controlling your heart rate, breathing, and the entire digestive system, among other essential functions. Stimulating the vagus nerve usually causes the heart rate to slow, one of the first steps in stress reduction. Regular yoga practice can tone your heart muscle, banish depression, boost energy levels, and balance your hormones and blood chemistry.

SCIENTIFIC STUDIES PROVE IT

The Center for the Study of Complementary and Alternative Therapies at the University of Virginia Health Systems reviewed more than two dozen scientific studies on yoga for type 2 diabetes. Their research revealed impressive healing benefits of yoga for people with diabetes, including lowering fasting glucose *and* after-meal glucose by 33%, plus decreasing A1C by up to 27%. Other benefits included lowering total cholesterol by 20% and LDL cholesterol by up to 8%, while pushing up HDL cholesterol by up to 4%. Decreases in body weight (up to 8%) were also shown.

Researchers at Ohio State University found that regular yoga practice can significantly lower inflammation. Fifty women participated in the study—half had just begun to practice yoga and the other half had been at it twice a week for two years. Blood samples were taken after yoga practice, light treadmill walking, and during a stress test. All the women who didn't regularly practice yoga had 41% higher levels of pro-inflammatory *cytokine IL-6*, a substance that increases dangerous inflammation in the body.

Keeping a regular schedule of moderate exercise such as yoga helps your body use blood sugar more effectively, serving as a sort of natural "active insulin." Increased physical activity pumps more blood into your muscles and puts glucose to work as fuel. More efficient use of blood sugar also makes your system more responsive to insulin. As you begin to reduce fat and build muscle, your entire cardiovascular system operates more efficiently as well, cutting your risk of further illness and complications.

YOGA FOR STRESS RELIEF

The physical benefits are only one part of yoga's appeal. Yoga is all about balance, both outer and inner, and that balance is what can free you from stress. Yoga calms the mind because it requires concentrated attention, not just on body postures but also on your breathing. This union of breath and body brings about a peaceful state of mind, as well as a more efficient and healthy body.

Another important aspect of regular yoga practice is its emphasis on mindful living (paying close attention) in a larger context. This isn't just reserved for your body and your breath during poses. The cultivation of mindfulness also extends into your everyday behaviors and choices. You've already learned the powerful health impact that comes from making good food choices and by understanding exactly what's in most of the processed foods you once ate. You've started paying closer attention by reading labels and expanding your awareness of the choices available to you. And you're learning to distinguish between a craving, appetite, and genuine hunger. Yoga helps you extend this practice by reinforcing it through a steady commitment to mindfulness in all aspects of life.

Mindfulness is yet another key to reducing stress, because just as paying close attention to your good health becomes habitual, so too does control over your responses to stress-producing circumstances, whether spontaneous, chronic, or avoidable.

EMBARKING ON A YOGA PRACTICE

Although yoga is a 5,000-year-old practice, it was perhaps inevitable that our contemporary culture would embrace yoga as a popular fitness activity. Yoga studios offer an alternative to weight lifting, aerobics, and conventional gym exercises—but all can be complementary and a comprehensive, integrated fitness program.

Practicing yoga with a class can provide motivation, support, and added commitment. But if joining a class at your local yoga studio seems a daunting prospect, you may want to search out a private teacher for a few sessions to get you started. Learning yoga privately with individual attention may help you create a positive new ritual to start your day, in the privacy of your own home. Yoga specialists who focus on therapeutic yoga for specific health conditions will have a better understanding of the challenges you face with diabetes. To locate someone near you, go online and Google "private yoga instruction" and the name of your town. Or just visit a local yoga studio and ask if instructors offer private sessions—many do.

SOME RULES OF THUMB

Keep it calm and gentle. Leave the "power yoga" classes to others. You're seeking a gentle and calm form of yoga to heal your diabetes. Avoid upside-down postures if you have retinopathy. Shoulder stands, head stands, and even forward bends can increase pressure in the eyes. If you have questions about this, ask your ophthalmologist before starting. Diabetics with neuropathy or foot problems will want to take extra care to position themselves near a wall so that support is readily available. It's also wise to get a pair of thick-soled shoes to protect your feet and toes against injury.

Like the new food choices you've been making, you'll find that yoga does lower your blood sugar. That's a beneficial effect, but if you're taking medication, ask your doctor to adjust your drugs to accommodate your new health status. It's often recommended that you not eat for several hours before practicing yoga, but again, if you're taking medication, this may upset both your blood sugar and your energy levels. Follow your own diabetes regimen, eat something light, and there won't be a problem.

Get started today. The free beginner's guide that accompanied your purchase of this book (titled *Healing Diabetes with Yoga,* by my coauthor Jim Healthy) contains a dozen basic yoga postures for people with diabetes, complete with photos and instructions.

TAKE ACTION TODAY: Begin the daily practice of yoga to heal your diabetes, reduce your risk of further physical complications, and gain a sense of inner peace and relaxation.

EXTRA CREDIT: Put on some comfy clothes and look through the basic yoga postures in Jim Healthy's Special Report on *Healing Diabetes with Yoga*. Pick just one and try it right now. Add a new one every day until you can perform the entire series.

DAY 19: ADD BETTER SLEEP

Sleep that knits up the ravelled sleave of care
The death of each day's life, sore labour's bath
Balm of hurt minds, great nature's second course,
Chief nourisher in life's feast.

WILLIAM SHAKESPEARE

HEALER: **How much—and how well—you sleep is directly linked to blood sugar and insulin levels. Establishing good sleep patterns will make an extraordinarily positive difference in your health. Here's how to sleep better…**

WHEN DID SO MANY OF US forget how to get enough sleep? One of our most important self-healing functions of the human body, good sleep, is being completely disrupted by the 21st century trio of overcommitment, overstimulation, and overwork. We pay dearly for our incessant physical and mental stress with shorter nights and less restful sleep. Studies show that a majority of Americans are walking through their day sleep-deprived. And that is making us sick.

HOW TO DEVELOP PREDIABETES IN JUST ONE WEEK

On Day 15, I explained the link between stress and insulin resistance. Sleep deprivation—which places enormous stress on your body—worsens insulin resistance, boosting your risk of developing diabetes and making it worse if you're trying to manage the condition.

Women who slept just five hours a night were 250% more likely to have diabetes compared with those who got seven or eight hours, a study published in the *Archives of Internal Medicine* reports. In other research, scientists looked at healthy young men who slept only four hours a night for six nights in a row. Their findings were shocking: Insulin and blood sugar levels of these young guys mirrored those of people with prediabetes. You read that right: In just one week of disturbed sleep habits, they developed a prediabetic condition.

Cortisol, the stress hormone. In a 2001 study published in *Journal of Clinical Endocrinology & Metabolism*, researchers showed that chronic insomnia leads to high levels of the stress hormone *cortisol*, in addition to hyperactivity of stress-response pathways in the brain.

Cortisol release is intended as a temporary energy-booster, activated during the fight-or-flight response to get you out of real danger quickly. It triggers a rush of glucose so you get an immediate burst of energy. But cortisol is also released during the drum-drum-drumbeat of chronic everyday stress, cranking up your cravings for fast-carb foods, which leads to weight gain. High cortisol levels also suppress your immune system *and* disrupt blood sugar metabolism. The solution is to sleep longer (and better) to keep cortisol levels lower.

A well-regulated appetite. Here's another major disruption caused by lack of sleep—appetite regulation. A delicate hormone balance normally keeps your appetite in check: The hormone leptin is responsible for signaling your brain: "I'm full, stop eating." *Ghrelin* is the hormone that tells your brain, "I need fuel. Let's eat." When you're deprived of consistent restful sleep, according to researchers at University of Chicago, leptin drops by some 18% (so you don't know when to stop eating) and ghrelin shoots up (making you feel even hungrier) by almost 30%. This is how sleep duration triggers overeating.[56]

Less sleep = more weight. Researchers at the Stanford School of Medicine found that sleep-deprived subjects had an increase in body mass index (BMI) *regardless of their diet or exercise activity.* Interpreted, this means that no matter how closely you watch your food intake or how much you exercise, less sleep will increase your weight regardless.[57]

STAY AWAY FROM PRESCRIPTION SLEEPING PILLS

Getting into a pattern of healthy sleep—eight or nine hours with minimal interruptions—takes a little know-how and some new "sleep skills." Sleeping pill manufacturers, on the other hand, are counting on you not wanting to go through the trouble. They're not interested in what might be contributing to your inability to sleep. They simply want to sell you a pill that will knock you out (even though these drugs disrupt your natural metabolism, leading to unpleasant side effects and the very real possibility of addiction).

Statistics show that 10% of the US adult population has trouble sleeping, with 3 in 10 experiencing occasional sleeplessness. In addition, our nation's economic woes have created an entire class of sleep-deprived worriers. In 2009, some 27% of Americans reported losing sleep over financial anxieties, according to a poll by the National Sleep Foundation. Along with all this sleeplessness, sales of sleep drugs are soaring. In 2008, we spent a whopping $56 million on sleeping pill prescriptions—up 54% over 2004—and that number is expected to grow exponentially during these hard times.

What else do you get along with this artificially derived sleep? Next-day drowsiness, depression, memory loss, and addiction. Those are just a few examples of how these chemical intrusions disrupt your delicate metabolic processes. More bizarre are the stories of sleep-walking,

---

[56] http://www.uchospitals.edu/news/2004/20041206-sleep.html

[57] http://www.ncbi.nlm.nih.gov/pmc/articles/PMC535701/

sleep-eating, sleep-cooking, and even sleep-driving that people on these heavily advertised sleep drugs have caused. In 2007, the FDA required strong warnings on the packaging of many sleep meds because of these dangerous side effects.

BE AWARE OF YOUR SLEEP HABITS

Today I want you to start becoming more aware of your sleep habits and to begin making positive changes in your life that can contribute to peaceful, restful nights. In the process, you'll be lowering your blood sugar, increasing your insulin sensitivity, and healing your diabetes. The first step to resetting your sleep patterns is to realistically assess your own sleep patterns so you can identify the reasons you're not getting a good night's sleep. Here's what I recommend…

Keep a journal. As simple as it sounds, just keeping track of how many hours you sleep (or don't sleep) and how you spend the last few hours of the day can help you make important changes. Jot down sleep-related issues, such as what you ate for dinner, how much coffee or tea you had throughout the day, whether you drank alcohol, what you watched on TV, how late you worked, or what thoughts dominated your evening conversations. These can all affect the quality and quantity of sleep, as can napping during the day.

Stress (again). Before doing anything else, go back to Day 15 and revisit our discussion on stress. Worry, anxiety, and fear fuel sleepless nights. So do relationship issues, being overcommitted, and having financial problems. If you haven't addressed the stresses in your life yet, you need to do this now so you can start sleeping well for your health's sake. Unraveling the underlying causes of your sleeplessness puts you on track to resolve it, instead of just covering it up with a prescription.

Time for tough choices. While it's true that some medications or illnesses contribute to sleep disturbances, in general sleep problems are caused by external activities interfering with your metabolism. That means changing your habits can most likely lead to positive improvements in your quality of sleep.

TIME TO WIND DOWN NATURALLY

These low-impact ideas can help create a calm, peaceful segue from your busy work day to a quiet night of restful sleep. Read on for some specific tips…

■ Limit coffee/tea consumption to one or two cups before noon and none after that. Caffeine is a stimulant and can take several hours to fully metabolize, but everyone responds differently to caffeine. One person's afternoon pick-me-up is another's insomnia, so adjust your intake according to your own responses—or eliminate caffeine entirely. Of course, sodas and "energy drinks" are already off-limits, because they are high in sugar (another stimulant).

Alcohol is another known sleep disrupter, which is one more good reason to limit your total consumption to one or two drinks with dinner.

- Stop work-related activity two hours before bedtime. This includes computer use, reading files, making calls, texting, and checking (and responding to) email. People who work at home may find it difficult to unplug, but even people who commute to an office often find it nearly impossible to separate home life from work activity in today's tight economy. This incessant involvement with work not only deprives you of family life and "me time," but it's also stressful. And this constant mental activity keeps your brain too revved up to sleep. Give yourself a break by taking time off work in the evening before bed.

- Turn off the TV and computer and put on some quiet music. Changing your TV/computer/video viewing habits might be one of the most important ways to ensure a peaceful night's sleep. Stop watching the news close to bedtime, and tune out anything else that is mentally stimulating. Instead of being discouraged by the nightly crime report, use the last couple hours of the evening for rote, calming tasks. Sort your laundry, clean the kitchen, prepare tomorrow's lunch. I like to make the rounds in my house, checking every room, putting things in order, and closing the curtains in a meditative mind state.

- If you're in the habit of staying up past midnight and yet get up at dawn, it's time to reset your inner clock. To do this, give your body all the necessary bedtime cues much earlier than usual: Put on your PJs, brush your teeth, and pretend it's bedtime a couple hours earlier than you usually retire. Keep your house quiet and the lights low so your body can adjust by winding down naturally. If you have a social life that keeps you out late several nights a week, it's time to reassess the value of that versus the damage your lack of restful sleep may be doing to your health.

- Find evening activities that are calming, such as reading, writing in your journal, or just listening to quiet music. Remember, you don't have to be doing something all the time. Sometimes just making a to-do list relieves you of the feeling you have to accomplish everything now. Evening is also a good time to practice gentle yoga, meditation, and other relaxation techniques.

- Here's how I fall asleep every night: Once in bed, I close my eyes and begin breathing consciously, counting each exhale backward from 100. I focus my mind fully on this activity and nothing else. It's a rare night that I make it to 80.

- A few other options: Exercise revs up your metabolism, so do it early in the day, not in the evening. Take a warm or hot bath in the evening to destress, detox, and relax. One of my patients who works at home uses a steamy hot bath to separate her work day from her evening. Sip a warm glass of milk (which contains calming calcium as well as slow-digesting fat and protein) 30 minutes before going to bed. Chamomile tea is another time-tested calming influence.

- If you wake up in the middle of the night and can't get back to sleep, get out of bed for a while and putter around your house (don't watch TV or turn on the computer, though). Instead, read a poem or a calming novel. On those rare occasions when this happens to me, I sit quietly and meditate until I'm sleepy again.

SLEEPY SUPPLEMENTS

Sometimes a supplement taken regularly over time can help reset your body's natural sleep rhythms. There are a wide variety of herbs, vitamins, and minerals that help support sound sleep and target different sleep-related problems. That's why it's best to understand your own sleep patterns and stress levels *before* trying supplements.

Most supplements work best over time, so do some research. Choose one that reflects your own experience, and give it a few weeks to see if it works before stopping or switching to another. Take the lowest recommended dosage, notify your physician of whatever you're taking and follow the guidelines on Day 16 for buying quality supplement products. Here are some that I recommend to my patients…

GABA. This neurotransmitter (brain chemical) has a calming effect. Some even call it the brain's "natural Valium." Low levels of GABA (*gamma-aminobutyric acid*) can lead to anxiety symptoms, palpitations, and irritability, all of which can result in disrupted or poor-quality sleep. Eating complex slow carbs increases the amino acid *glutamine*, which is a precursor to GABA. Other foods that can help increase your natural stores of GABA include almonds, bananas, brown rice, broccoli, spinach, and whole-grain oats. You can also take GABA supplements (500 to 1,000 mg spread out through the day with meals).

Taurine. This amino acid also works in the brain to calm anxiety as well as irritability and restlessness. It works by inhibiting the release of adrenaline, the "fight-or-flight" hormone released during stress. (Bonus: Taurine also improves insulin sensitivity.) A component of meat, eggs, dairy products, and shellfish, taurine is particularly beneficial to eye health by protecting the cornea from UV ray damage and preventing macular degeneration. It's also beneficial for cardiovascular health (it lowers blood pressure and cholesterol). You should be getting plenty of taurine in your diet if you're eating animal protein, but if you want to try a supplement to see if it helps you sleep, take 500 to 1,000 mg before bed and on an empty stomach.

5-HTP. *5-hydroxytryptophan* is an amino acid that's a precursor to serotonin (one of the "feel good" hormones) and is also involved in tryptophan metabolism. As we discussed on Day 15, serotonin and tryptophan are both involved in resolving stress and anxiety. When in balance, they promote a restful night's sleep. 5-HTP has become a go-to supplement for mild depression, and it's sometimes recommended for sleeplessness as well. Follow the dosage directions on the label.

Tryptophan. This amino acid is the one food writers like to mention around Thanksgiving in articles about people falling asleep after eating their turkey dinner. Turkey (like all protein sources) is high in tryptophan, which works with serotonin and melatonin to help you get enough sleep and also move through your day with a sense of harmony and balance. Follow dosage directions on the label and take tryptophan with vitamin B6 for maximum effectiveness.

Melatonin. This is Mother Nature's "sleep hormone"—but your body's production of it decreases with age and stress. It's often recommended as a supplement to combat jet lag. In a normal metabolism, levels of melatonin rise in the evening, stay high during the night, and then drop around dawn. The amount of light you're exposed to affects your body's production of melatonin, so when the winter days are short and dark, melatonin increases, often making us feel sleepy or depressed during the day. People who work at night can find it hard to sleep during the day because their melatonin levels drop just when they need more to help them get to sleep. Melatonin can have powerful effects on your metabolism and may cause next-day grogginess. Effective dosages vary widely, so I recommend you work with your physician in trying it.

Vitamin B6: This vitamin specifically counteracts high levels of the stress hormone cortisol. If you have chronically high cortisol levels (waking at 2 am, 4 am, and 6 am is a common symptom), take 50 to 100 mg of vitamin B6 before going to bed. But remember: No supplement can halt cortisol release as well as learning to deeply relax can. Please return to Days 15 and 18 and revisit the relaxation and yoga recommendations.

TAKE ACTION TODAY: Rearrange your pre-bedtime ritual to include the suggestions above. Replace your sleep-disturbing habits with a new "sleep easy" routine to help calm your mind and wind down from the activity of the day.

EXTRA CREDIT: Twenty minutes before bedtime, dim the lights and sit comfortably on a cushion or a chair (not your bed). Close your eyes, inhale through your nose and exhale through your mouth. With every out-breath, mentally count until you reach 10, then repeat. If thoughts encroach, let them go and return to counting your breath. You should find yourself drowsy in no time.

(+)

DAY 20: ADD MORE PHYSICAL ACTIVITY

The only exercise some people get is jumping to conclusions,
running down their friends, side-stepping responsibility, and pushing their luck!

AUTHOR UNKNOWN

HEALER: **Being active is some of the best medicine for diabetes. Now it's time to push your fitness to the next level…**

ONE WEEK AGO, you discovered walking as an excellent low-impact exercise. Your daily 30-minute walk (or three 10-minute walks) should be a comfortable habit by now. Today it's time to push yourself to a higher level of fitness.

If you enjoy walking, there are several ways to make your daily jaunts more vigorous for an extra calorie burn. If you'd prefer to add a new kind of exercise to your 30 minutes of daily walking, I've got you covered there as well. Read on for other options that add low-impact, low-stress movement to your exercise routine…

TAKE WALKING TO THE NEXT LEVEL

Add trekking poles. Using walking poles began as a summer training tactic for cross-country skiers. They caught on with hikers and quickly spread from Europe to the US. There are many kinds of walking poles, including carved wooden walking sticks, lightweight bamboo poles, and lightweight aluminum "trekking" poles that can be adjusted for different conditions (shorter for walking uphill and longer for downhill).

Try before you buy. If this approach interests you, borrow some cross-country ski poles or a hiking stick from a friend before you commit to buying them. Some people don't like the click-click sound of the poles on pavement or gravel, so they add rubber stoppers to the bottom. The added fitness benefits of walking with poles include…

■	A total body workout, because your upper-body muscles are used as well as your legs. Research at the Cooper Institute in Dallas found that using walking poles increases calorie burn by up to 46%. It is estimated that an hour walking with poles burns about 400 calories compared with only 280 calories walking without them, depending on body weight.[58]

- They help propel you, which means you're working harder than usual even as the support given by the poles makes it feel easier.

- Poles assist with balance and pace. Visualize a four-legged animal and its steady front-back walking rhythm. Perfect balance can make vigorous walking feel easier. And if you're hiking in uneven terrain, the extra support can really come in handy.

- They also relieve stress on your knees, hips, and other weight-bearing joints. This is important because people with diabetes also have higher rates of osteoarthritis (due to sugar-induced inflammation).

DIFFERENT STROKES FOR DIFFERENT FOLKS

Some people love using journals and gizmos to keep track of their progress, while others don't pay much attention to these details. And while some of my patients choose a highly ordered exercise regimen, others like to keep their walking schedule light and loose. Walking with a buddy or a group can be a fine motivator, but perhaps you prefer stepping out solo. No matter what your personal style is, here are some creative ways to kick it up a notch…

Try a pedometer. A pedometer is a device that counts your steps. (If numbers inspire you, fancier models also calculate mileage, calories burned, and distance covered. Some include a time/date or stopwatch feature.) There are many brands, so shop for one that has the features you like. Small and comfortable, they can be worn all day to keep track of how many steps you've taken—and to motivate you to take even more.

Studies show that walking 6,000 to 10,000 steps a day provides the ideal health benefits. This is the equivalent of walking almost four miles or about one hour, and you can probably work up to that faster than you think. (If that sounds like a lot of steps, it may surprise you to learn that the average sedentary couch potato already takes 3,000 or more steps just getting through a normal day. So doubling or tripling the amount of steps they take isn't really a big deal.) Remember, these steps can be accumulated throughout the day—while you're doing chores around the house or moving around your office—and not just on one long dedicated walk.

A pedometer is useful because it keeps count of your steps during the day and displays your total. This comes in handy because it gives you a goal to shoot for and shows you your progress any time you want to check. So if you're short of your 10,000-step goal by late afternoon, you can reach your target with an evening stroll.

---

[58] http://walking.about.com/cs/poles/a/polestudy00_2.htm

TAKING 10,000 STEPS A DAY

By walking 10,000 steps a day, you'll easily lose 10% of your body weight, with extremely good effects on your glucose metabolism. If you're prediabetic, 10,000 steps will significantly reduce your risk of getting diabetes. Here are some clever tricks for hitting that magic number…

- Park in the farthest corner of the lot at work, when shopping, or for appointments. This will easily add hundreds of steps to your pedometer, or extra minutes to your daily walking time.

- Add a brief walk to your breaks and lunches at work. The fresh air will improve your mood and attention as well as help metabolize glucose. Walk the few blocks to your local shops or from one errand to the next instead of driving. Carry a recyclable shopping bag and you'll be helping the environment while healing your diabetes.

- Ask a friend to walk with you. This can be quality time, which is becoming rare in our fast-paced world.

- Give your dog an extra daily walk. One study showed that dog owners get nearly twice as much exercise as people without dogs. Don't have one? Get one! It's also true that 40% of pet dogs are overweight because they're not walked enough. Plus, one of the most common complications of dog obesity is—you guessed it—canine diabetes.

- Be a little less efficient at home and work. Make several trips up and down the stairs, not just one. Carry grocery bags into the house one at a time to cover more ground. Take the long way around, whether it's from house to garage, or from your office to the restroom. Choose the stairs over the elevator. Skip shortcuts to increase your total steps.

- Be creative! Challenge yourself to think of new ways to increase the number of steps you take each day. Soon you'll hit the magic 10,000 number.

OTHER HELPFUL TIPS

Keep a walking log. Some of my patients find great inspiration in watching their progress on a chart or journal, and they often bring it to their appointment to share with me. It helps them look back and see the improvements they've made in increasing their speed and distance. Some of them even record their weight loss or how mood has improved.

If you want to try this, the first stat to track is the time you walked. You can also note the distance if you know it. If you use a pedometer, you can record the number of steps you took. Also include your route, the weather, and walking companions, if any. If daily record-keeping doesn't interest you, set aside time each week to catch up with your accomplishments and goals. Your walking log will be a fitness diary you can read months or even years from now, and you'll be amazed how much you've changed your life and your health.

Step out with a group. If walking solo doesn't inspire you, join a walking group (or start one yourself). Walking with others has many benefits. In some towns, it's safer than walking alone. Group walking also relieves boredom, is more motivating, and offers the chance to socialize and make new friends. For people who are naturally drawn to groups, it can increase commitment to a walking routine. Here are some ways to keep your group engaged…

- Set regular times to walk as a group. Regardless of who shows up…walk!

- Establish group goals and make time for everyone to announce how they're doing with their goals.

- Periodically meet to cook/share healthy recipes, like those you'll find at *www.myhealingkitchen.com.*

- Share articles and books on walking. Remind each other that walking can reduce stress, help prevent heart disease, improve sleep, help maintain or lose weight, and help heal diabetes or reduce the risk of developing it.

- Invite a speaker or a personal trainer to teach you more about the relationship between diabetes and fitness.

- Share ideas for interesting new walk routes.

Turn on the tunes. The evidence is undeniable: Music helps you walk faster and farther (and makes your walking a lot more fun!). A study published in 2002 by Ohio State University researchers found that people who listened to music while walking traveled four more miles than the control group who didn't use music. Reason? Music helps distract you from the tedium of exercise, makes it more pleasurable, and also increases your respiration and heart rate. Most of all, playing music you love provides motivation. Just be certain you're not missing any safety cues—like traffic noises.

WALK FOR CHARITY

You can help others while you're helping yourself by walking for a worthy cause. Charity walking events are great ways to meet others who share a cause. Here's a short list of organized walks for different causes…

- Walk for Diabetes. As someone living with diabetes, you can become a red strider and proudly wear the red T-shirt while you reverse your condition with my 30-day plan.

- JDRF Walk to Cure Diabetes. The Juvenile Diabetes Research Foundation walkathon is held in more than 200 locations to raise funds for diabetes research.

Other charity walking events include…

- American Heart Walk

- Race for the Cure

- Avon Walk for Breast Cancer

- MS Challenge Walk

- National Kidney Foundation Walk

- March of Dimes Walk America

- Leukemia & Lymphoma Society Light the Night Walk

- American Cancer Society Relay for Life

- Arthritis Foundation Walk

- Great Strides Walk for Cystic Fibrosis

SPINNING YOUR WHEELS

Another great way to burn calories and get in shape is by *spinning*. This is a cardiovascular workout done on a stationary bike that can be adjusted to simulate riding uphill on flat ground. Some spinning bikes have an onboard computer that tracks your mileage, speed, and distance—and even a heart monitor to keep track of your heart rate and calories burned.

Here's what's great about spinning: It's safer than riding a bicycle on the road. You aren't limited by the weather or the time of day. It's easy on your weight-bearing joints (unlike jogging). And it burns a lot of calories (a 30-minute spinning session can burn 500 calories, melting away extra pounds).

Gyms and health clubs usually offer spinning classes run by a highly motivating trainer who incorporates warm-up and cool-down periods, as well as plenty of heart-healthy routines in between. Here are some other health benefits of spinning…

It's aerobic and anaerobic. As an aerobic activity (meaning it increases your heart rate) spinning strengthens your heart muscle and lungs. Its anaerobic attributes include burning energy from stored fat and building muscle endurance, particularly in your legs.

You're in control. You can adjust resistance levels, regardless of what an instructor or video recommends, to progress at your own pace.

Group support. Spinning classes offer camaraderie and support as well as a sense of accomplishment and self-confidence. It's an opportunity for commitment, endurance, follow-through, and mental strength. (Of course, you can purchase your own stationary bike to use at home.)

HIT THE POOL RUNNING

Water-walking is even more low-impact than spinning, but it's a solid workout. It's easy on your joints because water's buoyancy reduces your body weight by 90% (really helpful if you're overweight). But because water is 800% more dense than air, it creates resistance that burns serious calories and strengthens your legs and core muscles as you walk, whether it's in the shallow end or the deep end (with a flotation belt). The deeper the water, the more strenuous your workout—and the more weight you'll lose.

Water-walking is so beneficial that it's the first physical activity elite athletes use when rehabbing after an injury or surgery. Ditto for patients in European hospitals immediately following joint replacement. It's also the therapy of choice for injured racehorses!

With water's buoyancy neutralizing the wear-and-tear pressure that gravity exerts on your joints, water-walking helps the surrounding muscles get strong enough to take up the slack. Plus, being in the water is comfortable for people who resist physical activity. You'll never again say "exercise hurts too much."

How to take the plunge. To start, stand in water that's waist deep or chest-deep. Walk as you would on dry land, but pump your arms more vigorously. Pay attention to these helpful tips…

Watch your form. Stand upright with your shoulders back and chest lifted. Stride forward, placing your whole foot (not just your tiptoes) on the bottom of the pool. Let your heel land first, followed by the ball of your foot. To avoid straining your back, engage the core muscles in your abdomen, tightening your stomach as you walk.

Add intensity. As you become more proficient, increase the challenge by lifting your knees higher. Let this naturally take you into a slow "water jog" for 10 strides and then return to walking. (This is called interval training because it mixes periods of exertion with less-strenuous segments.) Try walking backward and sideways to tone other muscles.

Try deep-water running (DWR). The aerobic and calorie-burning benefits of DWR can be superior to running on land. Both DWR and water-walking help reduce body fat and keep your heart muscle strong.

Benefits of water-walking…

- **Puts less stress on your heart.** While some exercises boost your heart rate, if you have health challenges, you may not want too much added stress on your heart, even while you're building new levels of endurance. Studies show that the exercising heart rate in water is up to 20 beats-per-minute *lower* than on land.

- **Builds muscle tone and strength.** Shallow-water aerobic exercise builds real muscle strength—the kind that keeps you strong and active. One study showed that untrained women who performed shallow-water aerobics for just eight weeks achieved significantly greater gains in several strength areas compared with the land-based control group—even though the aqua aerobics routine included no specific muscle-strengthening exercises.

■ **Leads to greater flexibility.** Four separate studies confirm that water exercise classes bestow increased flexibility (especially in the lower back and hamstrings). Researchers say the buoyant properties of water decrease joint stress while allowing a greater range of motion in joints and muscles.

With all that it has going for it, isn't it time you hit the pool? Plenty of public pools and gyms now offer aqua-aerobics and aqua-step classes. Some people like having an instructor and find it fun to work out in a group, although water-walking can be as simple as taking a stroll up and down a lap lane. To find a class near you, contact your local YMCA or fitness center.

MORE POOL TOOLS

If you're not big on swimming, the pool can still be your favorite workout arena. Besides water-walking, there's also a wide array of aqua exercise equipment, including aqua-steppers, aqua-cycles, and water workout stations. Check out *www.aquatic-exercise-equipment.com/Products.html* for a glimpse. For water shoes (I recommend them for better traction), aqua barbells, flotation belts, aqua joggers, and a mind-boggling array of water workout DVDs—everything from Aqua Samba to Aquatic Pilates—go to *www.waterworkout.com*. For the ultimate in aquatic exercise luxury, you must see the underwater treadmill at *www.activeforever.com*.

ONE FINAL WORD ON EXERCISE

I understand that you're busy. In fact, very few people have hours of free time just waiting to be filled with exercise. The reason healthy people exercise every day is because they make time for it. Even if you go from dawn until dark managing your home, family, and business, you can reserve 10 minutes three times a day in your schedule for a brisk walk. All it takes is your commitment. Once you get into the regular habit and feel the positive benefits, it will be easier to expand that time to do even more.

If your health condition limits you to a short walk once or twice a day, you'll still be better off than sitting on the couch. Physical activity gets your blood flowing, which improves circulation. Keeping your blood moving, your heart pumping, and your limbs swinging freely slows the production of inflammatory chemicals and limits the damage that free radicals can do.

Physical activity is not "optional" for people with diabetes. Consider it *medicine* that you must take every day to stay alive. But unlike most medicines that merely manage your symptoms, physical activity can actually heal the underlying cause of your condition and reverse it. That's just another way of saying "cure!"

TAKE ACTION TODAY: Make a commitment to take at least 10,000 steps every day starting now. Don't procrastinate. Go to your local sporting goods store or go online to purchase a pedometer. Slip it on your waistband and start tracking your steps immediately.

EXTRA CREDIT: Visit a nearby health club or your local YMCA/YWCA and sample a spin class or try water-walking today. It doesn't matter if you aren't a member. Most clubs will issue you a free temporary pass (sometimes good for up to a week) if you tell them you're investigating becoming a member. "Just do it!"

CASE STUDY: LINDA

"No more sugary fitness food for me!"

Case Study: Linda	Before	After
Weight	154	132
A1C	6.4	5.2
Blood Pressure	128/82	120/76
Triglycerides	194	138
Meds	-	-

Linda is a personal trainer in her 50s who followed a very healthy natural diet, but her energy drinks, protein bars, and smoothies were too high in natural sugars. Linda and I run in the same circles and one day she asked me for an appointment because she had started to feel unusually tired all the time. Linda ate a natural diet but she exercised hard all day long with her clients. She took in a lot of calories but she burned them too. Now she was having trouble recovering from her daily workouts with clients, and despite her best efforts, she was starting to get "soft." "Soft" is a word that athletic types use when they are starting to lose that beautiful, lean, muscle definition they strive for. And for Linda that spelled trouble. One of the ways personal trainers gather and keep clients is by looking fantastic. If her program didn't work for her, it threw everything she did into question.

Linda was sure her fatigue was just a hormonal problem rather than a dietary one. I didn't think it was "just a hormone problem." All the exercise in the world can't turn around an imbalanced diet and sooner or later it catches up with us. Linda got off junk protein bars and smoothies. After just two weeks on *The 30-Day Diabetes Cure*, things began to turn around. She got her energy back and soon lost 22 pounds.

PHASE III:

Ready for the Outside World

Days 21 to 30

The gem cannot be polished without friction,
nor man perfected without trials.

CHINESE PROVERB

(-)

DAY 21: ELIMINATE BAD EATING HABITS

He who does not mind his belly will hardly mind anything else.

SAMUEL JOHNSON

ANTI-HEALER: **Eating when you're stressed, driving, watching TV, or having a cocktail leads to overeating, extra calories, and poor food choices. It also dulls your sense of when to stop eating. Today let's take a closer look at unconscious eating patterns and how to transform them...**

HOW MANY DECISIONS did you make today about what to eat? At Cornell University, researchers asked study participants to estimate how many food decisions they make every day. Most said 15, but the researchers found that we actually make more than *200 choices per day* about what, where, and when we eat. The difference between 200 and 15 tells us a lot about how many of those choices are unconscious. You could even speculate that the folks in that study were making a whopping 185 unconscious food choices per day!

How can this be? Start by considering how often you eat while doing something else. Does food accompany you while you're driving, reading, working at the computer, or watching TV? If you automatically reach for something to eat when you curl up on the couch to watch a movie, it's easy to lose track of how much you've swallowed. And if you're not aware of how much you're eating, you won't know when to stop.

DISTRACTED EATING IS A BAD HABIT

In a study done at Johns Hopkins University, participants who watched TV while eating a bowl of macaroni and cheese were mostly unable to accurately report how much they'd eaten. Plus, research published in the *British Journal of Nutrition* found that participants who were given food while they played a computer game wanted to eat even *more* when they finished the game. A separate group (given the same amount of food without any distraction) not only knew how much they'd eaten but also didn't want any extra.[59]

---

[59] http://www.liebertonline.com/doi/abs/10.1089/bar.2006.9991

You may have experienced this yourself. Once your attention is diverted from the act of eating—whether you're online, watching a video, or reading a book—your unconscious mind takes over the eating process. There's no mystery here. Your conscious mind simply isn't paying attention to whether or not you're full because it's busy doing other things. It's almost as though you've entered a kind of trance. Suddenly the food is gone and you don't even remember eating it.

If you aren't aware of how much you're eating, you can't control consumption—and that means you'll gain weight. Researchers at Baylor College of Medicine in Houston queried a large group of fourth, fifth, and sixth graders about their TV and eating habits and discovered the overweight kids ate 50% of their dinners while watching TV. Compare that to the normal-weight children, who ate 35% of their dinners in front of the tube. (I'd say that's still too many kids eating in front of TV, wouldn't you?)

The youngsters who ate dinner with TV also ate more food overall—and more junk food and sodas in particular—consuming fewer healthy foods than the kids who had meals at the table with their families more frequently. While this indicates how closely family issues are related to calorie intake, the evidence is clear: It's easy to overeat when you're otherwise engaged. And when you plop kids down in front of TV with supper, you're setting them up for a lifetime of distracted eating.

SLOW THE PACE TO FEEL FULL

We also tend to eat *faster* when our attention is diverted, and so we miss internal signals that are there to help us. Eat too quickly and your body doesn't release the appropriate "I'm full" signal from the hormone leptin. A fascinating study by Greek and British researchers published in the *Journal of Clinical Endocrinology* found that when participants *slowly* ate a large snack broken up into small portions, their digestive tracts released hormones that made them feel full. Importantly, those hormones remained elevated for several hours, curbing their appetites even further.[60]

Participants who rushed through a snack of the same size didn't release the same amount of leptin, meaning their brains didn't receive the signal to stop eating. In this same study, researchers found that when participants were instructed to chew thoroughly and enjoy the experience of eating a meal, they ate fewer calories than those who were told to rush through it.

Not surprisingly, eating too quickly also triggers heartburn, acid reflux, and GERD (gastroesophageal reflux disease), Stephen Wildi of the Medical University of South Carolina found. That means more than just momentary discomfort. Those stomach acids washing back up into your throat can also permanently damage your esophagus. Bottom line? If you're distracted, rushing, or not paying attention to what you're eating, you're bound to overeat.

---

[60] http://jcem.endojournals.org/cgi/content/full/93/6/0

EATING AS AN EMOTIONAL BAND-AID

For many people, a stressful day, a fight with a loved one, or money worries often trigger eating ice cream directly from a carton. Who hasn't reached for food during times of emotional stress? Eating comfort foods during troubled times may satisfy you for a few minutes, but when they're high in sugar or fast carbs and low in healing nutrients, you run a serious risk of making your diabetes worse.

"Comfort foods" are those that are eaten to obtain a certain emotional feeling (or to maintain one). These foods produce emotion-altering effects in the brain that are as powerful as recreational or prescription drugs. This type of emotional eating accounts for a full 75% of overeating,[61] researchers say.

By understanding the signals of emotional eating, you may be able to see it coming and thwart it. Here are some clues from the University of Texas Counseling and Mental Health Center...

- Craving a specific food, such as ice cream or pie, because it's the only food that will "satisfy" your desire. That's eating to feed emotional hunger.

- Immediate gratification compels you. You want the food now. (With normal physical hunger mechanism, actual hunger comes on slowly.)

- Emotional eating can leave you feeling guilty.

- Eating to fill up an emotional need often leads to overeating. (You can fill a hungry stomach; but a hungry soul requires a lot more.)

Stress is also a major factor not only in overeating but also for eating the wrong foods. In 2005, researchers at Montclair State University ran two studies on the effects of stress on food choices. Stressed-out participants consistently chose M&M's over grapes, and more women than men turned to food when they were under stress. Researchers also found that twice as many participants who reported they were "dieting" turned to off-limits foods when they were stressed than participants who weren't on a diet.

If eating—or compulsive overeating—is your refuge during emotionally challenging times, consider the deeper emotional reasons for your distress and address the underlying causes.

WHAT YOU EAT...AND WHY

Emotional eating is usually driven by happiness, sadness, anger, or boredom. And just by recognizing your emotional state can help you solve the riddle of why you are eating. Here are some tips that may help...

---

[61] http://www.webmd.com/diet/features/emotional-eating-feeding-your-feelings?page=2

- Learn to recognize the warning signals of emotional eating. For instance, pay special attention to these issues: When and what do you eat? Why do you eat? What happened immediately before you reached for food? Keep a food journal and write down the dates and times you ate impulsively. Answer important questions about why you did it ("I was angry at my boss," "I felt trapped by my boyfriend," "Caring for my mother stresses me out"). Your growing awareness of these underlying motives can help ease you out of habitual and unconscious eating behaviors. And they'll certainly allow you to further unravel and resolve these complicated issues without resorting to food.

- Joining a support group, especially one for people with diabetes, can help you address the emotional or impulsive eating patterns that are sabotaging your efforts to heal your condition. I'll discuss this in more detail on Day 24.

- If your eating habits are out of control because of emotional factors, now is a good time to get help. Eating disorders are serious business and require professional treatment to help you sort out their deep emotional roots. Consider this a crucial part of your overall healing process. Ask your doctor to recommend a specialist who can help you with your eating disorder.

HOW TO FREE YOURSELF

You've learned an incredible amount about the health dangers in processed foods, including common breakfast foods, fast-food lunches, soft drinks, and snack foods. If you haven't fully eliminated these foods and replaced them with the whole, nutritious healing foods I've been recommending, you may need to return to Day 1 and start again. Quitting sugary foods is a big first step in helping you regain control over emotional eating. You really can't navigate the next step until you've mastered the previous one. It may take you longer than 30 days to get through this program. So what? The most important thing is that you complete every step. If emotional eating is a problem for you, try these suggestions to free yourself…

Find a new definition of "comfort foods." When she's looking for comfort in food, one of my patients bakes sweet potatoes with raisins and cinnamon and eats them with low-fat sour cream. Is she giving in to emotional eating? Yes, but she's choosing to satisfy it with health-giving diabetes healing foods. She's craving sugar, but she's getting it from naturally sweet potatoes and raisins. This is a wiser choice.

Get distracted. If you're a bored emotional eater, make a deal with yourself. Next time you think you need to eat, have a large glass of water and get outside for a 20-minute walk instead. Make sure you breathe as you stride. Still hungry? Choose any of the healthy snacks from Day 8.

Work your hands. One of most popular "boredom" foods is potato chips, and there's little wonder why. There's something curiously satisfying about all that hand, mouth, and crunch activity. Keeping your hands busy with something else—knitting, needlework, solitaire, an instrument, stroking a pet—can keep them distracted from junky foods (which you shouldn't have in the house anyway). If you really must snack, get a bowl of pistachios (in the shell). They'll keep you busy and you won't consume a lot of calories.

Try yoga or meditation. Put on some comfy clothes and move into several of your favorite yoga poses, concentrating on your breath and being mindful of nothing more than your limber body. Meditation is also good for diverting mindless eating habits. Return to Day 18 for more on yoga and managing stress.

POSITIVE EATING HABITS

Eat well all day long. By eating three meals a day all made of the Diabetes-Healing Superfoods—with satisfying snacks in between—you'll be able to move from meal to snack without the rampant hunger pangs that trigger impulsive, unconscious eating.

If a big project or a long meeting delays your lunch, select a healing snack combo (nuts, cheese, or garlic-yogurt with raw veggies or fresh fruit) to tide you over until you can eat a real meal. One of my patients always has cold chicken breast in the fridge for potential missed meals. Another eats avocado and salad greens for breakfast! It doesn't matter to me what you enjoy for breakfast or a snack, as long as you're eating a good variety of diabetes-healing foods.

Remember too: Whole, natural foods not only stabilize blood sugar but also trim your weight. High-quality meats, eggs, artisan cheeses, whole grains such as brown rice along with generous servings of fresh vegetables provide steady, stable sources of energy that will carry you through your day without being tempted by a sugary snack in your quest for energy.

Choose snacks you love. Keep a stash of your favorite diabetes-healing snacks on hand at home, in the car, and at work. If it's raw veggies and hummus, keep it handy and enjoy every mouthful. If it's fruit and cheese, go for it! Remember the dark chocolate we discussed on Day 8? A couple of small pieces with a few walnuts will nail cravings to the wall. One patient of mine finds immediate satisfaction in a tablespoon of natural peanut butter spread on a whole-grain slice of bread studded with a few raisins or banana slices.

Drink water. Honestly, if I had a dollar for every patient I saw who was trying to satisfy thirst with food, I could make a big charitable donation. Drink up, people! On Day 4, we talked about how you need 64 ounces a day. It's a common error to mistake hunger for thirst. Grab a large glass of water or some iced herbal tea. It's a good habit to develop and it will flood your belly and body with life-giving fluids.

Eliminate cocktail snacking. Sipping alcohol and nibbling bar snacks go hand-in-hand. This is an easy way to take in a lot of unconscious calories. That's why I recommend patients who want a glass of wine or cocktail have it with or after dinner. Your hunger's been satisfied by a nice diabetes-healing dinner and your stomach is full. If you do drink, this is the ideal way to do it, since the alcohol will be metabolized slowly via your full stomach.

TOP 11 WAYS TO CURB OVEREATING

1. **Eat on a regular schedule.** This means planning in advance what you'll be eating throughout the day—and preparing a healthy breakfast, lunch, dinner, plus snacks for yourself until you're ready for restaurants (coming tomorrow!).

2. **Go grocery shopping.** You can't prepare these healing meals and snacks unless you shop regularly—and wisely. Keep all the Diabetes-Healing Superfoods we've discussed on hand. Stock your fridge with fruits, vegetables, and high-quality meats, eggs, and dairy products. Fill your pantry with staples like beans, whole grains, and assorted nuts.

3. **Trash the junk.** If you still have junky snack foods in your cupboards, you'll be tempted to eat them. So make sure there are no sodas, crackers, chips, cookies, cheese puffs, boxed cereals, doughnuts, muffins, and frozen dinners hiding out in your kitchen. Ditch the processed lunch meats and juice boxes too. You can't indulge if it's not available.

4. **Enlist family support.** Don't use your kids as an excuse to keep unhealthy foods in the house. This junk is just as bad for them as it is for you. Tell your children there's plenty to snack on: apples, pears, bananas, cheese, nuts, fresh milk, plus raw veggies with nutritious dips. If they whine, put your foot down. The food habits they learn while growing up are the ones they'll cling to as adults—and pass on to their children. Your family may not have diabetes, but they could be heading that way if they eat the typical American diet. Teach your children how to cook with whole, natural foods instead of merely opening cans and boxes, or microwave frozen meals.

5. **Learn to cook with whole foods.** If *you* don't know how to cook, then learn. I believe one of the biggest reasons diabetes has reached epidemic proportions in the US is because we don't really know how to cook. Our parents got sucked into the lure of "instant" prepared meals and that's what we grew up eating. But these prepared foods are the very ones that are upsetting our blood sugar and making us fat. The situation is so bad that most young children can't even name fresh fruits and vegetables when they're held up in front of them! They have no clue where milk or cheese or eggs come from. It's up to you to educate them by example. Knowing how to really cook is not just a survival skill; it's a pleasurable, creative activity. It's an *art* that anyone can learn.

Where do you begin? The famous British chef Jamie Oliver suggests that every homemaker have five or six reliable "go to" recipes made from fresh, natural foods. If you're looking for a variety of easy and delicious Diabetes-Healing Meals, I recommend you become a regular visitor to the free *www.myhealingkitchen.com* Web site. I've eaten some of them—and they are truly delicious!

6. **Set a pleasant table and eat all your meals there.** (Never eat standing!) Eating while standing at the sink only encourages you to wolf down food when you don't need it—and can't keep track of it. Eating in front of the TV removes your attention from the flavors of food and the enjoyment of eating it. Set an artistic table (even if you're eating alone) and relax with all the accoutrements you'd find in an upscale restaurant: nice dinnerware, handsome flatware, and a cloth napkin. Include water with lemon and a small vase of flowers. Add some calming music and a candle. (Why bother? Doing so dignifies the act of nourishing yourself and honors life, as well as yourself.) If you eat lunch at your desk, put your computer to sleep and turn your phone off for 15 minutes. Clear a space that will allow you to eat without being distracted by unfinished projects. Better yet, find a spot outside to eat, weather permitting, and take a brisk walk afterward. You'll be refreshed and energized when you return to work.

7. **Create a food journal.** Keep a notebook handy and write down everything you eat and what time you ate it. In just a few days, you'll have black-and-white evidence of the choices you've made that don't serve your quest for health. You may also see patterns—such as a mid-morning run to the vending machine—that you can reroute by keeping healing foods at the ready. Return to Day 8 for some delicious snack ideas you can take to work.

8. **Trust your feelings.** When you find yourself reaching for comfort food in times of distress, recognize that your feelings need attention and real healing. Also recognize that food isn't the answer. If you have emotional stress that's causing out-of-control eating, get help. Call a friend, write in your journal, talk to a trusted spiritual advisor. Then join a diabetes support group. Just being with people who know what you're going through can nourish your soul. If you need more help, ask your doctor or local diabetes support group for a referral to a good therapist. More on getting support on Day 24.

9. **Eat when you're hungry.** Are you hungry on everyone else's mealtime schedule? Great. But if you're not, don't fight it. You don't have to eat a full meal just because it's time for dinner. Knowing that you're not very hungry is the first step toward voluntary portion control. Having a scrambled egg and salad for dinner is a fine choice if you have only a small appetite. Make good food choices…keep your blood sugar stable…and eat when you're hungry. One of my patients regularly eats like a longshoreman at breakfast, having lean protein and vegetables plus rice. She says it carries her through the day and she fills in later on with raw veggies and fruit. Who am I to argue!

10. **Become a unitasker.** Eating while driving is a good way to crash the car. Eat while working and you risk a moo-shu pork spattered keyboard. If you're ready to eat, *stop* doing everything else. If you're stuck on the road and need a quick bite, reach for one of the healthful snacks you stocked your car with to keep your blood sugar stable. But if you need a meal, stop the car and sit down in a restaurant, café, or roadside picnic area to eat. Or pop into a grocery for an apple, some cheese, and a plain yogurt and savor it before continuing on your journey.

11. **Enjoy eating!** Pay attention to your food—what it tastes like, what it looks like. Say a little prayer of thanks, even if you're not religious. Eat slowly and mindfully, as you chew, taste, and swallow. Invite a friend to eat with you—companionship over food is a human treasure. Remind yourself with every meal (and every bite) that the food you're sharing is directly healing your diabetes.

TAKE ACTION TODAY: Pay attention to when you eat, what you eat, and why you eat. You're in charge of your eating habits. By starting to understand what compels you to eat and how this contributes to your diabetes, you can take control and make changes.

EXTRA CREDIT: To develop (or rekindle) a burning passion for real food, rent the movie *Julie and Julia*. Starring Meryl Streep in the lead role as the famous chef Julia Child, this sweet story will give you a deeper insight into how eating and cooking with real food can elevate your overall *joie de vivre* (the French expression for "the joy of living").

(+)

DAY 22: ADD RESTAURANTS, PARTIES AND TRAVVEL

The greatest glory in living lies not in never failing,
but in rising every time we fail.

NELSON MANDELA

HEALER: **Yes, you're finally ready for the outside world! You know enough—and are strong enough—to tiptoe through the most dangerous dietary minefields out there. Here's how to sidestep the food bombs and tempting traps that make life in the "real world" so challenging for most people with diabetes…**

YOU'VE BEEN LEARNING and practicing for the past three weeks. Now it's time to spread your wings and fly off into the outside world and put your newfound skills and knowledge to the real test. It's out of the incubator for you! I want you to feel confident that you can have an active social life without constantly worrying about the temptations and pressures you're going to face—and the nagging doubt that you can't succeed. You can!

You may not succeed perfectly your first time out. In fact, you may slip and fall many, many times. But I have every confidence that, having come this far, you have what it takes to go all the way. Restaurants, parties, and traveling represent the most challenging situations that a person with diabetes faces. Finding healthy, healing meals in these circumstances will test you to the limits. And facing down those ooey, gooey splurge foods you couldn't resist in the past might make you sweat a little. (It's a lot like running into an old flame—you know, the one who trashed your heart so badly—and having him or her invite you over for a "friendly drink.") But you're wiser now; there are plenty of clever tricks you can employ to avoid the temptation—or else, just say no.

DINING OUT WITH SAVVY

Restaurants are redolent with memories of the days when you could eat whatever (and as much as) you desired. Those were the days before you knew there were consequences to this lasciviousness. Yet all those alluring triggers still linger. First comes the bread basket. Then the waiter asks if you want a cocktail or wine. The menu is filled with so many lavish indulgences: fried this…double-stuffed that…and outrageous entrées that haven't touched your lips for weeks. And—oh my God!—look at those desserts! Your friends are ordering to their heart's content. What will you do? What will you choose? How the heck will you ever manage not to indulge?

Awareness is your saving grace. I'm confident that you'll be fine because you have a powerful new force working for you now—and that's your *awareness*. You've developed the skill to watch your mind as all these temptations arise. You're no longer living unconsciously, reacting to every trigger compulsively. Instead, you're able to notice all these vivid sensations and seductions pestering you as if they were little children begging you to put every treat and goodie they see on the supermarket shelves in your shopping cart. Do you do it? Of course not; because you know that junk isn't good for them.

How to navigate the menu. By now you should be pretty adept at knowing what you should and shouldn't eat. Skip the bread basket. (If you're having wine, sip it with your meal instead of before.) Start with soup (not cream based) to fill you up. Follow that with salad with extra-virgin olive oil and balsamic vinegar on the side so you can control the amount. Then pick an entrée of either fish, poultry, or lean meat—surrounded by lots of veggies. If you must have a potato, request a small one (without the sour cream and bacon bits), add a small pat of butter, and eat it skin and all. If you're at a restaurant that serves exceptionally large portions, immediately divide your plate and ask your waiter to put half in a doggie bag so you won't be tempted to overeat.

What about dessert? You just ate a lot of food (volume-wise, but not in calories), so you should be stuffed. If you still have room for dessert, pick something sensible and split it with your dining companions. One or two spoonfuls should satisfy you. Studies show that after three bites, our taste buds don't register the sweetness anymore. So savor those first spoonfuls. Have a cup of herbal tea with dessert and alternate sips with bites.

Most of all, relax and enjoy yourself. Dining out shouldn't be a science project. (Nor should it be a self-indulgent "reward" for being "good" all week. The real treat is that you don't have to cook or clean up!)

THE MOST IMPORTANT DECISION: *WHERE* TO EAT

Planning is everything, right? You learned how important it is to have a shopping list at the supermarket…to pack your lunch whenever possible…and to never be without a baggie of safe snacks. Well, planning which restaurant you'll dine at is equally important. Why? Because you never want to be hungry in a place that doesn't offer you some healthy menu options.

Fast-food restaurants. You already know about the unhealthy ingredients that they pack into the menu. You're not going to get a satisfying meal in these establishments. Even their "healthy" salads are pretty bad. And the salad dressings they serve are loaded with excess calories and unhealthy fats, as well as high-fructose corn syrup, artificial flavors, and chemical preservatives. The point is, you're developing an appreciation of—and a hankering for—real foods that are artfully prepared. You won't find them at these places, so why waste your time or money? If the gang is headed off to the Golden Arches, excuse yourself, because it's not worth the stress and frustration.

National chains. The same is true for most of the big restaurant chains, although if you're skillful and disciplined, you can surely find something tasty and healthful. You may have to ask the waiter for substitutions (such as a side salad for the fries), but it is possible to get a good meal. A few chains offer humanely raised meats and organic produce (Chipotle Grill is one in particular). Olive Garden menu items are notoriously sodium saturated, so you'll have to request that the chef adds no salt. When ordering Chinese stir-fries, request minimum oil and no MSG. Don't be afraid to speak up for yourself. Most restaurants are happy to accommodate special needs and requests. After all, you're the one paying the bill. Here are some safe bets when deciding on a restaurant…

Seafood specialists. It's hard to go wrong with a nice piece of fresh fish or a pile of seafood surrounded by fresh veggies. Just be sure not to order anything fried (no matter how much you crave the Coconut Shrimp).

Thai food. Always a good choice because the cuisine is loaded with veggies, while featuring seafood, lean meat, and poultry. Stay away from the Pad Thai (which is fried noodles), but the soups, curries, and stir-fries are healthful and low in calories. Most restaurants even offer brown rice.

Asian cuisine. Not the Chinese buffet, please, with its chemically fluorescent sweet and sour sauces and oil-drenched veggies and meats. Stick to smaller Korean, Chinese, and Vietnamese restaurants offering homestyle meals. Go for the brightly colored vegetable stir-fries loaded on brown rice. Add some tofu or seafood for protein. Have the chef go easy on the oil.

Mediterranean. Probably not Olive Garden, but restaurants that feature fish, lean meat, lots of vegetables, and yummy salads are a great choice. "Italian-theme" restaurants are hit and miss because they usually feature pizza and pasta, which contain a lot of refined carbs. Some pizzerias offer whole-wheat or whole-grain crust. I usually request half the normal amount of cheese, plus extra veggies and tomato sauce.

Japanese. This cuisine sits high on my list of diabetes-healing restaurants. There's always fish, raw and cooked, and there may be brown rice instead of white for sushi. Nibbling steamed edamame (green soybeans) as an appetizer is a sure hit. You can usually get grilled wild salmon beautifully presented with a choice of vegetables. And you can't go wrong with soba noodles (made of buckwheat) with a veggie stir-fry. Avoid the white rice and anything "tempura" (deep-fried).

Diners. Believe it or not, most diners offer a wide array of real foods, starting with the ubiquitous omelet. Eggs are your friend any time of day and can be accompanied by a wide variety of diabetes-healing ingredients, including Spinach and feta in the classic Greek omelet…tomatoes and green peppers for the Denver…or a plain cheese omelet, one of my favorite comfort foods. Diners also offer veggie side orders. Feel free to order green beans, baked beans, and salad in place of toast and potatoes.

HOW TO SURVIVE THE HOLIDAYS

You've been invited to a holiday party, a potluck dinner, or you're meeting up with friends to watch the big game. You know there will be bowls of chips and snack foods, a cooler with sodas, and a fridge full of beer. Unidentifiable potluck casseroles will line the kitchen counter. No matter what the holiday, it seems there are always piles of cookies and bowls of candy. It's time to strategize (remember the power of planning)…

Eat before you go. This may sound counterintuitive—after all, you're going to a party and there's going to be a lot of food there! And that's exactly why you should eat a filling, balanced meal with plenty of protein and veggies shortly before you leave the house. With a full stomach, you'll be far less tempted by the snack table and dessert foods. When you arrive, find some club soda and sip a glass throughout the party.

But I'm going to a party right after work. The secret of living a diabetes-healing life in the outside world is planning ahead. When you know there's going to be an after-work party, plan the night before to take some leftovers you can microwave and eat before you leave work. Or put together a heftier snack pack than usual, including protein (hard-boiled eggs, turkey slices with cheese), plus some nice slow carbs (raw veggie crudités and a half-cup of kidney bean salad with bean dip or hummus), and don't forget to take a small bag of nuts.

Potluck jackpot. Potlucks are great news for us who enjoy eating well. Someone (maybe it's you) always brings a big salad. Someone (you again?) ensures that there's a colorful raw veggie tray filled with freshly cut carrots and celery sticks, chopped broccoli, and cherry tomatoes. "Someone" might include a tangy dip made with garlicky Greek yogurt and herbs. The possibilities are endless and healing. For instance: Cook up a pot of chili from grass-fed ground beef (or bison) with two or three varieties of beans. Make cole slaw with vinegar and oil dressing (instead of the traditional mayo) and lots of freshly chopped herbs. The bottom line? Bring diabetes-friendly dishes that you can enjoy.

Buffet survival skills. Cruise the offerings for those with maximum protein: Choose meatballs over pasta salad. Skip the mac-and-cheese and choose the chili. Load up on salad and veggies.

Nibble from the cheese tray, but leave the crackers behind. If you're having a cocktail, go for a Bloody Mary (or a white wine spritzer) and nurse it to the max.

Focus on friendship. You're at the party to enjoy being with friends and meeting new people. If you don't make food your primary focus, you can put time and energy into the people instead.

TIPS FOR TRAVEL

Travel presents an endless series of obstacles and hurdles to eating well. Whether you're on the road, in an airport, in a train or driving, don't be tempted to mess up your progress by eating what's available. Airports and conference hotels are virtual dead zones when it comes to finding fresh, nutritious food. So is much of the US highway system. Along with an abundance of packaged processed food, greasy-spoon restaurants, and fast-food chains, it's difficult to find truly healthy options. But it's not impossible. Here are some tips that can help…

Get a map. If you arrive at an airport or a train station without food, may the force be with you. Your only real option is to check a map, locate all nearby restaurants, and choose the places that at least offer a salad and fresh fruit. At breakfast, skip the fast-carb bagels and choose scrambled eggs. Ask for fresh tomato slices or fruit instead of potatoes. And pass on the processed and preserved breakfast meats.

Pack your snacks. Remember my advice to never leave home without a personal food supply? This is especially important when traveling long distances. You will never find a healthy meal or snack on an airplane (unless you're traveling First Class to Europe). Yes, you'll have a little more pretravel packing to do, but given flight delays and the absolutely dismal offerings in travel hubs, you'll be very glad you took the time.

One of my patients even takes a small cooler with her when she flies and packs her diabetes-healing snacks in it. She's never been caught hungry except for flights when she's neglected to prepare. She once told me about pacing the Birmingham, Alabama, airport trying to find a single piece of fresh fruit or other healthy food amid a sea of barbecue, burgers, and cinnamon buns. She's never been caught short since.

A cooler for your car or train trip. Long stretches of US highways are food wastelands, filled with convenience stores and fast-food chains. When you travel with a cooler full of your own food, you can enjoy all your favorites. Pack veggies, dips, hard-boiled eggs, canned tuna and sardines, plus artisan cheeses. Be sure you include lean meats, lettuce and tomato, plus condiments for making sandwiches on whole-grain bread. By keeping your cooler chilled, you'll have a meal option whenever you're hungry. (Take a blanket so you can park at the rest stop, get out, and enjoy a mini-picnic.)

Other food cultures. Traveling is all about adventure as we experience new vistas and other cultures with their own foods and preparation methods. Many other cultures take food far more seriously than we in the US do, meaning your food selections in other countries could actually be easier. With the spread of fast-food outlets, though, there's still a lot of junk food to be found in other countries. Avoid all fast foods, period. Small, family-run eateries often serve the most traditional fare: grilled fish with beans, salad, and corn tortillas in Mexico; antipasti along the Mediterranean; a perfect omelet with herbs in France. Healthy dining outside the US can be way easier.

AT A FRIEND'S HOME

As a guest in someone's home for a meal, honor your hosts by enjoying what they've prepared. Be vigilant about portions, choosing mostly veggies and lean protein. Of course, you'll try a small spoonful of any special dishes the host slaved over, and you'll relish every bite. If it's a close friend, be sure to confide in him or her about your condition, your food preferences, and what's off-limits. Your host should be more than willing to accommodate you.

TAKE ACTION TODAY: Go to lunch or dinner at a restaurant for practice. Invite your spouse or an understanding friend and outline your intentions. As you order and eat, explain your reasons for your menu choices and how they are helping to improve your condition. This "practice run" will give you valuable experience.

EXTRA CREDIT: Prepare for your next trip by making a list of the healthy foods you'll take along. Keep the list in your travel bag.

CASE STUDY: KEITH

"I'm now 30 pounds lighter and off two of my prescription drugs!"

Keith was on three blood pressure drugs and was heading toward diabetes medication, too. For years his doctor kept refilling—and adding—prescriptions without talking to him about the power of simple diet and lifestyle modifications. Keith was on the slippery slope to permanent decline. He was losing energy, listless, and depressed.

Case Study: Keith	Before	After
Weight	199	168
A1C	6.7	5.2
Blood Pressure	162/92	128/82
Triglycerides	180	146
Meds	Lisinopril, Atenolol, HCTZ	HCTZ (temporarily)

After looking at his lab work, I told him it would be much better to normalize his blood sugars and normalize his blood pressure without drugs. After only one month on *The 30-Day Diabetes Cure*, we eliminated one of his blood pressure meds. Keith's energy took off like a rocket! After the second month, we cut out a second blood pressure drug. He began walking and is now up to three miles every morning. He loves it so much that he even walks in the rain and snow. Now, after a year, he has lost 30 pounds and we're very close to getting him off all his medications.

(-)

DAY 23: ELIMINATE SELF-SABOTAGE

Be faithful in small things because it is in them that your faith lies.

MOTHER TERESA OF CALCUTTA

ANTI-HEALER: **Sabotaging your progress with self-defeating behaviors and negative thinking hurts your progress. Today you'll reaffirm your commitment, combat any negativity, and reaffirm your new habits.**

DID YOU THINK *The 30-Day Diabetes Cure* worked like a diet? That it was something you could stick with for a while, get "well" on, and then discard for your old patterns of eating and activity? By now you know this plan doesn't work like that. This is a new way of living that can actually *save* your life. Poor food choices and lack of physical activity are what cause diabetes—and reversing these habits is the way to heal it.

HOW TO HANDLE DISCOURAGEMENT

Have you stopped paying attention to your eating plan for days at a time? Did you decide to ignore your blood sugar when those cookies came out at work? Have you given in to some of your old cravings? Do you feel you're drifting back to the habits that got you in trouble in the first place? If you've "fallen off the wagon," the best way to regain your footing is to start again at Day 1. Repeating Phase I will put you on an even keel and bring your blood sugar and metabolism back into balance.

Don't feel discouraged. This is perfectly normal, because none of us are perfect. Trial-and-error is one of the most effective methods of learning. The important thing is that you noticed you're getting off-track and you correct your course as soon as possible. In the words of Nelson Mandela, "The greatest glory in living lies not in never failing, but in rising every time we fail." The old Japanese proverb, "Fall seven times, stand up eight," reiterates this wisdom.

Going back with the knowledge of where your weaknesses lie will help you become more aware of them so you can outsmart them when they pop up again. Here are some tips to take with you…

THE TOP 10 COMMITMENT-BUSTERS

You might be sabotaging your own best efforts by…

1. Keeping junky food in your home or office, so you can "sneak" a treat.

2. Creating "special food rules" that let you slip into old habits on various occasions, like birthdays, holidays, or celebration dinners.

3. Letting others sway your eating or activity schedule. Just because your mother-in-law wants you to eat her coffee cake doesn't mean you have to.

4. Giving in to "stress eating." After a hard day, it's easy to reach for a junky snack (especially if it's around the house).

5. Not recognizing that judgmental comments from family or friends over your new approach to diabetes are based in ignorance or their own insecurities.

6. Skipping your 30 minutes of daily walking because you "don't have enough time."

7. Not reminding your family that you need their support to succeed.

8. Forgetting to snack regularly (and healthfully) twice a day.

9. Still eating or drinking anything with sugar in it.

10. Skimping on sleep (one of the most healing aspects of your life).

"WE ARE WHAT WE REPEATEDLY DO…"

Aristotle said it, adding, "… Excellence is not an act, but a habit." Thousands of years later, scientists at Duke University confirmed this realization. They found that while people like to *think* they're in control of what they do, nearly half of all daily actions occur in the same location every single day. In short, humans are creatures of habit—for better or worse.

"Many of our repeated behaviors are cued by everyday environments, even though people think they're making choices all the time," says Wendy Wood, James B. Duke professor of psychology and neuroscience. "Most people don't think that the reason they eat fast food at lunch or snack from the vending machine in late afternoon is because these actions are cued by their daily routines, the sight and smell of the food or the location they're in. They think they're doing it because they intended to eat then, or because they like the food."[62]

Consider the positive side of this: You get up, use the bathroom, brush your teeth because you're in the bathroom. It's a habit based on location—and a good one. People who struggle with establishing good habits can apply this insight. Example: If you get the urge to eat while watching your favorite TV program, you should consider moving the TV. That's right; put it (or yourself) in a new location. Or get yourself a stationary bike and pedal while you watch. This creates

---

[62] http://news.duke.edu/2007/12/habit.html

a new habit that doesn't include a bowl of ice cream (like the couch did!). Sounds kooky, but it really works.

If you shop at a grocery store that hangs bags of trashy food at the register and you feel an overwhelming urge to grab one, shop at a new store. It's all about "habit."

HOW TO GET BACK ON TRACK

Changing your old unhealthy habits is central to my 30-day plan. But your new approach to eating and exercise won't happen without real effort and focus from you. Try these tips to get back on track …

Recognize your motivation. If you need motivation, reread my Special Report, *Dodging Diabetes Complications,* where I describe the terrible toll that unchecked diabetes can take.

Write it down. If I were sitting with you now, we'd put pen to paper and create a week's worth of diabetes-healing menus—from breakfast to dinner. Now make a grocery shopping list.

Declare your intentions. Tell everyone you know about your decision to follow *The 30-Day Diabetes Cure*—your partner, children, and coworkers. Declaring your intentions ups the odds you'll follow through. Put a reminder on the fridge too—just for yourself!

Get cookin'. Block out an hour to make a double batch of vegetable soup, three-bean chili, or a week's worth of Irish oatmeal. Portion it into meal-size containers and freeze some for later. Do this again with a new recipe two days from now. When hunger propels you, you'll reach for these diabetes-friendly meals just as easily as you once reached for a bag of chips. Trust me, you will.

Find a sponsor. In Alcoholics Anonymous, a sponsor is someone who's experienced in the recovery process. That experience comes from their ability to bounce back from "slips" and learn from them. A sponsor (or mentor) provides support and encouragement "one day at a time." Ask a friend who has diabetes to work through this program with you. Or find a local diabetes support group and seek out a mentor who can provide guidance. On Day 24 I'll talk about your support system in more detail.

Log it in. You may think you've made little-to-no progress in changing your eating and exercise habits, but is that really true? I mean, here you are at Day 23. You've hung tough for more than three weeks. You've learned a bunch. You're fighting the good fight. So acknowledge your progress and accomplishments. Keeping a daily journal and recording your meals, emotions, and activities can help jump-start new habits and keep you consistent.

Recognize triggers. All habits have at least one trigger. Is it the doughnut box at work? Dessert after a meal? The aroma of French fries? The stronger the trigger, the more powerful the habit. To break the hold these triggers exert, you first have to recognize them. Then you can create your own positive replacement habits. For example, when the doughnuts appear (as you know they will), make sure you have an apple and some walnuts to munch on. As for the postmeal expectation of dessert, enjoy an orange, yogurt with berries and cinnamon, a small square of dark chocolate. Create replacements you can learn to love.

Be mindful. Old habits haunt us, but being mindful focuses you on the present. Use the one-meal-at-a-time approach and make a healing choice *right now*. "For lunch, I'll have my yummy rice and veggies." Don't think about what your coworkers are eating. Eat well in the moment consistently, applying your new food choices one meal at a time.

Replace. If old bad habits are ganging up on you, arm yourself with specific replacements. For instance, if a cold soda beckons at your local gas station, make sure you've got a nice pomegranate spritzer along for the ride. If you crave a mid-afternoon sweet, reach for your healthy snack bag and enjoy a dried fig, or a couple of dried apricots or prunes, along with a small piece of cheese and five almonds. Never be far from your stash of healthy snacks.

REJECT NEGATIVE SELF-TALK

Negative self-talk is a real speed bump on the path to progress. Do you tell yourself you'll never be able to stick with a diet like this for life? Or that you simply hate walking for 30 minutes every day?

Stop creating self-fulfilling prophecies. There's reason for hope. Researchers at Duke University say the older we get, the wiser we become emotionally—and that includes not letting negative thoughts and feelings dominate.[63] One easy solution is to replace negative thoughts with positive ones. The more you do it, the easier it gets. If you think you're a negative self-talker, try these positive self-talk tips…

- When you feel yourself thinking or saying something negative, say "stop" out loud and affirm the opposite. "I can't eat a healing dinner because I didn't shop for food" becomes "I have a can of beans in the pantry, olive oil, and an onion, so I can make a yummy meal."

- Modify your wording to use less powerful phrases. "I can't" find a way to stay on the eating plan changes to "it's challenging to stay on the eating plan." Then, explore ways to make it less challenging and you'll be able to add "… but I'm getting better at it."

- "This will never work" becomes "how can I make this work?" Imagine the possibilities when you shift your mindset.

- Be optimistic—even if you're not! Count your successes every day and record them in your journal. Healing breakfast? Check. Diabetes-healing snack at 10:30? Check! Walked at lunch? Double check! You're on your way to being more optimistic already.

---

[63] AARP March-April 2010

- Draft a few positive affirmations and repeat them aloud or to yourself daily. Repetition is key. Create sentences phrased as if they're true right now. You can use these or write your own: "I'm reversing my diabetes with every step I walk." "I'm healthier with every bite of this delicious chili." "I feel peaceful and happy with my decision to stick with this plan."

- Jot down your affirmations and post them strategically on the bathroom mirror, kitchen fridge, and workplace drawer.

ARE *YOU* YOUR OWN WORST ENEMY?

I didn't say it would be easy, but I know you can do this. You *can* reverse your diabetes. You *can* get off your medications. You *can* reduce your insulin. You *can* avoid the deadly complications of diabetes. Most important is whether or not you believe it.

Henry Ford, a man who knew a thing or two about willpower, said: "If you think you can do a thing or think you can't do a thing, you're right." Everyone has a little voice inside telling us what we *can't* do. Making choices every day about what you eat is not difficult unless you believe it is. It's not any harder to go to the grocery store and buy fresh vegetables and a piece of wild Atlantic salmon than it is to pick up cookies, ice cream, a six-pack of Coke, and frozen pizza. A homemade salad loaded with fresh vegetables and beans, sprinkled with nuts and soft savory cheese crumbles and some cold sliced chicken breast is a snap! Your shopping list for this salad is: baby prewashed spinach, a red bell pepper, red onion, a can of kidney beans, raw walnuts, cheese, and a deli chicken breast. By buying double the ingredients, you can toss together another one on the weekend.

Now consider the alternative: eating a feedlot burger with an order of greasy fries, washed down by a HFCS-loaded soda handed to you by a clerk who may or may not have remembered to wash his hands after using the bathroom. That choice is easy.

When we're trying to recover from diabetes, we frequently meet the same obstacles that gave us the disease in the first place. Over and over, we are encountering the many ways in which we are our own worst enemy—instead of being our own best friend. In politics, this is called voting against your own best interests.

MORE TIPS TO SUCCEED

Exercise to curb your appetite. Researchers from the University of Colorado in Denver found that exercise diminishes hunger and appetite. That's one of the many reasons why regular physical activity is so important.[64]

---

[64] http://www.sciencedaily.com/releases/2009/09/090902112103.htm

Eat green. My meal plan is definitely good for your general health, as well as your diabetes. For instance, women who eat more folate-rich foods (one of the B vitamins) have 50% less chance of getting colorectal cancer than women who don't eat their folate foods, say researchers at Hallym University College of Medicine in South Korea.[65] You have my permission to "pig out" on broccoli, greens, oranges, and beans—all great sources of folate. Stay on your healing path and you'll conquer cancer at the same time!

Don't dine with overweight friends. Studies show that hanging out with people who are overweight makes you heavier. Recent research confirms that being fat is socially contagious—and just the opposite is equally true.[66] Choose your friends wisely.

HOW TO GET OUT OF A RUT

Step away from negative influences (and people) that stand in the way of your goals. Did your mother tell you that snacking would spoil your appetite? Does her voice still whisper as your hunger grows and dinner looms? Revisit Day 8 and be sure you nail those hunger pangs twice a day with healing snacks (along with filling diabetes-healing meals). Remember the hormone ghrelin? It signals that you're hungry now and then quiets down after you eat. So go ahead and enjoy a handful of pistachios (it takes half an hour for ghrelin to know you've eaten and send the "satisfied" signal).

Is a well-intentioned friend offering up "expert" advice? It's *not* true that nibbling on low-cal rice cakes is better than having a thumb-sized portion of parmesan cheese and an apple, no matter what he/she says. Gently remind your advice-giving pal that you're on a doctor-supervised plan and that you're loving your new food choices. (He/she may even be tempted to join you!)

Remember that fiber is your best friend. Fiber foods are slow-carb foods. Eating them for meals and snacks ensures that your body will be powered with a steady fuel supply. As a bonus, fiber digests more slowly, so you'll feel fuller longer. My most successful patients eat fiber-rich foods at every opportunity. If you haven't picked up the habit of eating fiber foods, start now.

Muscle burns calories. Muscle burns an astonishing 12 times more calories than fat. Have you added the extra exercise from Day 20? Literally lift yourself out of the doldrums by getting a pair of weights and starting to build muscle. Your newly lean body will keep you inspired to stay on the plan. Big bonus: Losing your obese profile adds an extra six years to your life span.

---

[65] http://www.nature.com/ejcn/journal/v63/n9/abs/ejcn200937a.html

[66] http://www.thecrimson.com/article/2007/8/3/study-weight-gain-most-prevalent-among/

TAKE ACTION TODAY: Decide now to eliminate anything that's sabotaging your success. Pick up a pen and write yourself a letter. In it, tell yourself why you're recommitting to reversing your disease. List your successes so far, and declare tomorrow a chance to start fresh. Seal the envelope, add your address, and stick on a stamp. Drop it in the mailbox tomorrow.

EXTRA CREDIT: Choose one self-sabotaging behavior you recognize in yourself and decide how you can transform it. Haven't walked yet? Hit the road right now. Haven't planned dinner? Go cut up a plate of raw veggies to snack on while you create your menu. Do you know what's for breakfast tomorrow? Hard-boil a few eggs so you'll be ready in the morning. It truly is that easy!

DAY 24: ADD A SUPPORT SYSTEM

The "I" in illness is isolation; and the crucial letters in wellness are "we."

MIMI GUARNERI, MD

HEALER: **Support groups, trusted friends, a skilled therapist—all can make an extraordinary difference in maintaining the good health you've worked so hard to achieve.**

WRAPPING YOURSELF in a blanket of support is one of the best ways to keep yourself uplifted and progressing in your recovery. We're social creatures by nature who need families and coworkers, neighbors, and friends. And yes, a condition like diabetes can make us feel separated, isolated, and alone.

Support really is essential—and you can find it in a friend's kitchen over a cup of tea, in a therapist's office, and even online. The key is to create a support system that's right for you.

LEAN ON ME: SUPPORT GROUPS

Since Alcoholics Anonymous started up in the 1930s, numerous support groups have emerged for just about every dysfunction imaginable. These types of groups are valuable for a number of reasons…

End of isolation. Nobody wants to be alone with a problem. People who go to self-help/support groups find real strength and insights in being with others facing the same challenges.

Boosting motivation. Groups can be "infectious" in success sharing. Just hearing others describe how they're managing something such as sugar cravings can motivate you to do the same.

Shared understanding. While friends and relatives may offer well-intentioned support, they just can't know the struggles you face. A support group provides compassion, empathy, and real-life wisdom and informed support from people who've "been there."

An accepting environment. You can talk about virtually anything in a support group without being judged or fearing embarrassment. That's hard to find in the outside world.

"Living the solution, not the problem." The best meetings follow this credo. Rather than a pity party or complaint session, support groups are energized by creative ideas and shared solutions.

Peer support. Well-run groups share personal experiences and practical strategies, instead of being told what you *should* do. Newcomers are welcomed warmly. Don't be shy. (Remember, everyone was new once!)

New trusted friends. Rock-solid relationships can sprout from these groups, often extending beyond official meetings to coffee talks, lunches, and dinner—even phone calls for emergency advice.

Low-cost anonymity. Many groups are offered at low or no cost. Members use first names to ensure privacy.

The salt of the year. Some of the best-adjusted and friendliest folks on earth attend support groups regularly. These members honor first-timers as VIPs. You should feel warmly welcomed to whatever group you choose.

P.S. ON SUPPORT GROUPS

- Experienced group members tend to recommend that you "take what you need and leave the rest." Translation: You won't find everything you hear to be immediately applicable to your situation. But don't disregard it. Group wisdom may be helpful later on, as your needs and situation change.

- Some diabetes groups function under the premise that it's an incurable condition. You know better, of course. Maybe you'll share what you've learned. If you sense a lack of openness, that's a sign this isn't the group for you.

- Choose well when you select a group, looking for a balance of newcomers and veterans coping with diabetes. Different perspectives add to the mix. Many groups have leaders—and the seasoned ones keep domineering members in line while encouraging more reticent contributors to open up. Empathy is essential—it's why you're there!

- Steer clear of groups that charge a lot of money, push you to abandon your medical treatment, or promise fast solutions and quick cures. Safe groups will never press you to purchase products or provide sensitive financial information—or even medical information you don't choose to share.

- Diabetes support groups come in all shapes and sizes, including those for children, teens, adults, couples, families, and women only. They're offered in many locations (and languages too). Ask your doctor, local hospital, or diabetes educator for a referral to a group near you.

- Online support groups can be an immediate help. Use good judgment when browsing online groups. To see what's out there, Google: "Diabetes Support Groups Online."

- Be especially on guard for depression. A study published in the *Journal of the American Medical Association* found that depressed people increase their risk of developing type 2 diabetes and vice versa.[67] Depression often causes people to eat more and gain weight, putting them at risk for diabetes. And if you have diabetes, you may feel discouraged about taking care of yourself, making it harder to manage your glucose levels, exercise, or make the necessary changes in your diet. You may even isolate yourself out of a sense of denial. But joining a diabetes support group could help you end that isolation and find new friends who are facing the same kinds of changes you are.

SET UP A "WISDOM COUNCIL" ON YOUR OWN

Would you believe that your success in managing diabetes is directly linked to the level of support you get from friends and your family? Research proves it—as long as you can recognize which type of support works best for you.

Not everyone in your life can be supportive. But all you really need are just a couple people you can always count on. It's essential to differentiate between those who will support you from those who will make it easy for you to have some cake, drink a few beers, and deviate from your goal. Here are some pointers on setting up a personal support group for yourself…

- Like any healthy relationship, tell your friends what you need. Educate them about diabetes and the 30-day plan you're following. Let them know you're asking for their support and be specific about how they can give it.

- Talk to your core group honestly and directly about your condition. Share your real feelings about the disease, and let them know how much you value their assistance and their support.

- Tell them up front that there might be times when you're going to need their help, and make sure it's okay to call upon them.

- Share your intention to take control over your health and body. Explain what you've learned about the foods that contribute to health and well-being—and the ones that don't. Talk to them openly about what's working for you and what isn't. This will help them support you when they see you're "slipping."

- Invite them over for a potluck of dishes containing your favorite Diabetes-Healing Superfood (see *www.myhealingkitchen.com*). Share your knowledge about how these foods heal diabetes.

---

[67] http://jama.ama-assn.org/cgi/content/full/299/23/2751

- Confess how hard it is to ask for help sometimes. You'll be breaking down barriers that keep you isolated, and you'll be marshalling the support you need just by letting them know that, in fact, you do need them.

- You could be saving their life in the process. While none of your friends or family may have diabetes now, it's entirely possible they eventually may develop it. A 2007 study published in the *New England Journal of Medicine* found that a person's chances of becoming obese increased a whopping 57% when a friend became obese. Diabetes and obesity, it seems, are indeed "contagious." (For close friends, the risk level was an astronomical 171%!) Researchers also found the effect was the same when friends lost weight. Imagine how powerful your recovery from diabetes could be for everyone's health! Get a pal to start eating better and walking with you. By sharing your healing experience with your friends, you could be saving lives.

CONSIDER PROFESSIONAL COUNSELING

Feeling like you hit a roadblock? Sitting with a counselor for a few therapy sessions can sharpen your awareness, rewire your old way of seeing life, and shift your behavior patterns.

It's no secret that food represents much more than nutrition. It's tightly bound up with emotional issues, habits, rules, memories, and social norms. Making the adjustments outlined in my 30-day plan can trigger some surprising (and sometimes disturbing) emotional responses. Here's where a trained therapist can really help. He/she can assist you in unearthing hidden associations with food so you can understand them and learn new responses. Together, you can define the problems, collaborate on solving them, set goals, and plan for continuing support.

Counseling can also propel you toward new ways of interacting with friends and family. It's true that family members don't always know how to accommodate a chronic illness. Even the person with diabetes may not realize the impact of the illness on the family. Professional guidance can open your eyes to the effect your condition and special needs are having on others. Here are some suggestions for locating a qualified counselor…

- Look for a therapist trained in cognitive behavioral therapy (CBT), which helps you identify negative thoughts and actions and replace them with constructive ones.[68] In a nutshell: You'll learn how to retrain your mind so it sees the glass half full, rather than half empty. CBT is not only highly effective at treating depression (which diabetics have a much greater risk of); it's also a documented way of lowering stress hormones—and when they drop so does your blood sugar.[69]

---

[68] http://www.diabetesselfmanagement.com/Articles/Diabetes-Definitions/cognitive-behavioral-therapy/

[69] http://www.dukehealth.org/health_library/health_articles/rxfordiabetes

- Start by asking your doctor or diabetes educator for a referral.

- Ask your support group for recommendations.

- Don't hesitate to ask the therapist about his/her qualifications and familiarity and experience in dealing with diabetes and the costs involved.

TAKE ACTION NOW: Assemble a support system tailored to provide you with encouragement and guidance. Choose an existing diabetes support group, a trusted friend, or a counseling-therapist. There's no need to carry this load alone (or overburden your spouse). Get the help you need. It's out there waiting for you.

EXTRA CREDIT: Call your doctor today and ask about diabetes support groups. Contact one and find out when they next meet. Ink it on your calendar. Commit to one visit to see if you find it helpful.

CASE STUDY: HAROLD

"After two weeks, I felt so much more energy. I lost 30 pounds in three months!"

Harold is an antiques dealer and is involved in very solitary work. He travels a lot—and the road offers nothing but junk food. But loneliness was his real problem, and food was his best friend. Harold is a perfect example of how emotional eating can get you stuck. You feel bad, you eat junk, and then you feel worse.

Case Study: Harold	Before	After
Weight	173.6	144
A1C	7.3	5.4
Blood Pressure	154/88	118/84
Triglycerides	193	92
Meds	Vitorin, Toprol, Ranitidine	None

But *The 30-Day Diabetes Cure* flips the situation: You eat well, you feel well, and then you eat better and feel better. When Harold came to me, he didn't feel well; he couldn't put his finger on it, but he knew something was wrong. He was tired all the time and felt miserable. But after just two weeks, he felt significantly better. And after three months, he felt like "a new man" and had lost 30 pounds! He still travels just as much—still eats at diners and truck stops—but now he makes smarter choices, so he's able to keep his weight and his A1C down. And he's off all his drugs!

(-)

DAY 25: ELIMINATE TOXINS

Food, one assumes, provides nourishment: but Americans eat it fully aware that small amounts of poison have been added to improve its appearance and delay its putrefaction.

JOHN CAGE

ANTI-HEALER: **A slew of evidence links chemical toxins to higher diabetes risk. Toxins disrupt the smooth functioning of your body, so minimize your exposure and strengthen your liver to help heal your diabetes. Here's how...**

THEY'RE EVERYWHERE. Persistent organic pollutants (POPs) from the environment accumulate in body tissues, stressing the liver as it tries to eliminate them, causing cell mutations (cancer), disrupting the endocrine system (that includes all hormones, blood sugar metabolism, and the reproductive system), and depressing your immunity, which leaves you vulnerable to infections, disease, and cancer. POPs are in our water, air, and household cleaners. They're in body care products such as shampoo and lotion. And they're present in our foods, plus their packaging and processing.

WHAT EXACTLY ARE POPS?

The EPA defines POPs as "toxic chemicals that adversely affect human health and the global environment. Because they can be transported by wind and water, most POPs generated in one country can and do affect people and wildlife far from where they are used and released. They persist for long periods in the environment and can accumulate and pass from one species to the next through the food chain."[70] Here are some specific POPs and where they "pop up" in your daily life...

- Antibiotics and growth hormones. These are routinely added to the grains eaten by factory feedlot animals. They lodge in their fat and in your body when you eat these meats. What your body is able to eliminate ends up in your neighborhood wastewater system (which is

---

[70] http://www.epa.gov/oia/toxics/pop.htm

271

recycled in tap water). The balance is absorbed into your body's fatty tissue. (Needless to say, the more body fat you have, the more accumulation you get.)

- Pesticides and fungicides are routinely sprayed on non-organic crops and absorbed by the plants themselves.[71] These have long been linked to the development of various cancers.

- Genetically modified (GMO) crops, which have already had their very DNA tinkered with. (There are no long-term studies showing these crops are safe for animals or humans who eat them.)

- Meats and vegetables packaged in plastic and Styrofoam, two sources of PVC (polyvinyl chloride), BPA (bisphenol A), and styrene—all known human toxins. In addition, BPA is linked to a higher incidence of diabetes![72] Most food cans are lined with BPA, and hard plastic water bottles and baby bottles are also made of it (though they're being phased out; I'll discuss all this more a bit later).

- Dioxins and furans are produced during industrial processes such as bleaching wood pulp to make paper and from burning trash (including medical and municipal waste). They're also in wood preservatives and garden and agricultural herbicides. Most of human exposure comes from eating animals (or dairy products) in whose tissues these chemicals have accumulated.[73]

IN YOUR HOUSE—AND YOUR BODY

The tremendous amount of plastic used in our food supply is simply incalculable—and some of its residue ends up in our bodies. Think of all those salad bar containers, milk jugs, yogurt tubs, and bags of peanuts. Add to that plastic spatulas, rubber scrapers, cups, and plates, all of which come into contact with heat via cooking or dishwasher.

Cleaning products are another source of toxic exposure. They contain dangerous chemicals such as formaldehyde, trisodium phosphate, hydrofluoric acid, and others labeled as "irritants." Shampoos are made with *sodium laureth sulphate*, a suspected carcinogen linked to kidney and liver damage. Parabens are known hormone disrupters, yet they remain in deodorant, cosmetics, and hair dyes. Hormone-disrupting *phthalates*—in hair spray, nail polish, and products containing "fragrance"—are banned in Europe because of their link to birth defects and cancer, but are largely unregulated in the US.[74] In 2008, Jane Houlihan, director of research for the Environmental Working Group, told a US House subcommittee that personal care products including shampoo and cosmetics are "the single largest source of risky chemicals that Americans are exposed

---

[71] http://www.epa.gov/oia/toxics/pop.htm

[72] http://www.ncbi.nlm.nih.gov/pmc/articles/PMC1332699/

[73] http://www.epa.gov/pbt/pubs/dioxins.htm

[74] http://www.ewg.org/water/downthedrain

to." Houlihan told the subcommittee, "Companies are free to use almost any ingredient they choose in personal care products, with no proof of safety required."[75]

RESEARCH LINKS TOXINS TO DIABETES

How do these ubiquitous toxins affect diabetes? The *Journal of the American Medical Association* reported in 2008 that people with the plastic chemical BPA in their bloodstream have "an increased prevalence of cardiovascular disease, diabetes and liver-enzyme abnormalities."[76] If you have diabetes, BPA is a very real danger to you. Canned foods are considered the main cause of BPA exposure, because the chemical is known to transmigrate from the lining of cans into the liquids or foods they hold.

Researchers who looked at populations exposed to massive toxic disasters say these people show a significant increase in the risk of diabetes over time, particularly women. These studies focused on a Taiwanese manufacturing accident that caused rice bran oil to be contaminated with PCBs (*polychlorinated biphenyls*) and PCD FS (*polychlorinated dibenzofurans*) and an Italian pesticide factory explosion that exposed thousands of residents to toxic levels of dioxin.

Other studies show that BPA causes a variety of female reproductive organ disorders, which women experience as ovarian cysts, fibroids, endometriosis, and several cancers. US soldiers who were part of the Vietnam Agent Orange campaign in the 1960s and '70s (which involved spraying a dioxin-based herbicide called *paraquat* over the jungles to kill foliage) experienced a 200% higher incidence of diabetes 20 years later than those who didn't participate. In fact, epidemiologists at the University of Texas Health Science Center actually found the diabetes risk correlated to the number of days the soldiers were exposed to spraying this deadly compound.

Even ordinary Americans who live far from factories, chemical waste sites, or large farming operations are at elevated risk. Toxic compounds are so pervasive throughout our culture that we all carry a toxic load. The Toxic-Free Legacy Coalition in 2005 tested hair, blood, and urine samples from study participants for an array of chemicals present in ordinary household products, including nonstick cookware, cleaners, and plastics. The researchers found a minimum of 26 toxic chemicals present in every person—with the highest toxic load 39 chemicals in a single human being!

HOW TO PROTECT YOURSELF

It's impossible to prevent your body from being contaminated by these environmental toxins. Even the Inuit Eskimos of Greenland, that generates no real pollution at all, have unacceptably high levels of man-made toxins that are produced in distant industrial countries.[77]

---

[75] http://www.ewg.org/node/28188

[76] http://www.womensconference.org/7-healthy-lifestyle-tips-on

[77] http://news.bbc.co.uk/2/hi/europe/2906357.stm

It's astonishing how far these toxins can travel to end up in the fat of the whale, seal, and polar bear meat that make up the traditional Inuit diet.

You can't escape today's toxic chemicals, but you can reduce your danger by changing your purchasing habits. More important, you can help the body's elimination system to naturally purge your bloodstream and fat tissues of toxins accumulated over time. Happily, your liver is your body's "toxin filter," which disarms them and sends them over to the kidneys for further processing before they're excreted via urine. (Yet another reason to keep your kidney function healthy.) Your colon is involved in this detoxification process too. Its mucous membrane keeps bacteria and other toxins from entering your body, and beneficial bacteria in your large intestine remove toxic wastes from the food you eat.

Here's the best news of all: You've been detoxing your body since Day 1 of *The 30-Day Diabetes Cure*! Here's how:

- By eliminating processed foods and factory meats, you've been removing a major source of toxic chemicals from your life.

- Loading up on vegetables, fruits, and whole grains provides extraordinary support to your digestive system—including your liver—in clearing toxins from your body.

- And our focus on fiber works in your favor too, since fiber binds to wastes and moves them out of your system.

- And on Day 13, with the start of your walking program …

- Your daily exercise began stimulating your respiratory system—heart and lungs—all natural detoxifiers!

- As the weight comes off, you shed the fat that stores toxins.

And as early as Day 3, when you quit sugary drinks and replaced them with water, you began flushing your body with one of life's greatest detoxifiers. Water is the best choice for washing away impurities. Well, *pure* water is, anyway.

HOW PURE IS YOUR WATER SUPPLY?

We couldn't survive very long without water, and yet our supply is swimming with toxins. Health officials stress that the levels are extremely low, but don't you believe it. A little later, I'll explain why you should get a good-quality water filter right away. For now, consider these facts…

- In 2009, a comprehensive survey of US drinking water found widespread levels of pharmaceuticals and "hormonally active" chemicals all across America. The Southern Nevada

Water authority tested tap water from 19 US locations and found the most common residues included atenolol, a beta-blocker used to treat heart disease; antidepressant drugs used by people with bipolar disorder; estrogen hormones; the tranquilizer meprobamate, an epilepsy anticonvulsant; plus numerous antibiotics.[78]

■ A 2010 Chicago Tribune story looked at the gender-bending effects of atrazine, the most common chemical found in US streams and rivers.[79, 80] Researchers at Indiana University discovered an increase in nine different types of birth defects in infants whose mothers were pregnant during the spring planting season (April through July), when atrazine is sprayed on farmland. Farmers, as well as golf course owners and homeowners, use this weed killer, which is banned in Europe but not in the US. The horror is that atrazine is a feminizing endocrine disruptor (a chemical that disrupts human hormones and turns males into females)—and it's more dangerous at lower concentrations than once believed, according to this research.

Atrazine ultimately ends up in our drinking water. Residents of corn-growing states have the worst contaminations, with up to 50% of them exposed to atrazine in drinking water (with levels spiking to 10 times the legal limit during planting season!). Even at concentrations that meet federal standards, atrazine is linked to low birth weight, birth defects, and menstrual problems. Independent researchers are finding that children's reproductive and nervous systems suffer disproportionately from exposure. So does wildlife: Male frogs reared in an atrazine environment turned into females and were able to breed with males. *That's simply mind-bending!*

DO YOU NEED A SPECIAL DETOX DIET?

Detox diets are all the rage in some corners, but do you need one? Let me remind you that you're already following one of the best there is. So keep up the good work. I don't recommend fad detox "cleansing" diets and fasting regimens because they dramatically disturb metabolism and may even do long-term damage. People with diabetes need a steady source of nutrients to support blood sugar, so avoid these quick fixes. It's essential for you to reject any dietary protocol that could overstress your body's metabolism.[81] But here's what you can and should do to reduce your body's toxic load…

HELP YOUR LIVER DO A BETTER JOB

We talked briefly about your liver as your body's filter for toxins. It's simply an amazing toxin clearinghouse! Literally all blood leaving your stomach and intestines heads first to the

---

[78] http://www.newscientist.com/article/dn16397-top-11-compounds-in-us-drinking-water.html

[79] http://chicagoist.com/2010/04/18/trib_tackles_gender_bending_chemica.php

[80] http://www.treehugger.com/files/2009/08/todays-toxin-atrazine.php

[81] http://www.webmd.com/balance/natural-liver-detox-diets-liver-cleansing?page=2

liver, which metabolizes nutrients and sends them off where they're needed. At the same time, it breaks down chemicals as it cleanses your blood of toxins such as alcohol and any chemicals you've ingested, absorbed, or inhaled. (Next to the pancreas, the liver is the most important organ in a diabetic's body.) The liver filters up to two liters of blood every minute.[82] It also screens out pathogenic bacteria from the bloodstream, helping you resist infection sickness. The bile your liver secretes helps break down fats in the blood so they can be absorbed for nourishment or stored for energy later. Your liver also produces cholesterol needed to carry fats through the body, for the creation of hormones, and to keep the walls of your cells stiff and impermeable.

So be extra kind to your liver! Given its role in cleaning up your body's toxic load, you shouldn't overload it or keep it so busy with one task (like clearing out alcohol by drinking too much); otherwise, it's not available when you need it to filter other environmental toxins.

DETOX HERBAL HELPERS

Chemical pollutants, exhaustion, poor eating habits, and chronic allergies can cause your liver to go sluggish.[83] It's fine to use herbs to help the detox process along. After all, people have been doing it for thousands of years. Remember, though, that as your liver gets assistance from herbs in clearing the junk from your body, the toxins themselves will move through your bloodstream on their way out the door. This can cause temporary fatigue, a little malaise, nausea, or even a mild skin rash. (These are common symptoms that detoxification is occurring.) Start gently on low doses of detox herbs so you don't have any extreme results. Here are some of my favorites…

Milk thistle. Also known as *silymarin*, this plant remedy has been used for more than 2,000 years[84] to protect the liver from damage and help it regenerate healthy cells. Multiple studies show that milk thistle is effective in protecting the liver from environmental toxins, including long-term alcohol use, plus pharmaceutical and over-the-counter drugs. Milk thistle's magic lies in the seeds that hold its active ingredient, *flavonolignans*, which actually alter cell membranes so that only tiny amounts of toxins can enter liver cells. It also stimulates protein synthesis for regeneration and repair of liver cells. In addition, these seeds contain essential fatty acids that serve as anti-inflammatory compounds in the liver.

Professional herbalists and alternative practitioners often recommend milk thistle as an herbal tincture for liver cleansing and healing—but you can also benefit from the capsule form. By stimulating the flow of bile through the liver, digestion improves along with elimination.

Visit a naturopath, clinical herbalist, or natural pharmacy for guidance on taking milk thistle. Generally, tinctures and extracts sold in natural foods stores can be taken by the dropper,

---

[82] http://www.detoxdietweb.com/turmeric-for-liver-detox

[83] http://www.detoxdietweb.com/turmeric-for-liver-detox

[84] http://www.wholehealthchicago.com/knowledge-base/m/milk-thistle/

added to a small amount of warm water. Start with one dropper once or twice a day and gradually increase it to two or three until you experience results. Milk thistle is often combined with licorice or dandelion, which also support liver health.

Burdock. This is another thistle herb used to cleanse the blood by helping your kidneys filter out impurities. I like to use a tincture of burdock along with milk thistle to ensure that toxins released from the liver don't hang around in your bloodstream very long.

Turmeric. Called the "king of spices," this Ayurvedic herb has long been used for liver cleansing. Its active ingredient is *curcumin*, a potent anti-inflammatory and antioxidant. Remember that your liver produces bile to move out toxins? Turmeric speeds the flow of bile and its toxic load. If you don't want to purchase supplements, just locate some organic turmeric and start sprinkling it on everything from eggs to chili. And while you're using it to boost liver function, you'll also be boosting brain power. A study published in the *American Journal of Epidemiology* looked at the link between curry consumption (curry is made with turmeric) and brain function in older Asian adults. The researchers found that those who ate the most had the lowest rates of cognitive decline.[85]

There's even more good news if you're concerned about Alzheimer's (and people with diabetes should be because they are at much higher risk). According to the *Journal of Neuroscience Research,* curcumin actually inhibits amyloid proteins from forming in the brain. These proteins are a hallmark of Alzheimer's.[86] Turmeric also helps with arthritis and prevents infections and also cancer, so shake it on liberally.

YOUR BODY'S LARGEST ORGAN RELEASES TOXINS TOO

Your body's largest organ is your skin—and it's a frontline detoxifier too. Just as skin absorbs toxins, it also purges them, releasing toxins in perspiration and body oils via sweat glands and oil glands. Sweat can even move out heavy metals such as mercury and oil-based toxins like petroleum products, which occur in many cosmetics. In keeping with the idea of a gentle detox, avoid extremes such as extended stays in any hot environment, which can be downright dangerous. Sweat it out in short spurts while keeping your cool by following these tips:

■ Work up a sweat by exerting yourself with vigorous exercise regularly to stimulate perspiration and detoxing.

■ Sweat in a sauna, steam room, or hot tub to open up pores and warm your body, which helps mobilize even more toxins to exit via the skin. Just a few minutes in any of these, with lots of fresh cool water after to replenish your liquid reserves, can be remarkably effective in releasing toxins through the skin.

---

[85] http://aje.oxfordjournals.org/cgi/content/short/164/9/898

[86] http://www.renegadeneurologist.com/turmeric-and-brain-health/

- Drink a liberal amount of fresh water throughout the day to support normal perspiration, which also eliminates unfriendly chemicals.

11 WAYS TO DETOX YOUR ENVIRONMENT

Believe me, I recognize that making big shifts in your lifestyle can be challenging and tough to implement all at once. That's why my 30-day plan gives you plenty of time to acclimate to new ideas, foods, and habits. It's the same with detoxing your environment and your body. You won't do it in a single day, but you *can* start taking steps that will clear your kitchen, bathroom, and cosmetics shelf of products that make it harder to heal your diabetes. Here are some pointers…

Get a water filter. Stop buying bottled water—it's bad for your budget and all those plastic bottles represent an environmental disaster. Instead, buy a high-quality water filter to remove pesticides, pharmaceuticals, and other impurities from your drinking water. You don't have to buy an expensive filter, but I actually recommend you make this investment if you can. You're now drinking 64 ounces of fresh water every day, so make your drinking supply as clean as possible. I recommend the Katadyn Combi Water Filter, with an attachment for your tap. Its ceramic element filters more than 13,000 gallons of drinking water before requiring replacement, removing bacteria and toxic chemicals.[87] You pay a little more up front, but you get water filtered to .2 microns, and that is as safe as you can get. Use a glass bottle, glass-lined thermos, or stainless steel bottle to carry your drinking water with you.

Pitch the plastic. Replace plastic wrap, bags, and storage containers with good old-fashioned wax paper and foil. Wax-paper sandwich bags are available in natural foods stores. Or just buy a roll of wax paper or foil. Wrap sandwiches with it and use it to cover glass bowls in the fridge. Then use it again.

Go with glass. Look for Pyrex storage containers with rubber lids, in a variety of sizes. They may seem heavy to carry to work, but they're far safer for your food, especially in the microwave (but no lids please!). Plastic containers and plastic wrap should never be heated in a microwave. Repurpose (or "upcycle") all your used plastic containers and yogurt tubs. Every workshop, mechanic, and gardener can use them for screws, nails, seeds, and small tools. Kids can play with them in the bathtub and sandbox; for craft projects; and to store collections. If they're overwhelming your kitchen, bid them "adieu" and toss into the recycle bin. Avoid buying more in the future (you can use them to make your own yogurt, remember?).

Remember code 245. If you must purchase plastic products, choose those with recycle codes 2, 4, and 5.

---

[87] http://www.thereadystore.com/katadyn-combi-water-filter

Nix the nonstick. Replace nonstick cookware with good old steel baking sheets, glass pans and casseroles, and cast-iron or copper-clad skillets. Teflon® and other nonstick coatings decompose at high heat—even if you don't cook at super-high temps. A study done by the Environmental Working Group showed that Teflon pans preheated on "high" on an ordinary stovetop can reach temperatures of 700+ degrees F in three minutes. At the same time, studies by DuPont (the manufacturer) show that Teflon off-gasses toxic particulates at 446 degrees F! At 680 degrees F, no fewer than six toxic gasses are released, including carcinogens, global pollutants, and other dangerous compounds. These fumes cause "polymer fume fever," which can disorient your brain. Long-term studies on these health hazards haven't been conducted yet, but why wait?

Un-plastic your utensils. Pitch plastic serving and cooking utensils—now that you've ditched your nonstick pans, there's no need for them anyway. Your cast-iron skillet will be fine with the same wooden spoons and metal spatulas your grandma used. Sorry about the picnic set, but re-place plastic cups and plates with lightweight reusable bamboo ones. Avoid plastic to the degree possible but when you can't, keep it away from the dishwasher and other heat.

Can the cans. Purchase tuna in foil packets. Buy frozen veggies and soups in waxed cardboard boxes (better yet, make your own soup). *Consumer Reports* in December 2009 published results showing that virtually every one of 19 name-brand canned foods tested contained some BPA, which leaches from the material that lines cans. The tests included juice, green beans, and tuna. In fact, they even found BPA in foods packed in cans labeled "BPA-free"! [88]

Clean green. Advertisers want you to believe you need a different product for every cleaning task (but, of course, you don't). There's a host of toxic chemicals in most cleaning products, and manufacturing them generates huge amounts of environmental waste. Wean yourself off standard household cleaners with a trip to the natural foods store, where you'll find products made with naturally derived ingredients—and without phosphates and other environmental pollutants. Or go completely natural: Ask your grandma or cruise the Internet for easy, inexpensive, clean and green cleaners made from ingredients like baking soda, lemon juice, and white vinegar. They'll leave your home clean and fresh with no toxic residue. Congratulate yourself for taking this step by buying a few glass spray bottles!

Avoid toxic chemicals in body care products. Using chemical-laden makeup and other body products can add an astonishing five pounds of toxic chemicals to your body each year. Among the worst offenders are parabens (*para-hydroxybenzoic acids*), the most widely used preserva-tives in cosmetics. They're in everything from shampoo and soap to makeup, deodorant, and baby lotions. Parabens have even been detected in breast cancer tumors. [89] (When you bring chemicals into contact with your skin, they're taken up directly by your bloodstream. [90]) One

---

[88] http://www.consumerreports.org/cro/magazine-archive/december-2009/food/bpa/overview/bisphenol-a-ov.htm

[89] http://www.telegraph.co.uk/news/uknews/1555173/Body-absorbs-5lb-of-make-up-chemicals-a-year.html

[90] http://blogs.mercola.com/sites/vitalvotes/archive/2007/06/22/Body-Absorbs-5-Lbs-of-Make-Up-Chemicals-Per-Year.aspx

study looked at 10,000 body care products and found that the average adult uses nine products daily—for a total of 126 unique chemical ingredients. Start reading the fine print (another great use for your magnifying glass) on the back of your shampoo, body lotion, and cosmetics. You'll be stunned by how many of them contain known toxic chemicals. Manufacturers say consumers are exposed to such small amounts that they're not dangerous, but researchers know better. Some European countries and Japan have banned many of these same chemicals to protect their consumers.

Better body care. Chemical-free products for your body are, predictably, more expensive than others. But just like buying organic produce, wild salmon, and grass-fed beef, the return is worth the extra outlay to protect your system from these ubiquitous toxins. Plus, you can offset the cost of chemical-free body products by making at least one of your own: shampoo. Use baking soda to wash your hair and a vinegar-water solution to rinse. Just wet your hair and gently massage in baking soda, adding more water to spread the love. Do you miss those chemical-laden bubbles? You'll get over it. Rinse with the vinegar-water solution and then rinse thoroughly with plain water. Now head back to your natural foods stores and look for skin products free of sodium laureth sulfate, parabens, and petroleum products. One of my patients dips into a jar of organic coconut oil (find it with the cooking oils at your natural foods store) and slathers it on her skin every night. No parabens in coconuts! These safe, low-cost options will offset the extra you pay for chemical-free cosmetics. You'll also discover that a lot of the products you thought you needed are actually unnecessary. Sticking to a few basic, natural products while eliminating the others will free up your budget as well as your toxic load. Finally, go online and Google "Campaign for Safe Cosmetics" or "Skin Deep" to see what's in the products you use or are considering for purchase.

Forget the fragrances.[91] Remove all air fresheners and scented dryer sheets, lotions, and candles from your house today, including anything with a fake "scent." The Natural Resources Defense Council released a study in 2007, which found most air fresheners and other scented products contain chemicals called phthalates—known hormone disruptors that affect reproductive development. Especially harmful to young children and babies, they affect testosterone levels and produce abnormal genitals and decreased sperm production. The state of California says no fewer than five kinds of phthalates are "known to cause birth defects or reproductive harm" and advises pregnant women to stay away. Get these scented products out of your house now! One last note: A study in the *American Journal of Respiratory and Critical Care Medicine* found that people using air fresheners and household cleaning sprays regularly have a stunning 30% to 50% higher incidence of asthma than people who didn't use them. Out at the University of Washington, professor Anne Steinemann did an analysis of some widely used scented products and discovered a whopping 100 unique volatile organic compounds, some of which are linked to cancer and problems with neurological, reproductive, and respiratory systems.[92]

---

[91] http://www.nhregister.com/articles/2008/11/26/opinion/doc492d4214d2c89772087215.txt

[92] http://ajrccm.atsjournals.org/cgi/content/full/176/8/735

TAKE ACTION TODAY: Commit to clearing toxins from your body and environment. Toss toxin-laden cookware, cleaning supplies, and body care products. Support your body's natural detox system by drinking lots of fresh water and kicking up your exercise until you sweat. Strengthen your liver with milk thistle and turmeric. And keep eating high-fiber foods to maintain good elimination.

EXTRA CREDIT: Order a water filter today and install it on your kitchen tap.

DAY 26: ADD STRENGTH TRAINING

I do now what others won't—so I can have later what others can't.

ANONYMOUS BODYBUILDER

HEALER: **Working your muscles boosts insulin sensitivity and lowers blood sugar. Plus, resistance training is the number-one way to strengthen your bones. Your heart gets a beautiful workout, too—and as lean muscle replaces body fat, you'll love the way you look! Here's how to get started…**

IF YOU THINK "ARNOLD" when I say weight lifting, get ready for some mind-blowing news. Strength training (also called resistance training) can make a powerful difference in the way your body processes blood sugar. Researchers in Austria observed 39 diabetic patients as they embarked on a simple weight-training program. After just four months, their A1C dropped from 8.3 to 7.1 and their daily blood sugars plummeted from 204 to147! Plus, their insulin resistance dropped an incredible 22%, while their lipid levels (total cholesterol, triglycerides, and LDL) fell significantly—with good HDL heading skyward. If these results came from a new pharmaceutical drug, you can bet it would bring in billions of dollars!

But this research undeniably shows that simply starting and sticking with strength training can improve blood sugar control just as effectively as taking a diabetes drug.[93] And this type of physical activity is even better for your body. Here's why…

"THE WHOLE-BODY DIABETES HEALER"

As you build lean muscle, your body clears more sugar from your blood. It's that simple. Lean muscle is highly sensitive to insulin and as you slowly but surely build it, your sensitivity to insulin improves. That's because your entire body responds to strength training by pumping more blood through your muscles. This in turn activates the glucose transporters and insulin receptors in your cells.

---

[93] http://diabetes.webmd.com/strength-training-diabetes

Resistance training, whether with free weights or strength-building machines, increases the amount of a compound called *Glut-4* in your body, which binds to cell membranes so it can transport glucose into muscle cells. Because diabetics are low on Glut-4, this is like getting a free extra supply.

Your heart and bones receive plenty of benefits too. Pumping iron kicks up blood flow throughout the entire body, strengthening your heart muscle and driving down your risk for heart disease. When you start strength training regularly, your body moves more glucose into cells for energy and more calcium into bones to make them strong enough to withstand your lifting.

And the benefits continue long after you've finished your workout. The more muscle mass you have, the more calories your body burns, even when you're sitting on the couch! University of Maryland cardiologist Michael Miller found that the number of calories you burn while doing absolutely nothing (called your "resting metabolic rate") increase by 7% after six months of weight training. Similar studies show you can boost your metabolism by a whopping 15% with regular strength training.

The lean bottom line: People who work with weights lose fat as they gain muscle, which is doubly important as we age. Starting in our late 30s, we lose a third of a pound of muscle every year, and it's usually replaced by fat. Strength training can slow this nasty trend—and even reverse it by adding extra muscle. And you're going to need that extra strength as you grow older. A review of 100 clinical trials discovered that strength training improves overall strength, stamina, balance, stair-climbing ability, and ease of standing from a sitting position. It also reduces the pain of osteo-arthritis. Even people in their 80s with other health problems achieve these remarkable benefits.[94]

START SMALL AND BUILD

The goal of strength training isn't to push for quick success with heavy weights—or to build massive muscles. You'll do best by starting with lighter weights and working up incrementally over time. Keep these tips in mind…

Weight. Beginners should start with light hand weights (also called dumbbells). This weight will be different for everyone. Experiment until you find a weight that you can lift straight over your head (called the "military press") 20 times in a row. The last five should be somewhat difficult and cause a slight burning sensation in your muscles. This is your beginning weight. You can also use a wall pulley, elastic bands, or wrist weights to get the same diabetes-healing benefits.

Repetitions. Also called "reps," this is the number of times you will perform the exercise at one time. I recommend you perform 20. The last three to five reps are the most important because they're the ones that actually build lean muscle mass. So keep your form good all the way to the end, increasing the weight only when your reps become easy.

---

[94] http://www.webmd.com/healthy-aging/news/20090708/strength-training-is-good-for-seniors

Sets. A "set" is one complete series of repetitions. Do three sets per exercise. The final set should be difficult, causing exertion. This is the goal; if it isn't difficult, you're not working. If you're not working, your body isn't getting any benefit. Remember that you're exercising your mind at the same time. You're building willpower as well as muscle power. Your mind may be whining: "This is too hard"…"This hurts"…"This is silly"…or "I don't have time for this." Let all that chatter be there and, just like the Nike slogan says, "Just do it!" I find it helpful to have some upbeat, energetic music on my iPod while I'm lifting to drown out all this mind dreck. Remember: Strengthening your willpower in the gym will make it stronger when you call upon it in the outside world.

Number of exercises. Some people prefer to spend an entire session on a region of the body (say, the entire torso, arms, shoulders, chest, and back or the lower body, legs, gluteals, and lower back). Other people like to mix muscle groups, alternating between exercises for the upper and lower body. This is completely up to you as long as you're sure to exercise the major muscle groups of your body throughout the week.

Days per week. Start with two or three days per week, always resting your muscles a day in between. Consistency is essential, so get in the habit. You're going to be strength training for the rest of your life. So learn to enjoy it!

Confuse your muscles! Our bodies are exceptionally adept at adapting to change. If you do the same workout with the same amount of weight week after week, your muscles will say "ho-hum" and won't improve. So mix it up (it's called cross-training). Add a new strength exercise or a slightly heavier weight. Your muscles will be challenged in different ways and you'll get better results.

CONSULT AN EXPERT

If you've never done this before, I recommend you work with a personal trainer in the beginning. That's because good technique is very important—especially for avoiding injuries. Doctors are well-acquainted with the knee injuries and other problems caused by patients who were strength training incorrectly. They'd never been taught the correct form for a squat or a lunge, a bicep curl, or an overhead lift. If you can afford it, hire a trainer at your gym or take a group class to get you going in the right direction. Many gyms offer free training on their equipment as part of a new membership. Working with a personal trainer is a worthwhile investment. You should only need a few sessions to get the hang of it.

Don't forget your core. A trainer can also show you several core-strengthening exercises. These are key to building total body strength, because your core (your abdominal and lower-back muscles) keeps you rock-steady while you work your various muscle groups. It's called your "core" because it's the center of all activity of strength. Ask the trainer to show you several core-strengthening techniques. Forget old-fashioned sit-ups and crunches. They won't get the job done, and they are a good way to hurt yourself. You should learn a variety of core exercises that target different abdominal muscles so you get a full midsection workout, front and back.

Location isn't everything. Where you work out is far less important than doing it with consistency. Some of my patients love the resistance machines at their local gym, as they do offer the advantage of providing support for your back. So if you're not in optimal shape yet, that's a great place to start. Others wouldn't dream of training anywhere but right at home using dumbbells and free weights. And some of my older patients prefer "resistant bands" (which are giant rubber bands that provide a sufficient workout for those not strong enough to handle weights). If you don't want to join a gym, there are plenty of strength-training DVDs that will walk you through the steps. Borrow them from the library or purchase online or at sporting goods shops.

Mirror, mirror on the wall. It's not vanity, its mindfulness. Strength-training in front of a mirror is extremely helpful in noticing a crooked arm or uneven lift and for monitoring your overall form.

TOP 10 STRENGTH-TRAINING TIPS

1. **Hydrate.** Drink two large glasses of water an hour before your workout, and keep your water bottle with you to sip between sets. Weight training should make you thirsty. If it doesn't, you may need to increase your weight.

2. **Eat something to power your workout**. Yogurt with nuts…whole-grain bread with a smear of peanut butter and a glass of milk…a banana. Whatever healing food suits you, keep it light and eat it 45 minutes to an hour before you begin.

3. **Raise your temp.** Climb on a stationary bicycle or Stairmaster to warm up. (You can also do five to 10 minutes of brisk walking.) Raising your body temperature primes your muscles for weight-bearing activity and gets your heart pumping, giving you more strength when you begin.

4. **Snack afterward.** Eating an apple, banana, or orange plus some protein after a workout feeds your muscles and replenishes your blood sugar. (You can add a piece of cheese to your fruit, or fork up a little canned tuna or salmon.) And keep hydrating, because water flushes toxins from your body.

5. **Get a lesson in good form.** Sloppy form leads to injuries. Ask a local trainer to give you a one-hour lesson on how to lift. Pay a trainer or find a free instructor at your local health club, YMCA/YWCA, or senior center. For a quality starter video, Google "Mercola how do I work out with weights YouTube." It's a great video with plenty of smart tips and pointers.

6. **Go slowly.** Weight training isn't about speed. In fact, it's more beneficial when done slowly and deliberately, with attention to form. Like yoga, this mindfulness creates a calming, meditative space while you're working out.

7. **Isolate muscles for best results.** When you first start working with weights, it's natural to tense up your whole body when you lift. Instead, focus all that tension solely on the muscles that you're working, relaxing those that aren't directly involved (like your other hand and your jaw).

8. **Breathe!** Holding your breath during a lift can spike your blood pressure. Remember: Inhale first and exhale while you lift. Inhale again as you release.

9. **Stretch.** After a lifting session (and between sets), stretching keeps your muscles loose and flexible. Always give yourself a day off between sessions so muscles can rest and repair.

10. **Pain isn't helpful.** Forget the adage "No pain, no gain." If an exercise hurts, stop immediately; you could be hurting yourself. Overworking (or poor form) can cause torn tendons and strained muscles. Sore muscles are another story. If you aren't a little sore the next day, you probably weren't working hard enough. Welcome the soreness as the sign of a good workout. Soon you'll grow familiar with the day-off feeling of muscles that have been well exercised.[95]

MORE STRENGTH-TRAINING BENEFITS

No one lives forever, but you do have control over how long you stay "young." After all, it isn't age that does most people in—it's *frailty*. When your muscles are weak, it's easy to lose your balance and fall. When you lack strength and stamina, you need others to take care of you. Strength begins with "mental toughness," which is the will to push through obstacles toward your goals. The real reason for exercising your body is to train your *mind*. And a strong mind will make it easier for you to say no to those temptations that can throw you off your path—and yes to the ones that will keep you true. But here are some other physical benefits of keeping your body strong…

- Builds energy, which improves your metabolism, which in turn helps you lose fat while gaining lean muscle. Muscle uses a lot more energy than fat, even when you're just relaxing on the couch.

- Leads to more efficient use of energy, including glucose and the calories your take in. Calories are needed to power your workout, and you'll be using plenty!

- Brings greater flexibility. Incorporating a range of motion in your routine improves flexibility in your joints. Flexing your muscles with resistance makes them work harder, so that your ability to stretch continues to grow.

- Strengthens your bones. Weight-bearing exercise has been proven again and again to build strong bones…and protect against osteoporosis…because it signals your body to send more calcium to bones, increasing their density.

---

[95] http://www.diabeteshealth.com/read/2005/09/01/4323/weight-training-and-diabetes/

- Boosts immunity. Studies show that moderate exercise (and strength training two or three times weekly certainly qualifies) increases your immunity to colds, flu, infections, and cancer.[96]

TAKE ACTION TODAY: Add strength training two to three times a week for better energy, stronger bones and heart, lower blood sugar, and a leaner profile.

EXTRA CREDIT: Contact a local gym or health club and ask for a "free one-week pass" to give their facility a try.

---

[96] http://well.blogs.nytimes.com/2009/10/14/phys-ed-does-exercise-boost-immunity/

DAY 27: ADD GREEN DRINKS

Even people who aren't sick may not have optimal wellness.

BRIAN CARTER

HEALER: Phytonutrients from plants become a concentrated superfood in green drinks, adding a nutritional punch to help you knock out diabetes!

HERE'S A WAY to get the massive nutrient power of leafy greens in a much smaller package. Yes, I want you to continue eating every dark leafy green veggie you can get your hands on—as much as you can every day—for their fiber content and for their rich supply of vitamins and minerals. Minerals, in fact, are extremely important in supporting insulin sensitivity…healthy blood sugar levels…a strong immune system…proper thyroid function…and a strong, steady heartbeat. Most of all, minerals provide your body's cells with incredible amounts of energy. And there's an ocean of minerals in the exceptionally nutrient-dense "green drinks" that I want you to include in your diet, beginning today.

"Nutrient density" means that, ounce for ounce, green drinks and supplements contain far more health-giving phytonutrients than an equivalent amount of their leafy green veggie cousins. These are true superfoods! The secret's in their blue chlorophyll (known to help boost the production of stem cells), which is plentiful in algae and other green plants. Green drinks offer the highest concentration of plant nutrients. Spirulina and chlorella are single-cell algae loaded with protein, amino acids, enzymes, chlorophyll, vitamins, minerals, and antioxidants with proven abilities to lower blood sugar and enhance metabolism, all in a form that's easily assimilated by the body. Green drinks are also made from dried-and-powdered grasses, including wheat grass and barley grass. Among other attributes, these grasses are high in omega-3, which is why grass-fed beef and dairy products are so good for you.

WHY YOU SHOULD DRINK THEM

Most of us don't get enough fresh organic greens in our daily diet no matter how many servings we try to eat. (These are Mother Nature's greatest healing foods!) One way to increase your intake is to juice them with other (sweeter) veggies such as carrots. But these green drinks are easier to whip up—and they contain even *more* nutrition. I'll discuss specific green drinks in a minute, but keep in mind that these green drink powders are powerfully effective in keeping your pancreas clipping along in peak health and at extinguishing all that inflammation that's damaging your tissues and organs.

Bottom line: A tall glass of green is like an insurance policy that covers you on days when your veggie drawer is running low, or on your high-stress days that might otherwise leave you flat-out exhausted.

SPIRULINA

Blue-green spirulina grows in warm, alkaline waters, mainly in Central Africa and Mexico. It contains 65% protein (the highest of *any* food!) and is twice as easily absorbed and used by your body as animal protein. Spirulina also contains more vision-protecting beta-carotene than carrots. Even the National Institutes of Health (NIH) admits that spirulina has a place in diabetes control. In a preliminary study of type 2 diabetics, the NIH says spirulina "may reduce fasting blood sugar levels" after just eight weeks of treatment.[97]

The sulphur in spirulina is essential to proper functioning of your pancreas, liver, and entire immune system. Research done on spirulina in India (published in the medical journal *Current Pharmaceutical Biotechnology*) showed it to be an effective "anti-diabetic" as well as anti-inflammatory, antioxidant, antibacterial, antiviral, and anti-allergenic.[98]

This tiny single-celled algae is especially mineral-rich, containing high amounts of potassium, calcium, chromium, zinc, iron, copper, magnesium, selenium, plus many other minerals that are essential for proper liver and pancreas function. It's also an outstanding source of vitamins B, E, and K, as well as important antioxidants, including *zeaxanthin* plus amino acids needed for optimal brain chemistry.

How can such a little package pack in so much goodness? Spirulina also contains SOD (*superoxide dismutase*), a protective antioxidant that fights free radicals and toxins in your body. It's also high in the essential fatty acid GLA (*gamma linolenic acid*), which has been shown to be an effective blood-sugar modulator.[99] What more could you ask for?

CHLORELLA

This miniscule, one-celled freshwater green algae, which grows in Australia and Southeast Asia, is a "dream food." That's because chlorella is loaded with protein (550% more than rice and 380% greater than soybeans!). It's extremely rich in vitamins and minerals, and contains nine es-

---

[97] http://www.nlm.nih.gov/medlineplus/druginfo/natural/patient-spirulina.html

[98] http://www.bentham.org/cpb/contabs/cpb6-5.htm

[99] http://www.chlorellafactor.com/chlorella-spirulina-27.html

sential amino acids (the building blocks of protein), which control the growth, repair, and maintenance of all your body's cells. It's bursting with magnesium, which is essential for balanced blood sugar, optimal blood pressure, and healthy nerve and muscle action. Magnesium is called "nature's antidepressant" because it helps us cope with stress (another benefit for people with diabetes).

- Research published in the *Journal of Medicinal Food* found that chlorella increases fat metabolism and insulin sensitivity, while reducing body fat, blood sugar, and serum cholesterol (all by affecting the biochemical pathways in the body).[100]

- Studies are under way at Virginia Commonwealth University, where Randall Merchant, professor of neurosurgery and anatomy, is examining the effect of chlorella on people with prediabetes (metabolic syndrome). According to Merchant, "It seems that chlorella turns on the genes that control the way insulin is normally used by the cells in the body. This research shows that chlorella could in theory help correct the problems of metabolic syndrome. It is not a magic bullet, but taking it is one other preventive thing you can do, like exercise or watching your diet."[101]

- Other research shows that chlorella encourages the growth of beneficial bacteria (called probiotics), while helping your gut with peristalsis, the contractions that move waste products from the food you eat through your intestines, thus keeping you regular and preventing toxins in stools from being absorbed by your bloodstream.

- In fact, chlorella and spirulina are both effective at toxin removal, be they the pesticides and environmental pollutants we're exposed to every day in our food supply, heavy metals in our water, or the excessive alcohol we may have overimbibed.[102]

- Back at Virginia Commonwealth University, clinical trials on chlorella for hypertension are now under way. The latest findings are hopeful: Chlorella lowered blood pressure in 50% of participants and also dramatically lowered cholesterol. People taking a blood-thinning medication such as Coumadin (*warfarin*) should talk to their doctors before taking chlorella, a rich source of vitamin K1, which encourages healthy blood clotting.

BARLEY GRASS

The young green shoots of barley grass are brilliant green, a clue to their concentrated chlorophyll content. Barley grass packs an iron punch (500% times more than spinach!) and has 1,000% more calcium than milk. Those are impressive numbers! Barley grass is also loaded with the super-antioxidant SOD, which researchers in Bucharest found to be a highly effective anti-inflammatory.

---

[100] http://www.ncbi.nlm.nih.gov/pmc/articles/PMC2788184/

[101] http://www.telegraph.co.uk/health/wellbeing/6028408/Chlorella-the-superfood-that-helps-fight-disease.html

[102] http://www.telegraph.co.uk/health/wellbeing/6028408/Chlorella-the-superfood-that-helps-fight-disease.html

So impressed were they with barley grass that they recommended it for people with rheumatoid arthritis.

You already know the devastating role inflammation plays in diabetes, heart disease, arthritis, and Alzheimer's. SOD is a known neutralizer of *superoxide*, the most damaging of all free radicals. SOD stops superoxide's effect on cell mutation in its tracks, essentially halting the proliferation of cancer cells. But SOD's benefits don't stop there. It also builds infection-fighting T cells and enhances retinal health to slow vision-destroying macular degeneration. Important for diabetics, SOD inhibits neurological degeneration (which means it helps prevent and repair neuropathy).

Evidence is building that barley grass can protect against heart disease and stroke by keeping the blood naturally thin. Researchers at China Medical College in Taiwan found that barley grass leaf extract drives down LDL cholesterol, the bad form that can accumulate in arteries and trigger stroke or heart attack. Scientists treating a group of heart disease patients over four weeks discovered that 15 grams of barley grass leaf extract drove down LDL along with destructive free radicals. Adding just 200 mg of vitamin E and C brought even greater LDL-lowering results.[103]

TIPS FOR DRINKING YOUR GREENS

Green drinks, powders, mixes, and supplements often contain one or more of the green superfoods spirulina, chlorella, and barley grass. You can try them separately or find a mix that has all three.

Pill or powder? Pills you swallow; powders you mix with water, vegetable juice, milk, or soy milk. Either way, you'll be getting plenty of the "green power." Avoid powdered mixes that contain added sweeteners or that recommend adding to fruit juice. You don't need the extra sugar. Stay away from products with added soy and gluten. These may aggravate your health condition.

Take your time. You don't need to jump into the green pool with both feet to reap the benefits of these miracle foods. Just a couple spoonfuls in your water bottle sipped throughout the day can make a difference. Or add them to a smoothie (my favorite choice!). You may notice physical improvements within days or weeks.

Tell your doctor. Keep your physician updated on all supplement choices you want to make, because your blood sugar, blood pressure, and cholesterol could drop like a lead balloon. If you're on medications for any of these conditions, you'll need to have them adjusted!

TAKE ACTION TODAY: Add a high-quality green drink or blue-green algae supplement to your daily diet for better blood sugar metabolism, enhanced immunity, and reduced inflammation. It's one more important step you can take in your quest for a long life of good health and well-being.

---

[103] http://www.thehealthierlife.co.uk/natural-remedies/herbs/barley-grass-health-benefits-00859.html

EXTRA CREDIT: Browse the Internet or your local health food store for these highly recommended brands and purchase a month's supply: Boku Super Food, Hawaiian Spirulina by Nutrex-Hawaii, New Chapter's Berry Green, Marine Phytoplankton by Ocean's Alive, Greens+, Emerald Energy Original, and NanoGreens by BioPharma.

CASE STUDY: LOUIS

"I said goodbye to diabetes a year ago—and it hasn't come back."

Louis refused to admit he was overweight and kept trying to fit 30 extra pounds of fat into his skinny clothes. His physician paid lip service to holistic care as a way to recruit patients, but believed deeply that type 2 diabetes isn't reversible. Louis started gaining weight fast (not uncommon as one's metabolism is progressing toward diabetes). At 30 pounds overweight, he began feeling bad about himself and was also losing energy and stamina. It was depressing, but he resigned himself to it.

Case Study: Louis	Before	After
Weight	209	176
A1C	8.1	5.6
Blood Pressure	158/92	134/80
Triglycerides	208	148
Meds	Metformin, Lipitor	Nothing

Then Louis got his minor miracle. He got sick and his doctor was too busy, so he called me. I saw what was going on immediately and put him on *The 30-Day Diabetes Cure*. After only a week, Louis was hooked. Today, 33 pounds lighter, Louis hikes at 12,000-feet altitude with ease. He has more stamina today than he had 10 years ago!

DAY 28: ADD SUPPLEMENTS

Adam and Eve ate the first vitamins, including the package.

E.R. SQUIBB

HEALER: **There are several high-quality supplements that can help if your blood sugar gets stuck on a plateau—or you simply want to accelerate your progress. Take a look….**

IN A PERFECT WORLD, the meals you're now eating would provide all the nutrients you need to turn your condition around. But even when your meals are based on organically grown whole grains, vegetables, and fruit, naturally raised meats and dairy products, plus wild-caught fish, sometimes you need a little extra nutritional support.

Much of our country's agricultural topsoil is depleted. Vital minerals and other soil nutrients are in short supply (or completely missing), which means that the food grown there is lacking as well. That's why it's so important to choose organic foods when shopping, but sometimes these are hard to come by. Another factor to consider is your body's ability to absorb these nutrients. You see, the older we get, the more difficult it becomes for our digestive system to extract all the nutrition in our food. The result is that we can end up poorly nourished even when eating a "perfect diet."

This is where high-quality supplements can make a real difference. Handfuls of supplements should never substitute for a nutrient-rich diet, but the reality is that your body is sometimes compromised in its efforts to regain its natural balance. When this occurs, you need all the help you can get.

BE SMART ABOUT SUPPLEMENTS

Supplement recommendations are often given with so many caveats about interactions and side effects that it's difficult to understand what makes them beneficial. I've avoided going into detail on the potential risks and interactions of the supplements in this chapter for one very good reason: I want you to talk to your doctor before taking any of them. That's because some of these supplements are so powerful that your blood sugar could drop significantly. You and your diabetes care team should be aware of their potential healing effects before you start taking them.

How to begin. Start on the Big Three described below as soon as you get your doctor's approval. For the rest of the healing supplements in this section, I suggest you try them one at a time. That's because you want to be able to track the results of what you're taking (so you can to say to your doc, "Look at my numbers after eight weeks on ginseng!") and by taking several supplements simultaneously, you'll never know which is responsible for the positive benefits you might experience.

Give them time. Introduce one new supplement and give it several weeks to work. Unlike drugs that act immediately, nutritional supplements take a while to build up in your system before you notice their beneficial effects.

Trust your intuition. In choosing which of these Diabetes-Healing Supplements to try first, read this entire chapter and see which ones might be right for you.

THREE TO TAKE FOR CERTAIN

Reread Day 16 for a quick refresher on how to recognize quality supplements. Along with your multivitamin and vitamin D, here are three more essentials that every diabetic can benefit from…

Fish oil. Wild-caught Alaskan salmon is one of the best food sources of omega-3 fatty acids there is, but it's difficult to find an affordable, reliable supply. Happily, fish oil supplements are a fine substitute. They're loaded with the same healing EPA (*eicosapentaenoic acid*) and DHA (*docosahexaenoic acid*), which have profound effects on your health.

DHA is like a big brake pedal that slows your liver's production of undesirable triglycerides. In addition, both EPA and DHA are incredibly effective at reducing overall inflammation. They do this by triggering the release of *prostaglandins* (natural substances that regulate immunity, inflammation, blood clotting, brain function, plus a host of other essential functions). They also have a profoundly healing effect in blood vessels, while thinning your blood and lowering your blood pressure. Omega-3s also improve the circulation, keeping blood flowing smoothly and reducing the risk of clotting, which limits your chances of stroke and heart attack. Finally, omega-3s are blood sugar stabilizers and are also helpful for depression. (I discussed this back on Day 11 in my discussion about good and bad fats.)

The American Heart Association recommends a daily dose of 500 to 1,000 mg of DHA and EPA from fish oil to reduce heart disease, one of your biggest risks. A 2006 study affirms the power of the individual omega-3s. Published in the *Journal of the American College of Nutrition*,[104] researchers found 1,000 mg of omega-3s lowered triglycerides in people with coronary

---

[104] http://douglassreport.com/2010/01/20/big-gift/

artery disease, whether the omegas came in the form of DHA combined with EPA or from DHA alone.

Here's the catch: To get enough EPA and DHA, your omega-3s must come from marine sources. Plant sources of omega-3s, including flax oil, flaxseed, borage oil, and evening primrose oil, are good for you and flaxseed is a wonderful source of fiber. But none of these yield a potent amount of EPA and DHA. The label of your fish oil product ought to give a quantity of each omega-3. To find out if you are getting enough DPA/EPA and not mysterious additives or toxins, take the total omega-3's and subtract EPA and DHA. If what is left over is greater than 50% of the pill, well, that's mysterious stuff that they can't account for—and that's when you need to worry about mercury and PCBs.

Krill oil may be an even better source of omega-3s than fish oil. That's because krill, a tiny crustacean eaten by the mighty whale, also contains a powerful antioxidant *astaxanthin*. It's responsible for the pink color of krill (and wild salmon) and makes krill oil 48 times more anti-oxidant-potent than fish oil, according to its ORAC (oxygen radical absorbancy capacity) score. The omega-3s in krill oil also have a different molecular form than fish oil, one that may be even more compatible with the human body.

Take one to three 1,000-mg fish oil or krill oil capsules three times daily with your doctor's approval. When shopping (take your magnifying glass), check the back of the label and make sure the product contains at least 500 mg of omega-3 per dose, in the ideal ratio of 3:2 (300 mg DHA to 200 mg EPA).

Fish oil can thin your blood, so if you're taking a blood-thinning drug like *warfarin* (Coumadin) or *clopidogrel* (Plavix), talk to your doctor before starting more than 2 grams daily. If you're on blood sugar-lowering medications, taking omega-3s may increase your fasting blood sugar levels. Use them with caution if you're on blood sugar-lowering medications, such as *glipizide* (Glucotrol and Glucotrol XL), *glyburide* (Micronase or DiaBeta), *Glucophage* (metformin), or insulin. Omega-3 supplements may increase your need for these medications, so be sure to consult your doctor first.

Like other supplements, fish oil capsules can be made from inferior products or contain undisclosed toxins. In a lawsuit filed in California in 2010, several fish oil producers were listed as having high levels of toxic PCB (*polychlorinated biphenyl*) compounds, even though they were labeled as purified. Go to www.FishOilSafety.com for more information and to check your brand. The Environmental Defense Fund (EDF) examined 75 brands of fish oil and created a Best Choice/Worst Choice list at *http://www.edf.org/page.cfm?tagID=16536*. I urge you to visit this site to check if your brand is on the safe list. Ultimately (as always), the responsibility rests with you, the shopper.

CoQ-10. Coenzyme Q-10 (also known as ubiquinol) is a nutrient made by the "energy factories" in your cells called *mitochondria*. Taking a CoQ-10 supplement boosts the way your cells produce and use energy. Studies show that the outcomes are very good for people with diabetes. CoQ-10 helps your body burn fat, improves cholesterol ratios, kicks up physical energy, and improves thyroid and pancreas functions. It's also essential for heart health.

By the way, the statin drugs so widely prescribed for high cholesterol (supposedly to protect diabetics from the disease's number one complication, heart attack) actually *deplete* your body's natural CoQ-10. That's because statins block production of cholesterol in the liver, where CoQ-10 is also made. Without sufficient CoQ-10, statins can cause liver damage, irregular heartbeat, muscle weakness, leg cramps, heart attack, and stroke. Isn't it ironic that statin drugs are supposed to protect you from heart attack, but put you at risk for the very same thing by depleting CoQ-10?

Here's another irony: Statin drugs *increase* the risk of diabetes! Because statins prevent the liver from making cholesterol, the blood sugar sent to your liver (where it's supposed to be converted into fats and stored for later use) gets pumped back into the bloodstream instead! Your blood sugar and triglycerides rise, and the next thing you know, you have a blood sugar metabolism dysfunction. In the recent AstraZeneca-sponsored JUPITER study, Crestor patients had a 27% *higher* risk of diabetes than patients who took a placebo.[105]

Lots of other medications can limit your body's production of CoQ-10. If you take diabetes drugs, antidepressants, female hormone replacement therapy, or blood pressure drugs, you definitely need to supplement with CoQ-10. But what to buy? The label may read "CoQ-10" or "coenzyme Q-10." A more active form will be labeled "QH" or "ubiquinol." This is a stronger version of CoQ-10, but it's not essential, especially if price is an issue. Take 50 to 150 mg once or twice a day. You should notice improvement in your energy levels fairly quickly.

Alpha-lipoic acid (ALA). If you have nerve pain, ALA can come to your rescue. It helps control blood sugar too. Your body makes some of this antioxidant fatty acid in tiny amounts, but it doesn't exist in food, so to get more you need to supplement. Studies show this potent neutralizer of free radicals improves circulation and helps insulin work better. Because it's both fat-soluble and water-soluble, ALA moves easily around your organs, bloodstream, and brain, neutralizing toxins and supporting the liver's detox function. It also helps generate vitamins C and E, as well as CoQ-10. Researchers say that ALA improves blood flow to the nerves by up to 44%. That increased flow can help relieve numbness and neuropathy, symptoms that traditional painkillers can't touch.

- A 2006 study[106] published in *Diabetes Care* found that ALA reduced the pain of diabetic neuropathy after just five weeks on a single daily dose. Half the study group got ALA and the others a placebo. The ALA takers reported an impressive 51% reduction in pain and numbness within two weeks.

---

[105] http://douglassreport.com/2010/01/20/big-gift/

[106] http://www.diabetesselfmanagement.com/Blog/Tara-Dairman/antioxidant_ala_eases_pain_from_diabetic_neuropathy/

- A German study discovered that after four weeks, ALA takers improved insulin sensitivity by 27%.[107]

Recommended dose. Take what the *Diabetes Care* researchers concluded was the lowest, most effective dose: 600 mg once a day, an hour before a meal for maximum absorption. If you can find *R-lipoic acid*, biologically most similar to human ALA, take just half that dose—300 mg once daily. Remember that ALA will lower your blood sugar, so if you're taking blood sugar medication, you might need to adjust your dose. (And isn't that the whole point?)

FOUR MORE HELPERS TO CONSIDER

Remember to check with your doctor before adding any new supplements to your regimen, because you don't want to end up in hypoglycemic territory. Here are four more supplements that are especially beneficial for diabetes…

Chromium. Here's the short story on the trace mineral chromium: It improves insulin sensitivity by increasing the number of insulin receptors on every cell. It also helps smooth out blood sugar spikes after eating by enhancing the action of insulin (and also because of its involvement in metabolizing fats, carbs, and proteins). Plus, chromium supports optimal thyroid function, which is vital for diabetics, since low thyroid leads to sluggish metabolism—especially the conversion of glucose to energy, as well as your ability to burn off extra sugar instead of storing it as fat.

Chromium deficiency contributes to high blood sugar, low thyroid, and weight gain. Chromium also appears to affect cholesterol levels favorably. Purchase *chromium polynicotinate*, most easily taken up by the body because it binds to niacin (vitamin B3). Or choose *chromium GTF* (glucose tolerance factor). Take 200 micrograms (mcg) one to three times a day—and don't exceed 1,000 mcg daily. Chelated chromium is more effectively absorbed than nonchelated.

Magnesium. A deficiency in this important mineral is fairly common among people with diabetes, and this can exacerbate insulin resistance and high blood sugar. Adequate magnesium levels are essential for proper insulin activity and a strong, healthy heart. Leg cramps and muscle spasms are relieved with adequate magnesium (and so is anxiety) thanks to this mineral's muscle-relaxing, calming effect. In fact, anxiety/agitation, restless leg syndrome, sleep disorders, and abnormal heart rhythms are all telltale signs of magnesium deficiency.

Ask your doc to test your levels, because there's no need to supplement unless you're deficient. Many Americans *are* deficient due to the low-quality, processed foods in the typical American diet. Produce grown in mineral-depleted soil won't provide much magnesium either. Keep eating lots of dark green leafy vegetables, but use a supplement if you need it. Take 250 to 350 mg once daily, but no more, especially if you have liver or kidney problems. Choose magnesium with *aspartate*, *malate*, or *glycinate*. These amino acids help the body process the magnesium

---

[107] http://care.diabetesjournals.org/content/26/5/1553.full

without stomach distress. Magnesium lowers blood pressure significantly (I use it for hypertension), and can give you diarrhea. If you are getting loose stools, then you are taking too much.

Gymnema sylvestre. Its Hindu name means "sugar destroyer"—and that tells the story. This herb has been used as a powerful diabetes medication in India for more than 2,000 years. It contains *gymnemic acids* that slow sugar's transport into your bloodstream. As a result, your own insulin has less sugar to process and your glucose levels are better controlled.

Gymnema also supports your pancreas function and helps neutralize carb cravings. Studies show that it's especially valuable for type 1 diabetes because it helps increase natural insulin production in the body. It may even repair and restore burned-out beta cells, giving type 1 patients the chance to reduce or even eliminate insulin injections. Take 250 to 1,000 mg daily, dividing the smallest effective dose throughout the day. Purchase a product that contains 75% gymnemic acids or one that's standardized to 25%.

Fiber supplements. You should be getting more than enough fiber from all the whole grains, vegetables, and fruits you're enjoying. But a fiber supplement can make the difference between "adequate" and "optimal" daily waste removal. No supplement is as ideally suited for people with diabetes as PGX (PolyGlycoplex). Made from the root of the Japanese konjac plant and other fibers, PGX is soluble fiber (meaning it forms a thick, viscous gel in the digestive tract), which slows the release of glucose into the bloodstream.

PGX is six times more viscous than psyllium, the fiber used in most commercial fiber brands (such as Metamucil®). In a study published in *Diabetes Care*, PGX reduced insulin-resistance by 40%—fully *double* the effect of other fiber supplements. Adding PGX to food can make a big difference too. *Diabetes Care* ran a study showing that a sprinkle of PGX on food led to a decrease in LDL cholesterol of 22%—about the same result you'd see with a statin drug, but without the adverse side effects.

EIGHT GREAT HERBAL HEALERS

Of course, you'll chat with your doctor before starting anything new, but the research on these Diabetes-Healing Herbs is too good to overlook…

Bilberry. A cousin of the blueberry, bilberry leaves and fruit are loaded with antioxidants called anthocyanins that prevent injury to delicate blood vessels, including the ones feeding the retinas in your eyes (damaged blood vessels cause retinopathy and also nerve damage). Animal studies done in 2010[108] suggest that bilberry can also reduce blood sugar, boost sensitivity to insulin, and help control obesity. It apparently works by activating *amp-activated protein kinase* (ampk), which controls insulin secretion, while encouraging the breakdown of fats in muscle and the liver. Try 80 to 120 mg of standardized bilberry extract twice daily.

---

[108] http://jn.nutrition.org/content/140/3/527.abstract

Bitter melon. *This* is actually a veggie whose seeds and fruit may lower blood glucose by helping cells use sugar more efficiently. Bitter melon also seems to block absorption of sugar by the intestines. Philippine researchers whose study participants took bitter melon capsules for 12 weeks had consistently lower blood sugar than a control group. Researchers publishing in a 1999 issue of the *Bangladesh Medical Research Council Bulletin* [109] found that average blood sugars dropped from 257 mg/dl to 222 mg/dl with bitter melon. Try 3 to 6 tablespoons (50 to 100 milliliters) of bitter melon juice every day.

Blueberry leaf extract. I have to chuckle when I see research from 80 years ago on using blueberry leaf extract (BLE) to treat diabetes. (Yes, the 1928 issue of the *Canadian Medical Association Journal* [110] is available online.) Talk about everything old being new again! BLE is a safe, natural source of *chlorogenic acid*, a workhorse that helps drive down blood sugar by keeping glycogen from turning into glucose. BLE also mimics the action of insulin to prevent sugar accumulation in your blood. In a 60-day placebo-controlled clinical trial,[111] patients (still on their meds) had their fasting glucose and triglycerides checked every two weeks. Some participants got 200 mg of BLE powder in capsule form three times daily before meals. By the end of the sixth week, the BLE takers had a notable reduction in blood glucose levels (from 169 mg/dL to 136 mg/dL). Bonus: By study's end, the BLE group recorded LDL drops from 141 mg/dL to 115 mg/dL—and their triglycerides plummeted from 179 mg/dL to 130 mg/dL.

Another study,[112] in 2006, found that 300 mg of BLE taken three times daily (15 to 30 minutes before meals) led to a 27% drop in fasting blood sugars and a remarkable 60% reduction in C-reactive protein (CRP), one of the body's inflammation markers. Try 300 mg of BLE standardized to a 15% concentration of chlorogenic acid three times daily before meals.[113]

Cinnamon cassia extract.[114] Our old friend cinnamon returns from Day 2! This time, researchers report that taking a gram (1,000 mg) or more every day can reduce blood glucose, LDL, total cholesterol, and triglycerides in people with type 2.

In the study, 60 people were randomly organized into six groups: The first three took 1, 3, or 6 grams of cinnamon daily. The other three groups took placebos. After 40 days, researchers found the three groups taking the real McCoy showed splendid improvements: Up to 29% drop in blood sugar…up to 30% reduction in triglycerides…up to 26% lower rate of total cholesterol…and up to a 27% drop in LDL. The placebo takers had no such improvements.

---

[109] http://www.diabeteshealth.com/read/2005/02/01/4095/bitter-melon/

[110] http://www.ncbi.nlm.nih.gov/pmc/articles/PMC1709814/?page=6

[111] http://www.ameriden.com/healthspot/category/diabetes/

[112] http://www.healthyfellow.com/315/blueberry-leaf/

[113] http://www.drdavidwilliams.com/legacy/order/0809_bldsgr_advmg.aspx?panelcode=be001933&listcode=1806 04&utm_campaign=bloodsugar&utm_source=full&utm_medium=email-loy&utm_content=bsug-180604

[114] http://www.pbrc.edu/division-of-education/pdf/pns/PNS_Cinnamon.pdf

Surprisingly, researchers have even found that cinnamon works with insulin synergistically, meaning the two working together produce an effect that's greater than the therapeutic effect of each one individually. But you need to take the right cinnamon. Cinnamon cassia is loaded with diabetes-healing MHCP (*methyl hydroxy chalcone polymer*), the spice's active compound, which boosts insulin receptivity of your cells. Studies of MHCP show it works like your body's own insulin to help clear sugar from the bloodstream. In effect, MHCP mimics insulin. There are two main varieties of cinnamon: *Cinnamomum cassia* and *Cinnamomum zeylanicum*. The latter is sweeter, lighter, and milder and comes from Burma or Sri Lanka. *C. cassia* is darker and stronger and, lucky for us, the most common type in the US. So keep sprinkling it on everything from fruit to smoothies, and if you want to try supplements, make sure they're made of cassia. Try 1,000 mg daily.[115]

Fenugreek.[116] Widespread in the Middle East, fenugreek's seeds hold the natural ability to lower blood sugar and cholesterol, while improving insulin sensitivity. That's because fenugreek seeds contain fiber, alkaloids, and other compounds that exert a hypoglycemic (glucose-lowering) effect, slowing the transport of glucose and the absorption of carbs, and delaying the emptying of your stomach. One amino acid in fenugreek may even stimulate secretion of insulin from the pancreas.

Fenugreek also increases the number of insulin receptors on red blood cells and helps your body utilize glucose better. A 1996 study published in *Nutrition Research* followed 60 type 2 patients for six months. They took 25 grams of powdered fenugreek seed each day with lunch and dinner. Result? Glucose (measured one hour and two hours after eating) dropped, and average A1C went from 9.6% to 8.4% after two months. After six months, participants' fasting glucose numbers plunged from 151 mg/dL to 112 mg/dL.

In a separate 1990 study published in the *European Journal of Clinical Nutrition*, type 1 diabetics taking insulin tried fenugreek. Half took 50 grams of defatted seed powder two times daily. Their fasting blood sugars nosedived from 272 mg/dL to 196 mg/dL and they also saw decreases in total cholesterol, triglycerides, and LDL. Try 5 to 30 grams with meals three times daily.

Gamma-linolenic acid (GLA).[117] GLA is an omega-6 fatty acid found in evening primrose oil, borage oil, and black currant seed oil. We need omega-6s for good health, but our bodies can't make them (which is why they're called *essential* fatty acids), so we have to get them from food. When omega-6s and omega-3s are out of balance, omega-6s become pro-inflammatory. However, GLA is a particular omega-6 that is converted into anti-inflammatory substances in the body. Some studies show that diabetics have lower-than-ideal levels of GLA, and that taking it for six months or longer can improve the function of damaged nerves.

---

[115] http://www.drdavidwilliams.com/legacy/order/0809_bldsgr_advmg.aspx?panelcode=be001933&listcode=180604&utm_campaign=bloodsugar&utm_source=full&utm_medium=email-loy&utm_content=bsug-180604

[116] http://www.diabeteshealth.com/read/2005/01/01/4193/fenugreek/

[117] http://care.diabetesjournals.org/content/16/1/8.abstract

In the Gamma-Linolenic Acid Multicenter Trial, patients with mild diabetic neuropathy took either 480 mg of GLA daily or a placebo for a full year. Researchers evaluated 16 different parameters (including sensation, muscle strength, tendon reflex plus heat and cold tolerance) and found improvement in all 16 in the GLA group. Try the dose that the study participants took—480 mg per day.

Ginseng.[118] Numerous studies show that it strengthens the immune system and fights a variety of diseases, including diabetes. This Chinese herb has been shown in multiple studies to help normalize blood sugar, improve insulin secretion from the pancreas, improve your cells' ability to use glucose, and slow down the absorption of carbs. In fact, taking ginseng capsules can lower blood sugar by 15% to 20% compared with a placebo. In one study, type 2 diabetics took North America-grown ginseng (along with a high-fiber supplement) three times daily for three months. An equal number took a placebo. After 12 weeks, the groups switched, with the placebo takers starting on ginseng-plus-fiber and the ginseng-plus-fiber folks taking the placebo.

Scientists found that A1C levels dropped into the normal range when participants were taking the active capsule but not during placebo periods. In a second study, participants took Korean red ginseng, which also improved insulin sensitivity against a placebo. Note: Asian ginseng is hot. It's guaranteed to raise blood pressure and possibly cause interactions with other medications. It's tough stuff! I recommend American ginseng (wild or organic if you can find it) because it's cool and the effect is moderated. Try 1 to 3 grams daily in tablets or capsules—or 3 to 5 milliliters of ginseng tincture three times daily. Ginseng is also available as a tea.

Prickly Pear Cactus.[119, 120, 121] Mexican traditional medicine uses this cactus, called *nopal*, to treat diabetes and high cholesterol. When scientifically tested, Mexican researchers found that type 2 diabetics who ate broiled nopal stems of the species *Opuntia streptacantha* had drops in blood sugar from 17% to 46%. That's impressive! The secret may lie in nopal's high levels of pectin and fiber, which help push down blood sugars by limiting sugar absorption in the stomach and intestines. Try a half cup of nopal daily or two 250-mg capsules three times daily.[122]

TAKE ACTION TODAY: In addition to taking your multi and vitamin D from Day 16, add the super supplements fish oil, coenzyme Q-10, and ALA to your daily nutritional regimen. This trio helps balance blood sugar levels, lowers cholesterol, relieves mild depression, increases your energy levels, and boosts immunity. Make a note to give your doc a call tomorrow and get his or her approval to start on the three. (Review the other healing supplements covered here and talk to your doctor about starting one.)

---

[118] http://diabetes.webmd.com/news/20030616/ginseng-may-help-treat-diabetes

[119] http://www.jfponline.com/Pages.asp?AID=2463

[120] http://www.webmd.com/vitamins-supplements/

[121] http://www.drugs.com/npp/prickly-pear.html

[122] http://www.rd.com/living-healthy/the-best-herbs-and-supplements-for-diabetes/article55702.html

EXTRA CREDIT: Decide now where you'll shop for fish oil, CoQ-10, and ALA. Do some price comparisons, too.

(-)

DAY 29: ELIMINATE BOREDOM

Until I discovered cooking, I was never really interested in anything.

JULIA CHILD

ANTI-HEALER: **Boredom results from habitual, mind-numbing behaviors and routines. It's the opposite of pleasure, passion, adventure, education, and perpetual growth. When a life lacks excitement, food fills the void. And when eating is a person's central entertainment, big trouble ensues.**

TOO MANY PEOPLE spend their time in front of the TV or sleepwalking through days so filled with boredom that they can't recall the last time they were actually "delighted." Mental boredom triggers physical stagnation, which in turn encourages disease and premature death. That's what researchers publishing in the April 2010 *International Journal of Epidemiology* discovered.[123] People who were severely bored by their jobs had a 250% greater risk of dying from heart disease than their non-bored cohorts.[124]

Playing it safe doesn't serve you or your health—in fact, just the opposite results. Chronic boredom numbs the senses and encourages destructive compensating behaviors such as overeating, alcoholism, smoking, plus recreational drug use and prescription drug abuse. When you're bored, your brain desires these quick fixes because it's either screaming "Make me feel alive!" or "Please stop the pain!"

Disease is not far behind once we lose our passion. And tragically, this is happening with greater frequency in our culture. "Virtual reality" is replacing the real thing—but living our life through others isn't satisfying us. Our senses are being numbed by lack of stimulation and the "use it or lose it" rule is taking its toll on us. Too many people are trapped "in a rut," which will all too soon turn into a grave.

One tragic result is that eating has become our chief source of pleasure and entertainment. Food serves as a powerful mind-altering drug that blunts our day-to-day existential pain. In the words of author Barbara Ehrenreich, "For the millions of us who live glued to computer keyboards

---

[123] http://www.hplusmagazine.com/articles/forever-young/boredom-killer

[124] http://ije.oxfordjournals.org/cgi/content/full/39/2/370

at work and TV monitors at home, food may be more than entertainment. It may be the only sensual experience left."

I believe the true key to reversing diabetes and obesity in our world (plus all the other chronic and degenerative diseases that plague us today) is for individuals to become passionate about something and pursue it with ardor. So today, we're going to reset your GPS for a new destination, one that takes you outside your comfort zone and pushes you toward new horizons. Today is about clearing out the limitations in your life and growing beyond them. Ultimately, this is what will keep you loyal to the principles of *The 30-Day Diabetes Cure* for the rest of your life—because you love your life so much that you'd never do anything to diminish it.

STEP 1: DISCOVER YOUR PASSION

It would take 50 more pages to tell you about the remarkable life transformations many of my patients have experienced as part of their diabetes-healing odyssey. These folks moved themselves from boring, unhealthy lives to ones full of enrichment, wonder, and passion. You can do the same. In Oprah's words, "Passion is energy. Feel the power that comes from focusing on what excites you!" Today, I'm prescribing it. I want you to sample a new variety of pleasurable activities—or perhaps an old hobby or skill that fell by the wayside long ago. Here are some pointers for your search…

Learn something new. People never stop learning. The lifelong learners are deeply curious, and you can acquire this habit too. What is it that you've always longed to do but never managed to get around to? Fly an airplane? Learn a new language? Sculpt? Become a health-care professional? It's not too late. Your local community college has a wide range of interesting adult education courses. (Sometimes they'll even let you audit them for free so you can see if you're really interested.) The point is: Keep growing! Your brain responds to the challenge of learning new information by increasing its number of neurons (brain cells). Studies show this helps to ward off dementia and Alzheimer's. And just the opposite occurs when you allow your mind to shift into neutral. ("Use it or lose it" applies to every part of your body.) As Bob Dylan sings, "He not busy being born is busy dying." Have you always wanted to learn to swim? How about gardening? Growing your own food has the added benefit of providing you with an on-site source of fresh food and a beautiful landscape.

Take a cooking class. James Beard said, "Food is our common ground, a universal experience." Taking a class will help you see why cooking is one of life's greatest pleasures. In his wonderful book, *Choice Cuts*, author Mark Kurlansky writes that "food is a central activity of mankind and one of the single most significant trademarks of a culture." If you followed the suggestion I gave on Day 21 and rented the movie *Julie and Julia* about the life of Julia Child, you know what I'm talking about. Learning to cook with real skill rewards you twice; first in the kitchen and then at the dining table. It's one of the most satisfying activities in life. Once you're engaged, visit *www.myhealingkitchen.com* for loads of delicious free recipes that are specially created to focus on the best Diabetes-Healing Superfoods.

Awaken your sex life. Has it become a routine? Has it disappeared entirely? You can enjoy the excitement and intimacy you experienced in your youth by rekindling that flame. Resparking your desire is possible at any age (and you should have already felt more than a few stirrings by following *The 30-Day Diabetes Cure*). Here are a few ideas passed on to me by my patients that helped them find their sexual passion. Write letters to each other as though you'll die tomorrow, describing what you love about your partner and your life together. Take a dancing class together, or just go dancing regularly. Remember to laugh. Put on some sexy music, light candles, and dress up for each other (perhaps enacting a secret fantasy you've held inside). Use aromatic oils to take turns giving each other a massage. (Don't know how to give a good massage? Take a class!) Go on a couple's retreat. Sign up for a yoga class that was specially designed for couples. Take a bath together. Get fit, lose some weight, tone your muscles, and pay attention to your appearance. Give yourself a new hairstyle, buy some sexy new clothes, create a new look for yourself, regardless of your age. Men especially: Take a look in the mirror and ask yourself if what you see is a "turn on." Remember what Mae West said about sexual attraction: "It's not the men in my life that counts—it's the life in my men."

Travel. Break your usual routine and head out for an adventure trip by hiking or biking in a foreign country you've never visited. Or choose a cultural tour of a particular city. Leave the typical tourist stuff behind and decide to discover something new. Maybe an eco-trip to learn about frogs in the Costa Rican rainforest. Or a journey to the mountains of Tibet. Even a local state park can offer you the pleasurable feeling of being in new surroundings. Check your state parks for lodges that welcome overnight visitors, and make it a romantic getaway. Hike the trails, go to the nature center, enjoy dinner near a roaring fire. Or stay at home and sleep in a tent one night, even if it's in your own backyard! Your neighbors won't think you're crazy—they'll find you fascinating. Why? Because it's a break from your humdrum routine. Be a tourist in your own city. One of my patients found a book of walking tours for her own city and was astounded by the history just three blocks from her house. As she strolled up streets she'd walked for years, the guide offered fascinating facts about the history of the area. She even ran into two Europeans who were there for the same reason.

Make time for pleasure. We all need "me time" regularly. Make a ritual out of taking a candlelit hot bath, scented with incense and/or essential oils. Schedule a regular massage to reacquaint yourself with the pleasures of your body. Have a facial. Go to the park every Sunday morning and take off your shoes so you can walk barefoot in the grass. Plan a picnic, alone or with friends. Schedule regular time exclusively for pleasurable pursuits. Sign up for colorpuncture. Have a Chinese face reading. Experience Reiki. If you're not sure what these exotic experiences are, Google them and choose one that intrigues you the most. Open yourself to life forces and pleasures beyond the four walls of your familiar life and living environment. Follow Mahatma Gandhi's advice and "Learn as if you were going to live forever. Live as if you were going to die tomorrow."

Become an artist. Have you always longed to express yourself creatively? Well, what are you waiting for? You can learn to paint, sculpt, write, or landscape by taking a class. (They're held everywhere, from libraries to the Y to local parks and recreation centers.) I just heard about a local class where for just $5 a session, students gather to draw the human form. Sign up for a photography class and decide what subjects intrigue you most. Is it nature…people…architecture? One fellow I know has a portfolio filled with photos of oddly shaped vegetables. If you're drawn to being an author, start by writing a short story about your triumph over diabetes. Illustrate it with drawings and/or a collage of magazine photos. Becoming absorbed in any artistic endeavor takes you out of your self and liberates you from mind-numbing TV and computer solitaire.

STEP 2: CLEAR OUT THE JUNK

Beat boredom by transforming your living space, as well as your "inner space." Clear out the old physical and metaphorical "stuff" that's been holding you back. You've made conscious choices about diabetes. Now be mindful about the things in your new life that support your health—and discard anything that might be a distraction or obstacle.

Start by tossing out those "plus-size" clothes that no longer fit. Get rid of leftover prescription medications your doctor has taken you off of. This project has everything to do with creating a clean white canvas on which you can paint a fresh energetic start. You can't sail to your next destination until you've lifted the anchor that's keeping you moored in the harbor. Here's a baker's dozen ideas to get you started…

1. Give away all those diet books that failed you.

2. Donate movies and CDs to the library or a women's shelter.

3. Take old clothes and kitchen utensils to your local community shop.

4. Pack up old photographs and mementos and send them to your son or daughter, niece or nephew—the new caretakers of this history.

5. Let go of people in your life who add nothing but drama, stress, or misery to it.

6. Stop picking at old wounds and endlessly rehashing injustices. Forgive everyone in your past who has ever wronged you. Release every resentment, anger, and bitterness in you. Remember that "to forgive is to set a prisoner free and discover that the prisoner was you." (Lewis B. Smedes)

7. Free yourself from the endless loop in which you're always the "innocent victim" of someone else's thoughtlessness.

8. Decide you'll never again utter the words "I can't" (even before you fully consider whether you actually can).

9. Clean out the basement. Then the attic. Then the garage. Celebrate your new "remarkable lightness of being" that comes from not being bogged down by all this stuff anymore.

10. Step away from relationships that no longer support you. In other words: Clean out your heart.

11. Stop listening to the "tape" in your head that defeats you. Change your actions into something positive.

12. Catch yourself when you complain about problems and see how you can become part of a solution instead.

13. Admit when you've made a poor choice, apologize if necessary, and move on. In short, forgive *yourself*.

STEP 3: SHARE THE LOVE

Today I want you to overcome one more limitation: the one that keeps you focused on your symptoms, your diet, your glucose numbers, your blood pressure readings, and your aches and pains. Now that you're feeling better, you're able to notice that there's a larger world that has nothing to do with your diabetes or your problems. It's a world full of need, pain, and suffering. And that world needs your help.

Remember that Beatles line, "The love you take is equal to the love you make"? It's absolutely true! Helping others is a joyful experience. I know of no greater satisfaction in life than volunteering two precious commodities: your love and your time. Ponder how your loving assistance and attention might change the lives of those in great need…

- Children with no shoes. Adults who can't read. The elderly stuck in nursing homes with no one to talk to.

- Veterans whose psyches and bodies are shattered. Parents who can't provide a meal for their family. Babies with no parents to care for them.

- Women, children, and pets who have been abused.

- Abandoned dogs and cats and imprisoned in cages and sentenced to death, without children to play with or a safe place to curl up at night.

- Even members of your own family who feel forgotten.

You're not the same person who began this plan 29 days ago. You're very different—and I'm not just referring to your health. You've developed a mindful approach to life by paying attention, being calm, and choosing the healing path. You've developed the wisdom and personal power to help and heal yourself. You've accomplished something that very few people are able to: You've transformed your life. What a miracle!

But there is an even bigger miracle in store for you—and that's by helping others to transform their lives. I urge you to step out into the world and give a helping hand. Spend one hour a week or one day a month—whatever you can fit in—to volunteer in your community. Visit the sick. Serve food to the hungry. Be a shoulder for someone's tears. Write a letter to a relative. Become a mentor in your support group. Share your wisdom and experience. Inspire someone who feels powerless. Join a movement. Register people to vote. Donate your old belongings. Search for ways you can be of service. Follow Sarah Bernhardt's advice: "Life begets life. Energy creates energy. It is by spending oneself that one becomes rich."

This is the next dimension of healing. Be the change you want to see in the world. You'll never be bored again as long as you live!

TAKE ACTION: Eliminate any tedious routine that doesn't stimulate or excite you. Expand your horizons beyond what you think you can do...who you think you can be... and where you belong in the world. Be inspired by the advice of philosopher William James, who said, "If you can change your mind, you can change your life." He was right.

EXTRA CREDIT: Turn off the TV for an entire day. Fix yourself a cup of tea and decide on one new activity in this section that you'll embark on immediately.

CASE STUDY: KASSANDRA

"I lost 30 pounds and at 65 have tons of energy for my new career!"

Kassandra is fascinating. At age 65, she went back to school in Film Studies, and was the oldest one in the class. She knew, in her heart, that she had stories to tell, and she graduated with a master's in Film Studies and into a new life. One day, she showed up in my office with a bad case of shingles. A conventional doctor might have treated her shingles with antiviral medication and sent her home (but I always look deeper into a patient's health).

Case Study: Kassandra	Before	After
Weight	162	138
A1C	7.4	5.8
Blood Pressure	154/94	112/72
Triglycerides	193	148
Meds	-	-

Imagine her surprise when her lab work showed that she had diabetes. She had high A1C, elevated triglycerides, and high blood pressure (all classic signs). Most physicians would have treated her diabetes, triglycerides and hypertension with medications. But I immediately put her on *The 30-Day Diabetes Cure*. Soon all of Kassandra's numbers plummeted back into the safety zone with a surprise bonus: She lost 24 pounds! What's the take-home message? Don't be afraid to let good eating habits heal you naturally.

DAY 30: CELEBRATE!

The more you praise and celebrate your life, the more there is in life to celebrate.

OPRAH WINFREY

HEALER: **Congratulations! You've just achieved what the "experts" claim is impossible: You're reversing a disease they've labeled "incurable." And you're getting off what would otherwise be a lifetime of medications. It's time for you to take a well-deserved bow!**

YOU MADE IT! You're actually saving yourself from diabetes and a lifetime of medicated misery. You looked diabetes square in the eye and decided to make your life an *exclamation*, instead of an excuse. In just 30 days, you turned your entire life around, transforming it from one of weakness, dependency, and sickness into one filled with personal power, wisdom, and new diabetes-healing skills. You are amazing!

WELCOME TO THE DIABETES-HEALING LIFESTYLE!

I don't know you personally (although I hope one day our paths will cross), but I bet you are looking, thinking, acting, and feeling much better than you were 30 days ago. Am I right? So let's celebrate your liberation from diabetic captivity with a "Total Diabetes Healing Day." That means starting the day with a diabetes-healing breakfast. Pack up your healing lunch, snacks, and beverages so you're not tempted to eat anything that will undermine your progress. Make time for physical activity. And plan to end the day with a special diabetes-healing dinner. This special day is just for *you*, so here are 10 suggestions on how to enjoy it to the max…

1. Arise earlier than usual to give yourself extra time to appreciate this day and your accomplishments. Spend 20 to 30 minutes quietly contemplating or meditating. (See suggestions below.)

2. Start your celebration with your favorite diabetes-healing breakfast. Enjoy creamy whole-milk yogurt with berries and walnuts…or a slice of whole-grain bread with almond butter… or an omelet with sautéed broccoli, cheese, and tomatoes. (If you want something fancier, see the recipe on page 317.)

3. Listen to some peaceful music as you eat and dress. Notice the changes you've made in the past four weeks, with a new body, attitude, and living space.

4. Remind yourself to buy a big bouquet of flowers.

5. Pick a new spot to walk, holding your head up proudly and smiling at every single person you encounter with pride and happiness.

6. Make a plan to share this remarkable day with your special friends and family members. Let them know what you've accomplished and thank them for their support. Let them shower you with accolades.

7. Do something special just for you. Take yourself out for a massage…spend the afternoon in a museum surrounded by beauty and creativity…or buy yourself a new outfit.

8. Remind yourself that you now have every tool you need to keep progressing toward a full, happy, peaceful, and healthy life.

9. Feel confident that you're well-equipped for the next phase of your life: living free of the chains with which disease, pharmaceuticals, and junk food bind you.

10. Let yourself feel gratitude for having made this transformation. (See Gratitude Exercise below.)

GET EVEN MORE INSPIRED

You've surely inspired friends and family who have observed your transformation. You're a hero to them and have set a wonderful example for them to follow. You've overcome diabetes! Plan a movie night with someone very special and view the moving true story of another person's determination and passion.

The film I want you to rent is *A Man Named Pearl,* and it follows Pearl Fryar, son of a poor sharecropper, as he creates a stunning 3.5-acre topiary garden from plants other people have discarded. In the process, Fryar rises to international prominence as an acclaimed topiary artist and brings together one of the poorest communities in South Carolina. Pearl will make your heart sing as you set a course for your future.

SEVEN STEPS FOR CULTIVATING GRATITUDE

Here's a small but enormously important exercise that I start my day off with. It only takes about 10 to 15 minutes, but the results last for an entire day. I find it especially helpful on days when nothing seems to go right.

1. Rise a bit earlier than normal. Go to a quiet spot and sit comfortably with your eyes closed. Pay attention to your breath as it naturally flows in and out, and let your mind clear. Scan

your body from the inside, beginning at the tips of your toes. Inhale and sense your flow of attention all the way to the top of your head as you exhale. Doing this a few times will calm and center you.

2. Invite a feeling of gratitude to overtake you with each inhalation, gradually surrendering to it. Feel grateful for the moment. For being alive. For your physical body. For the health and vitality you have. For the loved ones in your life. For all the things you are able to enjoy. And everything else in your life that you appreciate.

3. Allow a smile to form—even if you have to force it at first. Keep it there as you inhale and take inventory of each aspect of your present life for which you are grateful. In a short time, you should feel your smile blossoming into a delightful physical sensation of happiness that will spread throughout your body and your entire being.

4. Immersed in this joy, allow yourself to be thankful, in whatever manner suits you.

5. One by one, visualize the faces of people with whom you'd like to share this feeling of joyous well-being. As each person comes into your awareness, radiate your wish for health and happiness to him or her.

6. Finally, transmit this joy outward to our entire world and to the universe itself. Let it pour from your heart like a beam of golden light as you repeat three times:

> "May all beings be Peaceful.
> May all beings be Well.
> May all beings Prosper.
> May all beings be Happy."

7. Gather yourself by taking a big breath. Now open your eyes. Notice your surroundings in detail. With another large inhalation and exhalation, stand up and stride into your day with a giant step, open-minded and ready to learn the lessons that life has in store for you this day—and every day thereafter.

NOW IT'S TIME FOR YOUR GRADUATION

Congratulations for being such a good "student" these past 30 days! I urge you to continue keeping a daily journal of your activities and diet as a way of staying on track. This will also help you tune into your emotions and spiritual side, so you can see how they affect your physical comfort.

Remember, this isn't the end—it's just the beginning. Science is making new discoveries about diabetes every day. To stay in touch with new healing developments—and to discover other Diabetes-Healing Superfoods, plus hundreds of delicious free recipes that incorporate them—I invite you to visit *www.myhealingkitchen.com,* to continue your "education." Please write me at *DrRipich@30dayDiabetesCure.com* and let me know how this plan is working for you. I'd love to publish your story and tell the world about your success.

TAKE ACTION TODAY: Reinforce your success by sharing it with others. Take time to reflect on what you've accomplished. Express gratitude to those who've helped you, and inspire others with your story. Look forward to living a life of vitality, adventure, and good health.

EXTRA CREDIT: Prepare one (or both) of the special Diabetes-Healing Recipes on pp. 317–319 as part of your celebration. Enjoy!

CASE STUDY: RICHARD

"I don't have diabetes anymore!"

Richard is thin and thought of himself as a "health nut." Who'd have thought he could have type 2 diabetes with an A1C of 7.5?

The reason was he mistakenly believed that eating organic and low-fat food was a great diet—but he unknowingly was a "carbotarian," which caused his diabetes. He was eating way too many carbs and not enough protein. When I pointed out how all those "natural" sugars and other "health foods" were upsetting his metabolism, he "got" it immediately. By following *The 30-Day Diabetes Cure* plan, he began making educated food choices—and completely eliminated his blood sugar problems without ever needing medication.

Case Study: Richard	Before	After
Weight	122	124
A1C	7.5	5.6
Blood Pressure	112/72	114/82
Triglycerides	186	94
Meds	-	-

YOUR DIABETES-HEALING BREAKFAST

Poached Egg on Ezekiel Bread with Creamy Spinach and Roasted Red Pepper Sauce
Makes: 2 Servings
Total Time: 10 minutes

A plethora of powerhouse diabetes-healing ingredients combine in this quick-and-easy breakfast to make your morning healthy and hunger-free. Omega-3 eggs reduce inflammation, whole grains help stabilize blood sugar levels, and probiotics in the yogurt boost your immune system. Add the natural sweetness of roasted peppers and you have a true breakfast of champions.

INGREDIENTS:

1 medium roasted bell pepper

1 tablespoon lemon or orange juice

1 teaspoon pure olive oil

1 cup fresh spinach

1 clove garlic, minced

2 large omega-3 eggs

2 tablespoons nonfat yogurt

2 slices sprouted whole-grain Ezekiel bread, toasted

INSTRUCTIONS:

1. Puree the roasted pepper in a blender with the citrus juice. Leave some chunks if you like or blend until smooth.

2. In a sauté pan, heat the olive oil and saute the spinach for 2–3 minutes, stirring constantly. Add the garlic and cook for 1 minute more.

3. In a large sauté pan, heat 2–3 inches of water. Just before it starts to boil, lower the heat and add a splash of vinegar.

4. Use ring molds if you have them or just gently break the eggs and drop them in the water. Cook for 3–5 minutes or until the yolk is as hard as you like.

5. Stir the yogurt into the spinach.

6. Scoop the eggs out with a slotted spoon and serve on the toast with the spinach below and the pepper sauce on top.

TIPS AND NOTES:

Try this with sautéed mushrooms or caramelized onions instead of spinach. You can also try yellow or orange pepper in the sauce.

NUTRITION FACTS: *Serving Size 136 g, Calories 168, Total Fat 7 g, Saturated Fat 2 g, Cholesterol 161mg, Sodium 186 mg, Potassium 300 mg, Total Carbohydrates 16 g, Dietary Fiber 3 g, Sugars 5 g, Protein 10 g, Glycemic Load 7*

YOUR DIABETES-HEALING DINNER

Pink Peppercorn & Mustard Encrusted Lamb Chops, Faux Mashers & Steamed Broccoli
Makes: 4 servings
Total Time: 20–30 minutes

Protein-rich and succulent lamb chops, super protein and antioxidant-filled beans, and sulforophane-rich broccoli combine to make a delicious gourmet dinner that will celebrate your health and impress your loved ones. The pink peppercorns pop and the mustard gives zing to this amazing diabetes-healing dinner.

INGREDIENTS:

For the Lamb:

2 tablespoons pink peppercorns, crushed

1 tablespoon black peppercorns, crushed

2 tablespoons dried yellow mustard

1 tablespoon pure olive oil

Four 4–6 oz lean lamb chops

For the Bean Puree:

1 can butter beans, drained and rinsed

2–4 tablespoons low-fat milk

2–4 cloves roasted garlic, minced

2 teaspoons pure olive oil

2 cups broccoli florets, steamed

INSTRUCTIONS:

1. Turn the oven to broil.

2. Combine the peppercorns, mustard, and olive oil and spread evenly over each side of the lamb.

3. In a blender or food processor, mix the beans, milk, roasted garlic, and olive oil. Consistency can be as smooth or chunky as you like.

4. Broil the lamb chops for 3–5 minutes on each side depending on desired doneness and thickness of chops.

5. Heat the bean puree in a saucepan on low heat until heated through. Serve the chops over the beans with the broccoli.

TIPS AND NOTES:

Try this sweet and spicy peppercorn rub on anything from chicken to tofu to buffalo steaks. Add a tablespoon of yogurt to the bean puree to give it a creamy tang. If you like a creamier puree (mashers), add a few extra tablespoons of low-fat milk.

> **NUTRITION FACTS:** *Serving Size 302 g, Calories 310, Total Fat 14.2, Saturated Fat 3 g, Cholesterol 46 g, Sodium 204 mg, Potassium 591 mg, Total Carbohydrates 23 g, Dietary Fiber 7 g, Sugars 1 g, Protein 22 g, Glycemic Load 10*

BIBLIOGRAPHY

PHASE I

Agatston, MD, Arthur. *The South Beach Diet.* St. Martin's Press, 2003.

Cohen, RPh, Suzy. *Diabetes without Drugs.* Rodale, Inc., 2010.

Editors of Prevention. *Diabetes Breakthroughs 2010.* Rodale, Inc., 2010.

Esselstyn, Rip. *The Engine 2 Diet.* New York: Wellness Central, 2009.

Gottlieb, Bill. *Breakthroughs in Drug-Free Healing.* Bottom Line Books, 2008.

Hurley, Dan. *Diabetes Rising.* Kaplan Publishing, 2010.

Turner, ND, Natasha. *The Hormone Diet.* Random House Canada, 2009.

DAY 1

Cushman, William C., et al., "Effects of Intensive Blood-Pressure Control in Type 2 Diabetes Mellitus," *New England Journal of Medicine* (March 2010).

Editors, "Does Sugar Feed Cancer?" *ScienceDaily.com* (August 2009).

EPA lead toxin info: http://www.epa.gov/ttn/atw/hlthef/lead.html

Food industry lobbying information: http://www.opensecrets.org/lobby/indusclient. php?lname=n01&year=2009

Ginsberg, MD, Henry N., et al., "Effects of Combination Lipid Therapy in Type 2 Diabetes Mellitus," *New England Journal of Medicine* (March 2010).

Kawai, Kirio, et al., "Leptin as a modulator of sweet taste sensitivities in mice," *PNAS* (September 2000).

National Diabetes Information Clearinghouse: http://diabetes.niddk.nih.gov/dm/pubs/complications_heart/

Pierce, PhD, John P., Elizabeth A. Gilpin, MS, "Impact of Over-the-Counter Sales on Effectiveness of Pharmaceutical Aids for Smoking Cessation," *JAMA* (September 2002).

Romon, MD, PhD, Monique, et al., "Postprandial Leptin Response to Carbohydrate and Fat Meals in Obese Women," *Journal of the American College of Nutrition*, Vol. 22, No. 3, 247–251 (2003).

USDA sugar statistics: http://www.ers.usda.gov/Briefing/Sugar/

Wurtman, R.J., et al., "Brain serotonin, carbohydrate-craving, obesity and depression," *Obesity* (November 1995).

Zhang, Ping, et al., "Global healthcare expenditure on diabetes for 2010 and 2030," *Diabetes Research and Clinical Practice,* Vol. 87 (2010), 293–301.

DAY 2

Cinnamon research: http://www.ars.usda.gov/Research/docs.htm?docid=8877

Hlebowicz, Joanna, "Effect of cinnamon on postprandial blood glucose, gastric emptying, and satiety in healthy subjects," *American Journal of Clinical Nutrition*, Vol. 85, No. 6, 1552–1556 (June 2007).

Khan, Alam, et al., "Cinnamon Improves Glucose and Lipids of People With Type 2 Diabetes," *Diabetes Care* (December 2003).

DAY 3

Dept. of Pharmacology, Duke University, "Splenda alters gut microflora and increases intestinal p-glycoprotein and cytochrome p-450 in male rats," *Journal of Toxicology and Environmental Health* (2008).

Editors, "Missing Link Between Fructose, Insulin Resistance Found," *ScienceDaily.com* (March 2009).

Fowler, Sharon P., et al., "Fueling the Obesity Epidemic? Artificially Sweetened Beverage Use and Long-term Weight Gain," *Obesity* (2008).

National Institute on Alcohol Abuse and Alcoholism No. 16 PH 315 April 1992: http://pubs. niaaa.nih.gov/publications/aa16.htm

Nettleton, PhD, Jennifer A., et al., "Diet Soda Intake and Risk of Incident Metabolic Syndrome and Type 2 Diabetes in the Multi-Ethnic Study of Atherosclerosis," *Diabetes Care* (January 2009).

The Nurses' Health Study: http://www.channing.harvard.edu/nhs/

Parker, Hilary, "A sweet problem: Princeton researchers find that high-fructose corn syrup prompts considerably more weight gain," *News at Princeton* (March 2010).

Swithers, Susan E., Terry L. Davidson, "A Role for Sweet Taste: Calorie Predictive Relations in Energy Regulation by Rats," *Behavioral Neuroscience* (2008).

DAY 4

BPA information: National Institutes of Environmental Health Sciences: http://www.niehs.nih.gov/health/topics/agents/endocrine/

Dehydration information: http://www.mayoclinic.com/health/dehydration/DS00561.

Diabetes Friends Action Network: http://www.dfandiabetes.com/.

Dulloo, A.G., et al., "Green tea and thermogenesis: interactions between catechin-polyphenols, caffeine and sympathetic activity," *International Journal of Obesity* (February 2000).

Editors, "Black Tea May Fight Diabetes," *ScienceDaily.com* (August 2009).

Fei-jun, Luo, et al., "Effect of tea polyphenols and EGCG on nasopharyngeal carcinoma cell proliferation and the mechanisms involved," *Cancer Research* (December 2001).

Green tea information, University of Maryland Medical Center: http://www.umm.edu/altmed/articles/green-tea-000255.htm.

Huxley, DPhil, Rachel, et al., "Coffee, Decaffeinated Coffee, and Tea Consumption in Relation to Incident Type 2 Diabetes Mellitus," *Archives of Internal Medicine* (2009).

Kleemola, MSc, Paivi, "Coffee Consumption and the Risk of Coronary Heart Disease and Death," *Archives of Internal Medicine* (December 2000).

Starbucks calorie counts: http://www.starbucks.com/menu/catalog/nutrition?drink=all.

Tea research in the UK: http://news.bbc.co.uk/2/hi/5281046.stm.

DAY 5

Information about inflammation: www.americanheart.org/presenter.jhtml?identifier=4648.

Szkudelski T., "The mechanism of alloxan and streptozotocin action in B cells of the rat pancreas," *Physiology Research* (2001).

DAY 6

Vander Wal, J.S., et al., "Egg breakfast enhances weight loss," *International Journal of Obesity* (2008).

Yogurt benefits: http://www.naturalnews.com/010204.html

Zemel, M.B., et al., "Dairy augmentation of total and central fat loss in obese subjects," *International Journal of Obesity* (2005).

DAY 7

American Heart Association: www.americanheart.org

Grass-fed beef statistics and studies: www.eatwild.com

Jeffery, Robert W., et al., "Effects of portion size on chronic energy intake," *International Journal of Behavioral Nutrition and Physical Activity* (2007).

Junk food addiction information: http://www.scripps.edu/news/press/20100329.html

McDonald's nutrition information: www.mcdonalds.com

Moss, Michael, "Safety of Beef Processing Method Is Questioned," *The New York Times* (December 2009).

Salt recommendations: http://www.mayoclinic.com/health/sodium/nu00284

DAY 8

Adventist Health Studies: www.llu.edu/public-health/health/index.page

Fukuda, Toshiyuki, et al., "Antioxidative polyphenols from walnuts (*Juglans regia* L.)," *Phytochemistry* (August 2003).

Grassi, D., et al., "Cocoa reduces blood pressure and insulin resistance and improves endothelium-dependent vasodilation in hypertensives," *Hypertension* (August 2005).

Iowa Women's Health Study: http://www.cancer.umn.edu/research/programs/peiowa.html

Jenkins, David, et al., "Almonds Decrease Postprandial Glycemia, Insulinemia, and Oxidative Damage in Healthy Individual," *Journal of Nutrition* (December 2006).

Jiang, MD, Rui, et al., "Nut and Peanut Butter Consumption and Risk of Type 2 Diabetes in Women," *JAMA* (November 2002).

Josse, Andrea R., et al., "Almonds and postprandial glycemia—a dose-response study," *Metabolism* (March 2007).

Lamarche, Benoit, et al., "Combined effects of a dietary portfolio of plant sterols, vegetable protein, viscous fibre and almonds on LDL particle size," *British Journal of Nutrition* (2004).

Nurses' Health Study: http://www.channing.harvard.edu/nhs/

Physicians' Health Study: http://phs.bwh.harvard.edu/

Salas-Salvadó, MD, PhD, Jordi, et al., "Effect of a Mediterranean Diet Supplemented With Nuts on Metabolic Syndrome Status," *Archives of Internal Medicine* (December 2008).

Tapsell, PhD, Linda C., et al., "Including Walnuts in a Low-Fat/Modified-Fat Diet Improves HDL Cholesterol-to-Total Cholesterol Ratios in Patients With Type 2 Diabetes," *Diabetes Care* (December 2004).

Wien, M.A., et al., "Almonds vs complex carbohydrates in a weight reduction program," *International Journal of Obesity* (2003).

DAY 9

Farmed fish health info: http://www.whfoods.com/genpage.php?tname=george&dbid=96

Grass-fed beef studies: www.eatwild.com

Growth hormones: http://www.organicconsumers.org/toxic/hormone042302.cfm

Halkjaer, J., et al., "Dietary predictors of 5-year changes in waist circumference," *Journal of the American Dietetic Association* (August 2009).

Li, Lijun, et al., "Chronic Stress Induces Rapid Occlusion of Angioplasty-Injured Rat Carotid Artery by Activating Neuropeptide Y and Its Y1 Receptors," *Arteriosclerosis, Thrombosis, and Vascular Biology* (2005).

Processed meats: http://www.naturalnews.com/022288_sodium_nitrite_processed_meat.html.

Stier, Ken, "Fish Farming's Growing Dangers," *Time Magazine* (September 2007).

Trans fats: http://www.hsph.harvard.edu/nutritionsource/nutrition-news/transfats/

DAY 10

Ma, Le, et al., "Effects of lutein and zeaxanthin on aspects of eye health," *Journal of the Science of Food and Agriculture* (September 2009).

Manganese info: http://www.umm.edu/altmed/articles/manganese-000314.htm

Nurses' Health Study: http://www.channing.harvard.edu/nhs/

Yoshida, Makiko, et al., "Effect of Vitamin K Supplementation on Insulin Resistance in Older Men and Women," *Diabetes Care* (August 2008).

PHASE II

Agatston, MD, Arthur. *The South Beach Diet.* St. Martin's Press, 2003.

Cohen, RPh, Suzy. *Diabetes without Drugs.* Rodale, Inc., 2010.

Editors of *Prevention. Diabetes Breakthroughs 2010.* Rodale, Inc., 2010.

Esselstyn, Rip. *The Engine 2 Diet.* Wellness Central, 2009.

Gottlieb, Bill. *Breakthroughs in Drug-Free Healing.* Bottom Line Books, 2008.

Hurley, Dan. *Diabetes Rising.* Kaplan Publishing, 2010.

Turner, ND, Natasha. *The Hormone Diet.* Random House Canada, 2009.

DAY 11

"Did FDA Know of Avandia Dangers in 2002?" http://www.cbsnews.com/stories/2007/05/22/health/main2839924.shtml

"Fat in diet won't affect weight gain over time," http://www.reuters.com/article/idUS TRE5BA3C920091211

He, MD, Ka, et al., "Fish Consumption and Incidence of Stroke, A Meta-Analysis of Cohort Studies," *Stroke* (2004).

Kim, You Jung, et al., "Protection Against Oxidative Stress, Inflammation, and Apoptosis of High-Glucose-Exposed Proximal Tubular Epithelial Cells by Astaxanthin," *Journal of Agricultural and Food Chemistry* (September 2009).

Mathieu, C., et al., "Vitamin D and diabetes," *Diabetologia* (2005).

Omega-6 information: http://www.umm.edu/altmed/articles/omega-6-000317.htm

Omega-3 information: http://www.umm.edu/altmed/articles/omega-3-000316.htm

Shields, P.G., et al., "Mutagens from heated Chinese and U.S. cooking oils," *Journal of the National Cancer Institute* (1995).

"Trans fat is double trouble for your heart health," http://www.mayoclinic.com/health/trans-fat/cl00032

Trans fat regulation: http://www.bantransfats.com/

Visioli, Francesco, et al., "Olive Oil Phenols and Their Potential Effects on Human Health," *Journal of Agriculture and Food Chemistry* (1998).

DAY 12

http://www.womenshealthmag.com/nutrition/why-eat-fruit-peels?page=4

Kaplan, Marielle, et al., "Pomegranate Juice Supplementation to Atherosclerotic Mice Reduces Macrophage Lipid Peroxidation, Cellular Cholesterol Accumulation and Development of Atherosclerosis," *Journal of Nutrition* (2001).

Krishnan, DSc, Supriya, et al., "Glycemic Index, Glycemic Load, and Cereal Fiber Intake and Risk of Type 2 Diabetes in US Black Women," *Archives of Internal Medicine* (2007).

Riccardi, G., et al., "Effects of dietary fiber and carbohydrate on glucose and lipoprotein metabolism in diabetic patients," *Diabetes Care* (1991).

"Strawberries Reduce Inflammation in Blood Vessels," www.diabetesincontrol.com/index.php?option=com_content&view=article&id=5440&Itemid=0.

Weickert, Martin O., et al., "Cereal Fiber Improves Whole-Body Insulin Sensitivity in Overweight and Obese Women," *Diabetes Care* (2006).

DAY 13

Diabetes statistics: http://www.diabetes.org/diabetes-basics/diabetes-statistics/

Hyman, MD, Mark. *Ultrametabolism*. New York: Scribner, 2006.

Orchard, MD, Trevor J., "The Effect of Metformin and Intensive Lifestyle Intervention on the Metabolic Syndrome: The Diabetes Prevention Program Randomized Trial," *Annals of Internal Medicine* (2005).

Physical activity and walking information: http://www.cdc.gov/nccdphp/sgr/ataglan.htm

DAY 14

Chandalia, MD, Manisha, et al., "Beneficial Effects of High Dietary Fiber Intake in Patients with Type 2 Diabetes Mellitus," *NEJM* (May 2000).

Diabetes and Pima Indians information: http://diabetes.niddk.nih.gov/dm/pubs/pima/obesity/obesity.htm

Nurses' Health Study: http://www.channing.harvard.edu/nhs/

Stokes, RD, D. Milton, "Nature's Fat-Burning Breakthrough: Why eating carbs can help you slim down—and how to do it right," *Prevention.com*

DAY 15

http://emagazine.com/archive/3863

http://www.mayoclinic.com/health/relaxation-technique/sr00007

Antidepressants: http://www.psychotropical.com/ad_rev.shtml

Chopra, Deepak. *Ageless Body, Timeless Mind.* Three Rivers Press, 1994.

Editors, "Medical staff suffered severe stress after earthquake in Kobe, Japan," *British Medical Journal* (1996).

Gottlieb, MD, MPH, Daniel J., et al., "Association of Sleep Time With Diabetes Mellitus and Impaired Glucose Tolerance," *Archives of Internal Medicine* (April 2005).

"Job strain 'as bad as smoking'," http://news.bbc.co.uk/2/hi/health/763401.stm, (May 2000).

McGinnis, MD, Ronald A., et al., "Biofeedback-Assisted Relaxation in Type 2 Diabetes," *Diabetes Care* (September 2005).

DAY 16

Carroll, Linda, "Arthritis Supplements Often Lack Key Ingredient," *MSNBC.com* (April 2007).

Chiu, Ken C., et al., "Hypovitaminosis D is associated with insulin resistance and ß cell dysfunction," *American Journal of Clinical Nutrition* (May 2004).

Consumer Labs: www.consumerlab.com

Consumer Reports: www.consumerreports.org

Holick, M.F., "Sunlight, UV-radiation, vitamin D and skin cancer: how much sunlight do we need?" *Advances in Experimental Medicine and Biology* (2008).

Inzucchi, M.D., Silvio E., et al., "Efficacy and Metabolic Effects of Metformin and Troglitazone in Type II Diabetes Mellitus," *NEJM* (March 1998).

Mattila, Catharina, et al., "Serum 25-Hydroxyvitamin D Concentration and Subsequent Risk of Type 2 Diabetes," *Diabetes Care* (October 2007).

The Nurses' Health Study: http://www.channing.harvard.edu/nhs/

Teegarden, Dorothy, et al., "Vitamin D: emerging new roles in insulin sensitivity," *Nutrition Research Reviews* (June 2009).

"Vitamin D3 May Protect Against Nonmelanoma Skin Cancer," *MedPage Today* (2009), http://www.medpagetoday.com/MeetingCoverage/SID/14182

von Hurst, Pamela R., et al., "Vitamin D supplementation reduces insulin resistance in South Asian women living in New Zealand who are insulin resistant and vitamin D deficient—a randomised, placebo-controlled trial," *British Journal of Nutrition* (2010).

DAY 17

Akbaraly, PhD, Tasnime N., "Dietary pattern and depressive symptoms in middle age," *British Journal of Psychiatry* (2009).

Alpert, Jonathan E., et al., "Folinic Acid (Leucovorin) as an Adjunctive Treatment for SSRI-Refractory Depression," *Annals of Clinical Psychiatry* (March 2002).

Depression and diabetes information: American Diabetes Association, http://www.diabetes.org/living-with-diabetes/complications/mental-health/depression.html

Golden, MD, MH, Sherita Hill, et al., "Depressive Symptoms and the Risk of Type 2 Diabetes: The Atherosclerosis Risk in Communities Study," *Diabetes Care* (2004).

Lau, Thorsten, et al., "Antidepressant-induced internalization of the serotonin transporter in serotonergic neurons," *The FASEB Journal* (2008).

Sandy K. Reuven, "L-Tryptophan in Neuropsychiatry Disorders: A Review," *International Journal of Neuroscience* (1992).

Shih, RD, MS, Grace, "Diabulimia: What It Is and How to Treat It," *DiabetesHealth.com* (March 2009).

DAY 18

Dusek, Jeffery A., et al., "Genomic Counter-Stress Changes Induced by the Relaxation Response," *PLoS One* (July 2008).

Kiecolt-Glaser, PhD, Janice K., et al., "Stress, Inflammation, and Yoga Practice," *Psychosomatic Medicine* (January 2010).

DAY 19

Bouchez, MD, Colette, "The Dream Diet: Losing Weight While You Sleep," *webMD.com*.

Editors, "Stanford Study Links Obesity to Hormonal Changes from Lack of Sleep," *Science Daily.com* (2004).

Gottlieb, MD, MPH, Daniel J., et al., "Association of Sleep Time with Diabetes Mellitus and Impaired Glucose Tolerance," *Archives of Internal Medicine* (April 2005).

Sleep statistics: http://www.sleepfoundation.org/

Vgontzas, Alexandros N., et al., "Chronic Insomnia Is Associated with Nyctohemeral Activation of the Hypothalamic-Pituitary-Adrenal Axis: Clinical Implications," *Journal of Clinical Endocrinology & Metabolism* (2001).

DAY 20

www.activeforever.com

www.aquatic-exercise-equipment.com

Nordic Walking Study, Cooper Institute: http://www.cooperinstitute.org/research/past/nordicwalking.cfm

Water Aerobics and Water Walking information: http://www.diabetic-lifestyle.com/articles/jun01_burni_1.htm

www.waterworkout.com

PHASE III

Agatston, MD, Arthur. *The South Beach Diet.* St. Martin's Press, 2003.

Cohen, RPh, Suzy. *Diabetes without Drugs.* Rodale, Inc., 2010.

Editors of *Prevention. Diabetes Breakthroughs 2010.* Rodale, Inc., 2010.

Esselstyn, Rip. *The Engine 2 Diet.* Wellness Central, 2009.

Gottlieb, Bill. *Breakthroughs in Drug-Free Healing.* Bottom Line Books, 2008.

Hurley, Dan. *Diabetes Rising.* Kaplan Publishing, 2010.

Turner, ND, Natasha. *The Hormone Diet.* Random House Canada, 2009.

DAY 21

http://www.webmd.com/diet/features/emotional-eating-feeding-your-feelings?page=2

Brunstrom, Jeffrey M., et al., "Effect of Distraction on the Development of Satiety," *British Journal of Nutrition* (2006).

Carter, J.B., et al., "BMI Related to Number of Meals Eaten Watching TV as Reported by 4th to 6th Grade Students: Demographic Differences," USDA/ARS Children's Nutrition Research Center at Baylor College of Medicine (October 2000).

Editors, "Eating Food Too Fast Speeds Heartburn; Slow Eating Cuts Acid Reflux Risks," *WebMD.com* (2003).

Hendrick, Bill, "Eating Slowly May Help Weight Control: Study Shows Eating Too Fast Blocks Hormones That Make You Feel Full," *WebMD.com* (2009).

Wansink, PhD, Brian, "Mindless Eating: The 200 Daily Food Decisions We Overlook," Cornell University Food & Brand Lab (2007).

Zellner, Debra A., et al., "Food Selection Changes Under Stress," *Physiology and Behavior* (2006).

DAY 23

http://news.duke.edu/2007/12/habit.html

AARP March/April 2010.

Christakis, MD, PhD, MPH, Nicholas A., James H. Fowler, PhD, "The Spread of Obesity in a Large Social Network over 32 Years," *NEJM* (July 2007).

Editors, "Exercise Minimizes Weight Regain by Reducing Appetite and Burning Fat First, Carbs Later," *ScienceDaily.com* (September 2009).

Kim, J., et al., "Folate intake and the risk of colorectal cancer in a Korean population," *EJCN* (June 2009).

DAY 24

http://www.diabetesselfmanagement.com/Articles/Diabetes-Definitions/cognitive-behavioral-therapy/

http://www.dukehealth.org/health_library/health_articles/rxfordiabetes

Christakis, MD, PhD, MPH, Nicholas A., James H. Fowler, PhD, "The Spread of Obesity in a Large Social Network over 32 Years," *NEJM* (July 2007).

DAY 25

Persistant Organic Pollutants information: http://www.epa.gov/oia/toxics/pop.htm

http://www.epa.gov/oia/toxics/pop.htm

http://www.epa.gov/oia/toxics/pop.htm

http://www.ncbi.nlm.nih.gov/pmc/articles/PMC1332699/

http://www.ewg.org/water/downthedrain

http://www.ewg.org/node/28188

http://www.womensconference.org/7-healthy-lifestyle-tips-on

http://news.bbc.co.uk/2/hi/europe/2906357.stm

New Scientist, 12 January 2009

http://www.treehugger.com/files/2009/08/todays-toxin-atrazine.php

http://www.webmd.com/balance/natural-liver-detox-diets-liver-cleansing?page=2

http://www.detoxdietweb.com/turmeric-for-liver-detox

http://www.wholehealthchicago.com/knowledge-base/m/milk-thistle/

http://www.renegadeneurologist.com/turmeric-and-brain-health/

http://www.thereadystore.com/katadyn-combi-water-filter

http://www.consumerreports.org/cro/magazine-archive/december-2009/food/bpa/overview/bisphenol-a-ov.htm

http://www.telegraph.co.uk/news/uknews/1555173/Body-absorbs-5lb-of-make-up-chemicals-a-year.html

http://blogs.mercola.com/sites/vitalvotes/archive/2007/06/22/Body-Absorbs-5-Lbs-of-Make-Up-Chemicals-Per-Year.aspx

http://www.nhregister.com/articles/2008/11/26/opinion/doc492d4214d2c89772087215.txt

Houlihan, Jane, et al., "EWG finds heated Teflon pans can turn toxic faster than DuPont claims," *Environmental Working Group Reports* (May 2003).

vom Saal, PhD, Frederick, et al., "Bisphenol A and Risk of Metabolic Disorders," *JAMA* (2008).

Diabetes and Agent Orange: http://www.diabetes.org/living-with-diabetes/complications/agent-orange-and-type-2-diabetes.html

Toxic Free Legacy Coalition: http://toxicfreelegacy.org/

DAY 26

http://diabetes.webmd.com/strength-training-diabetes

http://www.webmd.com/healthy-aging/news/20090708/strength-training-is-good-for-seniors

http://www.usatoday.com/news/health/2001-07-12-weight-training.htm

http://www.diabeteshealth.com/read/2005/09/01/4323/weight-training-and-diabetes/

http://well.blogs.nytimes.com/2009/10/14/phys-ed-does-exercise-boost-immunity/

DAY 27

http://www.nlm.nih.gov/medlineplus/druginfo/natural/patient-spirulina.html

http://www.chlorellafactor.com/chlorella-spirulina-27.html

http://www.telegraph.co.uk/health/wellbeing/6028408/Chlorella-the-superfood-that-helps-fight-disease.html

http://www.telegraph.co.uk/health/wellbeing/6028408/Chlorella-the-superfood-that-helps-fight-disease.html

"Barley Grass: How a Plant Remedy May Offer Vital Protection Against Heart Disease, Stroke and Ulcerative Colitis," http://www.thehealthierlife.co.uk/natural-remedies/herbs/barley-grass-health-benefits-00859.html

Chlorella information: http://www.naturalnews.com/028017_chlorella_diabetes.html

DAY 28

Schwellenbach, Lisa J. "The Triglyceride-Lowering Effects of a Modest Dose of Docosahexae-noic Acid Alone Versus in Combination with Low Dose Eicosapentaenoic Acid in Patients with Coronary Artery Disease and Elevated Triglycerides." *Journal of the American College of Nutrition*, Vol. 25, No. 6, 480-485 (2006).

http://douglassreport.com/2010/01/20/big-gift/

http://www.diabetesselfmanagement.com/Blog/Tara-Dairman/antioxidant_ala_eases_pain_from_diabetic_neuropathy/

http://www.diabeteshealth.com/read/2005/02/01/4095/bitter-melon/

http://www.ncbi.nlm.nih.gov/pmc/articles/PMC1709814/?page=6

http://www.healthyfellow.com/315/blueberry-leaf/

http://www.drdavidwilliams.com/

http://www.drdavidwilliams.com/legacy

http://www.diabeteshealth.com/read/2005/01/01/4193/fenugreek/

http://care.diabetesjournals.org/content/16/1/8.abstract

http://diabetes.webmd.com/news/20030616/ginseng-may-help-treat-diabetes

http://www.webmd.com/vitamins-supplements

http://www.drugs.com/npp/prickly-pear.html

http://www.rd.com/living-healthy/the-best-herbs-and-supplements-for-diabetes/

DAY 29

http://www.hplusmagazine.com/articles/forever-young/boredom-killer

INDEX

BPA (bisphenol A), 272, 273
brain chemical imbalances, 213–14
brain fogginess, as sign of insulin resistance, 13
"brain specific" diabetes. *See* type 3 diabetes
bran, 171
brands, vitamin choices and, 206
bread, healthy *vs.* white flour, 103–4, 165–67, 169
breakfasts, diabetes-healing, 109–15, 167–68, 174–76, 194, 317–18
brown rice, meal suggestions, 195
brown-bag lunches, 112
buddies, for walking, 185
buffets, survival skills at, 252–53
burdock (herb), 277
burgers, vegetarian, 193
burrito, breakfast, 174
butter, 111

C

cactus, prickly pear, 303
caffeine, cutting back on
    and conquering sugar cravings, 72
    sleep problems and, 225
    tea and coffee, 92–94
calcium-rich foods, weight loss and, 112
calories
    burning, using trekking poles, 229–30
    empty, alcohol as, 89
    in fast foods, 118
    in grass-fed meats, 139
    in olive oil, 161
    in processed meats, 138
    strength training and, 284
cancer
    inflammation and, 180
    sugar as linked to, 70
    See also specific types of cancer
canned foods, toxicity of, 279
canola oil, 158
carbohydrates
    carbohydrate craving cycle, 55, 70, 106–7
    complex, for sustained energy, 112
    eliminating "fast carbs," 99–105
    fast carb foods *vs.* "slow carbs," 16, 21
    as fat substitutes in processed foods, 154
    metabolism, beans and, 189
cardiovascular disease
    beneficial fats, 159
    diabetes-related deaths and, 23

drugs for, and diabetics, 23–24
    exercise and, 179
    type 1 diabetes and, 27
    vegetable consumption and, 146
Carey, Drew, 40
celiac disease, 103
central obesity, description of, 15–16, 19
    See also belly fat
cereals, whole grain, 175
chain restaurants, 251
charity, supporting, 232–33, 309–10
cheese
    CLA content of, 140
    weight loss and, 112
chemical pollutants, 271–73, 274–75, 278–80
cherries, 173
children, vitamin D for, 212
chlorella, 290–91
chocolate, as a snack, 128–29
Chopra, Deepak, 202
chromium content of vegetables, 147
chromium supplements, 299
cigarettes, quitting, 60–63
cinnamon
    cinnamon cassia extract, 301–2
    to lower blood sugar, 79–81, 168
circulation, exercise and, 178–79
CLA (conjugated linoleic acid), 140
cleaning products, toxic exposure from, 272–73, 279
coconut oil, 160
coffee, 93–94, 95
cognitive behavioral therapy (CBT), 268
colds, frequent, 13
cold-turkey approach to dietary change, 53–55
comfort foods
    and emotional eating, 243–45, 247
    pasta, 169
    whole grains, 167
conjugated linoleic acid. *See* CLA (conjugated linoleic acid)
Consumer Labs, 207
Consumer Reports, 207
cooking, learning, 246, 306
coolers, traveling with, 253
CoQ-10 (Coenzyme Q-10), 297–98
core-strengthening, 285–86
corn, suggestions for eating, 195
cortisol, 197–98, 223–24
cosmetics, 272–73, 279–80
costs of conventional diabetes care, 6, 9, 35
counseling
    professional, making use of, 268–69

for stress-related issues, 200, 204
    support systems, 62
coworkers, stress and, 200
cranberries, 173
cravings
    for carbohydrates, 106–7
    emotional eating, 243–45
    for fast food, 120
    for sugar, conquering, 71–73
C-reactive protein. *See* hsCRP (high-sensitivity C-reactive protein) testing
creditors, stress and, 200
crepes, garbanzo flour, 193–94
cruciferous vegetables, 146
curcumin, 277
curried beans, 193

D

deep-water running (DWR), 234
dehydration, in type 2 diabetes, 20, 91
dental hygiene, and conquering sugar cravings, 72
dental problems, insulin resistance and, 13
depression
    diabetes and, 213–14
    diet and, 215–16
    professional counseling for, 268–69
    as sign of insulin resistance, 12
    supplements to help, 216–17
    support groups and, 267
desserts at restaurants, 250
detoxification
    on the 30-Day Diabetes Cure, 274, 275–76
    herbs for, 276–77
    via the skin, 277–78
    of your environment, 278–80
DHA (docosahexaenoic acid), 157, 296–97
diabetes
    dehydration and, 91
    depression and, 213–17
    drugs, complications from, 44–45
    exercise and longevity, 182
    false information about, 37
    genetic susceptibility, 191
    research on diet and lifestyle changes, 39–40
    statistics on, 3–4
    supplements for, 296–300
    toxins and, 273
    types of, 25–29
    understanding, 9–10
    victory over, celebrating, 313–15

fruit juice, 85, 94, 172
fruit spritzers, 95
fungicides, on food crops, 272

G

GABA (gamma-aminobutyric acid), 227
gas, from eating beans, 190
gastric bypass surgery, 33–34
genetically modified (GMO) crops, 272
genetics
    and calorie hoarding, 180–81
    lifestyle factors and, 191
    and type 1 diabetes, 25–26, 46
GERD (gastro-esophageal reflux disease), 242
germ, whole grain, 171
gestational diabetes, 25
ghrelin (hormone), 224
GI (glycemic index)
    fast *vs.* slow carbs, identifying, 105
    fermented foods and, 111
    maltose and maltodextrins, 89
ginseng, 303
GLA (gamma-linolenic acid), 302–3
glass storage containers, 278
Glucophage medication, 14, 39
glucose
    as bodily fuel, 10
    carbohydrate cravings and, 106
    damage from, in type 2 diabetes, 19–20
    exercise and, 178
    insulin resistance and, 11–12
    levels, spikes in, 85
    tolerance, and beans, 189
glucose monitoring (SMBG), ineffectiveness of, 41–43
glucose tolerance tests, for diabetes and prediabetes, 23
gluten intolerance, 103
glycation, 11
glycemic index (GI). *See* GI (glycemic index)
GMO (genetically modified) crops, 272
GMP (Good Manufacturing Practices) seal, 206
grains. *See* whole grains
granola, whole grain, 169
grass-fed beef, 139–41
gratitude, 248, 314–15
green drinks, 289–92
green tea, 92–93
greens, leafy, 147–48
grocery shopping, wise, 246
group walking, 232

growth hormones, in meat production, 137, 271–72
gymnema sylvestre (herb), 300

H

habits, breaking, 100
    See also addictions
habits, healthy, 258–62
healthcare system in the US, 31–35
hearing problems, and type 1 diabetes, 27
heart attacks, and diabetes, 23
heart disease. *See* cardiovascular disease
heart health
    improving, with cinnamon, 80
    strength training and, 284
    vegetables consumption and, 146
heartburn, 242
hemoglobin A1C tests
    and glucose levels, 42–43
    for prediabetes, 13–14
    and symptoms of MetS, 17
herbal teas, 95
herbs for diabetes care, 300–303
HFCS (high-fructose corn syrup)
    damaging effects of, 15, 83–84, 137
    as fat substitute in processed foods, 154
    "hidden" sugars, 73
    in snacks, avoiding, 133
high blood pressure. *See* hypertension
high-fructose corn syrup. *See* HFCS (high-fructose corn syrup)
high-sensitivity C-reactive protein. *See* hsCRP (high-sensitivity C-reactive protein) testing
holidays, surviving, 252–53
home environments, clearing out, 308–9
homocysteine, 217
hormones, stress, 197–98
hot cereals, whole grain, 168
household products, toxicity of, 272–73, 279–80
hsCRP (high-sensitivity C-reactive protein) testing, 23
hunger
    vs. appetite, 71, 100
    comfort foods and, 167
    eating habits and, 245, 247
    emotional eating and, 243
    exercise, to curb, 261–62
    fats, satiety and, 153
    snacking, 127–28
    tips for conquering cravings, 71–73
hydration, 71, 91–92, 95, 245

hypertension
    chlorella and, 291
    drugs for lowering, and diabetes, 23–24, 44–45
    as symptom of MetS, 17
    testing for prediabetes, 14
hypnotherapy, to stop smoking, 63

I

inactivity *vs.* exercise, 178–85
infections, frequent, 13
inflammation
    exercise and, 179–80
    fast carbs and, 101
    reducing, with cinnamon, 79–81
    reducing, with olive oil, 161
    yoga and, 220
insoluble fiber in beans, 188
insomnia. *See* sleep problems
inspiring others, on the 30-Day Diabetes Cure, 59–60
insulin
    and exercise, 179, 182
    increasing production of with drugs, 43–44
    role of, 10–11, 41
    sugar addiction, effects of conquering, 70
    and type 1 diabetes, 28
insulin receptors
    fenugreek seeds and, 302
    function of, 10
insulin resistance
    description of, 11–12
    reversing, with whole grains, 166–67
    salmon consumption and, 160
    screening for, standard, 13–14
    signs of, 12–13
    stress and, 223–24
    type 2 diabetes and, 22
    See also prediabetes
insulin sensitivity
    ALA and, 299
    beans and, 189
    chromium supplements, 299
    improving, with cinnamon, 79–81
    increasing, with exercise and weight loss, 28
interval walking, 184
intestinal bloating, 13

J

jams and jellies, 172
Japanese cuisine, 251–52
journaling, food, 247, 259

ABOUT THE AUTHORS

Dr. Stefan Ripich, ND, CNP. While modern medicine is failing to stem the spread of diabetes, Dr. Ripich is achieving 100% success in getting his patients completely off diabetes medicine and related drugs and back on the road to a healthy, normal life. His groundbreaking book, *The 30-Day Diabetes Cure,* is the first step-by-step guide to reversing type 2 diabetes and prediabetes. This easy plan also shows individuals with type 1 how to dramatically reduce their insulin dose, while virtually eliminating their risk of deadly diabetic complications.

Jim Healthy is a prolific health writer with a life-long dedication to researching and publishing the most important health discoveries of our time and creating practical "action plans" that help readers incorporate these new medical findings in their daily lives. He is also the co-author of *The Healthy Body Book* (Penguin Books, 1991), *The Fast Food Diet* (Wiley, 2006), *Arthritis Interrupted* (Jim Healthy Press, 2009), and *The Healing Kitchen* (Bottom Line Books, 2010). He is the founder/editor of the popular Web site *www.myhealingkitchen.com.*